County Council

Libraries, books and more . . .

2 4 SEP 2019		

Please return/renew this item by the last due date.
Library items may be renewed by phone on
030 33 33 1234 (24 hours) or via our website
www.cumbria.gov.uk/libraries

Cumbria Libraries

Interactive Catalogue

Ask for a CLIC password

Manchester University Press

The Beethoven song companion

Paul Reid

Manchester University Press
Manchester and New York

distributed exclusively in the USA by Palgrave

Published by Manchester University Press
Oxford Road, Manchester M13 9NR, UK
and Room 400, 175 Fifth Avenue, New York, NY 10010, USA
www.manchesteruniversitypress.co.uk

Distributed in the United States exclusively by
Palgrave Macmillan, 175 Fifth Avenue,
New York, NY 10010, USA

Distributed in Canada exclusively by
UBC Press, University of British Columbia, 2029 West Mall,
Vancouver, BC, Canada V6T 1Z2

British Library Cataloguing-in-Publication Data is available

Library of Congress Cataloging-in-Publication Data is available

ISBN 978 0 7190 7571 1 paperback

First published by Manchester University Press in hardback 2007

This paperback edition first published 2010

Printed by Lightning Source

Contents

Foreword

Beethoven's central position in the development of Classical music is almost universally acknowledged, and his extraordinary contribution to instrumental music, especially the symphony, is widely recognised. His vocal music, however, despite including many notable masterpieces, has often fared less well, and much less has been written about it. This is conspicuously true for his songs, and his massive contribution to the development of German song or *Lied* has sometimes been overlooked – partly because of the outstanding achievement of Schubert in this field. Schubert and Beethoven were living in Vienna at almost exactly the same time, and Schubert died only a little over a year after Beethoven. But Beethoven was a much older man, and, by the time Schubert began composing, around 1810, Beethoven had already made a major contribution to the genre, developing it in significant ways and using almost all the types that Schubert was to use later. His songs cover the entire range from simple, strophic settings, of the type favoured in North Germany in the eighteenth century, to extended cantata-like compositions in several sections, in which procedures derived from Italian opera and even from instrumental music are incorporated. And in his *An die ferne Geliebte* of 1816 he composed what is often regarded as the first song cycle – a genre that was to be so successful with later song composers.

There are many wonderful treasures amongst Beethoven's songs, and he put as much effort into composing them as he did for any other type of composition, as is evident from his intensive sketching of them. In fact he may have put even more effort into composing songs than other works, for he once remarked that 'an original good air' was just about the most difficult undertaking in composition (letter to George Thomson, February 1815). Like his instrumental music, his songs have a depth of expression that requires them to be heard several times to be properly appreciated.

The full extent of Beethoven's song output was known only to a few specialists until Helga Lühning's complete edition of the songs appeared in 1990, with its detailed textual commentary. Even this, however, has been of limited use to those not fluent in German, and a comprehensive guide in English has been sorely needed. The present book fulfils that need, and provides everything that readers are likely to want to know about Beethoven's songs. Particularly noteworthy is the provision of full texts (including, in some cases, stanzas that have often been omitted), with new and accurate English translations, and an account of where these texts originally appeared. Also valuable are the numerous critical and historical comments about both music and text, which the author has provided for every one of the songs. Leaving no stone unturned, he has also included songs that Beethoven began but did not complete. As with Beethoven's completed songs, there are far more of these fragments and abandoned drafts amongst his sketches than many have realised, and the fact that he began these settings is as interesting as the fact that he did not complete them. Thus the book is a mine of information for singers, listeners and scholars alike, and should be warmly welcomed by readers in all three categories.

Barry Cooper
University of Manchester

Preface

When *The Schubert Song Companion* was published in 1985, John Reed stated that he had compiled it because, unlike Everest, 'it wasn't there'. How much truer this is of the present volume, the first full-length published study of Beethoven's songs in English. Henri de Curzon, author of the first compact survey of the songs (in French), stressed the importance of a chronological study in 1905; Hans Boettcher, in a fine study of 1928 (in German), drew attention to the songs as an integral part of Beethoven's total oeuvre. Yet, despite the availability of recordings and the excellent complete critical edition of the songs from Henle, Beethoven's songs remain comparatively little known. The relative neglect of an entire aspect of Beethoven's output is difficult to understand, as the songs are important in their own right, in relation to other areas of Beethoven's creative endeavour and in the development of the Romantic German *Lied*. Few other song composers relate their choice of texts so consistently to their personal situation or reveal more of themselves through their settings. The songs offer us an unrivalled insight into Beethoven's personality and tastes.

One reason put forward to explain the neglect of Beethoven's songs (others are discussed in the Introduction) is the huge achievement of Schubert and the later Romantics in this field. While no one could sensibly claim that Beethoven's songs are the equal of Schubert's, it is none the less Beethoven who oversees the transition from Classical to Romantic song, from the eighteenth to the nineteenth century – a transition similar in kind to that which he achieved in the more public and ear-catching sphere of instrumental music. In particular, Beethoven's gradual liberation of the accompaniment, his exploitation of the new pianos as an expressive means of creating images and moods, and his related development of subtle tonal analogue, anticipate central aspects of the later Romantic *Lied*. It must be remembered that *Adelaide* was published as early as 1797, just days after Schubert was born, and that Schubert himself did not neglect Beethoven's songs, taking songs from op. 75 as models for his own settings and starting to make a copy of *Abendlied unterm gestirnten Himmel*, one of Beethoven's greatest songs and recognised as such by Schubert.

The present book includes all the songs composed for voice and piano, including a handful of choral works with piano accompaniment. Also included are unfinished songs, sketches which were or may have been intended for solo voice and piano, and even a couple of lost songs. The folksong settings made for Thomson, with accompaniment for piano trio, are not included, although two isolated folksong arrangements (*Das liebe Kätzchen* and *Der Knabe auf dem Berge*) sneak in on account of their authentic, if rudimentary, accompaniment for piano alone. Vocal works with orchestral accompaniment are included only if an authentic piano reduction by Beethoven exists (although an exception is made for two songs in this category which are familiar from the Peters song edition). After the Introduction has aired some central issues, the principal section of the book comprises entries in alphabetical order by title. Each entry includes a catalogue reference; for completed songs this is the number given by the standard Kinsky–Halm catalogue, while for other songs it is the number allocated by Willy Hess in his catalogue of the works not included in the old complete edition of Beethoven's works; a few sketches for unfinished songs are identified with numbers from Giovanni Biamonti's chronological catalogue or by their entry in Hans Schmidt's listing of the sketches. Musical incipits are given, except in a very few cases where a sketch was unavailable or indecipherable.

With the exception of the song cycle *An die ferne Geliebte*, op. 98, and the six Gellert songs, op. 48, songs are discussed individually rather than by opus. Full details of the publication of the songs are given in an appendix. Several songs are known by alternative titles (for example, *Plaisir d'aimer* is listed as *Romance*, and *Mignon* as *Kennst du das Land*). Readers are referred to the indexes (by title and by first line) for redirection, if a song cannot immediately be found under a particular title.

Apart from a few minor fragments, texts are given in full. Readers who are already familiar with recordings of songs such as the six Gellert settings may be surprised at the number of stanzas. Beethoven has always suffered in editions, performance and recordings from ruthless cropping of texts. Until 1990, when Helga Lühning's invaluable edition of the songs appeared (Henle), together with a scholarly Critical Report in German, almost all editions of the songs slavishly followed the text of the first complete edition (GA) of 1864; songs published in a later supplementary volume in 1888 were generally disregarded completely. Full texts are reinstated here, giving singers the opportunity to make performance decisions based on full and accurate information Translations are my own in every case, and accuracy of rendering was always the overriding consideration; the translations aim to be readable, but not to be singable. In the notes on each song, factual details concerning text and music are given, which often include reference to the cultural context and to Beethoven's personal situation, as a deliberate autobiographical subtext is so frequently identifiable. Musical points of particular interest are highlighted. I have not shrunk from expressing a personal view from time to time, knowing that the reader can adopt, modify or reject it as he or she pleases.

Notes on unfinished and even lost songs may initially seem excessively long, but they frequently offer a fascinating insight into Beethoven's literary interests and his compositional methods; indeed, the possible reasons why a song remained unfinished are often of interest in themselves.

I have avoided footnotes by the use of parentheses for details of references, autograph locations and translations within the main text. In song texts, both 'ss' and 'ß' are rendered as 'ss', but, in quotations from Beethoven's own writings, the composer's original and frequently eccentric orthography has been preserved, as this is part and parcel of the man who wrote them. Anyone who wishes to gain an understanding of Beethoven's character is recommended to read through the full three-volume set of *The Letters of Beethoven* (EA) in Emily Anderson's translation, while German-speaking scholars will delight in the beautifully produced German edition of the letters in eight volumes (BB), edited by Sieghard Brandenburg. Since the letters offer such a frank and often endearing composite portrait of their author, I have quoted from them frequently, generally in the original language with a translation.

I am grateful to a number of people for encouragement and support. Mark Zimmer and Willem Holsbergen of the 'Unheard Beethoven' project helped me to track down and decipher several autograph sketches; Richard Byrn of the University of Leeds gave helpful advice on elusive poems; Hartmut Krones of the Institut für Musikalische Stilforschung at the University of Vienna sent copies of relevant articles; Otto Biba, Director of the Gesellschaft der Musikfreunde Archive in Vienna, provided copies of fragmentary song settings; and Matthew Oglesby of the University of Leeds set the music examples with patient dedication. Barry Cooper of the University of Manchester has offered enthusiastic support and encouragement since I first mooted the idea of the study, answering frequent electronic queries promptly, reading the entire manuscript in draft and making valuable suggestions for improvement. He also generously agreed to provide a Foreword to the book.

Although our active collaboration on Beethoven songs (as opposed to Schubert songs) did not go much beyond playing the piano duet variations on *Ich denke dein*, I owe a unique debt to the late John Reed for his advice, encouragement and friendship. His children Jim, Jane and Kate not only agreed unhesitatingly to my adapting the format of the *Schubert Song Companion* for the present work but have shown keen interest throughout and have graciously allowed me to dedicate the present book to their father's memory.

Paul Reid
Sherburn-in-Elmet

Abbreviations

Principal locations of autographs

BH	Beethoven House (Beethoven-Archiv), Bonn
BJ	Biblioteka Jagiellońska, Krakow
BL	British Library, London
BN	Bibliothèque Nationale, Paris
CMMC	Central (Glinka) Museum for Music Culture, Moscow
DSB	Deutsche Staatsbibliothek, (formerly East) Berlin*
GdM	Gesellschaft der Musikfreunde, Vienna
ÖNB	Österreichische Nationalbibliothek, Vienna
RCM	Royal College of Music, London
SPK	Staatsbibliothek Preussischer Kulturbesitz, (formerly West) Berlin*

* Since the reunification of Germany, the two libraries have been officially reunited as 'Staatsbibliothek zu Berlin-Preussischer Kulturbesitz', but the two sites remain separate.

Song editions (see Bibliography for full details)

GA *L. van Beethovens Werke: Vollständig kritisch durchgesehene überall berechtigte Ausgabe* (Gesamtausgabe). Complete edition, Breitkopf und Härtel, Leipzig: volume 23 (1864) and supplementary volume 25 (1888).

Henle *Beethoven Werke XII/I: Lieder und Gesänge mit Klavierbegleitung*, ed. Helga Lühning (Munich 1990). Complete song edition in one volume, published with a critical report in German.

Peters *Beethoven. Sämtliche Lieder für eine Singstimme mit Klavierbegleitung*, rev. Max Unger (Frankfurt, London, New York, 1936).

Supp *Beethoven. Supplemente zur Gesamtausgabe*, ed. Willy Hess: *Band V: Lieder und Gesänge mit Klavierbegleitung, Kanons und musikalische Scherze* (Wiesbaden 1962, rev. 1980).

Catalogues

KH Georg Kinsky and Hans Halm: *Das Werk Beethovens. Thematisch-bibliographisches Verzeichnis seiner sämtlichen vollendeten Kompositionen* (Munich/Duisburg 1955).

Bia   Giovanni Biamonti: *Catalogo cronologico e tematico delle opera di Beethoven* (Turin 1968).

Hess   Willy Hess: *Verzeichnis der nicht in der Gesamtausgabe veröffentlichten Werke Ludwig van Beethovens* (Wiesbaden 1957).

Hess2   *The New Hess Catalog of Beethoven's Works*, ed. James Green (West Newbury 2003).

SV   Hans Schmidt: 'Verzeichnis der Skizzen Beethovens', *Beethoven-Jahrbuch VI* (Bonn 1969).

Other sources

EA   *The Letters of Beethoven*, translated and edited by Emily Anderson (3 vols) (London 1961).

BB   *Ludwig van Beethoven. Briefwechsel. Gesamtausgabe*, ed. Sieghard Brandenburg (8 vols) (Munich 1996). German edition of complete letters, including letters written to Beethoven.

T   Maynard Solomon, 'Beethoven's Tagebuch of 1812–1818', in *Beethoven Studies 3* (ed. Tyson) (Cambridge 1982) (numbers indicate the numbers allocated by Solomon to entries).

Introduction

A question of image

In his book *Für Freunde der Tonkunst* (For friends of music) of 1832, the influential Leipzig music critic Friedrich Rochlitz reported a one-sided conversation he held with Beethoven in 1822, with the composer holding forth and Rochlitz responding with nods and gestures. Beethoven explained enthusiastically how his meeting with Goethe in 1812 had fired him with enthusiasm. Goethe's poetry, he stated, cries out to be set to music, but then added 'Ich schreibe nur nicht gern Lieder' (I'm just not keen on writing songs). By 1822 Beethoven had, of course, virtually abandoned song composition, and we cannot in any case be sure whether Rochlitz's account is strictly accurate, but, in making this or a similar negative comment about his attitude to song composition, Beethoven was himself contributing to a complex image problem which has consistently prevented his songs with piano from receiving the attention they richly deserve.

Although the songs are an essential part of Beethoven's total oeuvre, they have always been overshadowed by his large-scale instrumental and orchestral works, and in the vocal sphere by *Fidelio* and the *Missa Solemnis*. It is these works which have moulded the popular image of the composer. The songs, works of a predominantly personal, even intimate nature, will never stand unscathed beside the large-scale, public works while they are approached with expectations and preconceptions derived from the popular image of the 'heroic' composer, taming the musical elements by sheer force of will. Only when we lay prejudice aside and regard the songs as representing another, complementary aspect of Beethoven as man and composer, will we appreciate their true merit and significance. Hans Boettcher wisely chose to entitle his 1928 study of the songs *Beethoven als Liederkomponist* (Beethoven as song composer), stressing that the songs are an integral part of the whole work and the whole man. They are the product of the same man who wrote the symphonies, the sonatas and the quartets; they offer a different, but complementary and frequently revealing view of the same creative genius.

Boettcher (p. 7) points to another aspect of the image problem which has dogged Beethoven's songs and prevented them from achieving true popularity. Just as Beethoven the song composer is unfairly judged by standards defined by his large-scale works, so he suffers from expectations which the post-Romantic generation harbours regarding 'the German *Lied*'. Beethoven's songs conform only erratically to a vague ideal image of German art song, which derives from and thrives on our familiarity with those composers who dominate recitals and recordings. Many of

Beethoven's songs can seem distinctly old-fashioned by the standards of Schubert and Schumann and the later Romantics, and such songs are relegated to an almost total neglect or to the circumscribed sphere of 'historically informed performance'. Songs which happen to conform to the image of the heroic composer (*Die Ehre Gottes aus der Natur*, say, or the second setting of *An die Hoffnung*) and songs which chime with our image of the true German *Lied* (such as *Adelaide* or *An die ferne Geliebte*) are promoted, in performance as in academic studies, at the expense of those songs which do not. It is essential to a full understanding of the composer to accept the songs as an integral part of his total output, just as it is necessary to consider *all* the songs to gain a rounded and accurate picture of the song composer, and to understand his key role in the development of the *Klavierlied*.

Beethoven's work all springs from the same essential source. In instrumental works as in vocal works, the impulse which drove him was frequently a lyrical one, and he sought to express and evoke emotion in his listeners. This much is stated, for example, with reference to his 'Pastoral' Symphony. Between sketches for his Choral Fantasia in op. 80, the composer writes: 'pastoral Sinfonie keine Malerey sondern worin die Empfindungen ausgedrückt sind welche der genuss des landes im Menschen hervorbringt' (Pastoral Symphony not painting but in which are expressed the emotions which the enjoyment of the country produces in a man). This comment (quoted by Nottebohm, *Zweite Beethoveniana*, p. 504) indicates that even overt programme music aims to express emotions first and foremost. Beethoven was apt to use vocal designations for instrumental movements (see entry for *Süsser Ruhegesang*). Indeed, a further reception problem for the songs lies in the fact that many of Beethoven's instrumental slow movements are actually more lyrically expressive than some of his more intellectually inspired songs. There was even a vogue which began during Beethoven's lifetime and continued for many years for setting words to instrumental movements to convert them into songs. In his *Thematic Catalogue* (Leipzig 1868), Nottebohm lists over thirty examples of instrumental and even orchestral movements arranged as songs. In one of the earliest examples, Franz Wegeler's *Die Klage* (set to the *Adagio* from the Piano Sonata op. 2/1 and appended to his *Biographische Notizen*: Wegeler and Ries 1838), it is instructive to observe how comfortably this process is achieved.

Texts-contexts-subtexts

Despite his ambivalent attitude towards song-writing, Beethoven seems to have been constantly on the look-out for suitable poems to set to music. He was an avid reader of books, and of the numerous periodicals and almanacs which offered recent prose and poetry, with occasional musical supplements (indeed, nine of Beethoven's songs were first published in this form). The composer's interest in literature is witnessed by frequent references in his correspondence, in a diary which he kept between 1812 and 1818, and in his conversation books. It is clear from the latter that a stream of visitors kept Beethoven fully informed of the latest publications and cultural gossip. The composer, meanwhile, meticulously copied details of recently published books he wished to acquire, with their prices, although he was happy to cadge free copies from publishers where this was feasible. Books from his library, many of which survive in Berlin (DSB), testify to his intense personal engagement with what he read, with turned-down corners, bold underlining of key passages and marginal exclamation marks and comments – generally, an affirming 'ja!'. It is interesting to note in this connection that Beethoven often inserted an emphatic 'ja' into song settings, partly for musical reasons, but also to confirm his solidarity with the poetic sentiments.

We shall see that some of Beethoven's greatest songs are those which demonstrate a close identification with the textual content, but his was a complex and often self-contradictory character, and his choice of texts derives from a variety of contexts.

Beethoven's two earliest songs, *Schilderung eines Mädchens* and *An einen Säugling*, are ill-suited bedfellows; the one is a stylised paean to female beauty, whose poverty of expression Beethoven's exuberant setting fails to disguise, while the other offers a thoughtful reflection on man's relationship with God as loving father. Perhaps the poems reflect passing enthusiasms of the 12-year-old composer, but it is more likely that they were recommended to him by his teacher Christian Gottlob Neefe or by the publisher Heinrich Philipp Bossler, in whose periodical they first appeared. The first poem in particular would have sounded amateurish and dated, had the composer revisited it in later years. Although *Der freie Mann*, a choice possibly influenced by a dalliance with freemasonry in Bonn, is an exception to the rule, several early songs set rather insipid poems of conventional sentiment: a list would include *Gretels Warnung, Das Liedchen von der Ruhe* and *Die Liebe*. Before the end of the eighteenth century, however, Beethoven had discovered some lyric verse of the highest quality. Matthisson's picturesque *Adelaide* and the linguistic and rhythmic vitality of Goethe's *Maigesang* and *Neue Liebe, neues Leben* led the composer to set new standards in lyric song composition – nothing less than the aim to recreate in heightened form the original emotional response of his poets.

Meanwhile, a witty strand of youthful humour informs a number of songs, of predominantly early date. The influence of *Singspiel* and opera is evident here, Beethoven having had generous opportunity to experience both in Bonn, as a spectator and chiefly from the orchestral pit of the court opera theatre, where he played the viola. These songs include *Urians Reise um die Welt* and the bitingly satirical *Aus Goethes Faust* (both with chorus participation), *Marmotte* and *Ein Selbstgespräch*, the latter a compendium of *buffo* devices. The overtly comical *Der Kuss*, despite its late publication date, is also a youthful work. While not directly humorous, the vital exuberance and sheer *joie de vivre* which glitter through *Schilderung eines Mädchens* and *Maigesang* are of a type with these comic songs. The theatrical credentials of *Maigesang* are confirmed by the ease with which Beethoven quickly reworked the song for insertion, with new words and orchestral accompaniment, into a popular *Singspiel* by Ignaz Umlauf.

Throughout his life, Beethoven was happy to write 'occasional' compositions, marking very specific events and generally of a convivial nature, solidarity often bolstered by the inclusion of a refrain in which the whole company could join. It is tempting to think that the 'drinking song of farewell' *Erhebt das Glas* was penned by Beethoven to commemorate his own final departure from Bonn, although the *Punschlied* of similar date lacks any specific context. The two songs written for the Viennese volunteer force in 1796–97, *Abschiedsgesang* and *Kriegslied der Österreicher*, as well as the unfinished *Östreich über alles* of 1809, were the direct product of intense outbursts of patriotic euphoria which swept Vienna as Napoleon's armies approached the city. Beethoven was following the general trend in composing *Kriegslieder* (war songs) at this time, but the two earlier songs mark highly specific events, their title pages detailing both the exact nature and precise date of the occasion commemorated. Happier occasions are celebrated in songs which Beethoven composed as favours for friends: the wedding song *Auf Freunde* for Anna Giannatasio, the birthday ode *Es lebe unser teurer Fürst* for Prince Ferdinand Lobkowitz, and the *Cantata campestre*, composed for the name-day of Johann Malfatti, a distinguished doctor.

Beethoven clearly received and responded to several paid commissions. One suspects that the English song *La Tiranna* was commissioned by its author William Wennington as a special memento of his European grand tour. *Elegie auf den Tod eines Pudels* was perhaps commissioned by the bereaved mistress of a specific canine. A theatrical commission led to the composition of the songs from *Egmont*; had Beethoven been allocated *Wilhelm Tell* (the composer's preferred commission according to Czerny), we should now have some complete solo settings of Schiller poems. Songs were also composed at the request of publishers. Thus, Beethoven contributed a setting of *In questa tomba oscura* to the grand collection of settings of the text by several composers, financed by a countess. Other songs were written specifically for publication in periodicals, including *Der Bardengeist, Andenken, So oder so* and *Resignation*. In one case at least, that of *Abendlied unterm gestirnten Himmel*, the composer had been invited to choose from a selection of texts provided by the publisher and opted for a text in which he found an extraordinary personal resonance.

The composer generally responded courteously and sympathetically to requests from poets to set their verse, although he was clearly unable to satisfy all but a few requests, many of which arrived at a period when he had virtually abandoned song composition. His first group of songs to texts by Reissig resulted from an appeal by the poet, a war veteran. Beethoven was clearly taken with the patriotic-picturesque *Merkenstein* and wrote a gracious letter to the poet Rupprecht (EA506 / BB759) to tell him so. On the other hand, he wrote to a certain Wilhelm Gerhard (EA788 / BB1141), declining to set his verse since it was too descriptive, stating that 'descriptions of a picture are the province of painting'. It is true that few close descriptions of natural scenes are found in Beethoven's song texts, and *Merkenstein* no doubt appealed to him more for the linking of natural scenes to emotional responses. *An die Geliebte* seems to have been written specifically for Beethoven to set, and there is a possibility that Beethoven actually requested the poem from Stoll, in recompense for the composer's active support when the poet was in financial straits.

It is not clear why Beethoven turned to Italian texts for a number of songs, although the habit had been encouraged by Antonio Salieri, for whom a large group of unaccompanied partsongs to Metastasian texts had been composed as exercises around 1801 or 1802. The composer's developing love for Therese Malfatti, of Italian descent, with whom he was to contemplate marriage the following year, may also have influenced his choice of several Italian texts during 1809. The composer's determination to master the language is evidenced by an Italian dictionary and grammars found in his effects and attempts at translation in his diary (T11/12). The Italian songs are elegantly handled, but even the fine songs of op. 82 never demonstrate that intimate engagement with poetry which characterises the greatest songs.

This intense personal engagement with his texts and identification with the poet's sentiments are unprecedented in the history of German song. Poems are no longer the mere pretext for a song, but carefully and deliberately chosen by the composer to reflect and parallel his own world view: his beliefs, his opinions, his emotions and his personal situation. An autobiographical subtext is thus seldom far below the surface in many of Beethoven's serious songs, and, in assimilating the poet's sentiments, the composer forges new creations of a rare (and often rarefied) intensity. It is to these texts which we now turn our attention and enter thereby the very heart of Beethovenian song.

From his earliest years Beethoven was an idealist with a fierce sense of personal and public morality and responsibility. He considered that a major part of his vocation was to uphold and promote the ideals in which he believed and which are the distinguishing mark of humankind. This helps to explain his continuing interest in setting words to music, despite his declared preference for larger instrumental and orchestral forms (EA1111 / BB1516), as music can enhance words and thereby the ideas they represent and bring them to wider public attention. *Der freie Mann* (The free man), as the title suggests, is a manifesto of the Enlightenment, celebrating the man who can live his own life on his own terms and by the power of his own will, the man who does not recognise tyrannical rulers, nor priests who seek to suppress personal freedom of belief, nor differences of race, birth or creed. *Der gute Fürst* (The good prince), which I have fitted to a song melody (see Appendix II), is a portrait of a wholly enlightened ruler, and by implication a condemnation of the many unenlightened petty despots around 1800, when the entity we now know as Germany contained well over three hundred sovereign territories, many of them feudal fiefdoms. It is probable that Beethoven encountered Goeckingk's poem in the Hamburg *Musenalmanach*, and quite certain that he would have applauded its content. *Der freie Mann* demonstrates a premodern 'political correctness', but for the key fact that women are not deemed worthy of mention. This is still essentially a man's world, an impression strengthened by *Der Mann vom Wort*, celebrating the German and manly virtues of integrity and reliability. *Opferlied* too suggests a strictly men-only context, this time the world of freemasonry, which usurped Enlightenment ideals and cloaked them in a shroud of mystery and rite. Beethoven seems to identify himself with the subject of the initiation ceremony, the youth solemnly devoting his life to the service of freedom, beauty and truth; indeed, the final line of the poem 'Das Schöne zu dem Guten' (Beauty allied to goodness) became a favourite watchword for the composer, who twice set it as a canon.

Beethoven's complex attitude to religion is revealed strikingly in his song texts. His faith in God was not tied to a particular denomination, but was deep and sincere none the less. Eastern religions fascinated him for a time (T61/62), although he clearly sought out ideas which found a resonance with his existing beliefs, such as an invisible and ineffable God who reveals his omniscient power in all creation

(T93). The composer owned copies of Tiedge's 'lyric-didactic poem' *Urania: Über Gott, Unsterblichkeit und Freiheit* (Urania: Concerning God, Immortality and Liberty) and Christian Sturm's *Betrachtungen der Werke Gottes im Reiche der Natur* (Observations of the works of God in the realm of Nature); both works seem turgid and rambling today, but enjoyed a vogue in Beethoven's day. In the six songs to poems by Gellert, Beethoven is closest to an orthodox Christian expression of faith. Prayer, humility, penitence and the hope of redemption are all covered in the poems selected by the composer for this group, which displays many characteristics of a miniature song cycle. An entry in his diary (T160), written at least fifteen years after the composer had written the songs, is a very clear echo of the first poem *Bitten*, indicating how thoroughly Beethoven had assimilated Gellert's text: 'Gott Gott mein Hort mein Fels o mein Alles' (God God my refuge my rock o my all). The fourth song, *Die Ehre Gottes aus der Natur*, introduces the idea of God revealed in Nature, the divine architect clearly visible in the miracles of his creation, and this image recurs in *Der Wachtelschlag*, a song which forms a bridge to the 'Pastoral' Symphony, a wordless celebration of the identical idea. Other songs treat ideals as the object of prayer, including *An die Hoffnung*, with its prayer to Hope, or Reissig's *Sehnsucht*, which apostrophises the 'silent God of Peace'. The second version of *An die Hoffnung* (op. 94), with its initial questioning of God's existence silenced by the command to hope for a better world to come, has an extraordinary intensity of expression, deriving from Beethoven's close personal involvement with his text. The composer makes no attempt to stand back in detachment from his text, but still manages to produce a song which is both finely crafted and deeply felt. Controlled intensity also marks the great *Abendlied unterm gestirnten Himmel* which describes the soul's final great journey, emancipated and transfigured, through the starry firmament to claim its reward for earthly suffering before God's throne. It is not enough to say that these poems 'struck a chord' with Beethoven; they are the poems he would have written himself had his literary genius matched his musical genius, and with his musical enhancement he quite consciously conferred immortality upon them.

Such songs as these are as far removed from two-stave eighteenth-century models, or even the more ambitious experiments of Neefe or Reichardt, as the 'Eroica' Symphony is from a symphony of Pleyel or even Haydn, and for the same reason: because in both the vocal and the instrumental genres, Beethoven, breaking with convention, has placed at the centre of his work his own world view, his very self and his most intimate feelings. To achieve this in the field of vocal music, the composer clearly needed to find texts which chimed precisely with his own ideas and emotions.

While Beethoven selected several happy love poems for composition, including *Ich liebe dich*, *Der Liebende* and *Lebensglück*, other poems seem chosen to mirror his own lack of success in this field. Admittedly, the theme of the distant beloved was so widespread at the time as to be considered conventional, but *An die ferne Geliebte*, with its final message of shared song uniting lovers despite distance, seems (and possibly was) tailor-made for the composer. Speculation as to whom Beethoven had in mind while composing his song cycle or a song such as *An die Geliebte* is inevitable. As a young man searching for love, Beethoven had set

Bürger's lament *Seufzer* (why am I the only one left out?) and his anticipation of eventual sexual fulfilment, *Gegenliebe*, with a vivid vibrancy. Beethoven's setting of *Gegenliebe* is far removed from Haydn's coy strophic setting of ten years earlier because Beethoven is prepared to shun detachment and convention and reveal himself unashamedly in his music. In *Wonne der Wehmut*, which celebrates the cultivation of emotion itself regardless of associated pain, Beethoven once again exhibits the double achievement of combining intensity of expression with consummate craftsmanship.

Both Schubert and Beethoven set Hölty's *Klage (An den Mond)* when they were 19, at a happy time of their lives, dominated by an optimistic outlook (Schubert actually included the setting in a collection of song copies written out neatly for his girlfriend Therese Grob). The composers are exhibiting here the ability to empathise with the young poet's lament despite the difference in their personal situations, and the settings are finely crafted and apt. Later in life, both composers found in poetry exact parallels or analogies for their less happy personal circumstances and works of great poignancy resulted. Another lament, *Die laute Klage*, started life as an Arabic poem, elegantly contrasting the turtle-dove's loud song of love-lament with the silent sorrow of the poet whose heart has been broken. Herder, probably working from the English translation by the orientalist William Jones, artfully recast the poem in German hexameter couplets, in each case featuring enjambement, with a marked caesura in the second line. Beethoven clearly related the poem, with its reference to the dumb-struck poet, to his own isolation in his deafness, actually changing the final word to personalise the text (see main entry for discussion). The song is cast appropriately in C minor, otherwise sparingly used for song composition, with a wealth of expressive gesture, including sighing pauses suggestive of the tragedy of a mute poet (or a deaf composer). Ironically, it is Beethoven's appropriation and personalisation of the poem that has made it publicly accessible, although the song would no longer be recognised by the anonymous Arabian poet. The song *Resignation* likewise suggests that Beethoven's own despairing world-weariness was combined with that of the poet to produce a work which doubles the emotive force of the original text.

Beethoven sought to set himself, the composer, above the poet, seeking always to add something to the sum total of expression. His song as a work of art should be greater in kind than the poem set. This was not a matter of pride or prejudice, but an artistic standpoint which was to become the norm during the course of the nineteenth century. If Beethoven felt that he could not improve on the original work of art, the poem, his fierce artistic integrity prevented him from composing a text. Thus, there are no completed solo songs to texts of Homer, Klopstock or Schiller, whom Beethoven called the 'immortal poets' (EA1260 / BB1773); in each case, unfinished sketches show that he could not resist the temptation to attempt settings of these poets, but failed utterly to find worthy musical equivalents for their verse. Schiller, of course, was to achieve his apotheosis in the 'Choral' Symphony, where vast vocal and orchestral forces are called into commission to do justice to this champion of ideals, but a single voice and piano were not sufficient means. According to Carl Czerny (quoted by Boettcher, p. 45), Beethoven once said 'Schiller's works are extremely difficult for a musician. The composer must have the ability to raise himself far above the poet; who can do that with Schiller?' The only one of Beethoven's declared 'favourite poets' (EA224 / BB395) whose poems led to completed songs (and very fine ones at that) was Goethe. Yet while the rhythmic vitality of Goethe's early lyric verse proved irresistible and *Wonne der Wehmut* struck a chord, here too several sketches remained unfinished. *Erlkönig* would have been a unique Beethovenian essay in the dramatic ballad and anyone can fall at the first hurdle with the intractable *Gesang der Geister über den Wassern*, but of greater interest is why Beethoven failed to find a musical match for *Heidenröslein* despite several attempts. One suspects that he was trying too hard, but also that he found in the simple allegory no point of contact. Despite his long occupation with folksong arrangements for the Edinburgh publisher George Thomson, folksong-like poems do not feature often in his original solo songs.

Formal variety and innovation

It is important to remember that Beethoven was a composer of both the eighteenth and the nineteenth centuries. His teachers included Christian Gottlob Neefe and Joseph Haydn, born in 1748 and 1732 respectively and firmly rooted in the eighteenth century. Both men still regarded solo song with keyboard primarily as a domestic pursuit, although both made strides in widening the expressive range of song. Until the end of the eighteenth century, songs were most commonly notated on two staves, the voice part doubled at every point by the keyboard, facilitating performance by a single amateur performer at the instrument. Both Haydn and Neefe began to introduce a third stave for the voice, gradually liberating the keyboard accompaniment as an independent vehicle, expressing mood, sentiment and even ideas. By the end of Beethoven's songwriting career, around 1820, full-blown Romantic song had emerged as the new style. Composers were revelling in the emotive possibilities offered by the dynamic range of the new pianofortes; improved models were appearing almost annually, each hastening the demise of the harpsichord and more gradually ousting the gentle clavichord, which had been the domestic keyboard instrument of choice at the end of the previous century. Beethoven, who respected the past but never lived in it, was a leader in developing the newly expressive *Klavierlied*, exploiting the power of the new piano to recreate quasi-orchestral effects, enabling him in turn to bring operatic devices into lyric song and lift it into the professional and public spheres. It also enabled him to write into his songs, as into his solo piano music, those sudden dynamic contrasts which originated in orchestral practice and developed into a mannerism.

In Beethoven's songs, the mild expressive adornments of Classical song gradually give way to bold harmonic contrasts and a complex system of rhetorical gesture, expressing and developing nuances of sentiment and meaning through a wide variety of tonal analogue, while forms and devices from Italian opera add to the new repertoire of expressive techniques (consider the operatic structure of *Seufzer/Gegenliebe*, or the elaborate use of cadenzas in *Gesang aus der Ferne* or *Mit einem gemalten Band*). A select survey of Beethoven's songs, from the simplest strophic forms to the modified and varied strophic songs where the accompaniment plays such a prominent role, and thence to the through-composed songs where the composer variously exploits formal-instrumental models and meaningful musical symbolism to unify the whole, traces the gradual evolution of German song: from the eighteenth to the nineteenth century, from Classical to Romantic.

Beethoven's two earliest songs, *Schilderung eines Mädchens* and *An einen Säugling*, were published on two staves, in accordance with what was standard practice in 1783–84. A feature of the first song is that the composer sets two short poetic stanzas to a single musical verse; this works well, but creates a problem, as the poem has an uneven number of stanzas. The problem does not arise in *Feuerfarb'* or in the Gellert setting *Die Ehre Gottes aus der Natur*, which use the same device, or in *Maigesang*, where three of Goethe's short stanzas are set to a single musical verse, mirroring the unbroken flow of the poem.

Among Beethoven's earlier strophic songs are many where the song might as well be written out on two staves, as the vocal line clings faithfully to the treble line of the piano accompaniment. It is significant that these include a series of songs with choral refrain, where the piano's doubling of the melody adds to the general sense of solidarity or conviviality. One might mention the two songs written for the ill-fated Viennese volunteer force, *Abschiedsgesang* and *Kriegslied der Österreicher*, the comical narration *Urians Reise um die Welt*, or the drinking songs *Erhebt das Glas* and *Punschlied*. Another example is provided by the *Der freie Mann*, while the *Opferlied* with similar Masonic overtones, although conceived as a solo song, has the effect of a unison male chorus (it was later to be adapted for larger forces). The unison of voice and piano treble line fosters a sense of mock ingenuousness in *Marmotte* and of wide-eyed innocence in *Das Blümchen Wunderhold*. Elsewhere, this technique can make songs such as *Mollys Abschied* or *Die Liebe* sound rather feeble.

Beethoven did not reject strict strophic setting as his songwriting career progressed, but continued to use it as he deemed appropriate until 1817 (for *So oder so*). Strophic form was used for *Der Mann vom Wort*, a text dear to Beethoven's heart where clear declamation of the sober text was the transparent aim; interestingly, the performance direction 'soft and loud according to the varying expression of the verses' confirms that Beethoven, like other composers, expected the performers to express the meaning of each stanza sensibly. Strophic setting was the clear choice for the ballad *Der Bardengeist* and for *Merkenstein*, with its refrain in the first and final lines of each stanza. Four settings of Christian Ludwig Reissig from 1809, *Der Jüngling in der Fremde*, *Der Liebende*, *Der Zufriedene* and *An den fernen Geliebten*, show strophic form at its best, thanks to poems which have a regular metrical pattern and stress. The first five of the songs to religious texts of Christian Fürchtegott Gellert, however, highlight a problem common in strophic setting. If the meaning of the first stanza is mirrored with nuanced precision in the musical setting, or if subsequent stanzas vary in metre or stress, the song will work only partially; the first stanza is well catered for, but subsequent stanzas are left to fend for themselves as a 'best fit'. Readers who are used to hearing only one verse of each Gellert song performed will, in fact, be surprised to see how many stanzas exist in the case of these songs above all, and performers' decisions as to which stanzas to perform may well be based on how well Beethoven's music happens to fit successive stanzas. The problem of fitting identical music to several poetic stanzas is highlighted by *An Amarant*. The sketch for this unfinished song could have been easily realised (and has been recently by a Dutch enthusiast), but the music is so closely tailored to the words of the first stanza, with its very particular stresses, that it cannot be made to fit the remaining stanzas. Could this be why the setting was abandoned?

One of Beethoven's principal contributions to German song is found in the many ways in which he varied the strophic song. This ranges from the slightest modification, such as his writing out of a second verse to *Das Liedchen von der Ruhe*, precisely to accommodate a new poetic metre, to the boldly ambitious strophic variation of *Abendlied unterm gestirnen Himmel*, which affects both voice and accompaniment so radically as to give almost the effect of through-composition.

Maigesang is essentially strophic, although the song is written out in full to accommodate the important piano introduction (a variation of the vocal melody), the chirruping interludes and the 12-bar coda. Codas feature prominently in many of Beethoven's songs and can become somewhat autonomous, an end in themselves. When Beethoven begins to think as a pianist and instrumental composer, a song which started out as a gently attractive strophic composition can lose its way. Cases in point are *Andenken* and *Lebensglück*, in both of which the final stanza is elaborately varied and expanded into a coda, with excessive word repetition which leaves the actual meaning of the text out of account. Beethoven was to bring vocal techniques into his instrumental music to great effect (the use of recitative in the Piano Sonatas op. 31/2 and op. 110 is a prime example), but the use of extended quasi-instrumental codas in his songs often adds little of formal merit and can detract from the whole (see *Lebensglück* for a discussion of this issue and an alternative view).

A vastly more successful means of strophic variation, and a major contribution to the development of song, is Beethoven's use of a varying accompaniment below an unvarying vocal line to achieve intensification or nuance of expression. An early and obvious example occurs in *Kennst du das Land*, where the final stanza's rumbling bass accompaniment suggests the dangers of the mountain path, but the songs of Beethoven's full maturity demonstrate a more fluent mastery of the technique. Sketches show that the composer took great pains to find the perfect metrical match for Reissig's poem *Sehnsucht* ('Die stille Nacht'), settling finally on a two-part melody which, while unchanged through successive stanzas (aside from minimal expressive rests), gives an impression of rhythmical freedom. While the overall mood of the song is achieved by the melody in this case, the piano accompaniment reflects the specific content of each stanza: calm and chordal at first for the silent nightfall, then syncopated for the poet's sleepless lament, and finally flowing triplets for his hope of rest and a dreaming vision of his beloved. The song cycle *An die ferne Geliebte*, also of 1816, uses a similar technique of accompanimental variation throughout the first four songs; indeed, the consistent use of the technique is a unifying factor within the cycle. Admittedly, the strophic variation goes beyond this at times. In the second song *Wo die Berge so blau*, remembrance of the native valley is suggested by the transfer of the voice to a repeated inner pedal note (the symbolism is clearer when we recall that the German word for memory is 'Erinnerung'), while the piano, having hitherto supported the voice in two registers, takes over full responsibility for the melody. In the third song *Leichte Segler*, a turn to the minor mode alters the sentimental complexion of the whole, although the varying accompaniment continues to adumbrate wafting winds and whispering brooks (see *Klage, Sehnsucht/Was zieht mir das Herz so, Auf den Tod eines Pudels* and the Gellert *Busslied* for further examples of meaningful major/minor shifts).

It is fair to say that the piano, always a faithful and indispensable companion, achieves the status of hero in Beethoven's song cycle and fully deserves its solo cameo appearances in the interludes, the postlude and the eight-bar instrumental arietta which opens the final song. In *Abendlied unterm gestirnen Himmel* the pianist once again has the major task in expressing the profound ideas, the tremulous emotions and the specific images presented by the poet, although in this song additional expression is achieved by significant variation of the vocal line. The high-lying chords which open the song introduce a gentle moonrise, and nightfall is described to a chorale-like accompaniment. Mention of the vast starry firmament brings the pattern of full repeated chords which had already been unambiguously defined by the composer (for example, in *Die Ehre Gottes aus der Natur* of 1802) as a tonal analogue for the 'countless stars of the firmament' and by extension for the glory of God in all creation and a mood of praise and exaltation. Oscillating figures suggest the storms of life, and majestic fanfares the confidence that we shall one day (at the last trumpet) be freed from all fear and pain. The high-lying angelic chorale of the postlude ends by combining a right-hand chord above the stave with a left-hand chord deep in the bass: the hope of heaven among the earthbound. An accompaniment such as this would have been unthinkable without the possibilities offered by the new pianofortes, but here, as in the through-composed songs to which we now turn, Beethoven elected to use the piano rather than the orchestra. This predilection, shared by Schubert (who started to make a copy of this grand song), expanded at a stroke the range of the *Klavierlied*.

Beethoven's through-composed songs expand the repertoire of lyric song. Compositions of similar type had been produced before, but these generally set narrative ballads (such as Reichardt's setting of *Erlkönig*) or were episodic affairs, like Zumsteeg's setting of Schiller's *Die Erwartung* (which in turn provided a close model for Schubert's setting of the text in 1816). The latter seem like several disparate songs in one. It was Beethoven's achievement, through trial and error, to produce through-composed, often extended settings of lyric poems which preserve a sense of overall unity while simultaneously mirroring incidental nuances of sentiment and reference.

Beethoven's first two essays in through-composed song, *Adelaide* and *Seufzer eines Ungeliebten*, both of 1794–95, are popular and grateful concert pieces for a fine singer and pianist, but each ultimately sacrifices the interpretation of the text to considerations of pure musical form. Here, Beethoven is incorporating techniques of Italian cantata and operatic aria into the *Klavierlied*, but the formal origins of his conception remain uncomfortably self-evident in their new context. Despite many features which prefigure the Romantic *Lied*, *Adelaide* is a cantata and was designated as such upon its first publication in 1797 (just days after the birth of Franz

Schubert). In the first section, the flowing introduction sets the general mood and leads seamlessly into the vocal melody, while through-composition enables precise tonal analogues of the picturesque variety, which simultaneously aim to recreate the subtly varying emotional responses of the poet. Having allowed the music to follow closely the emotional contours of the poem in the first section, Beethoven then creates an inescapable contradiction by inclining to pure music in the second section; the words, freely repeated, are largely ignored as such and become the excuse for a purely musical excursion, revealing the song as a whole to be essentially an instrumental or operatic conception. The song can still be enjoyed on its own terms, of course, but it only partially conforms to Beethoven's own forward-looking idea of the solo song with piano, where the meaning of the words is heeded at every point. In *Seufzer eines Ungeliebten*, Beethoven combines two poems by Gottfried August Bürger, to create a concert aria with piano, on the lines of the recitative-cavatina-cabaletta model, each section with an appropriate key of its own, yielding a satisfying pattern (C minor–E flat–C major). Again, words are repeated for the sake of pure musical shape rather than to reflect their meaning. It is significant that Beethoven later reused the music to the final section (*Gegenliebe*) of this 'double song' in his Choral Fantasia, op. 80, in 1808, confirming that the music is not intimately linked to Bürger's words and that the music is at least equally suited to grander choral and orchestral forces.

Three songs from the first decade of the nineteenth century, *Der Wachtelschlag*, *Neue Liebe, neues Leben* and *Gesang aus der Ferne*, show real mastery of through composition. *Der Wachtelschlag* of 1803 is a large-scale song with changes of key and time signature, but the whole is unified by the development of the dotted motif, emblematic of the quail's song, which is presented at the very beginning of the song as a musical motto. Through-composition enables Beethoven not only to pay close attention to the varying moods of the poem but to reinforce and cross-reference them. The hopping triplets suggest the call of the bird as it sits innocently beside the newly sown field; then the harvest, and the big repeated chords familiar from *Die Ehre Gottes aus der Natur* and *Abendlied unterm gestirnten Himmel* create a hymn of praise and thanks, and a mood of exaltation; finally the rumbling storm and fears for those caught up in warfare, although here the many and varied musical metres distort the motto motif somewhat.

Beethoven wrote 'Gesang' above the title 'Lied aus der Ferne', and this term is clearly better suited to this extended composition than 'Lied', which suggests a simpler, often strophic song, or refers to the original poem. Indeed, *Lied aus der Ferne* is the title reserved in the present study for Beethoven's first, strictly strophic setting of Reissig's poem; this music was ultimately used instead for his setting of *Der Jüngling in der Fremde* after the composer decided to write a vastly expanded through-composed setting of the text, and the contrast between the strophic 'Lied' and the through-composed 'Gesang' is inescapable. Whereas in the 'Lied' (see Henle 37b) a single musical verse has to serve for all the poet's stanzas regardless of mood or meaning, the 'Gesang' enables Beethoven to reflect the varying moods of the poem, from a calm memory of past happiness to the sudden awareness of present longing and a declaration of love made with a fast-beating heart and thence to a joyful anticipation of reunion. The song, essentially in ternary form, opens with a

23-bar piano introduction which constitutes a full exposition of the first section of the song. This first section, describing in compound time happy memories of the past, will be repeated as the final section of the song, albeit in an explicitly marked brisker tempo and with a much more decorated accompaniment, as the poet excitedly anticipates reunion and marriage. The middle section, in 2/4 time, starts in a tentative *poco allegretto*, although the syncopated accompaniment already suggests unease, but the poet's wildly beating heart is graphically portrayed, as the accompanimental quavers become syncopated semiquavers. The human heartbeat is, of course, the ultimate definer for tonal analogue, as in the late string quartets, where tempi varying from serene calm to manic activity, occasionally in rapid alternation, reveal the full range of Beethoven's constantly varying emotions and summon up equivalent feelings in the sympathetic listener. At the end of this rapid section of the song, the composer breaks the spell by allowing formal musical considerations to override true sentiment with an elaborate vocal cadenza and brief *adagio* recitative leading blatantly into a varied recapitulation of the first section.

Neue Liebe, neues Leben of 1809 marks a further progression in through-composition, as Beethoven manages here to reflect the twists and turns of the text and to achieve a remarkable faithfulness to actual speech rhythms in his declamation, without the need to vary his chosen musical metre. This move away from bipartite or episodic structure to a consistent underlying musical pulse which characterises the whole poem anticipates one of the principal features of many of Schubert's greatest songs, and we can confidently guess that Schubert knew, admired and learned from Beethoven's song (see *Kennst du das Land* and *Der Zufriedene* for evidence that Schubert was thoroughly familiar with the songs of op. 75). The whole song, in the manner of a rondo, is unified by its basic musical pulse, while the voice is liberated from the accompaniment, allowing real flexibility of declamation. The initial metre (crotchet – quaver) is a rapid heartbeat, rendered irregular *de facto* by the 6/8 time signature. When the *ostinato* quavers cease and the accompanist holds long chords at 'Ach, wie kamst du nur dazu?' the effect is of a 'freeze-frame', while the singer's question, a quasi-recitative but in strict time, is the 'voice-over'; the effect of a pause for reflection is beautifully accomplished. Later, the identical long sighing phrases used for 'dieser Blick' and 'zu ihr' make a clear association between the girl's physical attractiveness and her irresistible appeal, through purely musical means. Above all, through his choice of a relatively jaunty rhythm Beethoven exhibits a subtle understanding of the poem and its context: this is not a tragic tale of ill-fated longing, but an infatuation which will pass as fleetingly as the music, if it is kept in perspective.

Wonne der Wehmut and *Resignation* both exhibit the use and development of musical motif of a more specific kind. Interestingly, both songs set serious, intimate texts in major keys, illustrating how even bright major keys, here E and D respectively, can be rendered as poignant as minor keys. Admittedly, generous use is made of the tragic diminished seventh in the earlier song, and there is some tonal ambiguity in *Resignation*, but the point stands. *Wonne der Wehmut* exploits the familiar trope of falling couplets to represent tears, and this simple figure is developed throughout the song, in both voice and in the accompaniment, where descending scales become veritable fountains of tears, in a poem which pleads for tears never to dry up. As well as the falling couplet motif, the dotted figure of the opening 'Trocknet nicht' (coincidentally identical to the quail's song of *Der Wachtelschlag*) recurs throughout the song as a kind of motto refrain, always to the same words. *Resignation* is in ternary form, but the music is moulded throughout to the contours of the text. As well as the recapitulation of the opening stanza, the song is unified by the falling seconds, introduced at the outset and developed through the song as a motif for extinction. The mood of the poet is recreated by the composer at every point: the world-weariness which is part and parcel of the falling second motif, the fleeting recollection of past glories in C major, and the stoical resignation to fate *forte*, before the voice descends through an octave to final surrender.

The last of Beethoven's through-composed songs, *An die Hoffnung* (op. 94), the second setting of 1815, is grandly conceived in a clear attempt to do justice to the 'lyric-didactic' *magnum opus* from which the text is extracted. Beethoven knew and admired the poet, Christoph August Tiedge, which may account for the intensity of his setting. The recitative is a veritable compendium of rhetorical devices (see main entry), the carefully chosen key, B flat minor, already redolent of doubt and despair; and yet even within the recitative, a faster speed and a turn to the triumphant clarity of D major suggest doubts dispelled. The song proper, marked *Larghetto*, begins with a calm prayer, the voice floating serenely about a lulling triplet accompaniment. Word repetition threatens to become excessive until a series of short chords, marked *sempre pp* and separated by sighing rests, introduce a quasi-recitative section, where the words ('beloved voices fall silent') explain the generous rest to note ratio and the broken utterance which results. The brightness of C major as Hope seems to respond to the poet's appeal is short-lived, yielding to diminished sevenths and a turn to G minor, as the personified image of midnight as a figure leaning on a funereal monument is introduced. Big chords in D minor accompany the poet's railing against fate, before B major announces Hope's silver lining. A return to the opening verse of the *Larghetto* rounds off the song in traditional fashion.

Key decisions

Discussion of *An die Hoffnung* leads naturally to a consideration of the composer's use of particular keys in his songs and reminds us forcibly that it is not always sufficient to state that a song is 'in' a particular key, as Beethoven uses key as an expressive device and varies it, as meaning demands, within a work. Thus, in his larger songs he is always willing to undertake excursions of greater or lesser distance and duration outside his home key to illustrate, clarify or underscore images or emotional responses. It should, however, be added that Beethoven seldom loses sight of his chosen home key; indeed, *An die Hoffnung* (op. 94) is the only song which ends is a different tonic key from that in which it began, indicative of the sharply contrasting messages (despair and hope) of the recitative and the aria. A number of songs effect a similar contrast between sadness and the hope of better things to come by the move from a minor key to its tonic major: in *Elegie auf den Tod eines Pudels* grieving makes way for reassurance; in the Gellert *Busslied* contrition is followed by the assurance of God's forgiving grace; the self-pitying lament of

Seufzer eines Ungeliebten is relieved by the wish-fulfilment fantasy of *Gegenliebe*. Only in *Klage* does major become tonic minor, as the happiness of boyhood (E major) yields to the sadness and morbid introspection of maturity (E minor).

The briefest survey reveals that Beethoven uses *minor keys* sparingly in his songs. Hans Boettcher, whose 1928 study of the songs includes a valuable discussion of key choices (*Beethoven als Liederkomponist*, pp. 122–38), makes the interesting point that three songs extracted from larger literary works are in minor keys (*Marmotte, Aus Goethes Faust* and *Die Trommel gerühret*). A number of the unfinished songs are also in minor keys, including *An den Mond, Das Mädchen aus der Fremde* and *Heidenröslein*. Minor keys are used more predictably for Gellert's *Vom Tode* (in both sketches and the finished song), *Der Bardengeist* and, with telling poignancy, in *Die laute Klage*. The equation of minor keys with seriousness and major keys with happiness will never be more than an approximation, and Beethoven, like Schubert, can confound traditional expectations, nowhere more so than in his choice of major keys for *Wonne der Wehmut* and *Resignation* (see above).

It must be borne in mind when considering Beethoven's keys that each key had defined characteristics in the eighteenth century. While written definitions of each key's character seldom coincided exactly (see Rita Steblin's *History of Key Characteristics* for a convenient compendium of examples), most keys had clear associations and set up expectations in the minds of composer and listener alike. For composers of the Classical period, key choice could thus be a quasi-automatic process. Keys became effectively a metre for the emotions, indicating the type and degree of the feelings expressed and the response expected from the listener. If a song composer went outside the conventionally limited range of keys and added an excessive number of sharps or flats to the key signature (as rarely happened), serious grief or passion was afoot.

Before the arrival of equal temperament for keyboard instruments, a very gradual process which was only beginning in Beethoven's lifetime, the individual characters of keys were far more finely differentiated. The tuning of keyboard instruments is a matter of compromise, as only certain intervals are natural and other notes in the now traditional compass of the piano have to be falsely accommodated to the system (see David Grover's *The Piano*, London 1976, pp. 25–33, for a full explanation with accompanying mathematical formulae). Equal temperament, now universal, means that the octave is divided equally, so that all semitones are equidistant. Previous methods of tuning left the distance between the semitones unequal, either wider or narrower than a posited norm. Taking the semitone interval on a modern piano as a standard 100, semitones on pianos familiar to Beethoven had intervals ranging from approximately 112 (B–C and E–F) to 90 (C–C sharp). While we might deplore this lack of consistency, unequal temperament was not only widely accepted at the time but often viewed positively as what gave keys their true character. Keys were categorised as 'pure' (C, G, D, F and their relative minors), 'hard' (sharp keys) or 'soft' (flat keys), the degree of hardness of softness increasing with the number of sharps or flats in the key signature.

In addition to the rather obvious fact that remoter keys tended to raise the emotional quotient of the music, many writers and compilers of musical dictionaries tried to describe the true meaning of the different keys with greater precision.

These descriptions, many of which are reproduced by Rita Steblin (see above) in a helpful appendix with translations, are often fanciful and wordy, but give an insight into the fascination with the subject as part of the 'Affektenlehre' of the eighteenth century, which explored how best to create specific emotional responses in the listener. While Beethoven used keys in his own personal manner, which sometimes coincided with traditional definitions and sometimes did not, he was fully aware of the theories of such writers as Friedrich August Kanne, a personal acquaintance, and Christian Daniel Friedrich Schubart. Schubart's *Ideen zu einer Ästhetik der Tonkunst* (Ideas on the aesthetics of music) was written as early as 1784 (Schubart died in 1791), but achieved real influence only after 1806, when it was finally published posthumously in Vienna. According to Schindler, Beethoven knew Schubart's book well and defended it in discussion with friends. In the brief survey of key choices which follows, Schubart's descriptions of key characteristics are referred to, as it is important to bear in mind that Beethoven's close knowledge of such definitions implies that any departures from traditional usage were always conscious and deliberate. Many of the songs, of course, actually predate the composer's acquaintance with Schubart's writings, but these are quoted as typical of the many theories which abounded at the end of the eighteenth century.

Schubart characterises *C major* as 'totally pure . . . innocence, simplicity, naivety'. Beethoven uses the key in a much bolder guise. It is used for songs with chorus which exude conviviality or promote solidarity: the wedding song *Auf Freunde*, the war song *Kriegslied der Österreicher*, the drinking song *Erhebt das Glas* and for the assertive declaration of *Der freie Mann*. C major frequently expresses a newfound confidence and optimism after doubts, as in *Gegenliebe*, where C major is used to dispel the self-pitying stance which opened the song in C minor (the C minor–C major pattern is familiar from larger-scale works, including the Fifth Symphony and the final Piano Sonata op. 111, and the Choral Fantasia op. 80, where the music of *Gegenliebe* was indeed reused). In *Gott ist mein Lied* from the Gellert cycle, C major is used to express confident assurance. The optimism which accompanies the arrival of spring is expressed in C major in *Der Gesang der Nachtigall* and in *Es kehret der Maien* from the cycle *An die ferne Geliebte*, The fact that *Neue Liebe, neues Leben* is cast in the same key suggests that the lover's complaint is not to be taken too seriously. Beethoven's use of the key for the expression of a triumphant celebration matches more closely Schubart's definition of D major (see below). It expresses the glory of God in the Gellert song *Die Ehre Gottes aus der Natur* and briefly but vividly recalls the vigour of life's youthful flame in *Resignation* at the words 'Sonst hast du lustig aufgebrannt'. In this triumphant guise, C major recurs elsewhere, as in the Finale of the Fifth Symphony and those of the opera *Fidelio*: 'Heil! Heil sci dem Tag!' and the oratorio *Christus am Ölberge*: 'Preiset ihn, ihr Engelschöre!'

For Schubart, *G major* represents a pastoral idyll, 'true friendship and fidelity', 'gentle emotions'. The song of married contentment *Ich liebe dich* and the infinitely delicate *Das Blümchen Wunderhold* provide a reasonable match for this definition. *An den fernen Geliebten*, *Mollys Abschied* and *Feuerfarb'* are also gentle songs in G major, and it is instructive to note that the first two of these songs employ a feminine persona, while the second is by a female poet. Beethoven breaks the mould in *Abschiedsgesang an Wiens Bürger*, a companion piece to the war song in C major (see above), and in *Der Mann vom Wort*, where G major seems little more than a neutral support for vocal declamation.

D major is for Schubart the 'key of triumph, hallelujahs, war cries, victory rejoicing'. Among Beethoven's songs, only the sketches for *Östreich über alles* match this predictable and widespread definition, although it is used to great effect in the second setting of *An die Hoffnung*, when the poet commands us to hope and believe ('Hoffen soll der Mensch!'). Otherwise the songs in D major are a mixed bag, although they include several happy love songs: *An die Geliebte, Andenken, Nähe des Geliebten* and *Der Liebende*. D major in its traditional guise, as defined by Schubart and others, is employed in larger-scale works. It is the basic key of the *Missa Solemnis*, of the Second Symphony and the Violin Concerto. This is clearly a case where the same key bore different associations for Beethoven in the intimate sphere of solo song and in the public sphere of large concert works.

A major is characterised by Schubart as the key of 'innocent love, content-ment with one's lot, hope of reunion after parting, youthful gaiety and trust in God'. Most of these slightly disparate elements are encountered in Beethoven's songs in the key. *An einen Säugling* associates the innocent picture of a suckling baby with mankind nourished and protected by a loving God. Lost innocence is the theme of *Gretels Warnung*, while *Der Zufriedene* and *Lebensglück* are redolent of content-ment. Youthful high spirits inform *Der Kuss*, an early attempt at rococo humour, while absolute trust in God is witnessed in the second part of Gellert's *Busslied*. Two songs which do not match Schubart's descriptors are *Kennst du das Land* and *La Partenza*, where yearning and sorrow offer little hope of relief.

E major, the key of laughter and 'loud cries of rejoicing', acquires a some-what serener aspect in Beethoven's songs. Only the comical monologue *Ein Selbstgespräch* conforms to Schubart's definition. Elsewhere, the key is used for a prayer (Gellert's *Bitten*), for the ritual solemnity of *Opferlied* and the sublime anticipation of life after death in *Abendlied unterm gestirnten Himmel*. Two of Beethoven's finest love songs, one impassioned and one reflective, are cast in this key: *Wonne der Wehmut* and Reissig's *Sehnsucht*. The reference to starry skies in both *Abendlied* and *Sehnsucht* suggest that this image was associated for Beethoven with E major; indeed, Barry Cooper (*The Creative Process*, p. 43) adduces these two songs to lend credence to Czerny's report that the E major slow movement of the String Quartet op. 59/2 was conceived as the composer gazed at the stars. The accompanimental figuration of the delightful Italian love song *Odi l'aura* occasionally calls to mind the Piano Sonata in E major, op. 109, whose outer movements in this key frame a furious *Prestissimo* in the tonic minor. The *Adagio* of the Piano Sonata op. 2/3 compresses this pattern into a single move-ment, contrasting the serenity of E major and the seriousness of E minor. The song *Klage*, sketched a few years previously, explores a similar contrast of mood, the untroubled laughter of boyhood (E major) succumbing to the cares of maturity (E minor).

The remaining major sharp keys are used only incidentally in the songs. *B major*, for example, is used as a foil to B minor in *Sehnsucht (Was zieht mir)* and for the central section of *Odi l'aura*. It was left to Schubert to explore the possibilities of this key in masterpieces such as *Nacht und Träume* (D827) or *So lasst mich scheinen* (D877/3) where it acquires an ethereal quality far removed from the 'wild passions', 'anger' and 'despair' which Schubart describes.

F major is characterised by Schubart simply as 'complaisance and calm'. The 'little song of peace' *Das Liedchen von der Ruhe* provides a perfect match. Beethoven also used the key for the idyllic opening of *Der Wachtelschlag* and for the duet version of *Merkenstein*, a song which was marketed as a picturesque pastorale on its first publication. Despite some less likely uses of the key, such as in his setting of the quizzical *So oder so*, Beethoven seems to have associated F major with the untroubled and idealised image of the countryside, and it is no coincidence that he used this key for his 'Pastoral' Symphony and for the 'Spring' Sonata op. 24. It is also the key to which he instinctively turned when scribbling a brief sketch during a walk in the hills near Mödling, directly inspired by a beautiful sunset (see *An die Abendsonne*). The second section of each stanza of *Es kehret der Maien* from *An die ferne Geliebte* is set in the lower vocal register in F major (as subdominant); significantly, the fourth line of each stanza, referring successively to domesticity, fidelity and lovers uniting in the springtime, is entirely within that key.

B flat major, for Schubart an expression of 'happy love, clear conscience, hope, yearning for a better world', is chosen by Beethoven for two extended, cantata-like love songs: *Adelaide* and *Gesang aus der Ferne*. That Beethoven associated the key with love is suggested by his transposition of an Irish folksong melody into B flat (see Barry Cooper: *Folksong Settings*, p. 21). The melody had been sent to Beethoven by the Edinburgh publisher George Thomson, and the composer responded (in French): 'You wrote it in four flats, but as this key seems hardly natural and so little analogous to the heading *Amoroso* that it would change it rather to *Barbaresco*, I have treated it in the key that suits it' (EA405 / BB623). This rare recorded comment on the character of keys from the composer tells us something of his view of both B flat major ('amoroso') and A flat major ('barbaresco'). Two of Beethoven's most light-hearted convivial songs, the *Cantata Campestre* and the *Bundeslied*, were also cast in B flat major, the key of such larger works for public performance as the 'Hammerklavier' Sonata op. 106, the Second Piano Concerto and the Fourth Symphony.

Schubart designates *E flat major* 'the key of love, of devotion, of intimate conversation with God', its three flats symbolising the Holy Trinity. Beethoven uses the key to frame his cycle *An die ferne Geliebte* and in the Gellert setting *Die Liebe des Nächsten*, which reminds us to love our neighbour and states on a falling triad that 'God is love'. It is also the key which comes naturally to the composer when he sketches the words 'Gott allein ist unser Herr' (God only is our Lord) during a country walk. Otherwise no pattern seems to underlie the use of the key, although its lyrical qualities are exploited in songs as varied as *An die Hoffnung* (op. 32), *La Tiranna* and *Merkenstein* (solo setting), and only G major and C major are as frequently used in the songs. The song *Gedenke mein*, expressing sorrow at the departure of Archduke Rudolph, is written in E flat major, appropriately sharing this key with the Piano Sonata op. 81a ('Les Adieux'), whose first movement expresses the identical emotion. Beethoven's symphonic use of the key is quite different. The

'Eroica' Symphony and the 'Emperor' Concerto, works for public consumption where the grandest gestures abound, are far removed from the intimate ambiance of song performance.

A flat major, for Schubart the key of death, the grave and judgement, is little used by Beethoven for song composition. The associations with death are clear enough in In questa tomba oscura, but otherwise the key is used, more lyrically, only for two connected songs in the cycle An die ferne Geliebte (Leichte Segler and Diese Wolken), where the key is an integral part of an overall scheme. Boettcher (Beethoven als Liederkomponist, p. 125) tabulates the use of keys in songs and in slow instrumental movements, and one of his most striking results is that A flat major, virtually shunned by the songwriter, is used to keenly lyrical effect in no fewer than sixteen slow instrumental movements. Could it be that the traditional linking of this key to thoughts of death deterred Beethoven from using it in songs, where the texts might contravene established convention, whereas in instrumental 'songs without words', freed from the tyranny of textual associations, he felt at liberty to exploit the key's considerable expressive potential? Two uses of A flat major in larger vocal works match Schubart's description well: the aria 'In des Lebens Frühlingstagen' which opens the second act of Fidelio, where Florestan looks patiently towards death; and the duet 'So ruhe denn' from Christus am Ölberge, where Jesus accepts God's judgement and the Seraph shares his terror in the face of death and the grave.

Beethoven's relatively sparse use of minor keys has been adumbrated above. A minor, the key of 'pious womanliness, gentleness of character', is generally reserved for slighter songs, including three light-hearted songs: Marmotte, Urians Reise and Der arme Componist. It acquires gravitas in Gellert's Busslied, a penitential prayer, but here, as in the chorus of Urians Reise, the song turns to the brightness of A major to end in contrasting mood. E minor, characterised by Schubart as 'naive, womanly declaration of love . . . lament without grumbling, sighs with few tears', is used evocatively in Der Bardengeist for the nostalgic lament of the bard, and in the second part of Klage, where its lamenting tone is the more effective for following directly from the happiness of E major (see above). Three fragments in E minor (An den Mond, Das Mädchen aus der Fremde and Heidenröslein) confirm that Beethoven was not comfortable with this key for song composition.

B minor, famously referred to as a 'black key' by the composer, is used only for Sehnsucht (Was zieht mir), where it is followed by a turn to the major key as the expression of wild yearning is revealed to be no more than a poetical conceit, and for one of Beethoven's sketches for Heidenröslein, suggesting an unusually tragic interpretation of Goethe's little folksong parable. Those seeking a close match for Schubart's definition of B minor as 'silently awaiting one's fate, submission to divine dispensation' are referred to the opening section of the Agnus Dei from the Missa Solemnis, a uniformly sombre 'gentle lament'.

F sharp minor, described by Schubart as a 'dark key', full of 'resentment and discontent', was aptly employed for Gellert's Vom Tode, a severe reminder of transience and mortality. C sharp minor, the key of the 'Moonlight' Sonata, is used only for the sketches for a setting of Matthisson's Wunsch, a fond farewell to the untroubled world of childhood. Clearly, Beethoven here parts company with Schubart, who heard in this key 'penitential lamentation' and 'disappointed friendship'. For the song composer, it evokes only pleasant nostalgia.

A sketch for *Vom Tode* survives in *D minor*, a key of 'melancholy womanliness, engendering spleen and evil humours'. This was Beethoven's chosen key for his unfinished setting of the tragic ballad *Erlkönig* and occurs memorably in the second setting of *An die Hoffnung* as the poet rails against fate: 'Und blickt er auf, das Schicksal anzuklagen'. The key of the Ninth Symphony seems to have dark associations for Beethoven, evident in the 'Tempest' Sonata (op. 31/2) and in the earnest *Largo e mesto* from the Piano Sonata op. 10/3. It is also the key of Pizarro's aria of revenge 'Ha! welch ein Augenblick!' in *Fidelio* and of Klärchen's funeral music in *Egmont*. *G minor*, a key of 'discontent and unease' (and incidentally the key which Schubert chose for his *Erlkönig*), is used for Mignon's lament in *Sehnsucht (Nur wer die Sehnsucht kennt)* and for the bitter satire of Mephistopheles in *Aus Goethes Faust*.

C minor, 'declaration of love and at the same time lament of unhappy love', occurs in the personalised lament of *Die laute Klage* (see entry for a fuller discussion) and in the more stylised lament of *Que le temps me dure*. It is also the key of the self-pitying lament which opens *Seufzer eines Ungeliebten*, where the very title of the poem (Sigh of one who is unloved) must have suggested its use. As noted above, this song (as *Gegenliebe*) ends in C major. Through a series of works beginning with his very early Variations for piano on a theme of Dressler (WoO63) Beethoven sets up a virtual expectation that C minor will yield eventually to C major, so that the unrelieved minor lament of *Die laute Klage* appears atypical.

F minor is defined by Schubart in extreme terms as the key of 'deep melancholy, funeral lament, longing for the grave'. It would therefore have been considered appropriate for the *Elegie auf den Tod eines Pudels*, although it seems absurd that such a slight work should share the key of the 'Appassionata' Sonata, a work whose restless emotional energy speaks louder than words. The key is used to frame Klärchen's song *Die Trommel gerühret* from *Egmont*, and despite a middle section in F major, the use of F minor suggest that the tragic outcome of the play is already casting its shadow over this feisty and defiant song. Beethoven's unique use of *B flat minor*, for the opening recitative of *An die Hoffnung* (op. 94) where the poet at his lowest ebb doubts God's very existence, provides a perfect match for Schubart's description of the key: 'mockery against God, dissatisfaction with oneself and the world, preparation for suicide'. Together with other rhetorical devices (see main entry), the choice of key here is an aspect of tonal analogue; the very remoteness of the key, also described by Schubart as a 'Sonderling' (an odd misfit, an outsider), suggests the temporary alienation of the poet from everything he once believed in.

Directing performance

The direction 'Nach dem Sinn des Gedichts' (according to the meaning of the poem) which Schumann prefixed to his song *Mein Wagen rollet langsam* is unique and highly unusual in handing over total responsibility for interpretation to singer and pianist. Beethoven was not one to leave things to the intelligence and discretion of performers, and in preparing autograph manuscripts for publication he furnished them generously with tempo indications, instructions regarding expression, and dynamic markings. Posthumously published songs such as *Ein Selbstgespräch* or *Man strebt, die Flamme zu verhehlen*, which were never subject to this final stage of composer intervention and are thus devoid of any performance indications, look distinctly bare beside, say, *An die ferne Geliebte*, which is littered with dynamic markings, along with detailed tempo instructions in a mixture of Italian and German. Such instructions have the clear aim of achieving a degree of homogeneity in performance. In striving in this way to retain some control over the realisation of his compositions, Beethoven is also giving us interesting information regarding his views on performance and interpretation.

Of the innumerable German song collections published in the latter half of the eighteenth century, most included simple *performance directions* in German. Indeed, from about 1760, there seems to have been an unwritten agreement that German should be employed in preference to Italian in the case of short, lyrical settings of German texts: 'Lieder' in the strict sense of the word. Italian was reserved for instrumental compositions, for opera, for songs in Italian, or for German songs composed in imitation of Italian aria or arietta. In many cases a single word is considered sufficient to define the intended mood: 'traurig' (sadly), 'munter' (gaily), 'mutig' (boldly), 'lockend' (enticingly) and so on. 'Mässig' is preferred to 'moderato', and 'gehend' to 'andante'. Beethoven's teacher Christian Gottlob Neefe invariably used German for performance directions, his striving for 'Affekt' (emotion) clear from the variety of his instructions. Thus, in his *Das Totenopfer* of 1798, we see 'Langsam und tief gerührt' (Slow and with deep emotion), 'Heftig' (vehemently), 'Langsam stöhnend mit der höchsten Emphase' (Slowly groaning, with the greatest emphasis) and 'Mit Ergebung' (with resignation).

Although some of Beethoven's most detailed and informative performance directions are in German, his use of Italian directions in a majority of his songs before about 1811 strikes one as essentially backward-looking. It also suggests that the composer often failed to draw a clear line in his musical mind between instrumental and vocal composition, as Italian was still used almost exclusively for instrumental compositions. It is almost certain that most composers at that time would have used German indications for such simple songs as *Die Liebe* or *Das Blümchen Wunderhold*. The only song from the op. 52 collection with German indications is the first, the comical narrative of *Urians Reise um die Welt*, reflecting its earthy and non-lyrical character. Elsewhere the use of Italian often points to the Italian style of the composition. Of the six Gellert settings, only the last, *Busslied*, has directions in Italian, as Beethoven moves from chorale-like strophic form to an extended Italianate composition. Similarly, the strophic settings to poems by Reissig (*Der Jüngling in der Fremde, Der Liebende, An den fernen Geliebten, Der Zufriedene*) have instructions in German, but the elaborately through-composed *Gesang aus der Ferne*, complete with vocal cadenza, uses Italian (although Beethoven includes a German exhortation to increase the tempo at the reprise of the original 6/8 section). After 1811 Beethoven generally wrote performance directions in German, but the extended second setting of *An die Hoffnung* (see

above) has Italian directions, and Beethoven uses both German and Italian, sometimes together, in the song cycle *An die ferne Geliebte*, in his determination to
make his frequent subtle changes of tempo clear to all performers.

Regarding his German directions, Beethoven is not afraid to state the
obvious, in his concern to obtain the performance he prefers. Frequently he simply
takes his cue from the words of his text, as in *Kriegslied der Österreicher*, where
the direction 'Mutig' pre-echoes 'Mut', or *Des Kriegers Abschied*, where
'entschlossen' recurs in the poem. Directions in strophic songs are invariably based
on the words of a poem's first stanza; thus, in *Gottes Macht und Vorsehung*, the
direction 'Mit Kraft und Feuer' (with strength and fire), reflecting the reference to
a 'God of strength' in the second line, is, like the music itself, more appropriate
to the first stanza than to any of the fourteen stanzas which follow. The tendency
to underline the obvious in performance directions means that we learn little about
Beethoven's specific interpretation of a text, but we do learn that he sets great store
by appropriate performance which conveys the correct mood. How else could
Bitten, the prayer which opens the Gellert cycle, be sung than 'Feierlich und mit
Andacht' (Solemnly and with devotion)? Such directions conjure up an image of
Beethoven as a frustrated singing teacher repeating over and over to a pupil: 'Just
look at the *words*, for pity's sake! It's all there in the poem!'

Although most of his performance directions simply stress and summarise
the mood of a text, a few songs have unusually precise instructions to the performers. In the overtly comic song *Der Kuss*, the performers are instructed rather
superfluously to make it sound comic ('scherzend vorgetragen'); the tempo is
'lively', but Beethoven adds his habitual caveat 'but not too fast' (see below).
Beethoven's sense of comic timing is nowhere more evident than in this song, and
it is all clearly laid out for the performers, along with the endearing instruction
'lächelnd' (smiling) at the final punchline. Beethoven, himself more a 'growler'
than a singer and deaf by the time this early song was finally edited for publication
in 1825, has a clear image in his mind's eye (or ear) of how this song should be presented to achieve maximum effect.

Beethoven approached the composition of Hölty's fine poem *Klage* with
unusual care, possibly benefiting in this fine early song from the advice of Neefe.
In addition to marginal reminders to himself concerning tempo and notation (see
entry), there are longish performance directions which seem addressed to the
pianist. Above the introduction the composer has written a reminder to keep notes
sustained and legato throughout the song and at the interlude leading to the minor
section he asks for a gradual slowing. Both directions give specific and practical performance advice. In *Resignation* the comments are clearly addressed to the singer;
Beethoven seeks to determine the emotional ('with feeling, but resolutely') and the
technical ('well accented, as if speaking') aspects of the performance.

It is clear from Beethoven's *tempo indications* that he was at pains to avoid
extremes. Indeed, instructions not to perform *too* fast or *too* slowly are frequently
appended to the basic indication. Thus, in the Gellert songs, *Vom Tode* is marked
'Mässig und eher langsam als geschwind' (Moderate speed and slow rather than
fast), while *Die Liebe des Nächsten* is marked 'Lebhaft, doch nicht zu sehr' (Lively,
but not too much). The selfsame indication is given for *Neue Liebe, neues Leben*,

which addresses the poet's passionately beating heart, suggesting that clarity of declamation took pride of place for Beethoven (interestingly, Zelter's setting of the same text has a virtually identical marking: 'Lebhaft, doch nicht zu geschwind'). Three songs of Beethoven's maturity carry a contrary indication not to go too slowly: both *Merkenstein* (duet) and *Das Geheimnis* instruct 'nicht schleppend' (Don't drag), while *Sehnsucht* (WoO146) reads 'Mit Empfindung, aber nicht zu langsam' (With feeling, but not too slowly).

The other striking feature of Beethoven's tempo indications is their frequent occurrence within the course of a song, as the composer underlines words, ideas and changing moods through fluctuations of tempo. The brilliant comic timing of *Der Kuss* has been discussed, and examples abound elsewhere. The song cycle *An die ferne Geliebte* is notably rich in tempo indications, both to control the smooth linking of songs within the cycle, and within individual songs; the tempo is particularly finely nuanced in *Leichte Segler in den Höhen*, where the speed is relaxed before each of the final two verses to give the listener time to reflect respectively on the poet's pain and his sighs which fade with the setting sun before *Tempo I* returns each time with ever-renewed optimism, as the breezes which will carry his message of love pick up again.

As Maelzel's metronome was not available until 1814 or 1815, it is unsurprising that only two songs bear authentic metronome marks. The final version of *Resignation* dates from 1817, a somewhat fallow time, when Beethoven was deciding on metronome marks retrospectively for his first eight symphonies; the tempo indication (incidentally shared with the opening song of Schubert's *Winterreise*) is 'In gehender Bewegung' (at a walking pace) and the beat is set at 76 M.M. The same beat is given for *Abendlied unterm gestirnten Himmel*, marked 'ziemlich anhaltend' (quite steady). J. Fischhof stated, in an article on the significance of tempo (*Caecilia XXVI*, 1847, p. 94) that Beethoven had written a fascinating note on tempo and interpretation on the (lost) autograph of *So oder So* of 1817: '100 MM, but this can apply only to the opening bars, since feeling also has its own beat, but this cannot be completely conveyed at this level (i.e. 100)' (see entry). The statement that 'feeling has its own beat' is telling, allowing flexibility, to reflect the varying emotions of the text (*So oder So* does indeed bear indications for 'slight hesitations' in the final two verses, where this quizzical poem turns to thoughts of old age and death). It must be a source of regret that some metronome speeds were not given retrospectively for other songs, but the songs were evidently at the end of a long queue in this process.

Beethoven was unusually generous in his provision of *dynamic markings*. As in many larger works there are frequent juxtapositions of loud and soft dynamics. At times these seem arbitrary, as in *Kriegslied der Österreicher*, where the alternate marking of two-bar phrases as loud and soft bears no apparent relation to the text, but elsewhere sharply contrasting dynamics are used interpretatively. *In questa tomba oscura* begins quietly, but rises to *f* on the words 'ingrata' (ungrateful one) as the spirit recalls the cruelty of his lover. The voice then falls back resignedly to *p* and the central section begins *pianissimo*, rising swiftly to *fortissimo* as the spirit rejects the 'idle venom' of his lover's tears which have come too late. The song ends with a final repeated 'Ingrata!', where the second syllable falls on a sudden *forte* and the final syllable is marked *piano*; the effect, reminiscent of the 'Kyrie' which opens the *Missa Solemnis*, sums up the whole song: now that the spirit has said his piece he will for ever rest in the peace of the grave. A very similar ending occurs in *An die Geliebte*, where 'Mein!' is heard twice in the final bar, separated by a rest, the first time *forte* (suggesting a joyful proclamation) and the second time *piano* (suggesting a more inward satisfaction).

The strongly contrasted dynamics of *Die laute Klage*, one of Beethoven's most personal utterances, suggest almost a bipolar condition, as the lovelorn and sleepless poet expresses his pain through the envied persona of the turtle-dove as a 'loud lament' only to fall back into a quiet, sobbing realisation of his own inability to mitigate his anguish through song.

Another favourite dynamic effect is to rise through a crescendo to a sudden *piano*. Again, this can seem arbitrary, as in *Bitten*, where the breaks fall at 'so weit die / Wolken gehen' and at 'merk / auf mein Wort'. The opening phrase of the final Gellert setting, *Busslied*, on the other hand, demonstrates the meaningful use of the effect; to the words 'Against you only have I sinned' the voice rises through a *crescendo* which yields to a *subito piano* at 'sinned', as if the penitent is bowing his head in shameful acknowledgement of his guilt.

When Beethoven decides that a uniform dynamic is appropriate for an entire song, he is at pains to remind the performers of the fact. The unrelieved loudness of *Abschiedsgesang* with its doubled octaves is reinforced by frequent *sf* indications. The rococo delicacy of *Mit einem gemalten Band* is stressed both through the soft, but gently shaped dynamics (*sempre pp* occurs four times) and by separate expressive directions to singer ('delicately and gracefully') and to pianist ('delicately, not slurred'). The opening of *Wo die Berge so blau* from the song cycle is uniformly quiet. When the singer, on an unvarying pedal note, remembers his homeland ('Dort im ruhigen Tal') and time and pain are for a moment suspended, Beethoven is so concerned that the louder dynamic and more urgent mood of the next stanza should not be anticipated that five consecutive bars at the end of the section carry a *pp* marking.

The *ppp* marking does not occur in the songs, although it is implied in *Resignation* in the final bar before the reprise (b. 31) where the phrase 'lisch aus', which calls for the light of life to be extinguished, begins *pp* and carries a *decrescendo* mark. In the first version of *Der freie Mann* (Hess 146), marked 'feurig' (fiery), the young Beethoven is so carried away by the ideals of true freedom expressed in the verse that he allows himself a *fff* indication at the end of the fanfare-like postlude. This marking is unique in the songs and very rare within Beethoven's work as a whole.

The nearest Beethoven approaches to handing full responsibility for interpretation to the performers is in *Der Mann vom Wort*, where the direction reads: 'Gemäss dem verschiedenen Ausdruck in den Versen piano und forte' (Soft and loud according to the varying expression of the verses). The direction is a little surprising here, as the strophic song is provided with clear dynamic markings anyway and the stanzas do not differ greatly in expression, as this is a declamatory song about moral issues and not a lyrical piece. The composer is giving little away after all.

Examples of interpretative dynamics abound. *In questa tomba* has been mentioned above. In *T'intendo sì, mio cor*, where the poet addresses his heart, begging it not to reveal his pain, the tonal analogue of the anxiously beating heart is strongly underpinned by the dynamics. The beating is at first quiet but persistent, almost a sobbing. After two bars the singer (or poet) can no longer ignore the palpitation and is forced to analyse its cause and relive his pain. While the musical pulse remains constant, the varying dynamics provide a kind of emotional pulse as painful memories return and the singer becomes terrified of revealing his pain to the outside world, before falling back into silent suffering. Dynamics reflect the fluctuating moods of the poet in the second setting of *An die Hoffnung*. The quiet despair of the opening recitative with its wealth of rhetorical gesture (see above) is relieved by a rapid *crescendo* to the appeal to hope and trust in God ('Hoffen soll der Mensch!'). The prayer to Hope begins in quiet assurance, rising in volume as thoughts of the guardian angel up above come to mind. Successive images of despairing solitude and defiant railing against fate are underpinned by appropriate dynamics, before a powerful *crescendo* leads to the image of the sun appearing around the edge of the cloud which is 'life's dream'. After this confirmation that hope is real, the song ends very quietly, with a tone of calm assurance, 'all passion spent'.

Although Beethoven was often modest about his talent as a song composer, the sheer originality of his musical thinking enabled him to produce a range of work in which we can observe the emergence of the fully fledged Romantic *Lied*. Unlike his immediate predecessors, he had no inhibitions about expressing openly his own intellectual and emotional responses to verse in music and chose precisely such verse as occasioned a strong response. Perhaps only in the late string quartets, strangely intimate works with the tone of personal confession, does Beethoven wordlessly reveal so much of his inner self. The songs meanwhile offer us a vivid and verbally explicit commentary on the complex personality behind the music, but, like the quartets, they need to be performed to permit others to understand the personality which created them.

Despite isolated initiatives by a few enterprising individuals, it has generally required a powerful fillip to encourage performers to explore the full extent of Beethoven's achievement in song. Thus Peter Schreier's outstanding three-disc survey, recorded between 1968 and 1970, was enabled by the publication of Willy Hess's supplementary volume in 1962 (reminding us, incidentally, that a majority of songs are suited to a male voice). Deutsche Grammophon's edition of the complete songs in 1997 was made possible by the publication in 1990 of the outstanding Henle edition, with the editor of that edition providing a useful short essay in the accompanying booklet. Hopefully the publication of the present volume will encourage and enable performers from English-speaking countries to consider the full range of songs when planning a recital and thereby share with others the humour, the passion, the conviction and the awe which variously inform Beethoven's songs.

I *The songs*

ABENDLIED UNTERM GESTIRNTEN HIMMEL
Evening song beneath the starry firmament

H. Goeble

March 1820

E major WoO150 Peters 57 Henle 68 GA XXIII/247

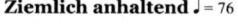

Wenn die Sonne nieder sinket,	When the sun sinks low
Und der Tag zur Ruh' sich neigt;	And day bows down to rest,
Luna freundlich leise winket	Luna beckons, quiet and friendly,
Und die Nacht herniedersteigt;	And night descends;
Wenn die Sterne prächtig schimmern,	When the stars sparkle in full splendour,
Tausend Sonnenstrassen flimmern:	Creating a thousand sunlit highways:
Fühlt die Seele sich so gross,	The soul feels so immense,
Windet sich vom Staube los.	And wrests itself free from the dust.
Schaut so gern nach jenen Sternen	It loves to look towards those stars,
Wie zurück ins Vaterland,	As though looking back to its native land;
Hin nach jenen lichten Fernen	Towards those bright distant expanses,
Und vergisst der Erde Tand;	Forgetting earth's tawdry pleasures.
Will nur ringen, will nur streben,	It desires but to struggle and strive
Ihrer Hülle zu entschweben:	To float free from its mortal shell:
Erde ist ihr eng und klein,	The earth is too small and restrictive,
Auf den Sternen möcht' sie sein.	It wishes to be among the stars.
Ob der Erde Stürme toben,	Though earthly storms may rage,
Falsches Glück den Bösen lohnt:	And false fortune reward the sinner:
Hoffend blicket sie nach oben,	It looks aloft, filled with hope,
Wo der Sternenrichter thront.	To where the celestial judge reigns.
Keine Furcht kann sie mehr quälen,	Fear can torment it no longer,
Keine Macht kann ihr befehlen;	Nor powers command it;
Mit verklärtem Angesicht	With transfigured countenance
Schwingt sie sich zum Himmelslicht.	It soars aloft to the heavenly light.
Eine leise Ahnung schauert	I feel the shiver of a presentiment
Mich aus jenen Welten an;	From those distant worlds;
Lange, lange nicht mehr dauert	My earthly pilgrimage

Meine Erdenpilgerbahn;	Will not last very much longer;
Bald hab' ich das Ziel errungen,	Soon I shall have achieved my goal
Bald zu euch mich aufgeschwungen,	And soared heavenwards to join you.
Ernte bald an Gottes Thron	Soon I shall reap beside God's throne
Meiner Leiden schönen Lohn.	The fair reward for all my sufferings.

Sadly, nothing is known about the poet whose text inspired this magnificent song. He is named variously as H. Goeble and H. Göble, which amounts to the same thing. 'Goethe', for example, was interchangeable with 'Göthe' at the time, with the latter spelling predominating. Goeble did not acquire a first name (Heinrich) until speculatively christened by Gustav Nottebohm in his Thematic Catalogue of 1868. Goeble's poem about the soul's ultimate release was among a group of texts offered to Beethoven by Johann Schickh, editor of the *Wiener Zeitschrift für Kunst, Literatur, Theater und Mode*, in which the song was first published in late March 1820 as a musical supplement.

One of the best known of Beethoven's own entries in the voluminous conversation books, reads 'Das moralische Gesez in unß, u. der gestirnte Himmel über unß – Kant!!!' (The moral law within us and the starry firmament above us – Kant!!!). The large writing and exclamation marks suggest a sudden epiphanic realisation. Barry Cooper (*Beethoven*, p. 275) explains that this entry was written early in February 1820, a month before the composition of the present song, after Beethoven had read a newspaper article by Joseph Littrow, a professor of astronomy. The final sentence is quoted from Kant's *Critique of Practical Reason*: 'There are two things which raise man above himself and lead to eternal ever-increasing admiration: the moral law within us, and the starry firmament above us.' Beethoven's desire to embrace both mankind and the entire cosmos in his work was to culminate in his setting of Schiller's *An die Freude* in the Ninth Symphony.

A more mundane, but still valid interpretation of Beethoven's complete identification with Goeble's text would consider his understandable desire to escape from the earthly sufferings connected with the guardianship dispute over his nephew Karl. On this interpretation, his sister-in-law Johanna is the sinner, enjoying temporary success before an earthly magistrate, while Beethoven himself anticipates his reward after death, before a heavenly judge. All possibilities are discussed in an excellent article on this song by Barry Cooper ('*Abendlied*').

The autograph of the song is in Vienna (ÖNB: Cod. 15514) and is dated 4 March 1820. A pencilled dedication to Dr Anton Braunhofer confirms that Beethoven certainly knew the doctor by this time, and had probably consulted him recently. Although Braunhofer became the composer's regular doctor only from April 1825, his name occurs in a conversation book entry in the very month this song was composed. Franz Schubert, no doubt recognising the exceptional qualities of this song, began to make a copy of it, but transposed it from E to D major and wrote out only the first 24 bars; he also altered the accompaniment figure in bar 6 and paid scant attention to Beethoven's dynamic markings (see Ernst Hilmar: *Verzeichnis der Schubert-Handschriften in der Musiksammlung der Wiener Stadt-und Landesbibliothek*, Kassel 1978). Nevertheless, the copy is one of the very few documentary links between the two great Viennese contemporaries. This song, described by Schumann as 'ein hehres und schönes Lied' (a gloriously sublime, beautiful song), represents the apotheosis of Beethoven's song-writing. Although the composer had seven years left to live, it has a valedictory quality and is indeed the last of his serious essays in solo song.

Some commentators have regarded *Abendlied* as 'through-composed' (see Stuber: *Die Klavierbegleitung*, p. 90f.), but this misinterpretation merely underlines Beethoven's achievement in the song, which is to match the changing tone and content of the verse within the formal constraint of the 'modified' or 'varied' strophic form. In Beethoven's songs of the modified strophic type, it is generally the evolving figuration of the accompaniment which carries the principal weight of expressive variation, while the vocal line is essentially unaltered (see *An die ferne Geliebte*); but in this song the composer treats the vocal melody too with a meaningful flexibility of line.

After four chords lying aptly high in the keyboard have fixed the tonality and introduced the starry firmament, eponymous hero of the piece, the first stanza opens with a solemn homophonic statement, suggestive of religious ceremonial. As the stars come out, throbbing repeated chords are used as a clear tonal analogue, representing not just the stars themselves but the very idea of divine glory and the sublime (Lesley Orrey identifies the analogue as an 'exaltation' technique in *The Beethoven Companion*, p. 426). The *topos* echoes throughout the Romantic song literature, as in Schubert's sublime male-voice part song *Nachthelle* (D892) or Schumann's *Mondnacht* (op. 39/5). The first six lines have set the scene in a dependent clause. For the final two lines, the main clause which introduces no less a subject than the ultimate emancipation of the human soul, Beethoven returns to bold, homophonic declamation.

At the opening of the second stanza, the vocal line rises 'towards those stars' just as it had previously descended with the setting sun. Throughout this song, Beethoven manages such subtly meaningful inflections of the vocal line with supreme confidence, acquired slowly and often laboriously during his long career as a song-writer. The varied accompaniment for each stanza sets the general mood, but it is the inflections in the vocal line which capture nuance.

It is the third stanza where the accompaniment is most richly and meaningfully varied. The opposed semiquavers in each hand at the start, not just providing a pictorial image of 'earthly storms' but also evoking the 'false fortune' which is the sinner's reward, are contrasted with a passage endearingly marked 'liebevoll' (affectionately) which refers to the soul's hope of salvation and reward. After a brief reminiscence of the 'exaltation' motif of repeated chords to introduce the judge who sits amid the stars, heavily dotted fanfare-like chords represent the certainty of redemption. (These fanfare-like chords are reminiscent of Schubert's great Klopstock setting *Dem Unendlichen* (D291), but, although this was written a full three years before Beethoven's song, it was not published until four years after Beethoven's death.) In the perorating final lines of the stanza, set again as homophonic declamation, the vocal line rises gloriously as the 'transfigured countenance' beholds the light of heaven.

The presentiment of the final stanza is expressed in a passage accompanied throughout by throbbing quavers, which must never rise above *pp*, making the poet's achievement of his final goal, expressed with an intensifying triplet accompaniment, all the grander when the delayed *crescendo* finally begins. Performers must take great care to ensure that the song's final winding down to a quiet close, with a brief coda and very quiet piano postlude, is not an anticlimax, but rather an expression of serene assurance, all doubts expelled, 'all passion spent'. A great performance of the song should be, as its composition seems to have been for Beethoven, a truly cathartic experience.

ABSCHIEDSGESANG AN WIENS BÜRGER
Song of farewell to the citizens of Vienna
Josef Friedelberg   Autumn 1796
G major WoO121 Peters 39 Henle 15 GA XXIII/230

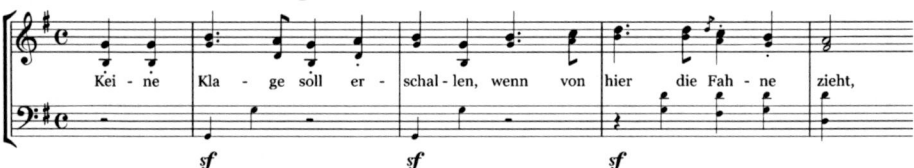

Keine Klage soll erschallen,	Let no lament sound forth
Wenn von hier die Fahne zieht,	When the flag departs from here,
Tränen keinem Aug' entfallen,	No tears fall from the eyes
Das im Scheiden nach ihr zieht.	Which follow its departure.
Es ist Stolz auf diese Zierde	It is our pride in this banner
Und Gefühl der Bürgerwürde,	And a feeling of civic dignity
Was auf aller Wangen glüht.	Which glows on every cheek.
Freunde, wünscht in Siegestönen	Friends, in tones of victory
Uns zur edlen Reise Glück.	Wish us good fortune in our noble mission.
Heiter folg' uns nach, ihr Schönen,	May your soulful glances
Euer seelenvoller Blick.	Follow us brightly, beautiful ladies.
Unsres Landes Ruhm zu mehren,	To increase our country's fame,
Ziehn wir mutig hin und kehren	We depart boldly and shall return
Würdiger zu euch zurück.	To you with greater honour.
Trotzend stehn vor Donnerschlünden	Even the rogue can stand defiantly
Kann wohl auch der Bösewicht.	In front of thundering cannons,
Milden Sinn mit Mut verbinden,	But he cannot combine a generous spirit with courage,
Menschheit ehren kann er nicht.	Nor can he honour humanity.
Nie das Glück der Tugend trüben,	Never to dull the bright joy of virtue
Brüderlich den Landmann lieben,	And to love one's compatriot as a brother:
Das ist deutscher Helden Pflicht!	This is the duty of German heroes!

Freut euch, Väter, jubelt, Mütter!	Fathers, be glad; mothers, rejoice!
Nirgend, wo der Korps erscheint,	Nowhere the corps appears,
Nicht bei Feinden, wird ihm bitter	Not even when facing the enemy,
Von der Unschuld nachgeweint.	Let innocence shed bitter tears for us.
Edel wollen wir uns rächen,	We want to avenge ourselves nobly,
Schweigen, bis die Taten sprechen;	Remain silent until our deeds speak for us;
Sie bewundre selbst der Feind!	May the enemy himself admire them!
Bessre Menschen, bessre Bürger,	Better people, better citizens
Als wir nun von hinnen gehn,	Than now leave this place,
Keine sittenlose Würger	No immoral thugs
Sollt ihr in uns wiedersehn.	Will you behold in us upon our return.
Unser Wien empfängt uns wieder,	Our Vienna will welcome us back,
Ruhmbekränzet, stark und bieder;	Crowned with fame, strong and upright.
Auf! Lasst hoch die Fahne wehn!	Rise now and let the flag wave on high!
Lasst uns folgen dieser Fahne -	Let us follow this flag,
Durch Theresens Kunstwerk reich -	Enriched by Theresa's artistry,
Deren Goldband uns ermahne:	Whose golden stripe reminds us
Tugend mach' uns Fürsten gleich.	That virtue renders us the equal of princes.
Ha! Wenn wir zurück sie bringen,	Ha, when we bring it back,
Wollen wir im Jubel singen:	We shall sing in triumph:
Dieses Band hielt Österreich!	Austria retained this stripe!

The patriotic verses were penned by a certain Joseph Friedelberg, who had already had poems published in the *Wiener Musenalmanach* between 1794 and 1796, when he was still in his teens. When volunteer corps were set up to counter the French invasion of southern Austria, he immediately enlisted in the Viennese regiment of 'Freiwillige' (volunteers), becoming a sub-lieutenant the following year. He was to die young from battle wounds in May 1800. This poem is known only from Beethoven's setting, published by Artaria in Vienna in November 1796. No autograph survives.

It would be facile to mock the poem as a hollow-sounding patriotic rant, but, at a time when the threat of foreign invasion was very real, it struck a chord with the Viennese. War songs (*Kriegslieder*) are a recognised subdivision of German song throughout the Napoleonic era and were performed at mass gatherings as a way of bolstering national confidence during a dangerous situation (see *Östreich über alles*). The French, whose urbane culture and literature had long been respected and imitated, at least by the lettered classes, now became the common enemy, following the terror of the French Revolution and the rise of Napoleon. This poem emphasises civic and national pride, the virtue and loyalty of the Austrian soldiers, and the morally ennobling effect of the forthcoming experience. It was written to celebrate the departure of the 'Fahnendivision' (colour division) of the volunteer force, explaining the references to the Austrian flag in the first, fifth and sixth stanzas. The first edition of the song carries a long subtitle explaining this precise context, making it one of the most specific of Beethoven's many 'occasional' compositions.

Beethoven's setting, marked 'resolute and fiery', has few artistic pretensions, but is appropriate to its function, with a four-square march rhythm, liberal scatterings of *sf* accents and *fortissimo* double octaves. The postlude introduces the military fife. If it had not been urgent to publish the song for a specific occasion, Beethoven might well have taken the trouble to orchestrate it. Although not marked as such, it is certain that the repetition of the refrain is intended to be sung by a chorus. *Kriegslied der Österreicher*, a companion piece to the present song, clearly designates similar choral repetitions.

Kühnel published the song in 1806, with new words by an unnamed author, as a 'Trinklied' (drinking song), celebrating a rather less elevated form of male bonding. In his defence, Kühnel clearly realised that the original words had lost their topical appeal following the French occupation of Vienna in November 1805. Swords had not yet been beaten into ploughshares, but a helmet made an adequate drinking vessel from which to drown one's sorrows, and a stirring tune was not wasted.

ADELAIDE Adelaide
Friedrich von Matthisson   1794–95
B flat major Op. 46 Peters 2 Henle 14 GA XXIII/216

Einsam wandelt dein Freund im Frühlingsgarten,	Lonely your friend wanders in the springtime garden,
Mild vom lieblichen Zauberlicht umflossen,	Gently bathed in the lovely magical light
Das durch wankende Blütenzweige zittert,	Which shimmers through the flowering branches,
Adelaide!	Adelaide!
In der spiegelnden Flut, im Schnee der Alpen,	In the reflecting waters, in the snow of the Alps,
In des sinkenden Tages Goldgewölke,	In the gold-fringed clouds of day as the sun sinks,
Im Gefilde der Sterne strahlt dein Bildnis,	In the star-spangled firmament, your image radiates,
Adelaide!	Adelaide!
Abendlüftchen im zarten Laube flüstern,	Evening breezes whisper among the delicate leaves,
Silberglöckchen des Mais im Grase säuseln,	The little silver bells of May rustle in the grass,

Wellen rauschen und Nachtigallen flöten:	Waves roar and the nightingales flute:
Adelaide!	Adelaide!
Einst, o Wunder! entblüht auf meinem	One day, o miracle! on my grave will
Grabe	blossom forth
Eine Blume der Asche meines Herzens;	A flower from the ashes of my heart;
Deutlich schimmert auf jedem	Upon every crimson petal will gleam:
Purpurblättchen:	
Adelaide!	Adelaide!

Matthisson's poem was first published, along with *Opferlied*, in the *Musenalmanach* for 1790, then edited by Johann Heinrich Voss. The almanacs were pocket-sized anthologies of recent poetry with fold-out musical settings of one or two of the poems. In the latter part of the eighteenth century they were a popular hunting ground for composers hungry for new verse to set to music, to satisfy in their turn the apparently insatiable appetite of the educated classes for new collections of songs. It is not known, however, whether Beethoven found Matthisson's two poems in the *Musenalmanach* or in the third volume of the poet's works, published in 1794. The surviving sketches for the song, including a sketch for the first section in Bonn (BH: Mh62) and extended sketches in the Kafka Album (BL: Add.Ms. 29801), have been dated to 1794–95.

The song was published in February 1797 by Artaria in Vienna as 'Eine Kantate', and Matthisson certainly received his due share of the credit. The title was printed as 'Adelaide von Matthisson' and it was also dedicated to the poet. It was, however, three years before Beethoven finally sent a copy of the song to its dedicatee with a sycophantic accompanying letter (EA40 / BB77):

> Mein heißester Wunsch ist befriedigt, wenn Ihnen die Musikalische Komposizion ihrer himmlischen Adelaide nicht ganz Mißfällt, und wenn sie dadurch bewogen werden, bald wieder ein Ähnliches Gedicht zu schaffen, und fänden sie meine Bitte nicht unbescheiden, es mir sogleich zu schicken, und will dann alle meine Kräfte aufbieten, ihrer schönen poesie nahe zu kommen.

> (My most fervent wish is satisfied if my musical setting of your heavenly Adelaide does not displease you, and should you be moved thereby to create another similar poem soon and, if you do not find my request immodest, to send it to me at once, whereupon I shall offer up my whole strength to do justice to your beautiful verse.)

The poet did not reply, but, when his poems were republished in Tübingen in 1811, the Appendix appeared to praise Beethoven's setting, despite the ambiguity of the reference to the text being 'put in the shade' by the music:

> Mehrere Tonkünstler beseelten diese kleine lyrische Phantasie durch Musik; keiner aber stellte, nach meiner innigsten Überzeugung, gegen die Melodie den Text in tiefere Schatten als der geniale Ludwig van Beethoven in Wien.

(Several composers enlivened this little lyrical fantasy with their music; none, however, according to my innermost conviction, put the text more in the shade in comparison with the melody than the brilliant Ludwig van Beethoven in Vienna.)

The poem is in the form of a Sapphic ode, each stanza consisting of three eleven-syllable lines, followed by a final 'Adonius' – a short line of five syllables (long-short-short-long-short). Matthisson uses the form to excellent effect, each stanza ending with the name of his beloved, 'Adelaide', which neatly forms the final Adonic line by itself. The frequent repetition of this name (four uses in Matthisson's poem become fourteen in Beethoven's song!) makes the performance of the song in English immediately problematic; does one simply sing the name with five-syllabled German pronunciation, or find an Adonic equivalent, such as 'déarest belóved'?

The designation of Beethoven's song as a 'Cantata' is telling. Matthisson's poem is the starting point for a musical structure of outsize proportions, unprecedented for the musical setting of a lyrical poem for voice and piano. Charles Rosen (*The Classical Style*, p. 380) states baldly that *Adelaide* is 'as much Italian Romantic opera as anything else', but the point is that Beethoven has deliberately chosen to set a German text in this style for voice and piano, expanding at a stroke the range of expression within the specifically German form of the *Klavierlied*. The composer ruthlessly appropriates and manipulates the text in the interests of musical form, repeating words *ad libitum* to fill his chosen phrase mould. Matthisson's poem consists of 76 words; Beethoven's song has 179 words.

The handsomely shaped introduction dovetails into a long-breathed vocal phrase of eight bars, illustrating the poet's lonely walk through the garden, with a delightful evocation of the 'magical light' shining through the moving branches, in a phrase of floated triplets. There is word-painting too in the heavier repeated triplet chords which suggest the snowy vastness of the Alps, which yield to broken triplet figures as day closes with a glorious sunset; and then the repeated chords return to greet the starry firmament with exaltation, a pre-echo of the same technique in other great songs, such as *Abendlied unterm gestirnten Himmel*. This use of tonal analogue, with a musical figure suggesting both a natural phenomenon (the stars) and an associated mood (exaltation), is a Romantic feature that anticipates a central Schubertian technique by some twenty years. The composer is not merely depicting Nature, but communicating to us what the poet must have *felt* in the presence of Nature, the whole linked and heightened by his being in love. The practice continues, with the evocation of whispering zephyrs, rustling lilies of the valley and fluting nightingales. All the musical images and phrases flow seamlessly into one whole, and we feel that here (almost twenty years before *Gretchen am Spinnrade*) we are witnessing the birth of the German Romantic *Lied*.

After a pause, no doubt much appreciated by the singer at least, the *Larghetto* makes way for an extended second and final section, *Allegro molto*. Beethoven's decision to interrupt himself in full flow and create a bipartite song akin to Italian operatic models seems almost perverse, although the poem, with its change of emphasis from present joy to the anticipation of future events, seems to invite such a process. Whether the poem's final stanza, speaking of flowers on the poet's grave, merits such a buoyant musical finale is questionable. Certainly a reviewer in the *Berlinische Musikalische Zeitung*, writing in 1805, criticised the over-jolly treatment of this final verse, feeling that it appears rather as if the composer is mocking the miracle of the petals' message and creating almost 'den Charakter einer Parodie' (Kunze: *Die Werke im Spiegel*, p. 41). This final section has also been criticised for the instrumental handling of voice and accompaniment. One almost feels that the voice could be replaced by, say, a violin. The instrumental handling of the voice is apparent from the very beginning of the section, where, after two bars of accompaniment, the voice answers to complete what is clearly a four-bar phrase ('Einst, o Wunder!'). This instrumental approach is unsurprising when one recalls that Beethoven was working simultaneously on the three piano trios of op. 1 and the three piano sonatas of op. 2.

Adelaide is by any standards a great song and has always been popular with both singers and listeners. Despite initial quibbles about the wisdom of through-composition, its popularity was virtually immediate and it was performed by the tenor Franz Wild and Beethoven for the dignitaries attending the Congress of Vienna, on 25 January 1815. Beethoven has not only illustrated the content of the poem but recreated the poet's every nuance of mood. Like other contemporary listeners, Matthisson may well have been overwhelmed when, perhaps for the first time, a poem was not just enhanced by music, but transfigured.

ADORATA, O NICE   Adored one, o Nice
After Metastasio   spurious

Hess 138 / WoO92a

This title is included in a scribbled list of works with target prices, prepared by Beethoven with a view to sales and later offered to Peters (EA1079 / BB1468). When Otto Jahn transcribed the price list, he read the entry as 'Odorata, o Nice', which was corrected by Willy Hess to the more feasible 'Adorata, o Nice', and both men took it to refer to a song. However, more accurate decipherment by Alan Tyson (see 'Price List of 1822') suggests that the entry actually refers to *No, non turbarti*, a Scena and Aria for soprano and string orchestra. This Scena, to a text from Metastasio's *La Tempesta*, was included in Kinsky's catalogue as WoO92a, having been published in 1949 in an edition by Hess (Wiesbaden, Brucknerverlag).

Hess failed none the less to realise that the Scena and the supposedly lost song are probably one and the same, and included the pieces as separate entries in his 1957 catalogue: *Adorata, o Nice* as Hess 138, and *No, non turbarti* as Hess 119. The confusion is explained in Hess2.

AH! PERFIDO O faithless one
Pietro Metastasio / unknown

1795–96

C major–E flat major Op. 65 Peters 65 Henle X/3 GA XXII/210

Allegro con brio

Ah! Per-fi- do, sper-gui-ro, bar-ba-ro tra-di- tor, tu par- ti?

Scene:

Ah! perfido, spergiuro, barbaro traditor, tu
  parti?
E son questi gl'ultimi tuoi congedi?
Ove s'intese tirannia più crudel?
  Va, scellerato!
Va, pur fuggi da me, l'ira de' Numi

Non fuggirai! Se v'e giustizia in Ciel,

Se v'e pietà, congiureranno a gara
Tutti a punirti! Ombra seguace!
Presente, ovunque vai,
Vedrò le mie vendette; io già le godo
  immaginando;
I fulmini ti veggo già, balenar d'intorno.

Ah no, ah no! Fermate, vindici Dei!
Risparmiate quel cor, ferite il mio!
S'ei non è più qual era, son' io qual fui;

Per lui vivea; voglio morir per lui!

Aria:

Per pietà, non dirmi addio,
Di te priva che farò?
Tu lo sai, bell'Idol mio!
Io d'affanno morirò.
Ah crudel! Tu vuoi ch'io mora!
Tu non hai pietà di me?
Perchè rendi a chi t'adora
Cosi barbara mercè?
Dite voi, se in tanto affanno

Non son degna di pietà?

Scena (recit.):

O faithless one, deceitful, barbarous traitor,
  you desert me?
And are these your final words of farewell?
Where is found a crueller tyranny?
  Go then, ingrate,
Go, yet flee from me only, you will not
  flee
The wrath of the Gods! If there is any
  justice in Heaven,
Any pity, they will all join together
To punish you! My shade will pursue you,
Ever-present, wherever you wander,
I shall see my revenge; I relish it already in
  my imagination.
Already I behold the lightning strike around
  you.
But no, oh no! Cease, gods of vengeance!
Spare him for my sake, strike me instead!
Even if he is not what he was, I am still the
  same;
I lived for him; I wish to die for him!

Aria:

For pity's sake, do not bid me farewell,
What shall I do without your love?
You know it well, my fair idol!
I shall die from my anxiety.
O cruel one! You see that I should die!
Do you take no pity on me?
Why do you give her who adores you
Such barbarous recompense?
Say yourselves whether I do not deserve
  pity
In such a state of anxiety.

This large-scale concert aria with orchestra is included here because it appears in the Peters edition of the 'collected songs' and in other popular editions which obediently follow Peters, such as Pauer's edition for Augener. It was first published by Hoffmeister & Kühnel in Leipzig in July 1805 as a collection of orchestral parts and a solo soprano part which incorporated a piano reduction, but neither this piano reduction nor the separate edition of the piano arrangement which the publishers issued the same year was prepared by the composer. The full score appeared only in 1856, from Peters in Leipzig. Only a fragment of a first autograph version of the score survives (BN: Malherbe), but a full copy, corrected by Beethoven, displays two title pages. The first of these is in French and states that this 'grande scène' was composed in Prague in 1796; the second, in Italian, bears a dedication to Josephine Clary. Sketches (including BL: Add.Ms. 29801) date from the previous year and suggest that Beethoven may have begun this work in 1795 in preparation for his visit to Prague.

The composer was in the Bohemian capital from February until April 1796, where he met the young Countess Josephine Clary (1777–1828), whose soprano voice was 'charming' rather than powerful and who also played the mandolin. The dedication of the work to Clary is unambiguous: 'Recitativo ed Aria composta e dedicata alla Signora di Clari di L v. Beethoven'. Nevertheless, it was the dramatic soprano Josefa Dussek (1754–1824) who gave the first performance, in Leipzig on 21 November 1796, and the announcement of the concert two days previously in the *Leipziger Zeitung* claimed that the concert aria had been composed for her. The printed edition bore no dedication: perhaps composer and publisher had decided that discretion was the better part of valour.

It was wholly appropriate that Dussek should have given the first performance. Not only was she famed for the expressive and dramatic quality of her singing, but she had impressed Mozart sufficiently for him to write two concert arias (or 'scene') for her: *Ah, lo previdi* (K272) and *Bella mia fiamma* (K528), the latter while Mozart was a guest at the Dusseks' villa, Bertramka, on the outskirts of Prague. *Ah! perfido* is clearly a true successor to the Mozart concert aria, as well as benefiting from Beethoven's contemporary studies with Salieri.

The text of the Scena (recitative) is by Metastasio. The author of the Aria text has not been identified; its poetry is undistinguished, although this does not deter Beethoven from lavish word repetition. The extended Scena incorporates many tempo changes after the initial brio opening has commanded our attention. These mirror the swiftly varying emotions of the deserted lover, from name-calling to threats of vengeance to self-sacrifice. The contrasts between slow and fast sections become even more extreme in the Aria. The *Adagio* sections would not be out of place in a selection of Beethoven's more Italianate *Klavierlieder*, but the very fast (*allegro assai*) sections are the province of the opera singer. One certainly imagines that Josefa, rather than the 19-year-old Josephine, would feel at home amid the descending chromatic scales and the high B flats.

Ah! perfido was among the works performed at Beethoven's marathon benefit concert at the Theater an der Wien on 22 December 1808, which also included the Fifth and Sixth Symphonies, the Fourth Piano Concerto and the Choral Fantasia.

ALS DIE GELIEBTE SICH TRENNEN WOLLTE
When she deserted him
Stephan von Breuning (after François Benoît Hoffman) 1806

E flat major WoO132 Peters 44 Henle 30 GA XXIII/235

Der Hoffnung letzter Schimmer sinkt dahin!	The last glimmer of hope is fading!
Sie brach die Schwüre all mit flücht'gem Sinn;	She broke all her vows with flighty abandon;
So schwinde mir zum Trost auch immerdar	Then may the awareness that I was once too happy
Bewusstsein, dass ich zu glücklich war!	Also vanish for ever, to give me some consolation.
Was sprach ich? Nein, von diesen meinen Ketten	What am I saying? No, no power, no resolve
Kann keine Macht, kann kein Entschluss mich retten;	Can save me from these my chains;
Ach, selbst am Rande der Verzweiflung	Ah, even on the brink of despair,
Bleibt ewig süss mir die Erinnerung!	Her memory remains ever sweet to me.
Ha, holde Hoffnung, kehr zu mir zurücke;	Ha, sweet hope, return again to me;
Reg all mein Feuer auf mit einem Blicke!	Kindle all my burning passion with one glance!
Der Liebe Leiden seien noch so gross;	However great love's sufferings may be,
Wer liebt, fühlt ganz unglücklich nie sein Los!	He who loves never feels his lot to be totally miserable.
Und du, die treue Lieb' mit Kränkung lohnet,	And you, who reward faithful love with callous rejection,
Fürcht nicht die Brust, in der dein Bild noch wohnet;	Do not fear the breast where your image still dwells;
Dich hassen könnte nie dies fühlend Herz;	This feeling heart of mine could never hate you.
Vergessen? Eh' erliegt es seinem Schmerz.	Forget you? It would sooner succumb to its anguish.

The poem is a free translation by Beethoven's long-standing friend Stephan von Breuning of a 'Romance' from *Le Secret*, a one-act drama by François Benoît Hoffman with music by Jean Pierre Solié, first produced in 1796 and popular in Vienna around 1800. The original was sung in the seventh scene and begins 'Je te perds, fugitive espérance'. Breuning's translation was completed in May 1806, and it is likely that the song was composed shortly after this.

The song first appeared as a supplement to the *Allgemeine musikalische Zeitung* in Leipzig on 22 November 1809. No autograph survives, but Gerhard von Breuning later made a copy of the song for Franz Wegeler from a manuscript in his father's papers. This version was published as a fold-out appendix to Wegeler's supplementary volume to his biographical notes on Beethoven (*Nachtrag zu den biographischen Notizen über Ludwig van Beethoven*) in Koblenz in 1845, wrongly announced as a first publication. Simrock, who had set the fold-out sheet, published it simultaneously as a separate edition in Bonn. This version is entitled 'Empfindungen bei Lydien's Untreue' (Sentiments upon Lydia's infidelity). As it differs from the first edition, it must be assumed that the young Breuning had copied from Beethoven's original manuscript, now lost. It is reasonable to suppose that the composer had made a revised copy of the song before its publication in 1809 and then returned the manuscript to the elder Breuning.

The text is set strophically, the only variation occurring in the final verse, where the accompaniment is syncopated, before an interrupted cadence leads to a brief vocal codetta. The choice of strophic form brings with it problems of declamation which are aggravated by the uneven metre of the text.. The fit of 'Süss mir die Erinnerung' in the second verse is clumsy despite an attempt at rhythmic assimilation. On the other hand, the melody is shapely. The emphasis on the first syllables of the last line of each stanza, repeated sequentially before a pause, works particularly well for 'Vergessen?' in the final verse. Although the jilted lover is still in denial, the fast tempo indication and the cheery piano postlude, which we hear four times, give a distinctly jaunty tinge to his plaint.

AN AMARANT / KRANK VOR LIEBE
To Amarant / Sick with love
Leopold von Goeckingk   1792
C major Bia 43 unfinished sketch

Allegretto

Mei-ne Mut-ter frägt mich im-mer: trinkst du auch den Man-del-trank? Trink ihn: Trink ihn:

Meine Mutter frägt mich immer:	My mother is always asking me:
Trinkst du auch den Mandeltrank?	Are you drinking that tonsil tonic?
Trink ihn! täglich wirst du schlimmer! -	Drink it up! You're becoming worse every day! -
Ach! die Liebe macht mich krank!	Alas, it is love which is making me ill!
Nimm doch, spricht sie oft bey Tische,	Have some, she often says at table,
Wirst so mager und so matt,	You're becoming so skinny and exhausted,
Nimm ein Stückchen von dem Fische! -	Have a little bit of the fish! -
Ach! die Liebe macht mich satt!	Alas, it is love which has overfed me!

'Siehst du nicht die Scheere liegen?   'Can't you see the scissors?
Liegt ja grade vor dir, Kind!   They're lying right in front of you, child!
Kann dich so das Auge trügen?' -   Can your eyes deceive you so?' -
Ach! die Liebe macht mich blind!   Alas, it is love which makes me blind!

'Bist so still? was mag dir fehlen?   'You're so quiet. What can be wrong with
                                      you?
Geht dir was im Kopf herum?   Have you something on your mind?
Weisst du gar nichts zu erzählen?' -   Have you nothing at all to say to us?' -
Ach! die Liebe macht mich stumm!   Alas, it is love which strikes me dumb!

'Ey! ich mögte fast dich schlagen!   'Oh, I almost feel like giving you a smack!
Zieh den Schlepp auf! was für Staub!   Lift your skirts up! All that dust!
Soll ichs dir noch zehnmal sagen?' -   Do I have to tell you another ten times?' -
Ach! die Liebe macht mich taub!   Alas, it is love which makes me deaf!

'O! die liebe Langeweile!   'Oh, this blessed boredom!
Wäre Amarant doch hier!' -   If only Amarant were here!' -
Hörst du Liebster? Eile! eile!   Can you hear, my darling? Hurry, do hurry!
Leben bringst du ihr und mir!   You will revitalise both her and me!
         Nantchen   Nantchen

The poem was published in the Göttingen *Musen-Almanach* for 1776. Leopold von Goeckingk had recently taken on the editorship of the almanac after Johann Heinrich Voss had left Göttingen and begun to publish his own new *Musenalmanach* in Hamburg. Two years later Goeckingk was to join Voss as co-editor, while Bürger took over the original Göttingen *Musenalmanach*. The issue for 1776 included a fluent but bland setting of the present poem by Ernst Christoph Dressler (1734–79), the same minor composer who had provided the theme for one of Beethoven's earliest compositions, the Variations on a March by Dressler WoO63.

The poem is part of a long exchange of poems between Goeckingk (using the pseudonym 'Amarant') and his wife Sophie Marie Philippine (writing as 'Nantchen'). Thus, the present poem is attributed to Sophie Goeckingk, and may indeed be entirely her work, rather than that of her husband. The poems were published as a collection in 1777 under the title *Lieder zweier Liebenden* (Poems of two lovers) and established Goeckingk's literary reputation. There is clearly no autobiographical subtext in the present poem, which caricatures a lovesick teenager of a bygone age.

Beethoven's autograph is in the so-called 'Fischhof Miscellany' (Berlin SPK: Aut.28, f. 43v) and is a fairly full sketch written on two staves, with the text to the first stanza underlaid. The melody is effectively complete and a simple accompaniment, largely 'Alberti bass', is sufficiently well adumbrated to make realisation of the song reasonably straightforward. Willem Holsbergen realised the song for the 'Unheard Beethoven' project in 2005 and the result can be heard on their website (www.unheardbeethoven.org). Holsbergen points out, in a letter to the author, that Beethoven's setting of 'Trink ihn!' as an isolated exclamatory phrase leads to severe problems in subsequent stanzas, where the third line cannot sensibly be split in this abrupt manner. Could Beethoven's awareness of this problem have been a factor in its remaining incomplete? The setting of 'Trink ihn! Trink ihn!' in the present song is reminiscent of the setting of 'Küssen, Küssen' in *Prüfung des Küssens*, an aria for bass solo and orchestra from 1790; the similar opening words of the present song ('Meine Mutter frägt mich immer') and of the aria ('Meine weise Mutter spricht') sparked a clear musical equivalence.

The sketch is published in facsimile and transcribed by Douglas Johnson (*Beethoven's Early Sketches*), although Johnson was unaware of the poem's provenance and authorship.

AN DEN FERNEN GELIEBTEN To her distant lover
Christian Ludwig Reissig   1809

G major Op. 75/5 Peters 21 Henle 44 GA XXIII/219

Einst wohnten süsse Ruh' und goldner Frieden	Once sweet repose and golden peace dwelt
In meiner Brust;	Within my breast;
Nun mischt sich Wehmut, ach! seit wir geschieden,	Now, alas, since we parted, every pleasure
In jede Lust.	Is joined to melancholy.
Der Trennung Stunde hör' ich immer hallen	I still hear the tolling hour of our parting echo,
So dumpf und hohl;	So dull and hollow,
Mir tönt im Abendlied der Nachtigallen	In the evening song of the nightingales I hear
Dein Lebewohl.	Your farewell.
Wohin ich wandle, schwebt vor meinen Blicken	Wherever I turn, your lovely image
Dein holdes Bild,	Hovers before me,
Das mir mit banger Sehnsucht und Entzücken	Filling my heart with anxious yearning
Den Busen füllt.	And delight.
Stets mahn' es flehend deine schöne Seele,	May it entreat your noble heart to recall
Was Liebe spricht:	The words of love:
'Ach Freund, den ich aus einer Welt erwähle,	'Ah friend, whom I have chosen above all others,
Vergiss mein nicht!'	Forget me not!'

Wenn sanft ein Lüftchen deine Locken kräuselt	Whenever a breeze stirs your curls
Im Mondenlicht,	By moonlight,
Das ist mein Geist, der flehend dich umsäuselt:	That is my spirit, as it whispers imploringly:
Vergiss mein nicht!	Forget me not!
Wirst du im Vollmondschein dich nach mir sehnen,	If you should ever pine for me by the light of the full moon,
Wie Zephirs Wehn	Like a zephyr
Wird dir's melodisch durch die Lüfte tönen:	My words will waft melodiously through the air to you:
'Auf Wiedersehn!'	'Until we meet again!'

Reissig's poem appeared in the first edition of his collection *Blümchen der Einsamkeit* (Flowers of solitude). The theme of separation recurs in other Reissig texts set by Beethoven, notably *Der Jüngling in der Fremde* and *Gesang aus der Ferne*, but here the speaker is feminine, rendering the poem a counterpart to *Der Jüngling in der Fremde*. We would gladly put our hands in our pockets to pay the coach fare for one or the other, so that they could be reunited, but this would defeat the purpose, as the actual longing for the absent one is the theme and pretext for the poems. An absent lover's longing and remembrance were to be explored more fully in Alois Jeitteles's poetic cycle *An die ferne Geliebte*, whose title may be a reminiscence of the present poem. There, particularly in the guise of Beethoven's song cycle (op. 98), the problem of separation will be gloriously resolved through the power of shared song; here, the lover's appeals are simply entrusted to the melodic capability of passing breezes.

There are sketches for the song in Berlin (DSB: Landsberg 5), dated to the autumn of 1809, one of which is close to the final version. The autograph (DSB: Artaria 173), which also contains Reissig's *Der Liebende* and *Der Zufriedene* is a fair copy. The song was first published in July 1810 by Artaria in Vienna in a collection of settings of Reissig poems by various composers, which also included *Der Jüngling in der Fremde* and *Der Zufriedene*, but appeared again in October 1810 as the fifth song of the op. 75 collection, published by Breitkopf und Härtel in Leipzig (*Der Zufriedene* also appeared as the sixth and final song of the set). Meanwhile, it had been published in August 1810 in London by Clementi, as 'The Distant Lover. A Favorite Arietta' under an arrangement agreed with the composer.

The final four bars of the Artaria edition differ from the autograph and the first printing of op. 75, upon which the collected edition and all subsequent editions are based. The Artaria version, which extends the vocal line and shortens the piano postlude, works perfectly well. It is printed in the Henle edition as an authentic alternative ending.

The song is a simple strophic setting in a bland 6/8 metre, and lacks the freshness of some other Reissig settings. It almost seems that Beethoven had a 'feminine' style for songs with piano which are clearly intended for a female singer. The preceding song of op. 75, *Gretels Warnung*, borders on the insipid, and two songs from op. 52, *Feuerfarb'* and *Mollys Abschied*, similarly suggest that Beethoven had difficulty in identifying strongly with a female persona in the sphere of solo song. Beethoven's 'feminine' style is no doubt an inheritance from the eighteenth century, when collections of simple songs designed to be sung by an amateur female performer, often to her own accompaniment, were commonplace. The unassuming key of G major, the slowish tempo (*larghetto*) and the narrow vocal compass of a sixth all encourage simplicity of performance and utterance.

The six songs of op. 75 certainly cover a wide range of dramatic personae, making performance of the whole set by a single singer utterly impracticable. Five of the poems are in the first person. Mignon (*Kennst du das Land*) is a waif, a girl who dresses as a boy for preference; the young Goethe speaks forcibly in his own voice in *Neue Liebe, neues Leben*; the tale of the flea is told in the third person, but through the explicit mouthpiece of Mephistopheles; *Gretels Warnung* is communicated by an ingenuous, but disillusioned young girl; the present song is sung by a restless girl in love; and the hero of *Der Zufriedene* is a man who is totally at ease with his lot in life. No one singer can command the range of interpretative dramaturgy implied, placing this mixed bag of an opus beyond the scope of a solo recital.

AN DEN MOND To the moon
Johann Wolfgang von Goethe   1826
E minor SV30 fragmentary sketch

Füllest wieder Busch und Tal	Once again you flood forest and dale
Still mit Nebelglanz,	Silently with your misty shimmer,
Lösest endlich auch einmal	Finally too you free and dissolve
Meine Seele ganz.	My soul entirely.
(Folgen 8 Strophen)	(8 further stanzas)

This tiny sketch in the 'Kullak' desk sketchbook (SPK: Aut.24, f. 48v), which Beethoven used in late 1825 and throughout 1826, is included merely for the sake of completeness and to illustrate Beethoven's continuing fascination with Goethe at a time when his song production had otherwise come to a complete halt. Only six ambiguous bars of music exist, of which only the first two are texted. Goethe's celebrated poem, in which the moon evokes feelings of melancholy and nostalgia, was not published until 1789 in the eighth volume of his works, but the original version, opening 'Füllest wieder 's liebe Tal', was written in January 1778 and set to music at once by Siegmund von Seckendorff from the manuscript.

The poem had already been set by all the usual suspects, including Reichardt (1790), Romberg (1793), Zelter (1812) and twice by Schubert (1815, c.1819), before Beethoven turned his attention to it for a fleeting moment. Like so many of his fragmentary song sketches, it is cast in a minor key. The composer was clearly relying on his memory, as the words are incorrectly rendered 'Stillest wieder Busch und Tal'. The use of 'stillen', which refers to satisfying hunger, quenching thirst or breast-feeding, is actually very apt here and points to Beethoven's unconscious assimilation of Goethe's poetic imagery: the verb occurs prominently, for example, in the second line of his *Wandrers Nachtlied*: 'Der du von dem Himmel bist, / Alles Leid und Schmerzen stillest' ('You who are from Heaven, / Who still (at your breast) all our sorrow and pain').

It would not be difficult to find an autobiographical subtext in Goethe's poem, which goes on to compare the fast-flowing river to female inconstancy, comments on the torture caused by the remembrance of happy times and seeks solace in song and the friendship of a kindred spirit.

AN DIE ABENDSONNE   To the evening sun
unknown   summer 1818

?C major Hess 323 sketch

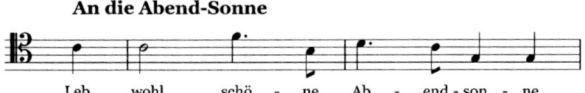

This tiny sketch, originally in tenor clef, appears in a pocket sketchbook (Vienna, GdM: A45, f. 20v) sandwiched between sketches for the 'Hammerklavier' Sonata op. 106. As the name suggests, the pocket sketchbooks were intended for use 'on the hoof', and Nottebohm suggests that the present sketch was written during a walk near Mödling, south of Vienna, as the sheet is headed 'In the evening on the path between and on the mountains' (see also *Gott allein ist unser Herr*). It may have been intended as a canon, but is included here not only for the sake of completeness, but because it gives an insight into Beethoven's use of his sketchbooks. This tiny fragment gives every impression of having been written on impulse in immediate response to a glorious sunset, which probably inspired both words ('Farewell, beautiful evening sun') and music. The brief moment of inspiration did not survive beyond the sunset and did not lead to a longer work when the composer returned home to recollect the scene and consider the larger-scale musical possibilities of his sketch.

The sketch was first quoted by Nottebohm (*Zweite Beethoveniana*, p. 137), and the sheet is reproduced in Johnson et al., *The Beethoven Sketchbooks*, p. 352.

AN DIE FERNE GELIEBTE   To his distant beloved
Alois Jeitteles   April 1816

Op. 98 Peters 33 Henle 63 GA XXIII/224

An die ferne Geliebte is the best known and most frequently discussed of Beethoven's works for solo voice and piano. It has the distinction of being the first musically linked song cycle, and as such looks forward to the song cycles of Robert Schumann, composed some 25 years later. There had always been song collections, where individual songs were linked by their common poetic theme or subject; indeed, Beethoven's own settings of six religious poems by Gellert (op. 48) is a prime example. The *Liederspiel*, a drama which included songs as a key element, and in its extreme form consisted entirely of a sequence of songs, moved from the theatre to the salon, reaching its apotheosis and ultimately the concert platform in Schubert's *Die schöne Müllerin*. But Beethoven established the principle of what Ruth Bingham (Parsons (ed.), *The Cambridge Companion to the Lied*, pp. 115–17) calls the 'musically constructed cycle', linking the six poems into an uninterrupted musical narrative, with a carefully organised sequence of keys and a final return to the music of the opening song to round off the cycle and gloriously affirm the message that music overcomes the bounds of physical separation.

Despite the work's popularity, it has not been established how Beethoven encountered this cycle of six poems by the young medical student and budding writer, Alois Jeitteles. The clearest common link between the two men is Ignaz Castelli, a leading 'mover and shaker' on the Viennese literary scene. He edited the journal *Selam*, in which Beethoven's song *Merkenstein* (WoO144) had appeared in 1815 and in which Jeitteles published poems from 1815 until 1817. The names of poet and composer appear frequently in Castelli's *Memoiren*, although never together. Castelli may well have recognised the suitability of Jeitteles's poetic cycle for musical setting and encouraged him to send his work to the composer. Beethoven was an obvious choice in view of his known predilection for the theme of the absent lover, evidenced in such songs as *Andenken*, *Gesang aus der Ferne* and *An den fernen Geliebten*.

The likelihood of an autobiographical subtext in the cycle has often been mooted. Barry Cooper hypothesises that, after the death of his brother in 1815 and his subsequent adoption of his nephew Karl, Beethoven's need for a female companion to love diminished. He became reconciled to the fact that his love for Antonie Brentano, now safely back in Frankfurt with her family, would become an exclusively spiritual liaison, although he could still 'communicate with her at the deepest level and express his love for her – through his art' (*Creative Process*, pp. 49–51). Cooper argues convincingly that writing the song cycle was 'a means of coming to terms with his plight by universalising it'. It is less easy to accept his suggestion that, as a means of coming to accept their separation, Beethoven may actually have asked Jeitteles to write this cycle of poems to his specification. The use of the word 'entfernte' rather than 'ferne' in the Bonn autograph (see below) is telling. 'Entfernte' has a sense of enforced separation and removal, as though someone he loved had been deliberately taken away from the composer, or deliberately removed herself from his company, just as Antonie took the hard, but irrevocable decision to return permanently to Frankfurt with her husband at the end of 1812, ending in the only way possible a love affair which had dragged on far too long.

The six songs are linked by interludes of varying length, making it impossible to extract a single song from the cycle, in the way that *Ungeduld* is often extracted from Schubert's *Die schöne Müllerin*, for example, or *Ich grolle nicht* from Schumann's *Dichterliebe*. Boettcher describes *An die ferne Geliebte* (*Beethoven als Liederkomponist*, p. 67) as 'gleichsam ein ungeheuer erweitertes Lied' (a single vastly expanded song, as it were), pointing out that, while each song is an 'image in itself', each 'offers its hand' to the following song. The musical *da capo* created by the return to the music of the opening song (to echoic words) in the final song closes the formal boundaries and underlines the essential symmetry of the cycle. This symmetry also encompasses the key pattern; the first and last songs are in E flat; the third and fourth songs share the common key of A flat; the second song is in G major, while the fifth song is in C major.

The third and fourth songs can be thought of as a continuum, sharing the common key of A flat, the same poetic metre and similar natural images; Kerman's view (*Beethoven Studies* I, pp. 126–7) that they might have been a single long stanza which Beethoven chose to split because of its length is fully credible and supported by the fact that Ludwig Nohl (in *Eine stille Liebe zu Beethoven*, Leipzig 1875) printed these two stanzas as one, although without quoting his authority for this. Kerman's theory that Beethoven may have written the final stanza of the first poem himself to set up a stronger correspondence between the first and last poems is, however, based on the flimsiest of circumstantial evidence, and his supporting assertion that 'Beethoven is known to have tampered with his original literary material in other cases' (p. 126) is misleading, as significant instances of this are very rare.

The autograph in Bonn (BH: BH 69) is entitled by the composer: 'An die entfernte Geliebte / Sechs Lieder von / Alois Jeitteles / in Musik gesezt / von L. v. Beethowen'. The manuscript is available in facsimile (Henle, Munich 1970). It is interesting to note that Beethoven himself did not refer to a 'song cycle' at this stage. There are also extensive sketches for the first five songs in the Scheide sketchbook (Princeton, NJ). Both are discussed by Kerman (see above). All sketches seem to date from the beginning of 1816, and the manuscript in Bonn is clearly dated by Beethoven '1816 im Monath April'.

The songs were first published by Steiner in Vienna in October 1816 as 'An die ferne Geliebte' and designated a *Liederkreis* (song cycle). The edition was riddled with errors, some of them traceable to oversights in the autograph. Beethoven wrote to Steiner around the end of October to ask for new proofs, suggesting that it was high time the worst errors were corrected by hand in the copies already printed (EA665 / BB985). The song cycle was dedicated to Prince Lobkowitz, but the composer refused to send an error-ridden copy 'aus der Barbarey' to his noble patron. The dedication copy from a revised printing, finally sent on 8 January 1817, arrived too late, Lobkowitz having died on 15 December 1816.

In the final song, the singer (or composer) claims that his songs come directly from his overflowing heart, artlessly, or at least seeking to avoid the ornamental trappings of art ('ohne Kunstgepräng'). There is certainly a move towards folksong-like simplicity in the vocal line of most songs, while strophic modification is achieved principally through the piano's contribution. The intensification of feeling generated by the increasingly urgent piano figuration is clearest, of course, in the first and last songs, and the extended coda to the cycle, marked 'allegro molto e con brio'. It is not difficult to trace connected motifs in the cycle which unite individual songs in a subtle and almost subliminal manner (see Christopher Reynolds: 'The Representational Impulse in Late Beethoven: I', *Acta Musicologica*, 1980, pp. 43–61). These points will recur in the discussion of individual songs which follows.

I AUF DEM HÜGEL SITZ' ICH, SPÄHEND   E flat major

An die ferne Geliebte (I)

Ziemlich langsam und mit Ausdruck

Auf dem Hügel sitz' ich spähend	I sit on the hill, peering
In das blaue Nebelland,	Into the blue mist-shrouded landscape,
Nach den fernen Triften sehend,	Seeking those distant country pastures
Wo ich dich, Geliebte, fand.	Where I first found you, my beloved.
Weit bin ich von dir geschieden,	I am separated from you, far away;
Trennend liegen Berg und Tal	The dividing mountain and valley lie
Zwischen uns und unserm Frieden,	Between us and our peace,
Unserm Glück und unsrer Qual.	Our happiness and our torment.
Ach, den Blick kannst du nicht sehen,	Ah, you cannot see the gaze
Der zu dir so glühend eilt,	Which speeds so ardently towards you,
Und die Seufzer, die verwehen	And my sighs disperse
In dem Raume, der uns teilt.	In the space which separates us.
Will denn nichts mehr zu dir dringen,	Will nothing then reach you any more,
Nichts der Liebe Bote sein?	Nothing be the messenger of love?
Singen will ich, Lieder singen,	I will sing, sing songs of lament
Die dir klagen meine Pein!	That tell you of my anguish!
Denn vor Liederklang entweichet	For all space and time recedes
Jeder Raum und jede Zeit,	At the sound of songs,
Und ein liebend Herz erreichet,	And what a loving heart has consecrated
Was ein liebend Herz geweiht.	Will reach another loving heart.

In keeping with the poet's later promise to avoid artistic embellishments ('ohne Kunstgepräng'), the first song is introduced by a single tonic chord. The 'fairly slow and expressive' vocal line rises and falls with natural ease. Here and throughout the cycle, word setting is predominantly syllabic (melisma would be artistic pretension), although Beethoven allows himself expressive appoggiaturas on 'dich', 'Glück', etc. in the penultimate bar of each stanza and for occasional meaningful nuances in subsequent stanzas, such as 'glühend' (bar 24) and 'Lieder (singen)' (bar 36).

Apart from these tiny variations, the vocal line remains constant throughout the five stanzas, and variation is the province of the pianist. Both the two-bar interludes between stanzas and the accompaniment to individual stanzas are varied. The variation intensifies the expression, but should not be seen as a process of intensification in a straight progression from stanza to stanza, as Beethoven is at pains to mirror the emotional content of individual stanzas within the voluntary constraint of the strophic outline. Thus the third stanza, with right-hand semiquavers and a syncopated bass line, is urgent and despairing, as the poet realises that his ardent glances (note the expressive vocal phrase at 'glühend') and his sighs (note the falling minor second which immediately follows the word) will never reach his beloved. The fourth stanza relaxes into a confident homophonic pattern, however, as the poet realises that the answer is to sing of his pain; 'Singen' (bar 35) is marked 'dolce' and the triplet figure on 'Lieder' (bar 36) is redolent of relief and emancipation.

Throughout the cycle, Beethoven uses a mixture of German and Italian performance directions, sometimes together and sometimes separately. The German directions often concern emotional expression: 'ausdrucksvoll' (expressively – I), 'angenehm und mit viel Empfindung' (pleasantly and with great feeling – IV), 'mit Ausdruck' (with expression – I/VI). The Italian directions (often with their German translations) refer more to the instrumental accompaniment and tempo variations, affirming the pivotal role of the piano in the cycle. The instrumental interludes between songs vary greatly in length, although by the fifth song there are a full 14 bars of transition, and the final song opens with an eight-bar set piece for piano ('andante con moto e cantabile') and ends with nine bars of piano alone.

In this first song, however, the voice accelerates in the final stanza into a brief *allegro* passage for piano, before G, having functioned as the third note of E flat major, is transparently redefined as the tonic of the second song.

II WO DIE BERGE SO BLAU   G major

An die ferne Geliebte II
Poco Allegretto

Wo die Berge so blau	Where the mountains so blue
Aus dem nebligen Grau	Peer forth out of the
Schauen herein,	Misty greyness,
Wo die Sonne verglüht,	Where the sun's rays fade,
Wo die Wolke umzieht,	Where the clouds gather,
Möchte ich sein!	There I long to be!
Dort im ruhigen Tal	There in the peaceful valley
Schweigen Schmerzen und Qual;	Pain and torment are silent;
Wo im Gestein	Where among the rocks
Still die Primel dort sinnt,	The primrose muses quietly,
Weht so leise der Wind,	And the wind wafts so gently,
Möchte ich sein!	There I long to be!
Hin zum sinnigen Wald	The power of love
Drängt mich Liebesgewalt,	And my inner anguish drive me
Innere Pein.	Off to the pensive forest.

Ach, mich zög's nicht von hier,	Ah, nothing would draw me away
Könnt' ich, Traute! bei dir	If I could be for ever with you,
Ewiglich sein!	Dearest one!

Beethoven finds a relaxed movement in compound time to fit the anapaestic metre of Jeitteles's verse here. The first stanza melody has all the apparent artlessness of folksong, introduced by stylised horn calls, evocative of a mountainous landscape. The entire melody is contained within the compass of a fifth (tonic to dominant) and involves simple sequences, with first two bars and then a whole five-bar section repeated at a raised pitch. This gives the melody fine shape and the satisfying feeling of inevitability.

The second stanza, marked *pianissimo* throughout, moves to the subdominant key, C major, setting the voice to an unvarying G, an inner pedal point, while the piano adumbrates the melody of the first stanza. This striking technique creates a sense of meditative calm, as the lover leaves contemplation of the mist-shrouded mountain tops and muses on the peaceful valley, but also a sense of unreality, for this is but a dream of happiness. The psychological subtlety of this second stanza as a representation of 'the complex process of memory', which he perceives in the entire cycle, is discussed with concision and clarity by Charles Rosen in *The Romantic Generation* (pp. 166–72). Schubert was to use the technique of transferring the voice to an inner melodic line while the piano outlines the true melody above, in such songs as *Der Kreuzzug* (D932), where the second stanza moves from exterior action to interior contemplation, or *An den Mond* (D296), where the final stanza refers to the intimate joys of friendship which cannot be shared or understood by outsiders. The technique, in its more sinister and dramatic ombra guise, was strikingly employed by Reichardt in his G minor setting of *Erlkönig* in 1794, to set the disturbing blandishments of the Erlking.

After the peaceful reflection of this second stanza, reality sets in swiftly. The return to the home key is a wrench rather than a smooth modulation. A brief four-note echo phrase in the accompaniment, appropriate to the mountain landscape, is gradually expanded into an obsessive motif, and both pace and harmonic complexity increase as the lover's 'inner anguish' overcomes him; the flow of the song is interrupted (bar 92) by a momentary dislocation of both tempo and harmony as the words 'innere Pein' are reiterated.

III LEICHTE SEGLER IN DEN HÖHEN   A flat major

An die ferne Geliebte III
Allegro assai

Leichte Segler in den Höhen	Light clouds gliding aloft
Und du, Bächlein, klein und schmal:	And you, little narrow stream:

Könnt mein Liebchen ihr erspähen,	If you can spot my sweetheart,
Grüsst sie mir viel tausendmal!	Bring her a thousand greetings from me!
Seht, ihr Wolken, sie dann gehen,	If, O clouds, you espy her walking
Sinnend in dem stillen Tal,	Thoughtfully in the quiet valley,
Lasst mein Bild vor ihr entstehen	Let my image arise before her
In dem luft'gen Himmelssaal.	In the airy vault of heaven.
Wird sie an den Büschen stehen,	Should she stand by those bushes,
Die nun herbstlich falb und kahl,	Now autumnally dull and bare,
Klagt ihr, wie mir ist geschehen,	Then, O birds, bewail my torment,
Klagt ihr, Vöglein! meine Qual.	The fate which has befallen me.
Stille Weste, bringt im Wehen	Calm west winds, as you waft over,
Hin zu meines Herzenswahl	Carry to my heart's chosen one,
Meine Seufzer, die vergehen	My sighs, which fade away
Wie der Sonne letzter Strahl.	Like the last rays of the sun.
Flüstr' ihr zu mein Liebesflehen,	Whisper to her my love's pleading,
Lass sie, Bächlein, klein und schmal,	O little narrow stream,
Treu in deinen Wogen sehen	Let her behold in your ripples
Meine Tränen ohne Zahl.	The true image of my countless tears.

As discussed in the introductory comments, there is evidence that the third and fourth songs set a single poem, which Beethoven chose to split for reasons of length. The two songs share a common key, although the shared poetic metre is not matched by a shared musical pulse. The transition between the songs is uniquely intimate; the voice sustains a high E flat, while the piano introduces the new metre and theme of the following song, so that there is here no break in the vocal line.

For the third song, Beethoven finds a jaunty rhythm, with triplets in the pianist's right hand pointed by chords in the bass which outline the vocal melody. The lightness of the gliding clouds is conveyed by the quaver-plus-rest pattern of the vocal line. As if he realised that the prevailing mood had been too cheerful for the girl's pensive stroll in the quiet valley, Beethoven turns to the minor key for the final three stanzas, but after a homophonic lament in the third stanza and hesitating tempo indications, the original mood returns in a new guise, with syncopated quavers for the fourth stanza and triplets in both hands for the final stanza. This happily conveys the lover's optimism as he entrusts his messages to the west wind and the brook (Rellstab's *Liebesbotschaft* is a similar example of the contemporary topos of poets' confiding in nature – not to mention *Die schöne Müllerin*), with the *pp* marking reflecting the lover's sighs and the whispered message.

The voice rises in volume only at the repetition of 'ohne Zahl' (countless (tears)) when the lover is overcome by present anguish, and the final word is held over almost three bars until relieved by the renewed hope and appeals of the fourth song.

IV DIESE WOLKEN IN DEN HÖHEN

A flat major

An die ferne Geliebte IV
Nicht zu geschwinde, angenehm und mit viel Empfindung

Diese Wolken in den Höhen,	These clouds high up above,
Dieser Vöglein muntrer Zug	This merry flight of birds
Werden dich, o Huldin! sehen -	Will see you, o gracious one -
'Nehmt mich mit im leichten Flug!'	'Let me join you in your easy flight!'

Diese Weste werden spielen	These west winds will dart
Scherzend dir um Wang' und Brust,	Playfully around your cheek and bosom,
In den seidnen Locken wühlen -	And tousle your silken tresses -
'Teilt' ich mit euch diese Lust!'	'If only I could share in your pleasure!'

Hin zu dir von jenen Hügeln	This stream hurries busily to you
Emsig dieses Bächlein eilt. -	From those hills.
'Wird ihr Bild sich in dir spiegeln,	'If her image is reflected in your water,
Fliess zurück dann unverweilt!'	Then flow back without delay!'

The fourth song, indissolubly linked by the held note in the voice to the previous one, continues the theme of clouds, birds, wind and brook reaching the beloved, but here the poet's fantasy leads him to wish that he could travel with them, rather than simply entrust a message to them. Beethoven used speech marks for the final lines of each stanza, as indicated above, as if the desperate poet breaks off from mere musing to shout his message aloud to sympathetic nature. In the first two stanzas, the final line is each time clearly defined by a rest and a striking off-beat vocal entry.

Again, it is the accompaniment which is varied and which illustrates the text. The first stanza has an appropriately high-lying right-hand figure for floating clouds, augmented by trills to suggest the little birds. Robert Stuber (*Die Klavierbegleitung*, p. 34) has described the extraordinary effect of spaciousness achieved by hearing the melody at three pitches here: in the tenor line of the accompaniment, in the voice, and in the high-lying trills at a quaver's delay. The oscillating octaves in the second stanza, which are regularly at odds with the pitch of the voice, together with the circling bass line, which again echoes the vocal melody at a quaver's delay, suggest the west wind's wayward tousling of the girl's hair. Descending scale extracts in the third stanza represent the brook's busy descent from the hills. The pace quickens at the end of the song, following the sense of the words 'ja unverweilt!' (without delay) and continuing the almost manic-depressive pattern of anxiety and reassurance which runs through the six poems. The poet's frequent mood swings explain the many tempo fluctuations in this song cycle. Whatever the autobiographical subtext in the cycle, Beethoven was fully aware of the proximity of hope and despair as a real part of his own experience and not just the province of hypersensitive poets.

V ES KEHRET DER MAIEN

G major

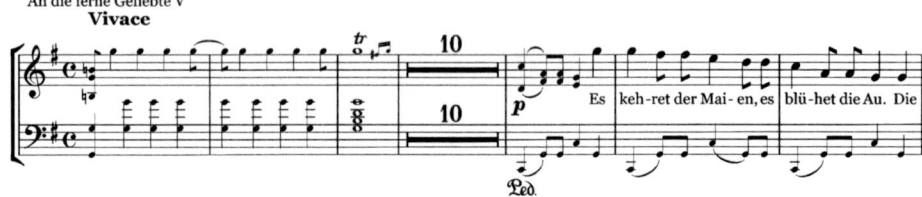

Es kehret der Maien, es blühet die Au.	May returns, the meadow is blooming.
Die Lüfte, sie wehen so milde, so lau,	The breezes waft by, so warm and gentle,
Geschwätzig die Bäche nun rinnen;	The brooks now babble along their course.
Die Schwalbe, sie kehret zum wirtlichen Dach,	The swallow returns to her hospitable roof,
Sie baut sich so emsig ihr bräutlich Gemach,	She constructs her bridal chamber so eagerly,
Die Liebe soll wohnen da drinnen	Love is to dwell within it.
Sie bringt sich geschäftig von kreuz und von quer	She busily fetches from every nook and cranny
Manch weicheres Stück zu dem Brautbett hieher,	Soft scraps aplenty for her bridal bed,
Manch wärmendes Stück für die Kleinen.	Warm scraps aplenty for her young ones.
Nun wohnen die Gatten beisammen so treu,	Now the pair live so faithfully together,
Was Winter geschieden, verband nun der Mai,	What Winter separated, May has now joined,
Was liebet, das weiss er zu einen.	He knows how to unite those that love.
Es kehret der Maien, es blühet die Au.	May returns, the meadow is blooming.
Die Lüfte, sie wehen so milde, so lau,	The breezes waft by, so warm and gentle,
Nur ich kann nicht ziehen von hinnen;	I alone cannot leave this place.
Wenn alles, was liebet, der Frühling vereint,	When Spring unites all things that love,
Nur unserer Liebe kein Frühling erscheint,	Our love alone beholds no Spring,
Und Tränen sind all ihr Gewinnen.	And its net profit is tears.

At the end of the previous song, Beethoven had modulated simply to C major by way of an augmented sixth on the final repetition of 'ja unverweilt!'. Now the dominant G takes centre stage in the introduction, making the eventual entry of the voice an even grander confirmation of the new key. The use of trills in the introduction, coupled with a falling minor third figure ('cuckoo' motif), leads us to anticipate feathered protagonists. We are not disappointed, although it is not a songbird that we encounter but the swallow, harbinger of early summer and model of conjugal fidelity.

Beethoven chooses an energetic dactylic metre (long-short-short) to match the longer lines of Jeitteles's poem. The singer enters quietly on a high G. The voice falls stepwise through an octave and then moves through a series of neighbouring notes. Nothing sounds more natural; nothing illustrates better the art which conceals art. The second section of each stanza is set in the lower vocal register in the cosy subdominant key of F major; significantly, the fourth lines of each stanza, referring to domesticity, fidelity and lover's uniting in springtime, are entirely within that key.

There is less variation here than in the previous songs. Here it is restricted to the piano interludes, which once again reflect the change from initial optimism to ultimate despairing resignation. The bitter repetition of 'all ihr Gewinnen' (its net profit), emphasised by Beethoven's inserted 'ja' (a favourite expressive device), is set in the minor mode. The tonic C is then redefined as the mediant of A flat major in the opening chord of the final song.

VI NIMM SIE HIN DENN, DIESE LIEDER E flat major

Nimm sie hin denn, diese Lieder,	Accept them then, these songs
Die ich dir, Geliebte, sang,	Which I sang for you, my love.
Singe sie dann abends wieder	Then sing them again at eventide
Zu der Laute süssem Klang.	To the sweet sound of the lute.
Wenn das Dämmrungsrot dann ziehet	When the red twilight glow travels
Nach dem stillen blauen See,	Towards the silent blue lake,
Und sein letzter Strahl verglühet	And its final ray fades
Hinter jener Bergeshöh';	Behind those mountain tops;
Und du singst, was ich gesungen,	And you sing what I sang,
Was mir aus der vollen Brust	What sounded from my overflowing heart
Ohne Kunstgepräng' erklungen,	Without the trappings of art,
Nur der Sehnsucht sich bewusst:	Conscious only of its longing:
Dann vor diesen Liedern weichet,	Then, in the face of these songs,
Was geschieden uns so weit,	What kept us so far apart will evaporate,
Und ein liebend Herz erreichet,	And what a loving heart has consecrated
Was ein liebend Herz geweiht.	Will reach another loving heart.

The final song, where the poet invites his beloved to accept his love songs and finally finds peace in the realisation that shared song can unite them despite distance, begins appropriately with a self-contained piano prelude of eight bars which is emblematic of pure music. The piano, marked *cantabile*, sings to its own accompaniment in a lyrical apotheosis of a slow Classical sonata movement, before the voice takes up the strain. The piano's right hand is then freed to adopt the oscillating semiquaver movement formerly heard in the bass, while the left hand supports with full chords, creating a new richness of texture. It is fitting that Schumann, that later champion of the song cycle, should have paid homage to Beethoven's cycle by quoting the opening of this final song at the end of the first movement of his Fantasie, op. 17 (see Charles Rosen, *The Romantic Generation*, pp. 101–6). Originally entitled 'Obolen auf Beethovens Monument' (Modest contributions towards Beethoven's monument), Schumann's work was conceived in connection with the fund launched in 1835 to erect a monument to Beethoven in Bonn, although this had been largely forgotten when Schumann's Fantasie was published in 1838, dedicated to Liszt.

When the poet turns in imagination to the dying rays of the setting sun, Beethoven responds with quietly throbbing repeated chords, usually associated with a spirit of wondrous exaltation in the face of natural glories and employed most memorably in *Abendlied unterm gestirnten Himmel*. Here the chords remain pianissimo throughout and are actually more closely related to a similar accompanimental figure in *An die Hoffnung* (op. 92) at the words 'von der Mitternacht umschauert' (surrounded by spectres of midnight). A short cadenza-like passage introduces the recapitulation of the opening music of the cycle with an arpeggiated chord outlining a dominant seventh in E flat, mildly suggestive of the beloved's lute. The music of the opening song returns in solemn vein with a simple piano introduction, but the vocal melody is immediately given new urgency by the ensuing syncopated accompaniment, and the music builds rapidly to a furious extended coda, marked *Allegro molto e con brio*. This coda, with its fragmentation of the text, its difficult octaves and occasionally complex figuration, clearly stresses the manic-optimistic side of the poetry. A piano postlude helps the music to wind down, almost literally, to a quiet doubled E flat in the bass, and a final emphatic statement of the opening theme rounds off the cycle aptly by confirming its cyclical aspect.

This glorious triumph of hope and powerful testimony to the power of song was sadly among Beethoven's final essays in solo song, although the folk-like simplicity of the themes, the treatment of tonality and the concentrated thematic development justify Joseph Kerman's memorable description of the cycle as 'a quiet herald of the third-period style' (*Beethoven Studies*, p. 154) – a formulation which correctly stresses the significance of the solo songs in the wider context of Beethoven's works.

AN DIE FREUDE To Joy
Friedrich von Schiller

1793

Hess 143 lost song

Freude, schöner Götterfunken,	Joy, beautiful divine spark,
Tochter aus Elysium,	Daughter of Elysium,

Wir betreten feuertrunken,
Himmlische, dein Heiligtum, usw.

We enter your sanctuary,
O heavenly one, our souls aflame, etc.

This is the text used, albeit selectively, for the Finale of the 'Choral' Symphony, but it is of interest that Beethoven turned to the poem on other occasions before his main work on the symphony in 1822–24. He was bound to feel an affinity with Schiller's ideals, although he found it very difficult to do justice to his high-minded poetry in a mere solo song and there are indeed no surviving, complete solo songs to Schiller texts.

The existence of an early solo setting of *An die Freude* is suggested by a letter written by Bartholomäus Ludwig Fischenich to Charlotte von Schiller, wife of the poet, on 26 January 1793. Fischenich was a law professor in Bonn who had known Schiller well during his studies in Jena and who was apt to interrupt his Bonn lectures to recite poems by Schiller, to the delight of his students, who included Beethoven at this time. Fischenich sent Frau von Schiller a copy of *Feuerfarb'* (p. 148) and promised a setting of *An die Freude* from his young protégé: 'He is also going to set Schiller's "Freude", in fact each and every verse. I anticipate something perfect, for I know him to be entirely devoted to what is great and sublime.' Frau von Schiller replied, praising *Feuerfarb'* and stating how pleased she was that Beethoven was setting *An die Freude*. No song survives.

Ferdinand Ries also lists *An die Freude* in a letter of September 1803 to the publisher Simrock, as the seventh in a list of eight songs, which was to become op. 52, although *An die Freude* was, of course, not included. There are brief melody sketches from 1798 (see below), but later sketches from 1812 and 1822 are clearly preparatory to the celebrated choral setting. Beethoven clearly decided that this poem demanded more than a lone voice with piano accompaniment, although the idea of treating the poem sectionally was already in his mind in 1793, as Fischenich's letter suggests a process of through-composition.

Biamonti 189 is a fragment in C major, dated to 1798–99, which sets a line from the poem: 'Muss ein lieber Vater wohnen' (There must dwell a kind father). While clearly unconnected with the lost setting, it confirms again Beethoven's ongoing preoccupation with this text:

Muß   ein   lie - ber Va - ter__ woh   -   nen.

The same autograph (Berlin, DSB: Grasnick 1, p. 25) includes a second sketch for the same words, which has received little attention, but can now be heard on the 'Unheard Beethoven' website:

Schubert, incidentally, had no inhibitions about setting the text strophically in May 1815. He sets the first eight lines of each stanza for solo voice and the final quatrain for chorus, in a composition (D189) which combines joyful exhilaration (solo) with due solemnity (chorus). The easy fluency of Schubert's setting points to an essential difference between the two great musical contemporaries.

AN DIE GELIEBTE To his beloved (first version)

Joseph Ludwig Stoll   Late 1811

D major WoO140 Peters 53 Henle 86/54 GA XXIII/243a

Andantino, un poco agitato

Oh, dass ich dir vom stillen Auge,	O that I might sip from your cheek
In seinem liebevollen Schein,	That tear which glistens so charmingly
Die Träne von der Wange sauge,	As it rolls from your silent eye,
Eh' sie die Erde trinket ein!	Before the ground swallows it up.
Wohl hält sie zögernd auf der Wange	It seems to linger, hesitating, upon your cheek,
Und will sich heiss der Treue weihn;	Wishing ardently to dedicate itself to constancy;
Nun ich sie so im Kuss empfange,	As I now receive it through my kiss,
Nun sind auch deine Schmerzen mein!	So too your heartache has become mine.

Stoll's poem was not published until 1814, when it appeared in two almanachs: *Selam. Ein Almanach für Freunde des Mannigfaltigen*, and Erichson's *Musen-Almanach für das Jahr 1814*. Schubert, who set the same text in October 1815 (D303), probably found the poem in *Selam*. Beethoven's settings of the text, however, date from the autumn of 1811, indicating that he must have received a manuscript copy from the poet. Stoll was acquainted with Beethoven, who knew him well enough to ask the orientalist Joseph von Hammer (later Hammer-Purgstall), who also worked as a government translator, to provide assistance to the poet in connection with a proposed trip to Paris (EA227 / BB391), and trusted him well enough to stand guarantor for a loan to the poet (EA293 / BB522) when Stoll was in financial straits.

Thus Stoll would have felt indebted to Beethoven and this supports a hypothesis that Beethoven may have actually commissioned the poem from Stoll, in order to set it for a specific dedicatee. Sieghard Brandenburg dates the second letter, concerning the loan guarantee, convincingly to the autumn of 1811 (see note on BB522), leading it to coincide neatly with Beethoven's first occupation with the poem. That the poem was written expressly for Beethoven is supported by a note on the Bonn sketch (see below): 'Nb: wenn noch 2 strophen dazu kämen, würde es noch schöner seyn' (NB: If there were to be a further two stanzas, it would be even more beautiful), which seems to be addressed directly to Stoll, although no further stanzas were forthcoming.

The idea that the song was composed by Beethoven as a personal expression of love is promoted by Maynard Solomon (*Beethoven*, pp. 175f.) who identifies the 'beloved' unhesitatingly as Antonie Brentano; in fact, this identification is an important strand of his argument for naming Antonie Brentano as Beethoven's 'immortal beloved'. The autograph in Paris (BN: Ms. 31), dated December 1812 by the composer, bears the inscription: 'Den 2n März 1812 / mir von Author erbethen' (2 March 1812, requested by me from the author). Solomon identifies the handwriting as Antonie Brentano's, although this neat identification is not universally accepted.

This version of the song was first published in *Lewald's Europa* 1836, I. Band, by Scheible in Stuttgart as a musical supplement, entitled 'Reliquie von Beethoven'. The main text comments that the song is 'a relic of Beethoven, one of his most passionate songs, which he once wrote in the album of the Bavarian court singer Regina Lang when she was residing in Vienna'. The album has not survived, and indeed the statement causes further controversy, as there is no record of the singer having been in Vienna at the appropriate time. Various sketches survive for the first version, now in Bonn (BH: Bodmer, Mh59) and Berlin (DSB: Grasnick 20a, and private ownership). It is thought that all the leaves belonged originally to the so-called Petter sketchbook, some leaves of which are now dispersed, and the Henle edition helpfully prints a reconstructed version of the combined song sketches (No. 106), which indicates how closely they resemble the final version.

The accompaniment of the first version, with broken-chord triplets almost throughout, supported at the opening by staccato quavers in the bass, seems to be better suited to a plucked instrument, and it is no surprise to learn that the familiar version in D major was actually preceded by a transposed edition in C major with both guitar and piano accompaniments. This was published by Gombart in Augsburg in March or April 1826, in his 'Lieder Kranz mit Begleitung des Pianoforte oder der Guitarre', with the vocal line sandwiched between the accompaniments for guitar (above) and piano (below). It is reprinted, with piano accompaniment only, in the Henle edition (No. 54).

The guitar as accompanying instrument was extremely popular in Vienna at the time and it was common enough to publish guitar arrangements of songs, but a Beethoven song conceived with the guitar in mind is more of a rarity. Solomon claims, to support his hypothesis concerning the secret dedicatee, that Antonie Brentano was an 'expert guitarist'. This can hardly be conclusive proof, as guitar-playing was so widespread. Intriguingly, the only picture in Robbins Landon's iconographical tome (*Beethoven*) which illustrates a guitar is *Concert at the Malfattis*, where Therese Malfatti, Beethoven's erstwhile intended, sits at the piano, while her sister Anna strums the guitar. A cancelled passage in a letter to Therese Malfatti (EA258 / BB442) actually refers to the guitar transcription of a song: 'übergeben sie gefälligst ihrer lieben schwester Nanette das lied für Guitarre übersezt' (please give your dear sister Nanette (Anna) the song transcribed for guitar). The passage continues to say that he did not have time to write out a further song, suggesting that Beethoven had made the guitar transcription personally in the case of this earlier song (possibly *Andenken*).

Although the guitar style may have had significant personal meaning for the composer, it must be admitted that the constant triplets make for a certain degree of monotony. The greater freedom which Beethoven permitted himself in the later, more pianistic version (see next entry) makes that the more passionate and more convincing interpretation of this intimate text.

AN DIE GELIEBTE To his beloved (second version)

Joseph Ludwig Stoll   Dec. 1811 (rev. 1814)

D major WoO140 Peters 52 Henle 55 GA XXIII/243

Andantino, un poco agitato

For text, translation and notes on the text, see first version (previous entry).

Although the autograph in Vienna (GdM: A10) is clearly dated '1811 im december' by the composer, Sieghard Brandenburg (in 'Ein Skizzenbuch Beethovens aus dem Jahre 1812' in Harry Goldschmidt (ed.), *Zu Beethoven, Aufsätze und Annotationen, Berlin 1979*) has dated the paper by its watermark to 1814. It seems possible that Beethoven revised the first version, or perhaps reconstructed the lost manuscript from memory, in 1814, when the opportunity for its publication arose. The date would then refer back to the song's first incarnation.

This second version was published as a music supplement to the journal *Friedensblätter. Eine Zeitschrift für Leben, Literatur und Kunst* in Vienna on 12 July 1814. Linked to the music supplement, the same issue carried an article which praised in fulsome terms the revised version of 'the immortal opera *Fidelio*', which had aroused 'general enthusiasm' when it was produced on 23 May 1814. The song was published again at the beginning of 1817 by Nikolaus Simrock in Bonn, his son Peter Joseph having purchased it, along with *Das Geheimnis* (WoO145) and the cello sonatas op. 102, during a visit to Vienna the previous September.

The accompaniment of the first version gave every impression of having been conceived for the guitar as much as for the piano. While the accompaniment in this second version is undoubtedly more pianistic overall, vestiges of guitar style remain, notably in the pulsing of the alternating monotone and chords which form the three-bar introduction. This introduction suits the new performance indication (*andantino, un poco agitato*), the foreshortening to three bars rather than the expected four proving unsettling and further emphasised by the minor-second dissonance set up in the third bar, which is resolved only by the singer's premature entrance.

Whereas in the first setting, triplets ran through the entire piece, reducing flexibility of expression, here subtle variations in the shape and weight of the accompaniment underline nuances of meaning within the text. In the first stanza, syncopation reflects the agitation of the hypersensitive lover as he anticipates the loss of the tear. After a briefly panicked interlude, the lover realises that the tear has not yet fallen and its lingering on the cheek is delicately conveyed by half-staccato markings and shaded dynamics. When he plucks up courage to kiss the tear from the girl's cheek, his newfound confidence is reflected first in the legato flow of the bass line and finally in repeated full chords which underline his certainty of having done the right thing. His anticipation of ultimate success in his suit is finely communicated in the last bar, where 'mein!' is heard twice; first loudly, in joyful affirmation, then quietly, to suggest inward certainty and contentment.

Even had the success of the first version not been torpedoed by its erratic publication history, this version would have won the palm. Its formal economy, its subtle enhancement of the text, not only reflecting mood, but creating a credible dramatic persona for the performer, and not least the perfect partnership of voice and piano, make it a fine example of the nineteenth-century German *Lied*.

AN DIE HOFFNUNG   To Hope (first setting)
Christoph August Tiedge   late 1804–05

E flat major   Op. 32   Peters 1   Henle 28   GA XXIII/215

Poco adagio

Die du so gern in heil'gen Nächten feierst	You who adore the holiness of the night
Und sanft und weich den Gram verschleierst,	And veil with your soft and gentle touch
Der eine zarte Seele quält,	The sorrow which tortures tender hearts,
O Hoffnung! lass, durch dich emporgehoben,	Oh Hope, uplifted by you, let the
Der Dulder ahnen, dass dort oben	Patient sufferer sense that high above
Ein Engel seine Tränen zählt!	An angel keeps record of his tears.
Wenn, längst verhallt, geliebte Stimmen schweigen;	When beloved voices die away and fall silent,
Wenn unter ausgestorbnen Zweigen	When remembrance sits desolate
Verödet die Erinnrung sitzt:	Beneath dead branches,
Dann nahe dich, wo dein Verlassner trauert	Then draw near, where the bereft mourner,
Und, von der Mitternacht umschauert,	Shrouded by the spectres of midnight,
Sich auf versunkne Urnen stützt.	Supports himself on half-buried urns.
Und blickt er auf, das Schicksal anzuklagen,	And should he look heavenwards to rail against fate,
Wenn scheidend über seinen Tagen	When in his final days the last, departing rays
Die letzten Strahlen untergehn:	Sink below the horizon:
Dann lass ihn um den Rand des Erdentraumes	Then let him behold behind this earthly dream
Das Leuchten eines Wolkensaumes	The golden glow at the cloud's fringe,
Von einer nahen Sonne sehn!	From a sun close at hand.

The verses come from the first 'Gesang' (canto) of Tiedge's *Urania: Über Gott, Unsterblichkeit und Freiheit* (Urania: concerning God, immortality and liberty). Tiedge's self-styled 'lyric-didactic poem' in six long cantos enjoyed a notable vogue and was frequently reprinted in the first half of the nineteenth century, before achieving virtual oblivion as tastes changed. *Urania* had first appeared in Halle in 1801, but Beethoven used the heavily revised second edition of 1803. A later edition was used for the more extended setting (op. 94). This poem within a poem appears in the first canto, subtitled 'Klagen des Zweiflers' (Lamentations of the doubter) at a point where the poet, acting as devil's advocate, questions the very existence of God. The wonders of nature suggest an orderly and benevolent world ruler, but the human world, where evil so often triumphs over good, suggests otherwise:

> Elend seufzet dort in dunkler Kammer!
> Laster stehen, wo die Tugend fällt!
> Ist ein Gott? Und so zerdrückt von Jammer
> Die hinausgestossne Welt?

> (Misery sighs in darkened chambers! Vices stand, while virtue falls! Is there a God? And the rejected world so crushed by sorrow?)

This poem, originally presented as a set piece entitled (in the index) 'Lied an die Hoffnung', is a plea for the patient sufferer to be uplifted by hope. It represents an early turning point in the work. Once doubts have been dispelled, humankind's innate need to search for God and immortality through faith bolstered by reason can begin in earnest. Despite references to God, this is more of a humanistic prayer to the abstract concept of Hope.

Beethoven's setting was first published by the Kunst und Industrie Comptoir in Vienna in September 1805. Sketches for the melody extend over seven pages in the 'Leonore' sketchbook in Berlin (SPK: Mendelssohn 15). They are discussed by Barry Cooper in *Beethoven and the Creative Process* (pp. 137–9). The six near complete sketches show substantial differences from each other and from the final version as published, but indicate the care which Beethoven took over the song. The later setting (op. 94) would demonstrate a totally different conception of song composition and is related to the present song solely by its text.

Beethoven presented the present setting to Josephine Deym (née Brunsvik) early in 1805. It is tempting to seek an autobiographical subtext in this new year's gift. The composer loved Josephine dearly and perhaps his own hope was renewed after the death of her husband in January of the previous year. The promise of a silver lining to the lifting cloud of mourning certainly has a resonance and relevance to the widowed Josephine. The gift was appreciated, Josephine writing to her mother in March 1805: 'Der gute Beethoven hat mir ein hübsches Lied, das er auf einen Text aus der Urania "An die Hoffnung" für mich geschrieben, zum Geschenk gemacht' (Dear Beethoven has made me the present of a pretty song 'An die Hoffnung', which he wrote for me to words from *Urania*) (quoted after La Mara (M. Lipsius): *Beethoven und die Brunsviks*, Leipzig 1929). Josephine had already shared the song with her sisters Therese and Charlotte in January 1805, swearing them to secrecy. Beethoven was alarmed when Lichnovsky noticed a manuscript copy of the song at his apartment and feared he must have suspected a romantic attachment (EA110 / BB216). This all points to an intimate dedication to Josephine, although this did not appear in the printed edition.

The song's impact is severely restricted by the strophic form. In the melody sketches Beethoven wrote out the words to the first stanza only. The music fits these words well, but struggles to convey the meaning of the remaining two stanzas. The melisma on 'Seele quält' in the first verse suits the tortured soul here and the setting sun of the third verse, but to use this phrase for '(Er-)innrung sitzt' in the second verse raises both metrical and semantic objections. Similarly, the falling phrase which closes the musical verse is appropriate to tears and half-buried urns, but completely wrong for the rising of a new sun in the third stanza. With their compass of over two octaves, the 'Moonlight Sonata' slow triplets which open and close the song, and form an interlude leading to the C major expression of hope relieving grief, illustrate the hope of a better life to come rising out of the depths of earthbound suffering.

Leslie Orrey (*The Beethoven Companion*, p. 423) criticises the instrumental thinking which controls the melodic extension towards an interrupted cadence at bar 22 ('Tränen zählt') and the section which follows, where the final three lines of text are each time repeated: 'a musical extension that again is determined more by instrumental musical logic than by any poetic compulsion'. One might go further and suggest that to have plumped for a full cadence to E flat at bar 22 and then cut at once to the postlude would have significantly improved the shape of the whole.

AN DIE HOFFNUNG To Hope (second setting)
Christoph August Tiedge   Spring 1815
B flat minor–G major Op. 94 Peters 32 Henle 61 GA XXIII/223

Ob ein Gott sei? Ob er einst erfülle,	Whether there be a God? Whether he will one day
Was die Sehnsucht weinend sich verspricht?	Fulfil those promises which human longing tearfully imagines?
Ob, vor irgend einem Weltgericht,	Whether this enigmatic being will reveal himself
Sich dies rätselhafte Sein enthülle?	At some last judgement?
Hoffen soll der Mensch! Er frage nicht!	Man must hope! His not to question!
Die du so gern in heil'gen Nächten feierst, usw.	You who prefer the holiness of the night, etc.

For remainder of text and translation, see earlier version (op. 32), (previous entry).

For this more grandly conceived setting of Tiedge's poem, already set strophically (op. 32), Beethoven decided to incorporate five lines of introductory verse, setting these as recitative. These lines were not included in the 1803 version of Tiedge's *Urania*, used for the earlier setting, and show that Beethoven used a later edition, no doubt the edition of 1808 found in the composer's effects after his death.

Beethoven had met Tiedge while staying at Teplitz in 1811 and regretted that they had not been able to spend more time together (EA324 / BB521). Tiedge was quick to suggest they used the informal 'du' in their letters, thus confirming a bond of friendship. In October, Beethoven wrote to say that he could not find the fine edition of *Urania* which Tiedge had recommended and asked the poet to send a copy, offering in exchange a marketable parcel of music (EA335 / BB525). Amalie Sebald, a gifted young singer from Berlin, had accompanied Tiedge and his female companion Elisabeth von der Recke to Teplitz in 1811 and had attracted Beethoven's attention. When she and the composer were both staying in Teplitz in September of the following year, Beethoven promised her that he would 'dip into Tiedge's poems': 'In Tiedge will ich blättern' (EA390 / BB601).

Despite his fondness for Amalie Sebald and his admiration of Tiedge, Beethoven did not act with undue haste, completing this song only in the spring of 1815. 'An die Hoffnung' remained the only text by Tiedge to be set by Beethoven, although it engendered two very different songs.

This later setting was published by Steiner in Vienna in April 1816, as op. 94, and dedicated to Princess Kinsky. There is an autograph, apparently a fair copy, in Harvard University's Houghton Library. The voice part is notated in soprano clef, an interesting throwback to Beethoven's earlier practice in his songs, at a period when he was turning increasingly to the modern treble (G) clef. At the recapitulation of the first stanza (bars 72–87) only the voice part is written out, with the piano marked '*come sopra*' (as above). The final two bars are fully written out.

The celebrated operatic tenor Franz Wild states that Beethoven wrote this 'Kantate' for him, following their successful public performance of *Adelaide* before a distinguished audience in January 1815. This is very likely the case, as he was entrusted with the first public performance of the present song on 26 April 1816. A fortnight earlier, there had been an impromptu private rendering in the Giannatasio del Rio household. Beethoven took the song with him when he visited on 9 April and it was performed by the two daughters, Franziska (Fanny) and Anna (Nanni). How well the girls, both in their twenties, coped with the song's demands in terms of emotional and technical resources is not recorded, although other reports suggest that they preferred more light-hearted fare (see *Auf, Freunde, singt dem Gott der Ehen*).

Whereas the first setting (op. 32) is strophic, with resultant limitations in the musical representation of the poet's meaning, here Beethoven sets the same text (plus a short introductory section) as a full *da capo* aria with recitative, allowing himself the luxury of through-composition with the safety net of a familiar formal framework. Hans Boettcher (*Beethoven als Liederkomponist*, p. 172) sees Beethoven's use of the *da capo* aria form, at a time when it was becoming outmoded, as a 'turning point'. Having paid his final homage to older models, with this apotheosis of the aria, the composer was free to follow his own path, enabling the original conceptions which ensued, starting with *An die ferne Geliebte*.

The introductory section, with languid chromatic meanderings, illustrates the anxieties of the poet whose belief in God has reached its lowest ebb. Indeed, this opening is a full compendium of rhetorical devices illustrative of religious doubt and human despair: B flat minor is the key which Schubart characterised as 'mockery against God, dissatisfaction with oneself and the world, preparation for suicide'; the chromatically descending bass line is an ancient *topos* of lament; the 'diabolic' tritone occurs continually as diminished fifth and augmented fourth; and the chord of the diminished seventh avoids harmonic certainty. The poet's tentative question word 'Ob' is thus well prepared and given further prominence by a pause, suggesting, as Hartmut Krones convincingly argues, 'fear at the enormity of doubting in God' (*Ludwig van Beethoven*, Vienna 1999, p. 90). The voice then rises through a perfect fourth to rest confidently on 'Gott', before the 'sei' which completes the question then alters the achieved interval to a sinister diminished fifth. Similar symbolic dissonances continue throughout the opening section, as the bass line, having descended through a diminished fifth before the voice entered (B flat to E) now continues its descent through a similar interval (E to B flat). After all this soul-searching, the move to the clarity of D major, *allegro*, as the poet affirms the nature of faith as hope beyond questioning, is a musical *coup de théâtre*. It is similar in kind to the opening of Haydn's oratorio *The Creation*, where light emerges triumphantly from the formless void of Chaos. Robert Stuber (*Die Klavierbegleitung*, p. 73) feels that this opening recitative also anticipates the final movement of the Ninth Symphony, where a meandering baritone solo leads to the solid clarity of the choral entry. Here it is Hope, there Joy which emerges triumphant.

The Aria opens in a gentle *larghetto dolce* movement, and in the first section, to be repeated as a written-out *da capo* at the end of the song, intensity is achieved chiefly through lavish word repetition. Thereafter variations in mood are achieved, within a stable basic tempo, through changes of key signature and note values. Indeed, Beethoven is at pains to find tonal analogues for images within the poem. The syncopation in the accompaniment at 'Dann nahe dich', reinforcing the poet's appeal to hope to 'draw near', is soon followed by bare descending octaves to illustrate the 'half-buried urns' and the sun's 'departing rays'. When the poet 'rails against fate', it is to angry full chords in the unexpected key of D minor. The progressive diminution of note values at 'Dann lass ihn', mirrored in an extended *crescendo*, as the poet sees the sun breaking through, produces a passage of extraordinary intensification, before the voice leads conventionally back to the first section. The song ends with a simple appended apostrophe to hope: 'O Hoffnung!'

Beethoven, in his determination to do justice to Tiedge's poem, has set new standards for the pianoforte song with this setting. Firstly, his striving for an appropriate tonal analogue for each poetic image and emotion is a Romantic feature and prefigures the extensive, consistent use of such devices in Schubert and the later Romantics. Secondly, Beethoven has managed to write a song of operatic proportions which works none the less as a German *Klavierlied* and in so doing has promoted voice and piano once and for all to the public concert platform. The two points are, of course, related. To descend meaningfully to a low B to evoke the setting sun, or rise gloriously to a ringing tenor A to convey its bright revival, is fine word-setting. But only a trained singer can meet the demands of such a wide tessitura. Song, which was the domestic province of the enthusiastic amateur throughout the previous century, has passed into the hands (and mouths) of professional musicians.

Henri de Curzon, author of the first monograph on Beethoven songs (1905), felt that the song required 'une grande voix de soprano dramatique' and even considered that the novelty and intensity of expression prefigure Wagner (*Les Lieder*, p. 35).

AN DIE MENSCHENGESICHTER To men's faces
Gottfried August Bürger

1794–95

G minor SV292 sketch

Ich habe was Liebes, das hab ich zu lieb;	I have found something lovely, I love it so much;
Was kann ich, was kann ich dafür?	How can I, how can I help it?
Drum sind mir die Menschengesichter nicht hold:	That's why men's faces have turned away from me:
Doch spinn ich ja leider nicht Seide, noch Gold,	But sadly I am spinning neither silk nor gold,
Ich spinne nur Herzeleid mir . . .	I am spinning only heartache for myself . . .
. . . Was dränget ihr euch um die Kranken herum,	. . . Why do you crowd round the lovesick patients
Und scheltet und schnarchet sie an?	Scolding and grunting at them?
Von Schelten und Schnarchen genesen sie nicht.	Scolding and grunting will not make them better.
Man liebet nur Tugend, man übet ja Pflicht;	We just love virtue, we act as duty dictates;
Doch keiner tut mehr, als er kann . . .	Yet no-one can do more than he is able . . .

The first and sixth stanzas of Bürger's eight-stanza poem are quoted to give a flavour of the text, in which the poet reiterates a favourite theme which many of his contemporaries found uncomfortable: the 'natural right' of individuals to seek happiness together even when their relationship cannot be sanctioned by social convention. His sonnet 'Naturrecht' (Natural right) argues the case for sex outside marriage with challenging explicitness (see *Seufzer eines Ungeliebten*). In the present poem, Bürger argues that a loving relationship concerns nobody but the lovers themselves and that love is as natural as sunshine and rain, day and night. He addresses his poem to 'human faces', whose frowns of disapproval he finds harrowing and unreasonable.

The sketch is fragmentary, sharing a sheet with other works (Vienna, GdM: A62), but it is interesting that Beethoven was attracted to this somewhat intractable poem (the only completed setting is that by Zumsteeg). The sketch is contemporaneous with Beethoven's setting of Bürger's *Seufzer eines Ungeliebten* and *Gegenliebe*, poems which broach the subject of love as a natural passion in similarly forceful language. At the age of 24, Beethoven clearly identified with Bürger's appeal for love to be given its head, regardless of social convention, an attitude which was later to lead to some problematic relationships with women, notably his deep feelings for Josephine Deym and Antonie Brentano, both married ladies.

The fragment is clearly headed 'An die Menschengesichter', but is only erratically texted. The first line of the sixth stanza (see above) is the only full line which is clearly decipherable, and one wonders whether Beethoven was not intending to set all the stanzas of a relatively long poem. The untexted melody in 6/8 which opens the fragment fits the words and catches the mood of the first stanza, which is petulant rather than seriously tragic.

AN EINEN SÄUGLING To a baby at the breast
Johann von Döring

?1783

A major WoO108 Peters 38 Henle 2 GA XXIII/229

Noch weisst du nicht, wes Kind du bist,	You do not yet know whose child you are,
Wer dir die Windeln schenket,	Nor who changes you,
Wer um dich wacht und wer sie ist,	Who watches over you and who that person is
Die dich erwärmt und tränket.	Who warms and suckles you.
Geneus, indes mit frommem Sinn,	Enjoy this for now in your innocence;
Geneus: nach wenig Jahren	Enjoy, and before too long
Wird sich in deiner Pflegerin	Your mother will be revealed
Die Mutter offenbaren.	As your carer.
So hegt und pflegt uns alle hier,	In the same way a good benefactor
Auf gleich verborgne Weise,	Tends and cares for us
Ein Geber, Dank sei ihm dafür!	With goods and food and drink:
Mit Gütern, Trank und Speise.	Let us thank him for it!
Zwar fasst ihn nicht mein dunkler Sinn;	Admittedly my benighted sense
Allein, nach wenig Jahren	Cannot comprehend him, but before long,
Wird, wenn ich fromm und gläubig bin,	If I do but humbly believe,
Er mir sich offebaren.	He will reveal himself to me.

Beethoven probably found the poem in the Göttingen *Musen-Almanach* for 1779. No autograph of this early song survives. The setting appeared in 1784 in the journal

Neue Blumenlese für Klavierliebhaber, published by Heinrich Philipp Bossler in Speyer, together with a Rondo (WoO49), also in A major. Here only one stanza appears below the music. The whole poem, as above, was printed in a separate collection of texts to accompany the songs for 1784. All four stanzas appear in modern editions, as is essential if Döring's central analogy is to become clear.

The poem threatens to become insipidly sentimental until we realise in the third stanza that the baby who is apostrophised in the title presents a model of our own existence. The baby, helpless, innocent and trusting, who will one day learn who it is to whom he owes his present material comfort, is no less than an analogy for every Christian adult, who must trust that one day his true benefactor will be revealed. To perform just the first two stanzas, as happens in a 'complete' CD edition, is to miss the point and settle for the mawkish suckling baby scenario. Despite the prevalence of autobiographical associations in Beethoven's later songs, Maynard Solomon's interpretation of this gentle song as part of the young composer's attempt to come to terms with the mystery surrounding his paternity (*Beethoven*, pp. 23–4) seems less than convincing.

The music is printed on two staves only, in customary eighteenth-century style, with the voice doubling the piano melody. The *arioso* marking is rather formal and flattering for so slight a piece, and there is an academic stiffness about the whole composition. Sixteen bars of song are framed by an eight-bar introductory section, reminiscent of an early Mozart sonata movement, and a four-bar postlude in similar style, far too cheerful for the poet's serious message. The only truly original feature, an unexpected move to an augmented sixth chord at 'wer sie ist' (bar 20), creates an overly sinister impression in relation to the poetic sentiment. For all this, the song is of documentary interest and throws light on Beethoven's serious-minded literary tastes, moulded by the offerings of the ubiquitous literary periodicals and annual almanacs.

AN GOTT To God
unknown

c.1795
G major sketches

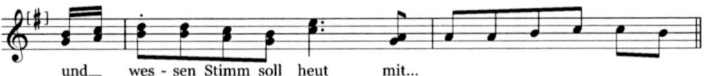

Und wessen Stimm soll heut	And whose voice should not today
Mit Jubel nicht erklingen,	Ring out with rejoicing,
Da unss der Höchste liess	Since the Highest One caused
Die Quell des Heils entspringen?	The well of salvation to spring forth for us?
Es kommt der güldne (Tag,	Here comes the golden (day,
Der uns entgegenlacht,)	Greeting us with laughter,)
Ein Tag der Lust und Freud,	A day of pleasure and joy,
Den Himlen selbst gebracht;	Reaching to the very heavens;
An dem sich konnt zuerst	The day on which the red glow of morning
Die Morgenröth erheben,	Could rise (as) for the first time,

Die unserer finstern Erd	Which gave to our dark earth
Die Helle Sonn gegeben.	The bright sun.

Sketches for a setting of this text are found on a leaf of the Kafka Album in London (BL: Add.Ms. 29801, f. 51r). In the right-hand margin Beethoven has written 'An Gott ist diess, wenn ich mich recht besinne' (This is (called) 'To God' if I remember rightly). Selected fragments of text make literal and poetical sense if the third line reads as above. Kerman's reading of 'Da *muss* der Höchste liess' makes no sense at all, and 'muß' is almost certainly a misreading of 'unß', Beethoven's usual spelling of 'uns' (us, for us). I have reconstructed the lines in square brackets to produce a probable version of the lost poem, which may be of interest to a scholar or enthusiast wishing to piece together the sketches in a realisation.

The sketches from the Kafka Album, helpfully transcribed by Kerman in his *Autograph Miscellany*, show Beethoven trying out various rhythmic gambits for the opening line, for one or two voices, as well as what appear to be short instrumental interludes, or *ritornelli*, and a homophonic setting of later lines in a broader tempo. All this suggests that the composer may have had a small-scale cantata in mind, incorporating soli and chorus, but this must remain speculation.

AN LAURA To Laura
Friedrich von Matthisson   1792
G major WoO112 Supp V/1 Henle 74 Not in GA/Peters

Freud' umblühe dich auf allen Wegen,	May joy blossom around you wherever you go,
Schöner als sie je die Unschuld fand,	More beautiful than innocence itself,
Seelenruh', des Himmels bester Segen,	May spiritual peace, Heaven's finest blessing,
Walle dir wie Frühlingshauch entgegen,	Waft towards you like a Spring breeze,
Bis zum Wiedersehn im Lichtgewand!	Until we meet again, clothed in light!
Lächelnd wird dein Seraph niederschweben,	The angel who bears the palm of judgement
Der die Palme der Vergeltung trägt,	Will float down to you, smiling,
Aus dem dunklen Tal zu jenem Leben	To lift your beautiful soul
Deine schöne Seele zu erheben,	From this dark vale up to that new life,
Wo der Richter unsre Taten wägt.	Where the Judge will weigh our deeds.
O dann töne Gottes ernste Waage	O, then God's sombre scales will ring out
Wonne dir, von jedem Missklang frei,	Your blissful salvation, free from all discord,

Und der Freund an deinem Grabe sage:	And the friend beside your grave will say:
Glückliche, der letzte deiner Tage	Happy one! Your very final day
War ein Sonnenuntergang im Mai.	Was a sunset in May.

It is not clear whether Beethoven used the first published version of the poem, in the Hamburg *Musen Almanach* for 1785, or the version published in Matthisson's collected poems in Mannheim in 1787. Interestingly, the title changes from 'An Serena' to 'An Laura' during the intervening two years, suggesting that the identity of the girl is immaterial in this poem of idealised love. The autograph was discovered by Georg Kinsky in a private collection in 1911 and the song was first published by him in Cologne in 1916, in *Musikhistorisches Museum von Wilhelm Heyer*, volume IV. The title 'An Laura' also derives from Kinsky.

The autograph in Bonn (BH: BH78) was virtually destroyed by fire in 1960, although it is well illustrated as a fold-out in Schiedermair's *Der junge Beethoven* (2nd edition, Weimar 1939). A double sheet in Vienna (GdM: A61) contains a partially texted sketch for the song, and can be confidently dated to 1792.

Although the song was not published until 1916, the music to the first and second stanzas was used by Diabelli to create a twelfth piano Bagatelle for his edition of op. 119, published around 1826. This set is generally known as a collection of eleven Bagatelles, with the spurious twelfth number expunged from all later editions. It is relegated to the Appendix in the Hess catalogue (Anhang 21). The issue is further complicated by the fact that these Bagatelles were generally designated 'opus 112' in early editions. Hess considers it possible that Beethoven arranged the Bagatelle himself from the song, but this is a minority view. Diabelli was more than happy to interfere with the works of other composers, as his embellishments to Schubert songs in the posthumous *Nachlass* editions make abundantly clear.

Although the song is hampered at times by a lack of subtlety and delicacy in the accompaniment, it is an interesting experiment in the incorporation of recitative. The first and second stanzas are set strophically to an aptly floating vocal line, redolent of springtime innocence and guardian angels. The song's flow is interrupted at the start of the third stanza for the dramatic interlude of the weighing of souls, set as recitative, but, once the anticipated 'not guilty' verdict has been pronounced, the music relaxes back into its steady rhythmic flow. The motivic figure of the rising octave, heard throughout the song, widens first to a tenth and then to a twelfth in the postlude; Laura has attained Heaven.

Although Schubert cannot feasibly have known this song, there is an uncanny similarity of formal outline in some of his own very early settings of Friedrich Matthisson. *Der Abend* (D108), *Lied der Liebe* (D109), *Erinnerungen* (D98) and *Der Geistertanz* (D116), for example, all show a strophic form interrupted briefly by recitative, before the original musical metre returns. It is fascinating to see how Beethoven and Schubert were experimenting along such similar lines in their early years, seeking a solution to the problem posed by individual lines or stanzas which provide a metrical or sentimental mismatch with the musical verse.

AN MINNA To Minna

unknown

c.1792

D major WoO115 Not in Peters Henle 99 GA XXV/280

Allegretto

Nur bei dir, an dei - nem Her - zen, flie - hen Sor - ge, Gram__ und__ Schmer zen,

Nur bei dir, an deinem Herzen,	Only with you, my head upon your breast,
Fliehen Sorge, Gram und Schmerzen,	Do cares, sorrows and pain flee away,
Und die Stifterin der Leiden,	And the cause of our suffering,
Unsre Liebe, schafft uns Freuden.	Our love, creates for us joys
Die kein Gott mir ohne dich.	Which no god could generate,
Die kein Gott dir ohne mich	Nor none give
Schaffen, keiner geben kann:	To me without you, to you without me:
Du mein Weib, und ich dein Mann.	You my wife and I your husband.
Wer wird diese Bande trennen,	Who will break these bonds, Minna?
Minna! Wer ein Unglück nennen,	Who can name any misfortune
Das wir nicht mit frohen Herzen	Which we cannot with glad hearts
Leicht ertragen, leicht verscherzen?	Bear lightly, treat lightly?
Deine Treue trinkt mein Mund;	My lips imbibe your constancy;
Ist mein Herz von Grame wund,	Should my heart be heavy with grief,
O! so scheut ihn mir ein Blick	Ah, then one of your loving glances
Deiner Liebe weit zurück.	Banishes it far away.
Minna, Minna, solche Freuden	Minna, Minna, such joys
Schafft die Liebe an uns beiden.	Does love produce in us both.
Lass durch Vorschmack sie versüssen,	May their foretaste add relish,
Jeden Tag uns neu genüssen!	May we enjoy each day afresh!
Lass uns ewig, ewig treu,	May we, for ever, ever faithful,
Unsre Liebe stündlich neu,	Our love hourly renewed,
Unsre Herzen gut und rein,	Our hearts good and pure,
Ewig unzertrennlich sein!	Be eternally inseparable!

The poet has not been traced, but the sentimental celebration of married love is reminiscent of Herrosee's 'Duett eines sich zärtlich liebenden Ehepaares' (Duet of a married couple who love each other tenderly), which Beethoven was to set in 1795 (see *Ich liebe dich*). The similarity of the subject matter and its expression is unsurprising, given the brief but intense fad for such hymeneal paeans during the second half of the eigtheenth century. Beethoven's sketches for the song text only one stanza, but the three-stanza poem was found by Gustav Nottebohm in another printed song entitled 'An Minna', whose composer has not been identified (Vienna: GdM).

Early sketches for the song in Vienna (GdM: A66) can be dated to 1790 through their proximity to the second version of *Klage*, but the principal sketches (GdM: A11) can be dated to 1792, partly through their proximity to the first version of *Feuerfarb'*, and partly through the note '6f40' in the lower margin of the autograph, which Nottebohm (GA, Critical Report to vol. XXV) recognised as the amount which Beethoven paid monthly for piano hire shortly after his arrival in Vienna!

There are three consecutive sketches: firstly, a single untexted melodic line; secondly, a smoother melodic line with underlaid text and a final *ritornello* appended; finally, the piano part alone on two staves. All three sketches are printed in Henle. The song would clearly have been further edited for publication, but the simple reconstruction in the old complete edition (GA) is sufficient for most purposes. The song, marked *Allegretto*, flows very pleasantly, and its air of calm assurance is most suitable for its subject. The comfortable vocal compass of a ninth (D to E) would make this a rewarding song for a tenor looking for interesting new repertoire.

ANDENKEN Thinking of you
Friedrich von Matthisson   c.1808

D major WoO136 Peters 58 Henle 36 GA XXIII/248

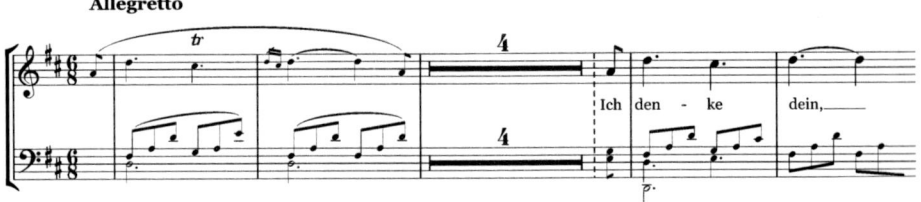

Ich denke dein,	I think of you
Wenn durch den Hain	When the chords
Der Nachtigallen	Of the nightingales
Akkorden schallen.	Sound through the grove.
Wann denkst du mein?	When do you think of me?
Ich denke dein	I think of you
Im Dämmerschein	In the twilight
Der Abendhelle	Of evening's glow
Am Schattenquelle.	By the shady spring.
Wo denkst du mein?	Where do you think of me?
Ich denke dein	I think of you
Mit süsser Pein,	With sweet torment
Mit bangem Sehnen	And anxious longing
Und heissen Tränen.	And warm tears.
Wie denkst du mein?	How do you think of me?

O denke mein	O think of me,
Bis zum Verein	Until we are united
Auf besserm Sterne!	In a better world.
In jeder Ferne	However far away,
Denk' ich nur dein!	I think only of you.

Matthisson's poem was written in 1792, but not published until 1802, when it appeared in Tübingen in the almanach *Flora, Teutschlands Töchtern geweiht* (Flora, dedicated to the daughters of Germany). Matthisson's close friend Friederike Brun was inspired by this poem to write a poem beginning 'Ich denke dein, / Wenn sich im Blütenregen / Der Frühling malt' (I think of you, when the spring is reflected in showers of blossom). It was Zelter's setting of Brun's poem which inspired in its turn Goethe's *Nähe des Geliebten* (see also *Ich denke dein*), which appeared in Schiller's *Musen Almanach* for 1796 and was thus published before Matthisson's poem. *Andenken* attracted the attention of numerous composers, including Weber, Schubert and Conradin Kreutzer.

Beethoven's setting was offered to Leo von Seckendorf in 1808, for inclusion in the periodical *Prometheus* where the first setting of *Nur wer die Sehnsucht kennt* had appeared in April of that year. In a letter accompanying the manuscript (BB337 / not in EA), the first unambiguous refrence to *Andenken*, Beethoven apologises for the delay in sending the promised song: 'Ich musste dieses Lied erstens suchen, dann noch obendrein, da ich das Manuskript in ein paar Schöne Hände schon längst gegeben, eine höchst fehlerhafte Abschrift wieder selbst abschreiben' (Firstly I had to look for the song and then on top of that, since I had long ago delivered the man-uscript into a beautiful pair of hands, I had to recopy an error-ridden copy myself). The 'beautiful pair of hands' probably belonged to Josephine Deym (née Brunsvik), for whom Beethoven had composed *An die Hoffnung* (op. 32) in 1805, together with one other song (EA115 / BB221). In a letter (in French) of 7 March 1806, Charlotte Brunsvik writes to her sisters, Therese and Josephine, requesting copies of *An die Hoffnung* (op. 32) and *Ich denke dein*. Since she refers to the works as 'deux airs', it seems certain that the second song is the present one, rather than the piano duet variations on 'Ich denke dein', which were in any case available in print by this time. Coupled with Beethoven's reference to the autograph having been presented to the lady with the beautiful hands 'long ago', the case for regarding *Andenken* as the other song presented to Josephine in 1805 seems proven.

In the event, *Prometheus* ceased publication in September and the well-travelled autograph was returned to the composer. The setting was sent to Breitkopf und Härtel in Leipzig as a present in 1809, as promised in a letter of 26 July (EA220 / BB392): 'Nächstens erhalten sie das Lied "ich denke dein" welches bestimmt war, in dem *Verunglückten Prometheus* aufgenommen zu werden, und worauf ich gän-zlich ohne ihre Erinnerung vergessen hätte – nehmen sie es als ein kleines Geschenk an' (You will shortly receive the song 'Ich denke dein' which was intended for inclu-sion in the *now defunct Prometheus* and which I should completely have forgotten about had you not reminded me – accept it as a small gift). It was duly published by the firm in March 1810. In a letter of 15 October (EA281 / BB474) Beethoven sug-gested rather belatedly that the song might be included in op. 75, but this did not happen. The surviving autograph (Genève-Cologny: Bibliotheca Bodmeriana) is a fair copy, demonstrating only minor corrections. An English edition, entitled 'Remembrance', was published by Clementi in London in August 1810.

Andenken begins with a six-bar piano introduction which pre-echoes the first long vocal phrase almost note for note. Having introduced the singer with an urbane musical obeisance (actually a figure of descending thirds), the pianist allows her to occupy centre stage and adopts a supporting role only. There is indeed something in the generous structure and public gesturing of this song which suggests the soubrette of light opera.

The first three poetic stanzas are set strophically. Beethoven sets the first four lines of each stanza to a confident, naturally flowing melodic line, the voice given momentum by a simple swinging figure which descends stepwise. Within this process, the first line, with its motto statement 'I'm thinking of you', cleverly occupies a space of its own while remaining connected to the lines which follow. This newfound command of the long-spun melodic thread was to stand the composer in good stead in the lyrical settings of Reissig texts which followed in 1809. The final line of each stanza is set as virtual recitative, with the varying question words (when? where? how?) each heard three times, allowing the listener ample time for reflection.

Beethoven follows the poet's lead in changing direction for the final verse, as the repeated assurances of the poet's love give way to an urgent injunction to his beloved to think of him also. This final verse, which occupies almost half of the whole song, disappoints after the natural flow of the previous verses. The fluency of the music is disrupted and violence done to the text, as the composer strives for emotional expression (or perhaps dramatic effect) by wholesale word repetition. Even after the whole stanza has been repeated, a short coda follows, and this despite the fact that the whole of this final stanza could already be interpreted as a single huge coda to the preceding verses. Beethoven even inserts an expressive 'ja!' on a long-held high G for extra impact; fine in opera, perhaps, but the effect seems out of place in the smaller form of the *Lied*. Just when it seems safe to applaud, a final vocal phrase repeats 'nur dein' (only of you) for the eleventh time. This phrase, incorporating a vocal appoggiatura which coincides with the final chord, prefigures a similar device at the close of the second setting of *An die Hoffnung* (op. 94).

AUF, FREUNDE, SINGT DEM GOTT DER EHEN
Rise, friends, and sing to the god of marriages (2 versions)
Anton Joseph Stein   January 1819
1st version (Hess 125) C major WoO105 Henle 90 Not in GA/Peters

Mit Feuer, doch verständlich und deutlich

2nd version (Hess 124)   A major WoO105 Henle 91 Not in GA/Peters

(Mit Feuer, doch verständlich und deutlich)

Eine Stimme:

Auf, Freunde, singt dem Gott der Ehen!

Preist Hymen hoch am Festaltar,
Dass wir des Glückes Huld erflehen

Erflehen für ein edles Paar!
Vor allem lasst in frohen Weisen
Den würd'gen Doppelstamm uns preisen,
Dem dieses edle Paar entspross!
Chor:
Vor allem lasst in frohen Weisen
Den würd'gen Doppelstamm uns preisen,
Dem dieses edle Paar entspross!

Solo voice:

Rise, friends, and sing to the god of
    marriages!
Praise Hymen greatly at the festive altar,
That we might beseech him to grant
    happiness,
Beseech him for this noble couple!
Above all let us praise in joyful strains
The worthy double lineage
From which this noble couple sprang.
Chorus:
Above all let us praise in joyful strains
The worthy double lineage
From which this noble couple sprang.

This little cantata was written for the marriage of Anna Giannatasio del Rio to Leopold Schmerling on 6 February 1819, when the second version was performed under Beethoven's direction. The words were provided by Anton Stein, professor of Classics at the University of Vienna, who was a friend of Anna's father, Cajetan. It is clear from the repeat indications, identical in both versions, that the original poem had four stanzas, but only one survives.

A letter to Cajetan Giannatasio of uncertain date (EA936 / BB1288), in which Beethoven explains that preparing works to send to London has held up work on 'your song', suggests either a commission or, more probably, the promise to set the cantata as a favour. Beethoven was indebted to both families. His nephew Karl was a pupil at Giannatasio's boarding school for boys between February 1816 and January 1818, and Cajetan had also agreed to Karl's staying at his house under close supervision in December 1818, after the boy had run away from Beethoven to his mother's flat. Beethoven became a frequent and welcome visitor to the Giannatasio household and enjoyed the company of Cajetan's two daughters, Franziska (Fanny) and Anna (Nanni); indeed, reports of laughter and pranks conjure up a portrait of the composer as a kind of favourite uncle to the girls, enjoying the carefree relationship he never achieved with his own nephew. The composer had an indirect connection to the bridegroom Leopold Schmerling through his brother Joseph Schmerling, a lawyer who had advised Beethoven in matters regarding the composer's guardianship of his nephew.

The autograph of the first version (Darmstadt, Hessische Landesbibliothek) was rediscovered in 1924. It had apparently lain forgotten for many years in the archives of Breitkopf and Härtel, publishers of the first complete Beethoven edition. The diligent archivist Wilhelm Hitzig finally rediscovered the manuscript, which was published in *Der Bär*, Breitkopf and Härtel's Yearbook, for the Beethoven anniversary year of 1927. This first version, dated 'am 14ten Jenner 1819', is written for a soprano or tenor soloist and a unison chorus, although the manuscript shows clearly that the use of a chorus to repeat the final three lines was an afterthought. Interestingly, this earlier version is cast in C major, a key it shares with three other songs for soloist and unison chorus: *Der freie Mann*, *Kriegslied der Österreicher* and *Erhebt das Glas*. It must be admitted that these four songs make odd bedfellows – written variously for freemasons, Viennese volunteers, a group of friends at a farewell gathering and a wedding feast – and yet they share a generalised context of sociability and solidarity. Encouraging the assembled company to join in a chorus clearly fosters cohesion.

The autograph of the second version (London, RCM: MS 4222) was sold by Anna Giannatasio's son-in-law to Edward Buxton in 1853, along with other Beethoveniana. One suspects that the items were sold without Anna's permission, as she reported to Thayer that the manuscript had been 'stolen'. However, it had been bought in good faith by Buxton, a partner in the publishing firm of Ewer & Co. This firm duly published the cantata in London in 1858, with new English words (only) by John Oxenford, as 'The Wedding Song', on the occasion of the wedding of Princess Victoria to Crown Prince Friedrich Wilhelm of Prussia in January of that year. (The whole affair of the two manuscripts is described with admirable clarity by C. B. Oldman in 'A Beethoven Friendship', *Music and Letters* 17 (1936), pp. 328–36.) The original version, with German words, was not published until 1962, when Willy Hess included it in his supplementary volume V. In the second version, lowered to A major, the soloist is notated in bass clef, and the chorus is in four parts. Perhaps new forces had presented themselves for the first performance.

Admittedly, the report of the first performance is at second hand and was not reported to Thayer until 1881, but it presents a delightful image of the composer at a family gathering. It was received from Anna Pessiak-Schmerling, daughter of the happy couple: 'When Mama came home from church after the wedding, she heard the sound of a very lovely male-voice quartet, and when it had died away, Beethoven stepped out from his hiding place and handed Mama the manuscript of the quartet she had just heard, with warm words of congratulation' (letter to Thayer of March 1881). As the chorus parts of the second version are notated in soprano, alto, tenor and bass clefs, suggesting a mixed chorus, Oldman assumes that the first version was performed at the wedding, as the account is specific about male voices. The second version seems, however, to be the revised and elaborated one. Perhaps Beethoven simply used the four clefs out of habit, or possibly he momentarily forgot that the chorus was to be exclusively male. (A reverse-parallel case is Schubert's part song *Ständchen* ('Zögernd leise', D920), which the composer set for alto solo and four male voices and then had to rewrite hurriedly when reminded that only female friends and singing pupils were to perform the serenade.)

The cantata, while of modest proportions, is a vigorous composition, opening *ff* with fanfare-like chords above a tremolo bass on the tonic, before a rising dominant flourish and ensuing pause give way to a simple and bold vocal line in the composer's declamatory mode. A three-bar interlude which echoes the vocal line forms a bridge to the second part of the poem, which is declaimed by the soloist and repeated, to a fuller accompaniment, by the chorus. A six-bar postlude brings the piece to a stirring close with three full chords on the tonic, hands far apart, covering almost the full extent of Beethoven's piano. A 'first-time bar' is marked for three stanzas, with a bar marked 'Ende' for the fourth stanza. To unearth the three missing stanzas now would be improbably serendipitous, although the song, with its accompanying history, deserves a performance, which would be greatly enhanced if the music were heard more than once.

AUS GOETHES FAUST From Goethe's *Faust*
Johann Wolfgang von Goethe   1809, sketched c.1790
G minor Op. 75/3 Peters 19 Henle 42 GA XXIII/219

Mephisto:

Es war einmal ein König,
Der hatt' einen grossen Floh,
Den liebt' er gar nicht wenig,
Als wie seinen eignen Sohn.
Da rief er seinen Schneider,
Der Schneider kam heran:
'Da, miss dem Junker Kleider
Und miss ihm Hosen an!'

In Sammet und in Seide
War er nun angetan,
Hatte Bänder auf dem Kleide,
Hatt' auch ein Kreuz daran
Und ward sogleich Minister
Und hatt' einen grossen Stern.
Da wurden seine Geschwister
Bei Hof auch grosse Herrn.

Und Herrn und Fraun am Hofe,
Die waren sehr geplagt,
Die Königin und die Zofe

Mephistopheles:

There once was a king
Who had a large flea.
He loved it more than a little,
Just like his own son.
So he summoned his tailor,
The tailor duly appeared:
'Now then, measure some robes
And breeches for this gentleman.'

It was now attired
In velvet and silk,
Had ribbons on its suit
And a cross on it too.
And at once became a minister
And had a large star.
Then all his siblings also
Became big shots at court.

And the ladies and gentleman at court
Were sorely plagued,
Both queen and maids

Gestochen und genagt,	Were stung and bitten,
Und durften sie nicht knicken	And were not allowed to squash them
Und weg sie jucken nicht.	And scratch them off their arms.
Wir knicken und ersticken	But we'll squash and suffocate
Doch gleich, wenn einer sticht.	Soon enough, if someone stings us.

Chorus (jauchzend):	*Chorus (cheering):*
Wir knicken und ersticken	But we'll squash and suffocate
Doch gleich, wenn einer sticht.	Soon enough, if someone stings us.

Goethe's viciously satirical song of the flea under royal protection, whose nepotistic advancement of his siblings causes much scratching of heads at court, is performed by Mephistopheles in the first part of *Faust*. As sketches for settings of the text date back to 1790, Beethoven must have used the version of the play which Goethe published in the final volume of a provisional collected edition of his works in 1790, as *Faust. Ein Fragment*. This version corresponds closely to the first part of *Faust*, published in 1808, but ends with the scene in the cathedral. A conversation book entry of April 1823 (quoted by Boettcher, *Beethoven als Liederkomponist*, p. 44) concerns Beethoven's desire to set Faust to music: 'So hoffe ich endlich zu schreiben, was mir und der Kunst das Höchste ist – Faust' (Then I hope finally to compose what for me and for art is the highest achievement – *Faust*). It was not to be. Apart from slight sketches for a setting of *Gretchen am Spinnrade* dating from the turn of the century, no other *Faust* music survives.

Having made a pact with Mephistopheles, whereby he will experience all that life has to offer in exchange for his eternal soul, Faust is transported from his brown study and introduced to some of life's more sensual pleasures. The odd couple call first at Auerbachs Keller, a renowned sixteenth-century tavern in Leipzig. One of the student regulars has just sung a cruel song about the death throes of a poisoned rat ('Es war eine Ratt' im Kellernest') and Mephistopheles is invited to sing them a new song. Claiming just to have returned from Spain, the 'land of wine and song', Mephistopheles launches into the Flea Song, the other drinkers joining lustily in the final chorus. He then performs some wild 'Hokuspokus' at the students' expense before he leaves with Faust, while the befuddled students are left to wonder whether it was all just an effect of the drink or real magic.

Beethoven's setting was published in October 1810 by Breitkopf und Härtel in Leipzig as 'Aus Göthe's Faust', the third song of the op. 75 collection. Clementi's parallel English publication had appeared in London in August 1810 as 'The Flea. A Comic Song and Chorus'. Like other songs from op. 75, the Flea Song was a completion and revision of earlier sketches rather than a wholly new conception. Fragmentary sketches in Berlin (SPK: Aut.28) and London (BL: Add. Ms.29801) bear scant resemblance to the finished article, but a sketch from 1792 in Bonn (BH: BH114) is closer to the final version. The autograph has disappeared, but a sketch in private ownership dates from 1809 and must have been its immediate precursor.

There is no wittier song by Beethoven. With a very restricted tessitura, the song is a grateful one for singers of any voice, but it is the pianist who has the fun and steals the show. The flea is introduced in the perky five-bar introduction; indeed, the first three bars, split between staccato figures in right and left hand, suggest a veritable plague of fleas, before the mock-seriousness of the trebled octaves in the fourth and fifth bars introduce the 'Once upon a time there was' opening of the satire. The flea interrupts cheekily half-way through each stanza with a nimble leap through three octaves and takes centre stage in the eight-bar interlude between stanzas, before finally getting his comeuppance in the final two bars when he is crushed not by the repeated protestations of the chorus, but physically, beneath the pianist's thumbs. The fingering of the six final descending right-hand couplets (all notes with the thumb) is Beethoven's own. This most physically graphic of tonal analogues was explained by Beethoven, as reported by Anna Pessiak-Schmerling: 'Als sie zum Schluss kamen, zeigte ihnen Beethoven lachend, wie das gespielt werden müsse, und nahm immer zwei Töne mit dem Daumen wie man einen Floh knackt' (When they reached the end, Beethoven laughed and showed them how it should be played, playing two notes with his thumb each time, as when crushing a flea).

This is one of Beethoven's songs with chorus, but here the chorus, as in the original context, is reserved for the final refrain, which then merges into an extended coda, as the drunken revellers repeatedly protest their indignation and their desire to exterminate all irritating parasites. Beethoven avoids descent into chaos by employing a steady tempo indication (*poco allegretto*), which should be observed throughout. The first German edition (i) set the final bars of vocal melody to a single word, encouraging an aspirated effect, while the English edition (ii) offered a repeated syllable; later German editions, including the GA and thus Peters (iii), repeated a phrase, simplifying performance, but reducing the opportunity for special vocal effects. The singer now has a choice:

BADELIED Bathing song
Friedrich von Matthisson   1817

C major Bia 677 lost sketch

Zum Bade! zum Bade!	Let us go bathing! bathing!
Vom Blumengestade	From the flowery bank
Hinab in die wallenden Fluten!	Down into the swirling waters!
Die Sonne gebietet,	The sun holds sway,
Sie wütet, sie wütet,	It rages, it rages,
Mit himmeldurchströmenden Gluten!	Its blazing rays permeating the sky!

Ha! Wie so gelinde	Ah, how softly
Die lispelnden Winde	The whispering winds
Die glühenden Wangen uns kühlen!	Cool our hotly glowing cheeks!
Wie schäumend die hellen,	How the brightly waves,
Lichtblinkenden Wellen	Sparkling in the sunlight,
Die schwebenden Hüften umspülen!	Splash around our floating hips.
Bald tauchen wir nieder,	Now we dive low,
Bald heben wir wieder	Now lift ourselves
Uns rudernd aus sandichten Tiefen!	From the sandy depths with flailing arms!
Und kämpfen und ringen	And struggle wildly
Stromüber zu dringen,	To get across the river,
Dass Loken und Wangen uns triefen!	Making our hair and cheeks dripping wet.
Auf Wogen zu schweben,	To float on the waves,
Sich jauchzend zu heben,	To rise up cheering loudly,
Welch Götterentzüken, ihr Brüder!	What heavenly delight it is, brothers!
Da rauschen den Kummer	Then the waves lull
Die Wellen in Schlummer,	All our cares to sleep,
Da stählt man die nervichten Glieder!	Then one can toughen frayed limbs!
Durchbrauset die Flächen	And so roar with delight
Von Flüssen und Bächen,	Through rivers and streams,
Von pappelumschatteten Teichen;	Through pools shaded round with poplar;
Bis Flokengewimmel	Until showers of flakes
Und Stürme vom Himmel	And winter storms
Die glänzende Bläue verscheuchen!	Chase the brilliant blue from the skies.

Gustav Nottebohm saw this unfinished song sketch on p. 5 of the Boldrini pocket sketchbook, which was in the ownership of the Artaria family until about 1890. It was subsequently lost and so Nottebohm's transcription of the incipit (*Zweite Beethoveniana*, p. 350) is all that survives of this song sketch. The setting had metrical markings above the notes, as illustrated. The reason for this is not clear, as there is no ambiguity in Matthisson's metre. Could it be that, at this later stage of his career, and with increasing deafness, he could less well imagine natural speech rhythms? Very few songs were to be completed after 1817, although *Abendlied unterm gestirnten Himmel* represents a glorious, if isolated, late flowering and consummation.

I am indebted to Dr Ruth Owen of Brasenose College, Oxford, for tracking down the poem, which was written in 1778 and possesses both rhythmic vitality and a pre-Romantic revelling in sounds for their own sake. There is sensuousness verging on sensuality in Matthisson's attempts to describe the joys of swimming, presented as a wholly masculine exercise. The energetic poem is presented here in full, as Beethoven clearly knew and admired it.

BUNDESLIED   Song of fellowship

Johann Wolfgang von Goethe   c.1795 (rev. 1820s)

B flat major Op. 122 Supp V/25 Henle 96 Not in GA/Peters

In allen guten Stunden,
Erhöht von Lieb' und Wein,
Soll dieses Lied verbunden
Von uns gesungen sein!
Uns hält der Gott zusammen,
Der uns hieher gebracht.
Erneuert unsre Flammen,
Er hat sie angefacht.

So glühet fröhlich heute,
Seid recht von Herzen eins!
Auf! Trinkt erneuter Freude
Dies Glas des echten Weins!
Auf! In der holden Stunde
Stosst an und küsset treu
Bei jedem neuen Bunde
Die alten wieder neu.

Wer lebt in unserm Kreise,
Und lebt nicht selig drin?
Geniesst die freie Weise
Und treuen Brudersinn!
So bleibt durch alle Zeiten
Herz Herzen zugekehrt;
Von keinen Kleinigkeiten
Wird unser Bund gestört.

Uns hat ein Gott gesegnet
Mit freiem Lebensblick,
Und alles, was begegnet,
Erneuert unser Glück.
Durch Grillen nicht gedränget,
Verknickt sich keine Lust;
Durch Zieren nicht geenget,
Schlägt freier unsre Brust.

On every happy occasion,
Heightened by love and wine,
May we sing this song
In united fellowship!
The god who brought us here
Keeps us together.
He revives the flame of friendship
Which he first kindled in us.

Glow then today in happiness,
Be truly as one in your hearts!
Come, drink to renewed joy
This glass of real wine!
Come, on this blissful occasion
Clink glasses and embrace
Your old friends faithfully
At every new gathering.

Who inhabits our circle,
And does not do so cheerfully?
Enjoy our relaxed ways
And true brotherhood!
Thus in all the times to come
Our hearts will stay attuned;
Our union will not be disturbed
By any trivialities.

A god has blessed us
With an open outlook on life,
And everything which happens
Renews our contentment.
No pleasure is wrecked
By the intrusion of idle fancies;
Our hearts beat more freely,
Unconstrained by social niceties.

Mit jedem Schritt wird weiter	With every step the swift path of life
Die rasche Lebensbahn,	Becomes broader,
Und heiter, immer heiter	And clearer, ever clearer,
Steigt unser Blick hinan.	Our gaze rises upwards and onwards.
Uns wird es nimmer bange,	We never become anxious
Wenn alles steigt und fällt,	At life's ups and downs,
Und bleiben lange! lange!	And we shall long remain, long,
Auf ewig so gesellt!	Eternally united thus.

Goethe's poem was written in 1775, during the age of sentimentality, when it was fashionable to express one's love for one's fellow men (women were generally excluded from key gatherings) in effusive terms. The cult of friendship led inevitably to the formation of numerous groups of young men, often devoted to high ideals and taking an established older man as mentor. The founders of the *Göttinger Hainbund* (Göttinger fellowship of the grove), for example, best known of the student literary groups, swore eternal brotherhood as they processed around an oak tree in September 1772, and venerated the work and person of Friedrich Klopstock. Goethe was only 26 when he wrote this poem celebrating and idealising friendship. It is ironical that, for today's German youth, a poem such as this has become a distinct embarrassment. While the traditional German ideal of male solidarity, liberally reinforced with alcohol, survives in the *Stammtisch* (regulars' table) and *Männergesangverein* (male voice choir), it appeals to a markedly more mature generation of social drinkers and singers.

Beethoven first made sketches for *Bundeslied* in 1795, but returned to it in about 1822, along with *Der Kuss* and *Opferlied*, reworking all three songs for publication. On 15 February 1823 he wrote to Carl Friedrich Peters (EA1137 / BB1570), announcing the dispatch of the three works to Leipzig. The composer was already stressing that the work, scored for two soloists and chorus, accompanied by two clarinets, two bassoons and two horns, could equally well be performed with piano accompaniment, and reiterated in a letter of 20 March 1823 (EA1158 / BB1575) that the piano reduction should be published along with the score. In the event, Peters did not publish the works and Beethoven offered them to other publishers. *Bundeslied* was finally published in July 1825 by Schott in Mainz, Beethoven's own piano reduction appearing simultaneously with the full score.

Despite the importance which the composer appeared to attach to the piano version, the autograph of the piano reduction (DSB: Aut.56) seems to have received scant attention. Specifically, tempo markings are omitted, some repeated passages are written in a shorthand version, and notes which could have been included without difficulty (such as doubled octaves) have not been included. Modern editors of *Bundeslied* in its piano version (Willy Hess for Breitkopf 1962, Helga Lühning for Henle 1990) have been forced to borrow tempo indications from the orchestral score.

Although on a grander scale, *Bundeslied* shares with the slightly earlier *Erhebt das Glas mit froher Hand* not only subject matter and a chorus but the use of regular four-bar phrases. It adheres rigidly to its chosen key. The first four stanzas are set to identical music, including a repeated introduction. As each stanza is followed in any case by a nine-bar postlude, which seems to lead directly back into the sung verse, it would seem eminently reasonable to omit the eight-bar introduction in the middle stanzas. The fifth stanza begins identically, but the word 'ewig' (eternally) is the pretext for a long held note, accompanied by celebratory sextuplet figuration in the upper voice of the accompaniment. (Composers have often found it difficult to resist word-painting on this word: in Schubert's *Elysium* (D584) 'ewig' extends over a full ten bars, to illustrate love's eternal wedding-feast in a classical heaven; one thinks too of Mahler's reluctance to take leave of the word at the end of *Das Lied von der Erde*.) The tempo is clearly meant to relax at this point, if only to accommodate the sextuplets with their very specific articulation, much better suited to the clarinet. The original tempo was 'In a swift, rapid movement' in *alla breve*; here the marking *Allegro* in common time allows for greater latitude. The piece ends with a long eighteen-bar postlude, which sums up the whole piece in miniature, to the extent of including a two-bar echo of the 'eternal' music in the altered tempo.

The marking 'Chor' always leaves open the question of how many voices should sing each part, but clearly the use of the piano arrangement allows the use of a small chorale, whereas the original horns and bassoons can support larger forces. A small-scale recital performance with piano seems more in keeping with the implied social context of the poem than a large-scale orchestral concert.

CANTATA CAMPESTRE
Clemente Bondi　　　　　　　　　　　　　　　　　　　　1814

B flat major WoO103 Henle 87 Not in GA/Peters

Allegro

Un lieto brindisi	We all raise
Tutti a Giovanni	A joyful toast to Johann
Cantiam così.	With this song.
Viva lunghi anni	May he live for many long
Sempre felici,	And always happy years,
Utile al mondo,	Helpful to society,
Caro agli amici,	Dear to his friends,
Nuovo Esculapio	The new Asclepius
Dei nostri dì!	For our age.
Viva Giovanni!	Long live Johann!
Viva ed al solito	May he live and as usual
Febbri e malani	Continue to cure
Segua a sanar.	Fever and sickness.

Viva Giovanni!	Long live Johann!
Viva ed il tempo	May he live and may time
Sospenda i vanni,	Stay its wings,
E si bei giorni	And be slow to cut short
Tardi a troncar.	Such beautiful days.

The cantata was composed for the name day of Dr Johann Malfatti (1775–1859), whom the composer had consulted on numerous occasions and who became a personal friend. Later they were to fall out: Beethoven explained to Countess Erdödy in a self-pitying letter of June 1817 (EA783 / BB1132) that he had changed doctors, since Malfatti, 'an artful Italian, had such blatant ulterior motives towards him and lacked both honesty and sense'. No trace of such animosity is evident in this boisterously convivial and unrestrainedly laudatory cantata of 1814. It was first performed on 24 June 1814, at Malfatti's house in Weinhaus, just outside Vienna, and the composer probably played the piano himself on this occasion.

The Italian text of the cantata was commissioned by Joseph Bertolini, formerly a student of Malfatti's, from Clemente Bondi, a Jesuit librarian, poet and translator. Beethoven seems to have composed the music very quickly, as indicated by sketches in the Dessauer sketchbook (GdM: A40). These sketches follow directly on sketches for the final version of *Fidelio*, notably a revision of Leonore's aria, which was first heard at the benefit performance on 18 July 1814.

The sketches in Vienna include a texted sketch, which is the only source for the original Italian text. The original autograph, used in the first performance, was presented by Bertolini to a celebrated pianist, Anna Caroline Belleville-Oury. This autograph is lost, but a revised copy was made, which was presented to Franz Liszt on the occasion of the Beethoven Festival in Bonn in 1845. This copy, now in Berlin (SPK: Mus.Ms. 1245), has German words, which celebrate the occasion, beginning: 'Was froh zum Feste / Beethoven brachte, / Das bringen wir nun, / Guter Liszt!' (What Beethoven happily brought to the celebration, we now offer, good Liszt!). A further copy (SPK: Mus.Ms. 1245/1), from the estate of Otto Jahn, superimposes a further corrupt German text, 'since the Italian original text was missing completely'. This version, based firmly on the 'Liszt' copy, begins 'Johannisfeier / Begeh'n wir heute! / Wie sonst es war, / Sei's heute auch' (Today we celebrate the feast of St John. As it was formerly, so let it be also today), and does similar violence to the scansion of the text and hence to the note values of the music.

The editor's task, therefore, is to combine the fragmentary indications of the Dessauer sketches and the complete copies with corrupt German text, to reconstitute the cantata with Italian text. The first modern edition by Willy Hess (*Jahrbuch der literarischen Vereinigung*, Winterthur, 1945, pp. 247–66.) was with German text. In 1975, Harry Goldschmidt went back to the Dessauer sketches and reconstructed the original version with Italian text (*Beethoven-Jahrbuch* VIII). Willy Hess includes an authentic Italian version (Supp V/20), as does Helga Lühning (Henle 1990). Lühning's very extended notes on the cantata in her Critical Report indicate the complexity of the sources, as well as their challenges, which she and other dedicated editors have gloriously overcome.

The cantata starts with a vigorous *Allegro* section, given both impetus and an Italianate tone by the choice of 6/8 metre. After two bars of piano introduction, the chorus proposes the toast to Johann unaccompanied, but thereafter the pianist is never silent and indeed kept extremely busy. The second section ('Viva', bars 13–33) is repeated at once, as well as forming the final *da capo* section. Cries of 'Viva' move up the voices and are reinforced offbeat by the piano. The busy piano writing in this section is reminiscent in mood and style of that in *Sehnsucht* op. 83/2 ('Was zieht mir das Herz so?). Beethoven's setting mirrors the words so closely in bars 43–47, where a turn to the minor mode and a *ritardando* at the words 'febbri e malanni' (fever and sickness) is followed at once by a bright *a tempo* at the words 'segua a sanar' (continue to cure), that one almost wonders whether sympathy or irony is intended. In view of Beethoven's own frequent illnesses, one suspects the former.

In the *Adagio* section, a prayer for long life, the contrast between the busy piano writing, as black with beams as the slow movement of an early piano sonata, and the serene flow of the vocal parts, is marvellously effective. Here too there is word-painting. The unexpected unison A flat in bar 75 on 'sospenda', a dramatic fall of a diminished fifth for the upper voices, does indeed suggest that the wings of time are for a moment 'suspended'. The long vocal lines on 'tardi' in the final pages are similarly evocative of the appeal to time to pass as slowly as possible. Beethoven, however, realises that this is no way to end the piece on this day of celebration, and returns to the second section, the cantata finishing with reiterated cries of 'Viva!'.

DAS BLÜMCHEN WUNDERHOLD
The little flower wondrous-fair
Gottfried August Bürger   c.1795

G major Op. 52/8 Peters 16 Henle 11 GA XXIII/218

Andante

| Es | blüht ein Blümchen | ir-gend-wo in | ei-nem stil len | Tal. | Das | schmei chelt Aug' und | Herz so froh wie |

sempre piano

Es blüht ein Blümchen irgendwo	Somewhere a little flower blooms
In einem stillen Tal.	In a quiet valley.
Das schmeichelt Aug' und Herz so froh	It delights the eye and the heart
Wie Abendsonnenstrahl.	Like the rays of the setting sun.
Das ist viel köstlicher als Gold,	It is far more precious than gold,
Als Perl' und Diamant.	Than pearls or diamonds,
Drum wird es 'Blümchen Wunderhold'	And so it is justly named
Mit gutem Fug genannt.	The little flower wondrous-fair.
Wohl sänge sich ein langes Lied	One could sing a long song
Von meines Blümchens Kraft:	About the power of my little flower;

Wie es am Leib und am Gemüt
So hohe Wunder schafft.
Was kein geheimes Elixir
Die sonst gewähren kann,
Das leistet, traun! Mein Blümchen dir;
Man säh' es ihm nicht an.

Wer Wunderhold im Busen hegt,
Wird wie ein Engel schön.
Das hab' ich, innerlich bewegt,
An Mann und Weib gesehn;
An Mann und Weib, alt oder jung,
Zieht's wie ein Talisman
Der schönsten Seelen Huldigung
Unwiderstehlich an.

Ach! Hättest du nur die gekannt,
Die einst mein Kleinod war –
Der Tod entriss sie meiner Hand
Hart hinterm Traualtar –,
Dann würdest du es ganz verstehn,
Was Wunderhold vermag,
Und in das Licht der Wahrheit sehn
Wie in den hellen Tag.

What miracles it can perform
On both mind and spirit.
My little flower performs indeed
What no other secret potion can;
You would never guess
To look at it.

He who cherishes wondrous-fair in his heart
Will become fair as an angel;
I have been moved to observe it
In both man and woman.
Whether man or woman, young or old,
It irresistibly attracts
The homage of the most noble souls
Like a magic charm.

Oh, if only you had known her
Who was once my jewel
(Death snatched her from my hand
Very soon after our wedding),
Then you would understand completely
What the little flower can do
And stare into the light of truth
As into the clear light of day.

The poem was published in the first part of Bürger's collected poems in Göttingen in 1789. It includes a further eight stanzas which add little except in term of intensification – or, to modern taste, overkill. In the final stanza, Bürger states that even the longest song would not do justice to the lady's bodily and spiritual charms, all attributable to the wondrous flower, and in the final line reveals the flower's name to be Modesty ('Bescheidenheit'). The poem is sufficiently celebrated to warrant its own entry in the *Oxford Companion to German Literature*. The biographical subtext is not far beneath the surface: Bürger had married Dorette Leonhart in 1774, but fell in love with her sister Auguste, who is the 'Molly' of his 'Mollys Abschied' and the lady referred to in the present poem. After Dorette's death in 1784, Bürger married Auguste, who however died in childbirth only two years later – hence, the reference to her death in the final verse as set. In the light of this stanza, the poem becomes a kind of eulogy to the departed, but in the form of a thanksgiving for a person of special qualities. She appears to exemplify the late eighteenth-century ideal of the 'schöne Seele', a woman who combines charm, beauty, modesty, wisdom and charity.

The song was first published in June 1805 by the Kunst und Industrie Comptoir in Vienna, as the eighth and final song of op. 52. As no source material survives, the dating must be conjectural. Although it is admittedly much more extended, the two-in-one song *Seufzer eines Ungeliebten – Gegenliebe* can be confidently dated to around 1795, and we can surmise that the other Bürger songs were first conceived at a similar time.

Beethoven's setting is deliberately simple, with voice doubling keyboard melody at every point. Beethoven seems to be stripping his music of all superfluous decoration, suggesting the delicacy of the little flower, responding to the statement that it is more precious than gold and jewels, and indicating that the composer was well aware of the true name of the flower: Modesty. The opening phrase has the merest adumbration of a bass accompaniment, and the middle section, where the words 'more precious than gold' actually occur, is left unharmonised, bare octaves doubling the voice. The naive outline of the melody, where intervals of a third predominate, is redolent of folksong.

This folksong quality has led to the song's inclusion in German anthologies, such as Ludwig Erk's *Deutscher Liederschatz*, where it sits comfortably enough among genuine folk melodies. It has also led publishers to superimpose different texts on the music. *Grasmücke* (Warbler) was originally included by Willy Hess in his 1957 catalogue as a separate entry (Hess 311), but cancelled when found to be identical with the present song, with a text by Hoffmann von Fallersleben added. It must be admitted that this poem, originally entitled 'Der Bekehrte' (The convert), fits the music very well; it is a moralising children's poem, where a mischievous boy is shamed into returning fledglings to the nest by the mother bird's lament.

It is difficult to imagine a greater contrast than that between *Das Blümchen Wunderhold* and the extrovert grandeur of many of Beethoven's mature symphonic works. While fully aware of the success of the symphonic Beethoven and proud of the part Viennese orchestras played in the spread of Beethoven's fame, the reviewer of the *Viennese Allgemeiner Musikalischer Anzeiger*, writing about the songs of op. 52 in 1830, still praises this small-scale masterpiece: 'Wie einfach ist der Schlußstein dieses zierlichen Gebäudes . . . gehalten! wie einfach und doch wie rührend, wie wahr!' (How simple the composer has kept the final keystone of this delicate structure! How simple, and yet how moving, how true!). It is difficult to disagree.

DAS GEHEIMNIS (LIEBE UND WAHRHEIT)
The secret (Love and truth)
Ignaz Heinrich Carl von Wessenberg   c.1815
G major WoO145 Peters 55 Henle 60 GA XXIII/245

Innig vorgetragen und nicht schleppend

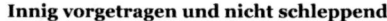

Wo blüht das Blümchen, das nie verblüht?	Where blossoms that little flower which never withers?
Wo strahlt das Sternlein, das ewig glüht?	Where shines that little star which glows eternally?
Dein Mund, o Muse! dein heil'ger Mund	May your mouth, o muse, your sacred mouth,

Tu' mir das Blümchen und Sternlein kund.	Be pleased to make flower and star known to me.
'Verkünden kann es dir nicht mein Mund,	'My mouth cannot reveal the secret to you,
Macht es dein Innerstes dir nicht kund.	Unless your innermost self makes it known to you.
Im Innersten glühet und blüht es zart	In the innermost self those who faithfully preserve it
Wohl jedem, der es getreu bewahrt!'	Will surely sense a glow and a delicate blossoming.'

The poem is not found in editions of Wessenberg's work and was presumably given to Beethoven by Johann Schickh, editor of the *Wiener Moden-Zeitschrift und Zeitung für Kunst, schöne Literatur und Theater*, in which the song first appeared on 29 February 1816 (a leap year), as a music supplement. This periodical, which aimed to keep its readers up to date with the latest fashions in art, literature, music and the theatre, seems to have targeted ladies of leisure in particular. Schickh's note accompanying the text to the song reads: 'Hr. van Beethoven has accompanied this delicate poem with one of his most delightful and urbane song compositions and thereby embellished this publication. We consider this work of art to be not only one of the most excellent ornaments of our journal, but also one of its strongest recommendations, and are happy to be able to bring our lady readers pleasure with today's music supplement.'

Schickh knew the tastes of his readership. Fanny del Rio, extracts from whose diary were published by Ludwig Nohl in Leipzig in 1875 in *Eine stille Liebe zu Beethoven. Nach dem Tagebuch einer jungen Dame*, records a visit from Beethoven, accompanied by Peter Simrock, who had asked if he might borrow a copy of this song: 'Gestern Abends war Beethoven bei uns und brachte einen jungen Menschen, seinen Landsmann mit . . . Wegen seinem Lied, das ich ihm leihen musste, sagte er auch, er müsse es mir wohl bald wiederbringen (da ich ihm darum bat) schon meiner Liebe zur Wahrheit wegen; es war Das Geheimnis, Liebe und Wahrheit von Wessenberg' (Last evening Beethoven was here with a young compatriot of his. Concerning his song, which I had to lend him, he said he would have to return it to me soon (since I asked him to do so) if only for my love of truth; it was *The Secret (Love and Truth)* by Wessenberg).

Helga Lühning assumes it was a once extant autograph which Fanny lent to Beethoven, but it was perhaps only a copy of the printed music supplement, as the diary entry of 29 September 1816 was made seven months after the song's publication. Peter Simrock duly took a copy of the song, together with a copy of *An die Geliebte* back to his father Nikolaus in Bonn, and Simrock senior published both songs early in 1817.

Although no autograph survives, there are sketches for the song in the Scheide sketchbook in Princeton, NJ. Although these cannot be dated with certainty, the second half of 1815 is a reasonable conjecture.

Das Geheimis achieves the effect of natural speech rhythm, starting with four bars of what is effectively accompanied recitative, before the voice settles into a regular flow with the appeal to the muse to reveal the secret. There is an appealing symmetry in the way the question rises through a sixth from G to E, while the imprecation to the muse returns stepwise to the tonic Indeed, throughout the song the melody never goes outside the first six notes of the G major scale, enhancing a tone of innocence. The second stanza is set to an identical vocal melody, but the accompaniment is varied to acknowledge the fact that the singer's persona has changed from questioner to answerer. The final two lines are repeated in a final coda-like section. The dynamic markings are predominantly *p* or *pp*, as befits a secret. There is nothing oracular about the muse's revelation; it is more in the manner of a friend's confidence.

In view of the song's proximity, in its date of composition and publication history, to *An die Geliebte* which was first published with optional guitar accompaniment, it is interesting to observe how easily this song might be transcribed for guitar: the detached chords at the opening, the long arpeggios at the pauses, and the undulating broken chords from bar 16; the final chord is also arpeggiated. Beethoven would certainly have been aware of a guitar tradition in German and Viennese households and this even seems to have influenced his accompaniment style in some of those songs which were clearly intended for domestic consumption. He fully expected some of his simpler songs to be transcribed for voice and guitar, and would not have been surprised when the present song was indeed included in a large collection of guitar transcriptions of operatic arias, duets, trios and solo songs, published by Simrock later in 1817. The collection also included *Die Liebe, Marmotte* and *Das Blümchen Wunderhold* from op. 52, along with the second, familiar version of *An die Geliebte* and, more surprisingly, *So oder so*.

The *Romanze* which Beethoven composed for Friedrich Duncker's drama *Leonore Prohaska* earlier in 1815 is the composer's only work for voice and harp. It is tempting to speculate that a verbal correspondence (the Romanze begins 'Es blüht eine Blume im Garten mein') and a similarity of poetical thought (both flowers have magical qualities) led to a musical correspondence, although this extends here only to the manner of the accompaniment.

DAS LIEBE KÄTZCHEN The sweet kitten
Austrian folksong   March 1820
A minor Hess 133 Supp V/16a BB1372

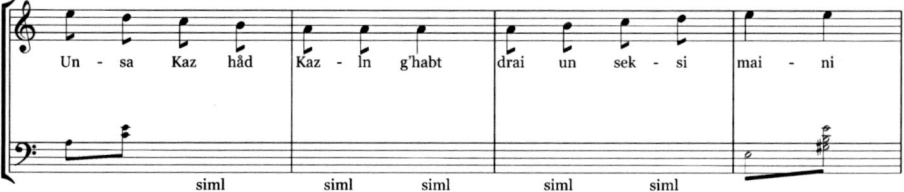

Unsa Kaz håd Kazln g'håbt,	Our cat has had kittens,
Drai un seksi, maini;	Sixty-three, I think;
Oan's håd a Ringerl af,	One of them sports a little curl,
Dås is schon dås maini.	That one's definitely mine.

This little folksong was sent to the publisher Nikolaus Simrock in Bonn, in a letter of March 1820 (EA1013 / BB1372), along with *Der Knabe auf dem Berge* (Hess 134). Beethoven explained that the folksongs were in reimbursement of Simrock's postal expenses: 'da ich weiß, daß die Kaufleute das Postgeld gerne sparen, so füge ich hier 2 österreichische Volkslieder als Wechsel bey, womit sie schalten u. walten können nach Belieben, die Begleitung ist von mir' (As I know that businessmen like to save on postal costs, I am adding here two Austrian folk-songs in exchange. You can do whatever you like with them. The accompaniment is my own). Beethoven went on to propose that trifles of this kind could easily be provided in exchange for future favours.

The words, melody and tempo indication are taken directly from *Österreichische Volkslieder mit ihren Singweisen*, ed. Franz Ziska and Julius Max Schottky, which had appeared in Pest the previous year. Beethoven's simple accompaniment for keyboard alone is far removed from the elaborate folksong settings he produced for the Scottish publisher George Thomson, accompanied by piano and strings and featuring prominent introductions and *ritornelli*; but then, those settings represented a major professional commission.

The song was first published in the *Niederrheinische Musikzeitung* No. 38, on 23 September 1865, and was included in Ludwig Nohl's *Neue Briefe Beethovens* (Stuttgart 1867) two years later (letter 232).

DAS LIEDCHEN VON DER RUHE Little song of peace
Hermann Wilhelm Franz Ueltzen c.1793, revised 1795
F major Op. 52/3 Peters 11 Henle 6 GA XXIII/218

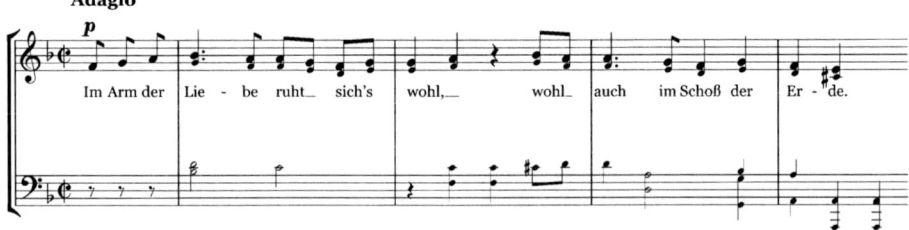

Im Arm der Lie - be ruht sich's wohl,— wohl auch im Schoß der Er - de.

Im Arm der Liebe ruht sich's wohl,	It is sweet to rest in a lover's arms,
Wohl auch im Schoss der Erde.	Sweet also in in the bosom of the earth.
Ob's dort noch oder hier sein soll,	Whether it be there or here
Wo Ruh' ich finden werde;	That I shall find peace,
Das forscht mein Geist und sinnt und denkt	This is what my mind wonders and ponders
Und fleht zur Vorsicht, die sie schenkt.	And pleads to the caring one who grants peace.
Im Arm der Liebe ruht sich's wohl,	It is sweet to rest in a lover's arms,
Mir winkt sie, ach! vergebens.	But love beckons to me, alas, in vain.
Bei dir, Elisen, find ich wohl	With you, Elise, I should doubtless find
Die Ruhe meines Lebens.	Peace in my life

Doch wehrt mir harter Menschensinn,	But the evil thoughts of men keep you from me,
Und in der Blüte welk' ich hin.	And I wither away in my prime.

Im Schoss der Erde ruht sich's wohl,	It is sweet to rest in the bosom of the earth,
So still und ungestöret!	So silent and undisturbed.
Hier ist das Herz oft kummervoll,	Here the heart is often sorrowful,
Dort wird's durch nichts beschweret	There it is not troubled by anything.
Man schläft so sanft, man schläft so süss	One sleeps so gently, so sweetly,
Hinüber in das Paradies.	As one drifts towards Paradise

Ach, wo ich noch wohl ruhen soll	Oh, where then shall I find peace
Von jeglicher Beschwerde;	From all troubles?
Im Arm der Liebe ruht sich's wohl,	It is sweet to rest in a lover's arms,
Wohl auch im Schoss der Erde.	Sweet also in the bosom of the earth.
Bald muss ich ruhen, wo es sei,	Soon I must rest, wherever it may be.
Das ist dem Müden einerlei.	It is all the same to the weary one.

Beethoven's source for the poem is uncertain. When the song was first published in June 1805 (Vienna, Kunst und Industrie Comptoir) as part of op. 52, the text was wrongly credited to Bürger. This makes it likely that Beethoven found the text in the *Musen Almanach* for 1788, which was edited by Bürger, rather than in a collected edition of Ueltzen's poems. The poem proved popular with composers. Max Friedländer lists fourteen settings in *Das deutsche Lied im 18. Jahrhundert*, including settings by Daniel Gerstenberg, Michael Haydn, Andreas Romberg and Johann Franz Sterkel, the latter a composer and celebrated pianist whom Beethoven had met in Aschaffenburg in the autumn of 1791.

Beethoven, who to a large extent shared the literary tastes of his time, was clearly attracted by this poem with its self-indulgent meditation on love, the travails of life and the sleep of death, the true peace which can be found only beyond the grave. Although no full autograph exists, there are extensive sketches in the Kafka album (BL: Add.Ms. 29801), which have been reproduced and tentatively reassembled in a transcription by Joseph Kerman (*Autograph Miscellany*) and which show that the song was complete in outline by 1793. Beethoven may have worked again at the solo song in 1795, when he composed a three-part canon (WoO159) on words from the poem, his very first canon in the collected edition and probably composed during his studies with Albrechtsberger. The song will have been revised again immediately prior to its publication in 1805.

The final song, when compared with the discontinuous and rather fussy sketches, demonstrates a confidence and smoothness in the vocal line which possibly owe something to Beethoven's early studies in Vienna, where his principal teachers had been Haydn, Schenk and Albrechtsberger. Like Schubert before him, Beethoven may also have gleaned an understanding of fluent word setting from his consultation lessons with Salieri, despite or because of the fact that Salieri presented him with Italian texts. Beethoven's understanding of Italian prosody as such was never outstanding, but stylistic principles of universal value will still have been acquired.

The song, in F major and marked *Adagio*, opens with a gently circling phrase within a four-note span, which evokes the peace of human love, before a smooth turn to the relative minor at the mention of peace in the bosom of the earth. There is close attention to the natural rhythm of the words throughout, notably in the repeated question as to where peace will be found. The uneasy spiritual search and intellectual debate at 'Das forscht mein Geist' is represented by major seconds in the right hand and a syncopated figure in the left hand, which are gradually smoothed over as the poet pleads to a caring and provident God. The music to the second verse of the song was printed in full, as the poetic metre changes, and it is the music to this second verse which also fits the remaining two stanzas. The jog-trot accompaniment in the interludes and postlude is the only aspect which detracts from this attractive and self-assured composition.

DAS MÄDCHEN AUS DER FREMDE
The girl from foreign parts
Friedrich von Schiller   1809/1810

E minor Bia 516/523 two sketches

| In ei - nem thal bey ar - men Hir - ten er - schien mit je - dem jun - gen Jahr |

In einem Tal bei armen Hirten	In a valley among poor shepherds
Erschien mit jedem jungen Jahr,	Early each year there appeared,
Sobald die ersten Lerchen schwirrten,	As soon as the first larks began to hover,
Ein Mädchen schön und wunderbar.	A beautiful and wondrous maiden.

Sie war nicht in dem Tal geboren,	She had not been born in that valley,
Man wusste nicht, woher sie kam,	Nobody knew where she came from,
Und schnell war ihre Spur verloren,	And all trace of her was quickly lost
Sobald das Mädchen Abschied nahm.	As soon as the maiden took her leave.

Beseligend war ihre Nähe,	She filled those near her with delight,
Und alle Herzen wurden weit,	And every heart opened to her,
Doch eine Würde, eine Höhe	And yet a certain elevated dignity
Entfernte die Vertraulichkeit.	Discouraged familiarity.

Sie brachte Blumen mit und Früchte,	She brought with her flowers and fruits,
Gereift auf einer andern Flur,	Ripened in some other land,
In einem andern Sonnenlichte,	In a different sunlight,
In einer glücklichern Natur.	In a happier realm of nature.

Und teilte jedem eine Gabe,	And distributed to every person a gift,
Dem Früchte, jenem Blumen aus,	To this one fruits, to that one flowers,
Der Jüngling, und der Greis am Stabe,	The young man, the old man with his stick,
Ein jeder ging beschenkt nach Haus.	Everyone went home with something.

Willkommen waren alle Gäste,	All guests were welcome,
Doch nahte sich ein liebend Paar,	But if a loving couple approached her,
Dem reichte sie der Gaben beste,	To them she presented the best of gifts,
Der Blumen allerschönste dar.	The most beautiful flower of all.

Biamonti 516 (SV127) is a full melody sketch for a song on Schiller's text (incipit given above). At the foot of the closely written autograph sheet (Bonn, BH: Mh80r), there is a brief *ritornello* for clarinet. The marking 'ritornell' suggests a clarinet interlude between verses, rather than a full-blown clarinet *obbligato* which might prefigure Schubert's *Der Hirt auf dem Felsen*. It is interesting that the mention of shepherds brought the clarinet to mind for both composers. Schubert's cantata of 1828 was to release a flood of songs with clarinet obbligato (some are usefully collected on the Divine Art CD 25025: 'The Obbligato Clarinet'), many composers finding in the soulful instrument an ideal means to evoke pastoral scenes and the related musings of the solitary rustic. A conjectural dating for Beethoven's song is 1809, as the Bonn sketch shares an autograph sheet with *Der Liebende* of that year. The meandering melody, cast like the majority of unfinished sketches in a minor key, seems to lack direction and the potential for further development. The 'Schiller block' which prevented Beethoven from completing a single solo song to a text by the poet he so much admired, is in contrast to the easy fluency of the Reissig songs, including *Der Liebende*. In this instance at least, a lesser poet yielded a greater musical harvest.

Biamonti 523 (SV198) is a brief sketch for a setting for voice and piano (Paris, BN: Ms. 48). Gustav Nottebohm (*Zweite Beethoveniana*, p. 282n) refers to it as a mere 'Ansatz' (opening) on a sheet with an Ecossaise in D major (WoO22) and a sketch for Goethe's *Sehnsucht* (op. 83/2). Hans Boettcher (*Beethoven als Liederkomponist*) guessed that Beethoven may have made these sketches in 1797, the year the poem was first published in Schiller's *Musen-Almanach*, but it can be confidently dated to 1810 through the other works. Boettcher lists the song as 'Das Mädchen *in* der Fremde', which is clearly a rare oversight.

DAS ROSENBAND   The garland of roses
Friedrich Gottlieb Klopstock   1803

D major Bia 393 / SV60 sketch

Im Früh-lings-schat - ten fand ich sie____

Im Frühlingsschatten fand ich Sie;	I found her in the Springtime shade;
Da band ich Sie mit Rosenbändern:	Then I bound her with ribbons of roses:
Sie fühlt' es nicht und schlummerte.	She felt nothing and slumbered on.
Ich sah Sie an; mein Leben hing	I looked at her; with that glance
Mit diesem Blick an Ihrem Leben:	My life was tied to her life:
Ich fühlt' es wohl und wusst' es nicht.	I clearly felt it, but was not aware of it.

Doch lispelt' ich Ihr sprachlos zu,	Yet I whispered silently to her
Und rauschte mit den Rosenbändern:	And rustled the ribbons of roses:
Da wachte Sie vom Schlummer auf.	Then she awoke from her slumber.
Sie sah mich an: Ihr Leben hing	She looked at me: with this glance
Mit diesem Blick an meinem Leben,	Her life was tied to my life,
Und um uns ward's Elysium.	And all around us turned to Paradise.

The poem was written in 1753 and first published, together with a musical setting, in Christian Ernst Rosenbaum's *Lieder mit Melodien, für das Klavier* (Altona and Lübeck 1762). Its title in early editions was *Das schlafende Mädchen* (The sleeping girl). The poem is one of the 'Odes to Cidli', the name by which Klopstock addressed Meta Moller, whom he was to marry the following year; indeed, the poem appears under the simple title *Cidli* in the Göttingen *Musenalmanach* for 1774.

Klopstock's finely crafted lyric poem, with its rococo plot and accessories, found wide favour with composers. Friedländer, in *Das deutsche Lied im 18. Jahrhundert*, refers to Rosenbaum's through-composed setting as 'among the very worst music published during the eighteenth century', but praises the settings by Steffan (1778), Zelter (1810) and above all Schubert (1815).

Beethoven's sketch is in the 'Eroica' sketchbook in Krakow (BJ: Landsberg 6, p. 145). Sadly, it is in pencil and has become virtually illegible since Nottebohm described the sketchbook (*Ein Skizzenbuch von Beethoven aus dem Jahre 1803*, Leipzig 1880), transcribing the first three bars. This is, in fact, about half of the entire tiny sketch, although Schmidt mentions a further sketch in the Grasnick 20b miscellany in Berlin (DSB, f. 18r; SV54).

It is of the greatest interest that Beethoven failed to complete a single solo song to a text by either Schiller or Klopstock, despite his known admiration for these poets. In a letter of uncertain date (EA708 / BB1522) he asked the publisher Steiner to lend him Klopstock's works and in 1824 (EA1260 / BB1773) he stated how much he desired to set texts by Homer, Schiller and Klopstock. It is as if Beethoven felt he could not do justice to these great literary figures and gave up at the first hurdle. Fortunately, Goethe fared much better, but numerous unfinished sketches, although lengthier, present a similar picture of a composer apparently inhibited by great poetry (see *Heidenröslein*, *Rastlose Liebe*, *Erlkönig*).

DER ARME COMPONIST The poor composer
unknown   1790–92

A minor Bia 15 / SV 172 sketch

der arme Componist

Schweiß trop-fen kos-tet mir je-de No-te und zu wei-len auch be geis tert mich mein ge-ni-us lang ohr

Du Gott der Musen, steh mir doch bei!	Thou God of the Muses, hasten to my aid!
Mir fällt gar nichts, mir fällt gar nichts ein.	Nothing at all occurs to me, nothing at all.
Ach, ich armes Genie!	Alas, poor genius that I am!
Zwanzig Schweisstropfen kostet mir jede Note	Every note costs me twenty drops of sweat
Und zuweilen auch begeistert mich	And at times too I am inspired
Mein Genius Langohr.	By my long-eared muse.

This comic song is sketched on a double-sided leaf in Bonn (BH: BSk 17/65c / SBH 705), sandwiched between the cello part of an unknown work in G major and what appear to be harmonic experiments and an elaborate unidentified cadenza. The Beethoven House experts have dated it, on the basis of handwriting and paper type, to 1790–92, during Beethoven's final years in Bonn. The text was first deciphered for the 'Unheard Beethoven' project by Robert Jodoin.

The impracticable tessitura of the piece suggests that it was never intended for performance, but was merely a personal whimsy, in which Beethoven (who may well have provided his own words) expresses his frustration during a bout of 'composer's block'. Despite this, Beethoven pays close attention to the natural speech rhythms of the text. The first phrase rises pleadingly, as Beethoven invokes the 'God of the muses', rather than St Cecilia, and reaches a comically exaggerated climax above the range of a normal voice as the composer laments his lack of inspiration. The humorously abrupt ending with its falling octave figure both suggests the long-eared donkey muse and gives an ironical sample of his dubious musical guidance. The vocal melody is complete, with sparse indications of a reiterated accompaniment figure, starting in A minor and turning to A major at bar 5, where a counter-melody in the right hand is also adumbrated.

The piece has been completed and can be heard on a midi file at www.unheardbeethoven.org. It would certainly provide light relief and a significant talking point if performed in suitably tongue-in-cheek style (and necessary use of falsetto) at an otherwise serious *Lieder* recital.

DER BARDENGEIST The bardic spirit
Franz Rudolph Herrmann

Nov. 1813

E minor WoO142 Peters 50 Henle 56 GA XXIII/241

Mäßig langsam

Dort auf dem ho-hen Fel-sen sang ein al-ter Bar-den-geist;

Dort auf dem hohen Felsen sang
  Ein alter Bardengeist;
Es tönt wie Äolsharfenklang
Im bangen schweren Trauersang,
  Der mir das Herz zerreisst.

Und wie vom Berge zart und lind
  Ins süsse Blumenland
Kastalias heil'ge Quelle rinnt:
So wallt und rauscht im Morgenwind
  Das silberne Gewand.

Nur leise rauscht sein Lied dahin
  Beim grauen Dämmerschein,
Und zu den hellen Sternen hin
Entschwebt sein Herz, sein tiefer Sinn
  In süssen Träumerein.

Und still ergriff mich mehr und mehr
  Sein wunderbares Lied.
Was siehst du, Geist, so bang und schwer?

Was suchst du dort im Sternenheer?
  Wie dir die Seele glüht!

'Ich suche wohl, nicht find' ich mehr,
  Ach! die Vergangenheit.
Ich sehe wohl so bang und schwer,
Ich suche dort im Sternenheer
  Der Deutschen goldne Zeit.

Hinunter ging die Sonne schon,
  Kaum blieb ein Widerschein;
Mit Arglist und mit frechem Hohn
Pflanzt nun die düstre Nacht den Mohn
  Ums Grab der Väter ein.

Ja, herrlich, unerschüttert, kühn
  Stand einst der Deutsche da;
Ach! Über schwanke Trümmer ziehn
Verhängnisvolle Sterne hin.
  Es *war* Teutonia.'

Noch auf dem hohen Felsen sang
  Der alte Bardengeist;
Es tönt wie Äolsharfenklang

There atop the lofty crag sang
  The ghost of an ancient bard;
One hears a sound like an Aeolian harp
In his anxious, solemn lament,
  Which tears my heart to shreds.

And just as Castalia's sacred spring ripples
  Gently and softly from the mountain
Into the sweet flowery plain,
So his silvered robe wafts and rustles
  In the morning breeze.

His song fades only softly away
  With the grey light of dawn,
And his heart, his deep thoughts
Waft away towards the bright stars
  In sweetest reveries.

And in the silence, his wondrous song
  Took ever greater hold of me.
Why do you look, spirit, so anxious and
  solemn?
What is it you seek in the starry legions?
  How your soul seems to burn!

'I seek indeed, yet no longer find,
  Alas, the past.
I indeed look anxious and solemn,
I seek there among the starry legions
  The golden age of the Germans.

The sun was already setting,
  Scarcely a reflection lingered;
With deceit and impudent scorn
Sombre night now plants its poppies
  Around the ancestral graves.

Yes, once the Germans stood there,
  Majestic, unshakeable, intrepid;
Now, alas, foreboding stars
Pass over fragile ruins.
  This *was* once Teutonia.'

And still atop the lofty crag sang
  The ghost of that ancient bard;
One hears a sound like an Aeolian harp,

| Ein banger, schwerer Trauersang, | An anxious, solemn lament, |
| Der mir das Herz zerreisst. | Which tears my heart to shreds. |

Herrmann's poem first appeared in Erichson's *Musen-Almanach für das Jahr 1814*, published in Vienna by Carl Gerold, along with Beethoven's setting. Beethoven must, then, have received the text directly from the poet or the editor with a request for its musical composition. In the music supplement, the date of Beethoven's song was stated as 3 November 1813, and, in the absence of any autograph or sketches, we must accept this date.

Herrmann's other writings evince an interest in the Germanic past, including a dramatic trilogy on the Nibelungs, although this has hardly worn as well as Wagner's later reworking of the legends. *Der Bardengeist* presents the spirit of a dead bard who laments the passing of the German golden age, as the sun sets symbolically on its fragile ruins. This is not bardic poetry as such, but a memorial of the patriotic bardic tradition in German poetry which reached its peak in the 1760s and was kept alive in succeeding decades by the disciples of Klopstock and the ancient bard Ossian. The latter was, in fact, an elaborate hoax, but was superbly timed by the true author James Macpherson to capitalise on the revival of interest in bardic lore and national folk literature.

The bard as hero still survived in Vienna in the early years of the nineteenth century. The old man who takes up his harp to sing his own swansong in Mayrhofer's *Nachtstück* (Schubert's D672) is a direct descendant of the Harper of Goethe's *Wilhelm Meister*. Bruchmann's 'angry bard' (*Der zürnende Barde*, Schubert's D785) seems so much on the defence, however, because he senses that the days of the true bard, with his lyre made from ancient oak, are now numbered. The topic is part of the Romantic preoccupation with the past, viewed through rose-tinted spectacles. It is one aspect of Romantic escapism: in order to evade the vale of tears which is the present, poets looked either to the good old days of the past, or yearned for peace in a truer reality beyond the grave. It is easy to see how such themes appealed to the Viennese, living between Napoleon's cannonades and Metternich's repression and censorship. Indeed, such escapism was positively encouraged, as it diverted the people's attention from musing on their sorry lot and listening to the voices of subversion.

Beethoven matches the poem with a narrative, ballad style in slow compound time. The use of block chords at the opening of each stanza give an air of folksong simplicity to the song; Zelter's setting of *Der König in Thule* and the opening of his *Berglied* (to a text by Schiller and sharing the key of the present song) have a similar intention and effect. But there is artistry aplenty in the on-flowing melody which Beethoven has woven to fit every stanza of the ballad.

Apart from the solo in the second version of the wedding cantata *Auf Freunde, singt dem Gott der Ehen*, this is the only Beethoven song where the vocal line is written in bass clef. This reflects the male persona, of course, but also lends gravitas to the solemn tone and subject matter of the text. The voice moves stepwise within the compass of only a minor sixth, making this a grateful song for any baritone. The song is framed by an introduction and a slightly extended postlude, which are heard only once, a technique which occurs in the roughly contemporary folksong settings and in one or two of the later solo songs. The introductory bars, which rise through four octaves, may, as Robert Stuber suggests (*Die Klavierbegleitung*, p. 67), symbolise the appearance of the ghost, or were possibly suggested by the mention of the Aeolian harp.

'Castalia's sacred spring' in the second stanza refers to a fountain on the flank of Parnassus, named after a nymph of Delphi who threw herself into it to escape the unwanted attentions of Apollo. The fountain was sacred to the muses who dwelt on Parnassus, and its waters were also credited with the power of prophecy – the Delphic connection. The reference is, then, appropriate to the bardic vocation, although it derives from a different mythological complex.

DER EDLE MENSCH May the noble man
Johann Wolfgang von Goesthe
20 January 1823

G major WoO151 Supp V/17 Not in GA/Peters/Henle

Der edle Mensch	May the noble man
Sei hülfreich und gut	Be helpful and good

The text is a corrupt version of the opening lines of Goethe's poem *Das Göttliche* (The Divine), in which he contrasts 'unfeeling' nature, which treats all creatures equally regardless of their merit, with man's ability to discriminate, judge, reward and punish. This ability implies an obligation for humankind to live a noble and useful life, and thereby offer a model of the divine. Thus, although Beethoven uses here only the first two lines of the ten-stanza poem, the resulting motto encapsulates its essence. Beethoven attached great importance to such carefully selected mottos, which became for him deeply personal bywords. The first two lines were used in their correct form for the six-part canon *Edel sei der Mensch, hülfreich und gut* (WoO185), also composed in 1823.

The present setting extends to a mere 11 bars and was written either for Baronin Caecilie von Eskeles or for her daughter Marie, on 20 January 1823. Bernhard Eskeles was a wealthy banker and had advised Beethoven on his purchase of shares in the Nationalbank in 1819. These shares were important to the composer, in order to guarantee his nephew Karl's financial security after Beethoven's death. The Eskeles hosted fine receptions at their mansion in Vienna and their country house at Hietzing. Marie married Count Franz Wimpffen in 1825 and assembled a large set of composer autographs, which were bequeathed to the Gesellschaft der Musikfreunde in Vienna after her death. WoO151 was naturally among them (GdM: Wimpffen).

The short song was first published by C. Lange in *Musikgeschichtliches* in Berlin in 1900 and is reprinted by Willy Hess in the fifth of his supplementary volumes (1962). Its modest proportions suggest the improvisatory nature of an album leaf, and, while it bears no direct dedication, it is dated 'am 20ten jenner 1823' and signed by the composer.

DER FREIE MANN The free man (final version)
Gottlieb Conrad Pfeffel   1792, rev. 1794
C major WoO117 Peters 41 Henle 3 GA XXIII/232

Wer ist ein freier Mann?
Der, dem nur eigner Wille
Und keines Zwingherrn Grille
Gesetze geben kann;
Der ist ein freier Mann.

Wer ist ein freier Mann?
Der das Gesetz verehret,
Nichts tut, was es verwehret,
Nichts will, als was er kann;
Der ist ein freier Mann.

Wer ist ein freier Mann?
Wem seinen hellen Glauben
Kein frecher Spötter rauben,
Kein Priester meistern kann;
Der ist ein freier Mann.

Wer ist ein freier Mann?
Der selbst in einem Heiden
Den Menschen unterscheiden,

Who is a free man?
He, whose laws are given
By his own will and not
By the whim of a tyrant.
He is a free man.

Who is a free man?
He who respects the law,
Does nothing which it forbids,
Desires only what he can do
He is a free man.

Who is a free man?
He whose radiant faith
Cannot be shaken by rude mockery
Nor suppressed by priests;
He is a free man.

Who is a free man?
He who can see the real person
And value virtue

Die Tugend schätzen kann;	Even in the heathen;
Der ist ein freier Mann.	He is a free man.
Wer ist ein freier Mann?	Who is a free man?
Dem nicht Geburt noch Titel,	He who can recognise his brother
Nicht Samtrock oder Kittel	Regardless of title or birth,
Den Bruder bergen kann;	Velvet jacket or smock.
Der ist ein freier Mann.	He is a free man.
Wer ist ein freier Mann?	Who is a free man?
Wem kein gekrönter Würger	He to whom a crowned thug
Mehr, als der Name Bürger	Can offer no more than
Ihm wert ist, geben kann;	The name of citizen merits;
Der ist ein freier Mann.	He is a free man.
Wer ist ein freier Mann?	Who is a free man?
Der, in sich selbst verschlossen,	He who, confident in himself,
Der feilen Gunst der Grossen	Can withstand the petty
Und Kleinen trotzen kann;	Blandishments of great and small.
Der ist ein freier Mann.	He is a free man.
Wer ist ein freier Mann?	Who is a free man?
Der, fest auf seinem Stande,	He who, firm in his position in life,
Auch selbst vom Vaterlande	Can suffer the ingratitude
Den Undank dulden kann;	Even of his own fatherland.
Der ist ein freier Mann.	He is a free man.
Wer ist ein freier Mann?	Who is a free man?
Der, muss er Gut und Leben	He who can lose nothing
Gleich für die Freiheit geben,	Even if he must sacrifice
Doch nichts verlieren kann;	Property and life for freedom.
Der ist ein freier Mann.	He is a free man.
Wer ist ein freier Mann?	Who is a free man?
Der bei des Todes Rufe	He who, when death summons him,
Keck auf des Grabes Stufe	Can look confidently towards the grave
Und rückwärts blicken kann;	And boldly back on his life.
Der ist ein freier Mann.	He is a free man.

Beethoven found the poem in the Göttingen *Musen Almanach* for 1792, where it was accompanied by a musical setting by Christian Schwenke, which may have influenced the young composer. The third, fourth and sixth stanzas were not included in the first edition and are reinstated only in Henle. As these stanzas deal successively with spiritual freedom from narrow-minded priests, treating heathens equally and paying no more respect to crowned heads than to anybody else, it is likely that they were suppressed by the publisher, valuing discretion more than valour. The poem certainly appealed to Beethoven's egalitarian sentiments and is almost a manifesto for some key principles of the German Enlightenment, which valued freedom of speech and religious tolerance, considering all people to be of equal value despite differences of social standing or creed, and judging them by their deeds. Lessing's *Nathan der Weise* of 1779 demonstrates and promulgates such a world view.

The song was composed in Bonn, but revised in Vienna in 1794 or 1795 with a view to its inclusion in a set of ten settings, which eventually became the eight songs of op. 52, the present song and *O care selve* ultimately being dropped. The autograph of this setting and that of an earlier version (BL: Add.Ms. 29801) are finely reproduced, along with transcriptions, in Kerman's *Autograph Miscellany*.

The song was published in 1808 by Simrock in Bonn, together with *Opferlied* (WoO126) and *Neue Liebe, neues Leben* (WoO127), but the poem's talk of intellectual and political liberty had already attracted the attention of the local community of freemasons. In 1806 a version of the song had been published, also by Simrock, with adapted words by Beethoven's lifelong friend Franz Gerhard Wegeler. The title of this adaptation was *Maurerfragen* (Masons' questions), subtitled 'Ein Lied für die Loge' (a song for the lodge), and the first stanza gives a taste of the way the text dealt with a series of 'frequently asked questions' of the age: 'Was ist des Maurers Ziel? / Stets edler sich zu heben, / Das Höchste zu erstreben, / Frey von des Zufalls Spiel' (What is the Mason's aim? To rise to ever higher nobility, to strive for the highest, free from the play of chance). Beethoven was attracted to the ideals of freemasonry during his Bonn years, under the influence of high-minded friends and of his teacher Neefe, who was a prominent member of the Masonic order of the Illuminati. One might reasonably suspect, however, that the wide appeal of freemasonry in intellectual circles had less to do with the lure of secret rituals than with embracing a general creed of high ideals in the context of the flourishing cult of friendship.

Like the original poem, Wegeler's version, which runs to seven stanzas and includes a French translation, deals in high-principled superlatives, but with rather less subtlety than Pfeffer, a gentleman of proven moral fibre, who ran a military academy for the sons of Protestant nobleman in his native Colmar after being blinded through illness at the age of 22. Living in Alsace, the poet spoke German and French fluently, and his translations to and from each language also fostered international understanding in a truly practical fashion.

Beethoven's setting is four-square. This is necessary for a song which is designed to be sung by a unison male chorus and a soloist, but, even if the choral aspect did not demand it, Beethoven tended to declaim words with simple repeated note-values when his text expressed noble sentiments (the Choral Fantasia, op. 80 and the 'Ode to Joy' in the Ninth Symphony are heightened examples of this procedure). Here the chorus opens proceedings to pose the question, and Beethoven's bold repetition of 'Wer?' neatly solves a metrical problem posed by the poet: in the poem, the important question word falls on a weak stress and the music transfers it to a stressed position. The soloist then replies with his varying answers before the chorus responds: 'He is a free man, a free, free man!', declaring their absolute agreement with the noble thoughts expressed on their behalf. One might well argue that the whole song represents a contradiction, in that talk of the individual's freedom is at odds with the inevitable loss of personal identity in a unison chorus.

Beethoven would not see it like that; for him it is a glorious confirmation of shared human values. Although the song is written on three staves, the piano doubles the vocal line at every point. The song's simple grandeur and serious-minded tone are wholly in keeping with the sentiments, which the composer, an idealist throughout his troubled life, would have warmly seconded.

DER FREIE MANN The free man (first version)
Gottlieb Conrad Pfeffel   1792, rev. 1794

C major Hess 146 Henle 75 Not in Peters Not in GA

See final version (previous entry) for text, translation and details of poetic source.

The autograph in the Kafka Album (BL: Add.Ms. 29801) is transcribed by Kerman in his *Autograph Miscellany*. It is a work of Beethoven's Bonn years from around 1792. While the vocal melody is identical with that of the final setting (see above), the differences in the accompaniment and the effect they have on the overall tone of the song fully justify its separate publication. This version was first published by Willy Hess in *Musika X*, Heft 6, in 1956, and is reprinted in volume V of his *Supplemente zur Gesamtausgabe* (1962) and in the Henle edition (1990).

The autograph has only one stanza below the music. It is written at a time when the composer's notation was still eminently legible and the corrections, carried out in three stages according to Kerman's analysis, are especially carefully indicated. The most striking of the amendments is the very neat rewriting of the four-bar postlude; the small handwriting here contrasts strongly with the large scrawled signature which follows: 'ipse fecit L: v Beethoven', which suggests that Beethoven was struggling with a refractory quill (requests for decent quills abound in his letters). The latest editions (see above) preserve the *fff* marking, unique in the songs, from the cancelled version of this postlude.

Whereas the final version has a high degree of solemnity, this version is full of a kind of triumphant exuberance, as if the composer has suddenly realised with delight the truth of the poetic text. This is achieved by the jaunty device of the descending bass jumps in bars 4 and 6, the occasional freeing of the voice from the treble piano line, by the marking 'feurig' (fiery) and particularly by the martial fanfares and final *fff* flourish in the postlude. Is it too fanciful to hear in this postlude a tiny pre-echo of the finale of the Fifth Symphony, also cast in C major?

Mention should be made of a further sketch in the Kafka Album, which starts with a bold statement of the question for 'four men's voices':

Vier männliche Stimmen

The full sketch is reproduced by Kerman. It would be a relatively simple matter to complete it, but the result would be of historical interest only. Even in the opening phrase quoted above, we see the young composer straining for a vague expression of grandeur, with little respect for basic prosody, the musical setting stressing the inconsequential 'ist'.

DER GESANG DER NACHTIGALL
The song of the nightingale
Johann Gottfried Herder   June 1813
C major WoO141 Not in Peters Henle 88 GA XXV/277

Höre, die Nachtigall singt, der Frühling ist wiedergekommen!	Listen, the nightingale is singing, Spring has returned!
Wieder gekommen der Frühling und deckt in jeglichem Garten	Spring has returned once again and in every garden
Wohllustsitze, bestreut mit den silbernen Blüten der Mandel.	He bedecks seats of pleasure with silver almond blossom.
Jetzt sei fröhlich und froh; er entflieht, der blühende Frühling.	Now be happy and glad; burgeoning Spring is fleeing fast.
Gärten und Auen schmücken sich neu zum Feste der Freude;	Garden and meadow bedeck themselves anew for the joyful
Blumige Lauben wölben sich hold zur Hütte der Freundschaft.	Feast. Flowered bowers' arches make a delightful sanctuary
Wer weiss, ob er noch lebt, solange die Laube noch blühet?	For friendship. Who can tell if it survives for as long as the bower flowers?
Jetzt sei fröhlich und froh; er entflieht, der blühende Frühling.	Now be happy and glad; burgeoning Spring is fleeing fast.
Glänzend im Schimmer Aurorens erscheint die bräutliche Rose;	The bridal rose sparkles in the shimmering light of dawn;
Tulpen blühen um sie wie Dienerinnen der Fürstin.	Tulips bloom round her like servants round a princess.
Auf der Lilie Haupt wird Tau zum himmlischen Glanze.	The dew forms shining halos on the heads of the lilies.
Jetzt sei fröhlich und froh; er entflieht, der blühende Frühling.	Now be happy and glad; burgeoning Spring is fleeing fast.
Wie die Wangen der Schönen, so blühen Lilien und Rosen;	Lilies and roses blossom like the cheeks of fair ones;

Farbige Tropfen hangen daran wie
  Edelgesteine.
Täusche dich nicht; auch hoffe von keiner
  ewige Reize.
Jetzt sei fröhlich und froh; er entflieht, der
  blühende Frühling.

Tulpen und Rosen und Anemonen, es hat
  sie der Sonne
Strahl mit Liebe geritzt, blutrot mit Liebe
  gefärbet;
Du, wie ein weiser Mann, geniesse mit
  Freunden den Tag heut
Und sei fröhlich und froh; er entflieht, der
  blühende Frühling.

Denke der traurigen Zeit, da alle Blumen
  erkrankten,
Da der Rose das welkende Haupt zum Busen
  hinabsank;
Jetzo beblümt sich der Fels; es grünen Hügel
  und Berge.
Jetzt sei fröhlich und froh; er entflieht, der
  blühende Frühling.

Nieder vom Himmel tauen am Morgen
  glänzende Perlen;
Balsam atmet die Luft; der niedersinkende
  Tau wird,
Eh' er die Rose berührt, zum duftgen Wasser
  der Rose.
Jetzt sei fröhlich und froh; er entflieht, der
  blühende Frühling.

Herbstwind war, ein Tyrann, in den Garten
  der Freude gekommen;
Aber der König der Welt ist wieder
  erschienen und herrschet,
Und sein Mundschenk beut den erquickenden
  Becher der Lust uns.
Jetzt sei fröhlich und froh; er entflieht, der
  blühende Frühling.

Hier im reizenden Tal, hier unter blühenden
  Schönen
Sang, eine Nachtigall, ich der Rose: Rose
  der Freude,

Coloured droplets hang from them like
  jewels.
Be not deceived; hope for no everlasting
  appeal from them.
Now be happy and glad; burgeoning Spring
  is fleeing fast.

Tulips, roses, anemones – the sun's rays
  have
Etched them with love, dyed them blood-
  red with love.
You, like a wise man, enjoy this day with
  your friends
And be happy and glad; burgeoning Spring
  is fleeing fast.

Remember that sad time when all the
  flowers fell sick,
When the rose's withered head drooped
  upon its bosom;
At present rocks are a-bloom, hills and
  mountains green.
Now be happy and glad; burgeoning Spring
  is fleeing fast.

Glittering pearls of dew from above form
  every morning;
The air breathes a balsam scent; the
  descending dew, even
Before it touches the rose, becomes as
  fragrant rose water.
Now be happy and glad; burgeoning Spring
  is fleeing fast.

Tyrannical Autumn wind had entered the
  garden of delight;
But the king of the world has returned again
  to reign,
And his cupbearer offers us the refreshing
  goblet of joy.
Now be happy and glad; burgeoning Spring
  is fleeing fast.

Here in the valley of delight, among
  blossoming beauties,
I sang, a nightingale, to the rose: rose
  of joy,

Bist du verblühet einst, so verstummet die Stimme des Dichters.	When you once wither away, then the poet's voice will become silent.
Drum sei fröhlich und froh; er entflieht, der blühende Frühling.	Then be happy and glad; burgeoning Spring is fleeing fast.

Beethoven completed only two songs to texts by Herder: *Der Gesang der Nachtigall* and *Die laute Klage*; a third, *Die Schwestern des Schicksals*, remained a fragment, while *Lerne schweigen, o Freund* (WoO 168) was set as a canon. It would be wrong, however, to measure the significance of Herder to the composer by this meagre harvest. Both completed songs are of the greatest interest, and the number of copies of Herder's poems made by Beethoven, five alone written on a sheet in the British Library and more entered in his diary between 1813 and 1815, suggest that Beethoven may even have envisaged a kind of Herder song cycle. The fact that the two completed songs were, unusually, not put forward for publication during the composer's lifetime encourages such speculation.

Herder was a difficult writer to ignore. His direct influence on the poets of the *Sturm und Drang* (storm and stress) movement, including the young Goethe whom he met in Strasbourg in 1770, as well as on subsequent writers, is difficult to overstate. Herder's most lasting achievement is his huge collection of so-called 'Volkslieder', which comprised not only German folksongs but translations from many languages and even songs from Shakespeare plays, as they had the immediacy of true folksongs. The collection, which appeared in 1778–79, set out to exemplify his many writings on the true nature of poetry. Herder felt that the culture of his time had become over-civilised and desensitised. German poets should aim to shake off the artificial conventions of 'art' and recapture the vigour and immediacy of the earliest folk poetry. This was a sharp reaction to the primacy of reason in the writings of the Enlightenment, with emphasis now shifted to the poet's intuitive expression of emotion, and in poetry to an emphasis on rhythm. Herder felt strongly that 'Lieder' (referring to poems) should be heard, not seen, and flow artlessly. In the Preface to the second part of the *Volkslieder* he stated: 'Lied muss gehört, nicht gesehen werden; gehört mit dem Ohr der Seele, das nicht einzelne Silben allein zählt und misst und wägt, sondern auf Fortklang horcht und in ihm fortschwimmet' (The poem must be heard, not seen; heard with the ear of the soul, which does not simply count, measure and weigh individual syllables, but attends to continuity of sound and swims along with it). It is important to add that, while these ideas were warmly embraced by the poets of the *Sturm und Drang*, they were not a formula for later Romantic poetry, where there is far more attention to the beauty of words for their own sake, coupled with a refined artistry which Herder would have rejected.

Beethoven found *Der Gesang der Nachtigall* in Herder's 1792 collection *Zerstreute Blätter* (Scattered leaves), subtitled 'Blumen, aus morgenländischen Dichtern gesammelt' (Flowers gathered from Eastern poets). Herder translates an original work by the Turkish poet Mesihi (not by the Persian poet Sadi, as the composer erroneously states on the autograph). The autograph of the song in Berlin (DSB: Grasnick 7) is dated 'am 3ten Juni 1813'. Beethoven has experimented with a new postlude, which he has then cancelled. Only one stanza is written out. It is clear that Beethoven expected further stanzas to be performed, as a marginal comment points out that subsequent stanzas do not refer to the nightingale itself, but always to spring. This is no doubt why the introduction, with its stylised imitation of birdsong, is not repeated before subsequent stanzas.

This is not Beethoven's only exercise in 'folksong', of course. His folksong settings for Thomson gave him an unrivalled insight into the appeal and potential of an artless melody in a strophic frame; brushing elbows with *An die ferne Geliebte* in the Scheide sketchbook, we find Beethoven's copy of a true folksong setting, *Die drei Reiter; Das liebe Kätzchen* and *Der Knabe auf dem Berge* are authentic dialect songs which have been left almost untouched by their accompaniment; while *Ruf vom Berge* sets a sanitised version of a folksong, included in Herder's volumes, incorporating musical techniques perfected in the Thomson folksong settings.

With the present song, Beethoven achieves a fine blend of folksong-like simplicity and artful endeavour. The introduction is remarkably unrestrained in its evocation of birdsong. Perhaps a real nightingale would not adhere quite so strictly to C major throughout his song; perhaps his note-values would not develop to a climax with such mathematical precision; but the effect, however stylised, is as appealing as the chirpy dactylic metre of the voice, when it enters, is irresistible. The gradual build-up to a measured trill is, of course, reminiscent of Beethoven's representation of the nightingale in the 'Pastoral' Symphony. We are too much captivated by the music to object that a nightingale, of all possible birds, should not be commenting on such sunlit daytime scenes as those described here. One word of caution: the irregularity of the hexameters – lines vary between 14 and 16 syllables, with only the final two feet remaining constant throughout – would swiftly become problematic, were one to attempt to sing beyond this first stanza without careful forethought.

As *Der Gesang der Nachtigall* was not published until 1888, in the supplementary volume XXV of the complete edition, it is missing from the ubiquitous Peters edition. While this means that it remains little known, those who discover this immaculate gem in the new Henle edition will savour a serendipitous encounter and tend to revise their image of the mighty symphonist, which must now be broadened to include the sensitive miniaturist.

DER GUTE FÜRST The good prince
Leopold von Goeckingk

c.1795

E flat major sketch

[Kräftig]

Die | Lie - be nicht, und | nicht der Wein drängt | un - ser Lied___ her - | vor.

    Die Liebe nicht, und nicht der Wein,   It is not love, nor wine,

      Drängt unser Lied hervor.   Which urges us to sing.

Des guten Fürsten Lob allein,
　Hebt unsre Brust empor.
O mögt' er doch unsterblich sein!
　Das sing uns nach, o Chor!
Chor　O mögt' er doch unsterblich sein,
　Der keinen Tag verlor!

Er kränkt der Menschheit Rechte
　nicht,
　Spricht dem Gesez nicht Hohn;
Verträge sind ihm kein Gedicht,
　Bleicht gleich die Zeit sie schon;
Der Schmeichler Skorpion-Gezücht
　Umkriecht nicht seinen Thron.
Chor　O Muster jeder Fürstenpflicht!
　Sitz lang' auf deinem Thron!

Auf unsern Frühlingsfeldern rangt
　Sein Wild nicht frech herum;
Die schlanken vollen Halme tanzt
　Sein Hirsch und Reh nicht krumm;

Was wir gesät, was wir gepflanzt,
　Wühlt nicht sein Eber um.
Chor　O kehre, Tod, so spät du kannst,
　Erst seine Fackel um.

Er brennt nicht unsre Hab' und Gut
　In Feuerwerken auf;
Nicht auf Maitreffen-Gunst beruht
　Der Preis im Wettelauf;
Auch trägt er unser deutsches Blut

Den Britten nicht zu Kauf.
Chor　Drum steige hoch, wie Aetnas Glut,

Sein Lob zum Himmel auf.

Kein gieriger Lotto-Pächter frisst
　Des armen Mannes Brod;
Kein Günstling und Monopolist
　Erstellt sich ein Verbot,
Das seines Handels Leben ist
　Und unsers Handels Tod.
Chor　Den Fürsten, wenn du billig bist,
　Nimmst du zuletzt, o Tod!

The praise of our good prince alone
　Is what swells our lungs.
Oh, that he might be immortal!
　Sing that in echo, oh chorus!
Chorus　Oh, that he might be immortal!
　He who wasted not a single day!

He does not offend against human
　rights,
　Does not mock the law;
Treaties are not a mere fiction to him,
　Even if they should fade with time;
The scorpion race of sycophants
　Does not crawl around his throne.
Chorus　O pattern of every princely obligation!
　May you reign long on your throne!

His game does not range impudently
　Around our springtime fields;
His stags and deer do not flatten
　The tender ripe ears of corn as they
　　prance.
His boars do not grub up
　What we have sown or planted.
Chorus　O lower your torch, o death,
　As late as you possibly can.

He does not burn our property
　In firework displays;
Competition prizes are awarded
　Fairly and without favour;
Nor does he sell our German
　bloodstock
　To the British.
Chorus　Therefore, let his praise rise
　heavenwards
　Like the fires of Mount Etna.

No greedy lottery concessionary
　Gobbles up the poor man's bread;
No favourite and monopolist
　Is allowed to draw up a decree
Which means life for his own business
　But spells the death of ours.
Chorus　If you are fair, o death,
　You will take our prince last.

	Er nimmt nicht neunen erst die Haut		He does not rob nine people naked,
	Und schenkt dem eilften Schuh;		Just to give the eleventh one shoes;
	Wenn er uns Dämm' und Brücken baut,		When he builds us dams and bridges,
	Und Krüppel bringt zur Ruh',		And comforts cripples,
	Und stattet aus des Armen Braut:		And decks out the poor man's bride:
	Wer giebt ihm was dazu?		Who offers him anything in return?
Chor	Drum fragen wir auch alle laut:	Chorus	And so we all ask aloud:
	Wo ist ein Fürst wie du?		Where is another prince like you?

	Sei Jude, Freigeist oder Christ:		Whether Jew, Freethinker or Christian:
	Bei ihm gilt nur die That!		Only deeds count with him!
	Sei fremd: Er wirbt dich nicht mit List		Be you a stranger: he will not cunningly
	Als Mietling für den Staat;		Recruit you as a state mercenary;
	Wer nicht Soldat sein will, der ist		Whoever does not want to be a soldier,
	Bei ihm auch nicht Soldat.		Will not be a soldier in his state.
Chor	Wohl dir, dass du kein König bist!	Chorus	It is well for you that you are not a king!
	Wohl unserm kleinen Staat!		It is well for our little state!

Among several unidentified song sketches in the so-called Kafka Album in London (BL: Add.Ms. 29801) is a full melody sketch in E flat (f. 133r), with the final five bars designated for a chorus. Using this clue, it was possible to find a poem which fits the musical metre perfectly in one of the many contemporary almanacs, much favoured by composers as the source of song texts.

Goeckingk's poem appeared in the Hamburg *Musenalmanach* for 1787, which he edited jointly with Johann Heinrich Voss at that period. It was published under the pseudonym '-tt-', used by Goeckingk for fourteen of his numerous contributions to the Hamburg publication between 1777 and 1787. All Goeckingk's contributions are listed by Gerhard Hay in *Die Beiträger des Voss'schen Musenalmanachs* (Hildesheim 1975). Hay suggests several reasons for the use of pseudonyms or 'Chiffren': poets, notably editors, did not want to be accused of contributing too much; some poets in professional positions did not want to reveal their identities; many poets contributed to several competing journals and courted anonymity to avoid giving offence to other editors; editors wished to give the artificial impression of a larger number of contributors; finally, readers enjoyed trying to solve the riddles posed by such pseudonyms.

To these reasons might be added discretion in the present instance, as the poem could be interpreted as a song of protest against tyrannical rulers. It may be that the poem was simply addressed as a sincere tribute to an enlightened ruler, on the lines of the Lobkowitz Cantata (see *Es lebe unser teurer Fürst*), but it seems equally probable that the poem is satirical. The 'good prince' of the title is a model of what princes should be, and in enumerating everything which the benevolent ruler is not, Goeckingk is attacking the abuses of too many petty despots, at a time when Germany was still carved up into numerous secular and ecclesiastical principalities.

The interpretation of the poem as satire justifies its adaptation to this lilting music, which swings along in compound time in the manner of a drinking song rather than a panegyric. Songs with chorus are a distinct genre among Beethoven's songs, and this melody has most affinity with the *Punschlied*. Like that song, it can be dated with some assurance to 1791 or 1792.

The music is offered in Appendix II to show how some of Beethoven's sketches can be brought to life and rendered performable with some research and imagination. The melody has been simply harmonised, with a short *ritornelle* added. Interested readers are recommended to visit the 'Unheard Beethoven' website (www.unheardbeethoven.org) for numerous realisations of Beethoven sketches in all genres (see also *An Amarant, Der arme Componist, Heidenröslein, Rastlose Liebe*).

DER JÜNGLING IN DER FREMDE
The young man far from home
Christian Ludwig Reissig   1809

B flat major WoO138 Peters 46 Henle 37a GA XXIII/237

Etwas lebhaft, jedoch in einer mäßig geschwinden Bewegung

Der Frühling entblühet dem Schoss der Natur,	Spring blossoms forth from nature's womb,
Mit lachenden Blumen bestreut er die Flur.	Covering the meadows with smiling flowers.
Doch mir lacht vergebens das Tal und die Höh',	And yet hill and dale smile upon me in vain;
Es bleibt mir im Busen so bang und so weh.	My heart remains so full of pain and anxiety.
Begeisternder Frühling, du heilst nicht den Schmerz,	Life-breathing Spring, you cannot heal my grief,
Das Leben zerdrückte mein fröhliches Herz;	Life crushed my carefree heart;
Ach, blüht wohl auf Erden für mich nicht die Ruh',	Ah, if indeed there is no peace for me on earth,
So führ mich dem Schosse der Himmlischen zu.	Then lead me towards the lap of the gods.
Ich suchte sie morgens im blühenden Tal,	I sought it in the morning in the flowering valley,
Hier tanzten die Quellen im purpurnen Strahl,	There the springs were dancing in the crimson rays
Und Liebe sang schmeichelnd im duftenden Grün,	And love sang caressingly amid the fragrant flowers,
Doch sah ich die lächelnde Ruhe nicht blühn.	And yet I did not find smiling peace blossoming.

Da sucht' ich sie mittags, auf Blumen gestreckt,	Then I sought it at midday, lying on a bed of flowers,
Im Schatten von fallenden Blüten bedeckt,	In the shade, bedecked with falling blossom,
Ein kühlendes Lüftchen umfloss mein Gesicht,	A cooling breeze played round my face,
Doch sah ich die schmeichelnde Ruhe hier nicht.	And yet I did not find gentle peace here.
Nun sucht' ich sie abends im einsamen Hain,	Now I sought it in the evening in the lonely grove,
Die Nachtigall sang in die Stille hinein,	The nightingale's song penetrated the silence
Und Luna durchstrahlte das Laubdach so schön,	And the moon shone through the lovely roof of leaves,
Doch hab' ich auch hier meine Ruh' nicht gesehn!	And yet here too I did not find my peace.
Ach Herz, dich erkennt ja der Jüngling nicht mehr,	Oh, my heart, this lad no longer knows you at all.
Wie bist du so traurig, was schmerzt dich so sehr?	Why are you so sad? What pains you so?
Dich quälet die Sehnsucht, gesteh es mir nur,	It is yearning which tortures you, just confess it,
Dich fesselt das Mädchen der heimischen Flur!	It is the girl from home who has enslaved your heart.

The musical composition was originally intended for another Reissig poem 'Lied aus der Ferne'. The autograph in Washington (Library of Congress: Whittall Foundation) has the text to the first stanza of 'Lied aus der Ferne'. When Beethoven set this text again as a through-composed song with the title 'Gesang aus der Ferne' (WoO137), it was clearly decided to put another poem of identical metre to the earlier composition, although it remains unclear whether the decision was the composer's or the publisher's. *Der Jüngling in der Fremde* was first published in July 1810 in the second part of 'Achtzehn deutsche Gedichte', a collection of eighteen Reissig poems in musical settings by various composers, dedicated by the poet to Archduke Rudolph. This second part also included Beethoven's *An den fernen Geliebten* (op. 75/5) and *Der Zufriedene* (op. 75/6), as well as Reissig settings by Moscheles, Dietrichstein, Reichardt, Gyrowetz, Leykam, Weigl and Hummel.

The first Reissig settings seem to have been composed in quick succession in the latter half of 1809. Reissig's collection of poems *Blümchen der Einsamkeit* (Flowers of solitude) had appeared in July 1809, although Reissig may have given manuscript copies of some poems to Beethoven before this. The poet, a veteran of the Austrian army, was wont to request musical settings from popular composers and then publish collections of his verse in musical settings. He gave himself top billing and dedicated each collection to a dignitary, hoping no doubt for a financial acknowledgement.

The setting is strophic. Hans Boettcher (*Beethoven als Liederkomponist*, p. 62) suggests that the melody was designed to fit the words of the second stanza, but this rare oversight ignores the fact that the melody was not designed to fit this poem at all, the words having been inserted by the publisher from a printed copy of the poem. The melody can be judged only in relation to the 'Lied aus der Ferne', the poem for which it was intended. It best fits the first stanza of the latter poem, which is indeed the only stanza written out on the autograph. The dancing, dotted figure on 'blühenden Kranz' (garland of flowers) and the stylised horn calls at 'Nachtigallwäldchen' (nightingale copse), evoking a general sense of rural peace, both make more sense in the context of the original poem.

Nevertheless, the song as published has an appealing confidence and fluency of line. The melody is flexible enough to be accommodated to the varying mood of each stanza, although something more wistful and less jaunty might have been preferred on the whole. The tempo indication (fairly lively, but in a moderately fast tempo) would certainly benefit from further moderation, as the poet's self-pitying search for peace continues to follow its circular path.

DER KNABE AUF DEM BERGE The boy on the mountain
Austrian folksong   March 1820
G major Hess 134 Supp V/16b BB1372

Duărt ob'n af 'm Beargerl gu gu! sizt just so a Biă-berl wiă du! Kumm

Duărt ob'n af 'm Beargerl gu gu!	There on top of the mountain, hey-ho!
Sizt just so a Biăberl wiă du!	There sits a lad just like you!
Kumm åba main Biăberl zu miăr,	Come to me then, my lad,
I zåhl d'r an'n Wain uns a Biăr,	I'll pay for some wine and some beer,
I zåhl d'r a Nuss mid an'm Kearn,	I'll buy you a nut with a kernel,
Kånnst glaiwŏlst main Biăberl no wearn.	You can gladly be my boyfriend now.

This simple folksong was sent to Simrock in Bonn in a letter of 18 March 1820 (EA1013 / BB1372), along with *Das liebe Kätzchen* (Hess 133) to compensate the publisher for his postal expenses. The letter is in Bonn (BH: Slg. Bodmer). For details see *Das liebe Kätzchen*.

Despite Beethoven's warning on the back of the envelope to open it carefully ('ouvrés la lettre avec bien de ménagement'), the opening bars of the song have been lost owing to the autograph having been torn, but can be reconstructed with ease from the original source, as both words and melody were taken directly from *Österreichische Volkslieder mit ihren Singweisen*, ed. Franz Ziska and Max Schottky (Pesth 1819).

First published in 1865 (see *Das liebe Kätzchen*), both folksongs were included a century later in the *Supplemente zur Gesamtausgabe*, vol. V, edited by Willy Hess.

DER KUSS (ARIETTE)   The kiss
Christian Felix Weisse   December 1822

A major Op. 128 Peters 36 Henle 69 GA XXIII/227

Allegretto
Mit Lebhaftigkeit, jedoch nicht in zu geschwindem Zeitmaße und scherzend vorgetragen

Ich war bei Chloen ganz allein,
  Und küssen wollt' ich sie;
Jedoch sie sprach, sie würde schrein,
  Es sei vergebne Müh'.

Ich wagt' es doch, und küsste sie
  Trotz ihrer Gegenwehr.
Und schrie sie nicht? Jawohl, sie schrie,
  Doch lange hinterher.

I was all alone with Chloe
  And wanted to kiss her;
But she said she would scream,
  And I was wasting my time.

I risked it nevertheless, and kissed her,
  Despite her resistance.
And didn't she scream? Oh yes, she screamed,
  But only long afterwards.

Weisse's poem was first published in his collection *Scherzhafte Lieder* (Light-hearted poems) in Leipzig in 1758, although it was later reprinted in the collection *Kleine lyrische Gedichte*. Beethoven may well have found the poem in a Viennese edition of 1793.

His earliest sketches for the song date from 1798, including a complete texted sketch in Berlin (DSB: Grasnick 1) which is fairly close to the published version. Max Friedländer (*Das deutsche Lied im 18. Jahrhundert* II, p. 104) suggests convincingly that Beethoven may have returned to the song in 1822 to provide some light relief from his work on the *Missa Solemnis* and the Ninth Symphony. Two autographs survive from December 1822. The autograph in Paris (BN: Ms. 33) is a heavily corrected fragment, consisting of bars 22 to 49, and displays some variants, which are fully discussed by Helga Lühning (*Kritischer Bericht*). A full autograph, dated '1822 im Decmb', is in London (BL: Stefan Zweig collection).

Beethoven wrote in the right margin of the autograph: 'Was für ein Titel?' (What title?), and when the song was published, it carried as the only title 'Ariette', followed by the first line. Weisse's poem was clearly headed 'Der Kuss' and the song was first given this title in Whistling's *Handbuch der musikalischen Literatur* in 1828 and then adopted in the first complete edition (GA). Beethoven offered the song to Peters and Probst (and possibly to Simrock), stressing each time that it was fully through-composed (EA1137/1266 / BB1570/1783). It was finally accepted by Schott and published in Mainz in the spring of 1825. The opus number was allocated after Beethoven's death, when Artaria and Schott reached agreement on the numbering of the late string quartets and realised that op. 128 was still available.

Notwithstanding arguments about unwinding, it can appear strange that Beethoven's final published essay in solo song should be a comic piece. It sets out to amuse, as is clear at the start from the performance direction 'scherzend vorgetragen' (performed jovially); when the final vocal phrase is marked 'lächelnd' (smiling), the singer is again clearly instructed to share the joke with the audience. Beethoven certainly reveals here a comic talent, and the 'timing', on which successful humour so often depends, is impeccable.

The song opens with a nine-bar introduction, which introduces the song's main theme and concludes with what sounds like an excerpt from some early bagatelle. The composer repeats 'küssen' three times, as the kiss is the main object of the exercise; the voice rises each time to a higher note, until the modified vowel of 'küssen' ensures that the singer's lips are pursed as for a kiss in the final slurred rise to top E. When the girl says she will scream, the vocal part ascends stepwise through the scale of E major, until the scream emerges on a long-held high E. As the voice descends symmetrically down the scale, the interrupted figuration suggests that the girl's protestations that the lover is wasting his time do not carry conviction. The setting of 'Gegenwehr' (resistance), with extended melisma on the first syllable, suggests the merest pretence of a struggle.

Superb comic timing is then demonstrated, as Beethoven in a calm *poco adagio* passage teases us with the question: 'Didn't she scream?', before the answer (yes!!) is given after a dramatic pause, the voice rising to a screeching high G sharp. But the joke is not over. She did not scream at the time. The handling of the transitional 'doch' (but) is masterly, and as the song hurtles to its conclusion the frequent repetition of 'lange' emphasises just how long afterwards she did think to scream.

It is a measure of genius that such a humorous masterpiece can be brought into existence in the immediate vicinity of such profound works as the *Missa Solemnis* and the Ninth Symphony, but anyone who has read through Beethoven's voluminous correspondence will have found similar contrasts of mood, and be fully aware of the composer's very lively sense of the comic.

DER LIEBENDE The lover
Christian Ludwig Reissig   1809

D major WoO139 Peters 47 Henle 39 GA XXIII/238

In leidenschaftlicher Bewegung

Welch ein wunderbares Leben,	What a wonderful life!
Ein Gemisch von Schmerz und Lust,	A blend of pain and pleasure,
Welch ein nie gefühltes Beben	What a new, quivering emotion
Waltet jetzt in meiner Brust!	Has taken control of my heart!
Herz, mein Herz, was soll dies Pochen?	O my heart, why this furious beating?
Deine Ruh' ist unterbrochen;	Your peace has been shattered;
Sprich, was ist mit dir geschehn?	Tell me, what has happened to you?
So hab' ich dich nie gesehn.	I have never seen you like this.

Hat dich nicht die Götterblume	Has not the divine flower,
Mit dem Hauch der Lieb' entglüht,	She who blossomed in the sanctuary
Sie, die in dem Heiligtume	Of purest innocence,
Reiner Unschuld aufgeblüht?	Set you aglow with the breath of love?
Ja, die schöne Himmelsblüte	Yes, the fair blossom of heaven,
Mit dem Zauberblick voll Güte	Her enchanting gaze radiating goodness,
Hält mit einem Band mich fest,	Holds me fast with a ribbon
Das sich nicht zerreissen lässt.	Which can never be severed.
Oft will ich die Teure fliehen;	Often I wish to flee from my dearest;
Tränen zittern dann im Blick,	Then trembling tears fill my eyes,
Und der Liebe Geister ziehen	And the spirits of love summon
Auf der Stelle mich zurück.	Me back the same instant.
Denn ihr pocht mit heissen Schlägen	For my heart pounds fiercely,
Ewig dieses Herz entgegen;	Drawing me eternally to her;
Aber, ach! Sie fühlt es nicht,	But, alas, she does not feel
Was mein Herz im Auge spricht.	What my heart speaks through my eyes.

Although the song was composed, along with four other Reissig settings, in the second half of 1809, this poem did not appear in print until 1815, in the third edition of Reissig's poems. Beethoven clearly received a manuscript copy from the poet, who was known to encourage composers to set his works to music. The present poem is based shamelessly on Goethe's *Neue Liebe, neues Leben*, borrowing from this poem not only its exact poetic form and its general theme but even specific phrases: 'Herz, mein Herz', 'das sich nicht zerreissen lässt', etc.

Reissig was hardly the only poet to flatter Goethe (as though that was necessary) with his imitation: Resemann's 'Herz, mein Herz, was will das geben?' had appeared in 1789; Eichendorff's 'Neue Liebe' begins 'Herz, mein Herz, warum so fröhlich?', and Heine will have had Goethe's poem in his mind when he penned 'Herz, mein Herz, sei nicht beklommen'. The question which concerns us here is whether Beethoven's settings of *Der Liebende* and *Neue Liebe, neues Leben* display similarities which are due to verbal echoes in the texts. These can be quite easily discerned in his setting of the phrase 'Herz, mein Herz', but not really elsewhere. A more interesting issue is whether the composer's encounter with Reissig's poem was one of several factors that led him to revise his earlier setting of *Neue Liebe, neues Leben* in 1809. It would have been a contributory factor only, as the main impetus for that revision was Simrock's unsanctioned publication the previous year of an earlier version of the song, coupled with Beethoven's renewed interest in Goethe's works at this time.

The song was first published in July 1810 by Artaria in Vienna, in the first part of 'Achtzehn deutsche Gedichte', a collection of eighteen Reissig poems in musical settings by various composers, dedicated by the poet to Archduke Rudolph. This part opened with Beethoven's *Gesang aus der Ferne* and included settings by Weigl, Salieri, Reichardt and Amadè, closing with the present song. *Der Liebende* appeared in London, as 'The Lover. A Favorite Arietta', in October 1810, printed by Clementi. The translation, which begins 'What new sense of pain and pleasure / Now pervades my troubled mind?', necessitates only slight adjustments in the melody.

An autograph in London (BL: Add.Ms. 47852) comprises *Gesang aus der Ferne* and *Der Liebende*. The manuscript of *Der Liebende* is hastily written, with many corrections. A second manuscript in Berlin (DSB: Artaria 173) is a fair copy in Beethoven's hand, showing the composer in a very human light, prone to err. Originally bars 20–1 were left out and were added later, Beethoven noticing his mistake when writing out the words, while bar 29 was written out twice and then the extra bar crossed through.

Although Beethoven was soon to fall out with Reissig over his presumption in publishing songs without the composer's permission (see *Gesang aus der Ferne*), the poet's verses certainly seemed to release in Beethoven a new lyrical fluency of expression, nowhere more so than here. The music lives up to its tempo indication ('passionately'). The five-bar introduction initiates the flow of semiquavers which will continue uninterrupted until the final bar. Their ripple is basically a simple matter of broken chords, but an anticipation of the opening vocal melody is neatly concealed within the figuration of the introduction and the postlude, which leads seamlessly back to successive stanzas. The double quaver upbeat with which the voice enters gives real thrust to the melody and dominates the first section, after which it is ousted by the crotchet–quaver pattern suggested irresistibly by 'Herz, mein Herz'.

Der Liebende is a true love song, in which Beethoven achieves the effect of a spontaneous outpouring of emotion. It is a grateful song for both pianist and singer, but it is essential to observe the composer's carefully placed dynamic markings to give the song its full impact.

DER MANN VOM WORT The man of his word
Friedrich August Kleinschmid c.May 1816
G major Op. 99 Peters 34 Henle 64 GA XXIII/225

Gemäß dem verschiedenen Ausdruck in den Versen piano und forte

Du sagtest, Freund, an diesen Ort	You said, my friend: I shall return
Komm' ich zurück, das war dein Wort.	To this spot; that was your word.
Du kamest nicht; ist das ein Mann,	You did not come. Is this a man
Auf dessen Wort man trauen kann?	Whose word one can trust?
Fast grösser bild' ich mir nichts ein,	I can hardly imagine a greater thing
Als seines Wortes Mann zu sein;	Than to be a man of one's word.
Wer Worte, gleich den Weibern, bricht,	Someone who breaks his word, like women,
Verdient des Mannes Namen nicht.	Does not deserve to be called a man.

Ein Wort, ein Mann, war deutscher Klang,	'A man's word' was a German watchword
Der von dem Mund zum Herzen drang,	Which went straight from mouth to heart,
Und das der Schlag von deutscher Hand	And which a German handshake
Gleich heil'gen Eiden fest verband.	Bound as with sacred oaths.
Und dieses Wort, das er dir gab,	And nothing could break this word he gave you:
Brach nicht die Furcht am nahen Grab,	Not fear of imminent death,
Nicht Weibergunst noch Menschenzwang,	Not women's favours nor human compulsion,
Nicht Gold, nicht Gut, noch Fürstenrang.	Not gold, not goods, nor princely rank.
Wenn so dein deutscher Ahne sprach,	If your German ancestors spoke thus,
Dann folg als Sohn dem Vater nach,	Then follow your father, like a true son,
Der seinen Eid: Ein Wort, ein Mann,	Who, as a man of his word,
Als Mann von Wort verbürgen kann.	can guarantee his oath: 'A man's word'.
Nun sind wir auch der Deutschen wert,	Now we too are worthy of the Germans,
Des Volkes, das die Welt verehrt.	The people whom the world reveres.
Hier, meine Hand; wir schlagen ein	Here, take my hand. We firmly shake hands,
Und wollen deutsche Männer sein.	And desire to be real German men.

Friedrich August Kleinschmid was born in Westphalia, but went to Vienna in 1776 at the age of 27 to study law. He rose swiftly through the ranks of the police force, becoming director of the Vienna prison in 1810 and finally a councillor (*Regierungsrat*) by 1812. Although he occasionally contributed to literary journals, this poem was apparently never published, and Beethoven must have received it in manuscript form. If Kleinschmid gave it to the composer in the hope that he would compose it, he chose the right man. Although the poem seems impossibly dated now, particularly in its incidental deprecation of the entire female sex and its jingoistic promotion of the German race above all others, the essential notion of keeping one's word as a serious matter of honour was extremely close to Beethoven's heart, as his letters frequently confirm.

In May 1818, Beethoven writes to Count Lichnowsky (EA901 / BB1257), echoing the first stanza of the present poem, complaining that he had waited in all morning, but his noble friend had not turned up as promised. In a letter of March 1799 (EA31 / BB41) the composer stresses that he does not vacillate, but sticks steadfastly to what he says: 'sondern fest bey dem beharre, was ich sage'. In April 1809 he is determined to disabuse Breitkopf when he feels the publisher has been misinformed, since for the truth to be known is important for his honour: '*da es für meine Ehre wichtig ist*' (EA209 / BB375). In January 1813 Beethoven writes to Archduke Rudolph in self-pitying vein (EA402 / BB615) to lament the tendency for people not to honour their word: 'um so mehr, da in der jezigen Zeit weder Wort, weder Ehre, weder Schrift jemanden scheint binden zu müssen' (the more so as nowadays nobody seems to consider themselves bound by either word or honour or written agreement). Finally, in a letter written in English in December 1815

(EA574 / BB867), Beethoven reassures Charles Neate that, while he is happy to agree a written contract with the Philharmonic Society, 'I would not have them think that I could ever act otherwise than as *a man of honour*.'

Sketches in the Scheide sketchbook (Princeton, NJ) date the song's conception to the early summer of 1816, immediately after the song cycle *An die ferne Geliebte*. In the late summer of 1816, Beethoven sent a song to the publisher Sigmund Anton Steiner as a small gift, which is assumed to be *Der Mann vom Wort* (EA674 / BB964), requesting its immediate publication. This flatly contradicts Schindler's improbable assertion that Beethoven was reluctant to publish the song, a story presumably intended to stress the personal significance of the text. The song was duly published by Steiner in Vienna in November 1816. The title was rendered as 'Der Mann von Wort', although in the autograph in Bonn (BH: Bodmer, Mh.35) Beethoven has written 'Der Mann *vom* Wort', underlining 'vom' three times. 'Vom', which incorporates the definite article (= von dem) seems intended to stress the absolute and inviolable essence of a man's word.

The song is of very modest proportions, strictly strophic, tonally unadventurous and with a vocal melody which only three times goes beyond the first five notes of the G major scale. The brief chordal introduction, heard only once, and the repeated postlude, with angular rhythmic figures and a final fanfare, lend military overtones, reflecting the references to patriotism and manly virtues. The singer's simple, purely syllabic declamation allows the words to speak for themselves. A similar declamatory style, within a similarly restricted compass of notes, characterises many of Beethoven's vocal works, including the choral setting of *An die Freude* in the Ninth Symphony. Indeed, the melodic germs of Beethoven's works are frequently modest, although in instrumental works they often become the subject of ambitious thematic development, freed from the tyranny of the word.

A point of particular interest concerns Beethoven's performance direction: 'Soft and loud according to the varying expression of the verses'. Beethoven, who clearly regarded the liberal sprinkling of dynamic markings as an essential stage of preparing works for publication, has here found the confidence to leave decisions to the common sense and intelligence of the performer. Although this is forced upon him to some extent by the strict strophic design, this handing over of major performance decisions to the performer is a big step for Beethoven. Only the singer is allowed this privilege; the four-bar piano postlude contains as many dynamic indications!

DER WACHTELSCHLAG The song of the quail
Samuel Ferdinand Sauter   1803
F major WoO129 Peters 43 Henle 27 GA XXIII/234

Larghetto

Ach, wie schallt's dor-ten so lieb-lich her vor! Fürch-te Gott! Fürch-te Gott!

Ach, wie schallt's dorten so lieblich hervor!	Oh, how delightful is yonder sound!
Fürchte Gott!	Fear the Lord!
Fürchte Gott!	Fear the Lord!
Ruft mir die Wachtel ins Ohr.	The quail calls out to me.
Sitzend im Grünen, von Halmen umhüllt,	Sitting in the field, protected by long grass,
Mahnt sie den Horcher im Schattengefild:	She admonishes me as I listen in the shade:
Liebe Gott!	Love the Lord!
Liebe Gott!	Love the Lord!
Er ist so gütig, so mild.	He is so kind and so gentle.
Wieder bedeutet ihr hüpfender Schlag:	Then again her dotted song means:
Lobe Gott!	Praise the Lord!
Lobe Gott!	Praise the Lord!
Der dich zu lohnen vermag.	Who is well able to reward you.
Siehst du die herrlichen Früchte im Feld,	When you see the splendid crops in the field,
Nimm es zu Herzen, Bewohner der Welt!	Think on this, dweller upon the earth:
Danke Gott!	Thank the Lord!
Danke Gott!	Thank the Lord!
Der dich ernährt und erhält!	Who feeds and preserves you.
Schreckt dich im Wetter der Herr der Natur:	If the Lord of Nature frightens you in the storm:
Bitte Gott!	Ask the Lord!
Bitte Gott!	Ask the Lord!
Ruft sie, er schonet die Flur.	She calls, he will spare the land.
Machen Gefahren der Krieger dir bang,	If warriors' dangers make you anxious:
Traue Gott!	Trust the Lord!
Traue Gott!	Trust the Lord!
Sieh, er verziehet nicht lang.	Behold, he will not leave you for long.

Samuel Sauter's real claim to fame is that some of his more naive verses were reprinted in the Munich *Fliegende Blätter*, a humorous weekly publication, as examples of unintentional humour, where he was named as Gottlieb Biedermeier. This ironical characterisation of his poetry as stolidly moral and provincial thus provided the label for the later period of taste and style known as 'Biedermeier'.

Sauter was by no means the first or only poet to notice the poetic potential of the quail's rhythmically distinctive call. Throughout the eighteenth century, anonymous poets celebrated the bird's piety, by interpreting its call as a command to love, trust and obey the Lord. One version was included in the collection of folk-songs known as *Des Knaben Wunderhorn*, beginning 'Hört, wie die Wachtel im Grünen schön schlägt, / Lobet Gott, lobet Gott!' (Hear how beautifully the quail sings in the fields / Praise the Lord!). Other examples share the same poetic metre, and it seems likely that Sauter simply refined pre-existing folksong versions. His version, first published in the almanach *Taschenbuch für häusliche und gesellschaftliche Freunde* (Pocketbook for domestic and sociable friends) in Heilbronn in 1799, has achieved immortality thanks to Beethoven's and Schubert's settings, but even now editors cannot agree on the text. For example, Henle has 'Ach, wie schallt's . . .' and '. . . im Schattengefild', while Peters has 'Horch, wie schallt's . . .' and '. . . am Saatengefild'. Through tracing common divergences from the original text, it is possible to demonstrate that Schubert almost certainly used Beethoven's song as the source for the text of his song (D742, published 1822), although there is no evidence of musical borrowing.

The Beethoven House in Bonn possesses a tiny texted sketch for the 'Fürchte Gott!' motif (Mh71), as well as a full autograph manuscript (Bodmer, Mh32), which are both dated to 1803. Numerous deletions and alterations in the autograph suggest that Beethoven was still in the process of composition rather than proof-reading prior to publication. *Der Wachtelschlag* was published early in 1804 by the Kunst und Industrie Comptoir in Vienna. Beethoven had offered the work to Breitkopf und Härtel in September 1803, pointing out that it was entirely through-composed (EA81 / BB158), but clearly did not give them long to make up their minds before offering it elsewhere. It was not unusual for him to have a work on offer to several publishers at once.

The song is indeed 'ganz durch komponiert' and amounts to a small cantata. The symbolic song of the quail is introduced at once and heard seven times in the short prelude; thereafter it appears numerous times and is subject to rhythmic vari-ation (see below) just like a purely instrumental motif. Although the song opens and closes in the pastoral key of F major, Beethoven explores other tonal realms as the poem evolves and becomes more reflective. There is plenty of meaningful word-colouring through music. On a light-hearted note, jumping triplets evoke the dotted (literally: 'hopping') metre of the bird's song; but such a concrete represen-tation is shallow beside the massive repeated chords at 'Danke Gott!', where a tonal analogue established in the Gellert songs the previous year and extending to *Abendlied unterm gestirnten Himmel* represents the glory of God in all creation.

The use of recitative at 'Schreckt dich im Wetter' and again at 'Machen Gefahren' is a calculated risk, as the flow of the music is interrupted, but the change of direction is in both cases justified by the words. The vigorously pumping *Allegro* interlude which precedes the mention of the warriors (bar 51) is closely related to the fiery last movement of the Piano Sonata op. 31/3 (*Presto con fuoco*), composed in 1802, the previous year. The final section (from bar 58) is marked *Allegretto*, but was originally designated as *Allegro* in the composer's autograph. There is every reason to consider Beethoven's first intention here, as the music may threaten to lose momentum, notwithstanding the evocation of rumbling thunder in the depths of the keyboard (bars 67–75) and the syncopation which oddly sug-gests the dangers of war (bars 76–9). In this final section, the stylisation of the quail's song, here assimilated to 6/8 time, can cause the music to wind down rather too early.

The quail has offered first the poet and then the composer a superb opportu-nity to exploit tonal analogue. The first stage is to attribute words and hence ideas to the rhythm of birdsong. The second stage is to create an inseparable bond in the ear and mind of the listener between the rhythmic motif and the idea of praising God. A third stage is to reuse the motif in a purely instrumental work and thereby impose extra-musical meaning on the work. This is exactly what occurs in the slow movement of the 'Pastoral' Symphony. The process is lucidly discussed by Barry Cooper (*Beethoven and the Creative Process*, p. 56), who explains the unexpected inclusion of the quail's song in the orchestral work: 'By incorporating the quail in the symphony Beethoven is recalling the words associated with its call and making this part of the symphony represent nature's song of praise and thanks to God, just as the last movement is mankind's.'

DER ZUFRIEDENE The contented man
Christian Ludwig Reissig   1809

A major Op. 75/6 Peters 22 Henle 45 GA XXIII/219

Froh und heiter, etwas lebhaft

Zwar schuf das Glück hienieden	Fortune, to be sure, never created me
Mich weder reich noch gross,	Either rich or great in this life,
Allein ich bin zufrieden	But I am still content
Wie mit dem schönsten Los.	As if I had the happiest of lots.

So ganz nach meinem Herzen A friend has been granted me
Ward mir ein Freund vergönnt, Exactly after my own heart,
Denn Küssen, Trinken, Scherzen For kissing, drinking and joking
Ist auch sein Element.   Is just his cup of tea too.

Mit ihm wird froh und weise With him I have, cheerfully and wisely,
Manch Fläschchen ausgeleert; Emptied many a bottle;
Denn auf der Lebensreise   For on our journey through life
Ist Wein das beste Pferd.   Wine is the best mount.

Wenn mir bei diesem Lose   If my present lot should ever
Nun auch ein trübres fällt,   Become even gloomier,
So denk' ich: keine Rose   Then I shall think to myself: no rose
Blüht dornlos in der Welt.   In this world blooms without thorns.

Reissig's poem appeared in the first edition of his collection *Blümchen der Einsamkeit* (Flowers of solitude) in 1809. The poet, who had been seriously injured while fighting against Napoleon, here manages to sound completely at ease with his lot in life, although the final lines point our that life is never completely happy, no rose without thorns. Similar sentiments are recorded by Beethoven in his diary (see Solomon, 'Beethoven's Tagebuch'), where he copies out phrases from Herder's *Müh' und Belohnung* (Effort and reward), stating (T56) that you cannot taste honey without being stung, nor obtain pearls from the ocean if you are afraid of a few crocodiles! This was part of Beethoven's determined attempts to come to terms with a sometimes unhappy lot, but also underlines his firm belief in hard work and sacrifice as the path to ultimate achievement.

The first extant sketch for the song is in Moscow (Central State Archive) with extensive corrections and revision by the composer. An autograph in Berlin (DSB: Artaria 173), which also contains Reissig's *Der Liebende* and *An den fernen Geliebten*, is a fair copy, dated to autumn 1809. The song was first published in July 1810 by Artaria in Vienna in a collection of settings of Reissig poems by various composers, which also included *Der Jüngling in der Fremde* and *An den fernen Geliebten*, and appeared again in October 1810 as the final song of the op. 75 collection, published by Breitkopf und Härtel in Leipzig.

The English version of the song was published in London by Clementi as 'The Contented Man. A Favorite Arietta' at the end of October 1810 – the nearest Clementi and Breitkopf ever came to achieving exact synchronisation of publication. Beethoven had instructed Breitkopf not to publish the songs (and other contemporary works) before 1 September (EA245 / BB423) and had clearly given similar advice to Clementi, as the English editions of the first five songs of op. 75 had been faithfully registered by him at Stationers Hall on 31 August. Breitkopf's delay in publishing the songs had no adverse effects on his sales, as the English editions would have been slow to reach the European mainland during the Napoleonic era and so could not provide material for a possible pirated edition.

Op. 75 comprises six songs of very different moods (see *An den fernen Geliebten* for a discussion of interpretative issues), but ends on a note of light relief, with this optimistic text. The perkiness of the setting is due largely to the dancing semiquaver triplets of the accompaniment, which are given a further lilt by a liberal sprinkling of grace notes, and the staccato markings of the quaver chords, which enliven an apt but predictable vocal line. Beethoven encourages observance of his instruction 'cheerful and bright, fairly lively' by carefully chosen dynamics, keeping the voice *piano* throughout, but allowing the piano some expressive contrasts.

The choice of A major for this song is wholly in accord with Christian Friedrich Daniel Schubart's description of the key in his *Ideen zur Ästhetik der Tonkunst* (Theories on the aesthetics of music), where the characteristics of this key are said to include 'Zufriedenheit über seinen Zustand' (contentment with one's situation). Although this important treatise was written around 1784, it was first published posthumously only in 1806, just three years before the composition of the present song, and Beethoven is known to have owned and studied Schubart's book. A major is also the key of the opening song of the op. 75 collection, *Kennst du das Land*, where its use seems more arbitrary, despite other characteristics listed by Schubart being more in evidence: 'declarations of innocent love', 'hope of seeing each other again when parted from a lover'.

Franz Schubert, then eighteen years of age, composed settings of both *Kennst du das Land* and *Der Zufriedene* on the same day, 23 October 1815. Both of Schubert's settings share Beethoven's key (A major) and are transparently influenced by the structure of the earlier songs. Schubert even employs semiquaver triplets in his setting of *Der Zufriedene* (D320). Schubert's song is little known, as it was not included in the Peters edition, but provides strong evidence that the younger composer was consciously learning from Beethoven's example at this stage of his career.

DES KRIEGERS ABSCHIED   The warrior's farewell

Christian Ludwig Reissig   Late 1814

E flat major WoO143 Peters 49 Henle 57 GA XXIII/240

Entschlossen

Ich zieh' ins Feld von Lieb' entbrannt,   I go off to war, aflame with love,
  Doch scheid' ich ohne Tränen;   Yet I depart without shedding a tear.
Mein Arm gehört dem Vaterland,   My arm belongs to my country,
  Mein Herz der holden Schönen.   My heart to my lovely beauty.
Denn zärtlich muss der wahre Held   For a true hero must always burn
  Stets für ein Liebchen brennen,   With tender love for a sweetheart,
Und doch fürs Vaterland im Feld   And yet be able to die resolutely
  Entschlossen sterben können!   For his country on the battlefield!

Ich kämpfte nie, ein Ordensband   I never fought in order to gain
  Zum Preise zu erlangen;   Honours or medals as my prize;
O Liebe, nur von deiner Hand   O love, I would wish to receive
  Wünscht' ich ihn zu empfangen.   Honours from your hand alone.
Lass eines deutschen Mädchens Hand   Let the hand of a German maiden
  Mein Siegerleben krönen!   Crown my life as victor!
Mein Arm gehört dem Vaterland,   My arm belongs to my country,
  Mein Herz der holden Schönen!   My heart to my lovely beauty!

Denk' ich im Kampfe liebewarm   When during the battle, aglow with love,
  Daheim an meine Holde,   I think of home and my sweetheart,
Dann möcht' ich sehn, wer diesem Arm   Then I would like to see the man
  Sich widersetzen wollte;   Who could withstand my onslaught;
Denn welch ein Lohn! wird Liebchens Hand   For what a reward, when my beloved's hand
  Mein Siegerleben krönen!   Will crown my life as victor!
Mein Arm gehört dem Vaterland,   My arm belongs to my country,
  Mein Herz der holden Schönen!   My heart to my lovely beauty!

Leb wohl, mein Liebchen, Ehr' und Pflicht   Fare well, my love. Honour and duty
  Ruft jetzt die deutschen Krieger;   Now summon German warriors;
Leb wohl, leb wohl und weine nicht!   Fare well, fare well and shed no tears!
  Ich kehre heim als Sieger;   I shall return as victor;

Und fall' ich durch des Gegners Hand,	And should I fall by the hand of the enemy,
Dann soll mein Ruf noch tönen:	My cry will yet resound:
Mein Arm gehört dem Vaterland,	My arm belongs to my country,
Mein Herz der holden Schönen!	My heart to my lovely beauty!

A sketchbook in Krakow (BJ: Mendelssohn 6) includes several melody sketches for this song and can be dated to late 1814. As the poem did not appear until 1815, in the third edition of Reissig's collection *Blümchen der Einsamkeit*, it is clear that Beethoven received it direct from the poet. Reissig was evidently planning further publications of his poetry in musical settings by various composers, akin to the 'Achtzehn deutsche Gedichte' of July 1810, where five of Beethoven's earlier settings had been published. *Des Kriegers Abschied* was duly published in June 1815 by Mechetti in Vienna as the fourth of 'Six German Songs' to Reissig poems; Beethoven found himself in the company of Gyrowetz, Gelinek, Hummel and Moscheles.

The composer had fallen out badly with Reissig over what he considered to be the unauthorised publication of his settings in the earlier collection (see notes on *Gesang aus der Ferne*). It is, therefore, surprising that he should have set two further Reissig poems at this later date. Although he clearly took unusual care over *Sehnsucht* (WoO 146), Beethoven appears to give the present poem short shrift. It is the poorest of the Reissig poems set by Beethoven, with its hackneyed theme of the soldier who gives his strength to the fatherland and his heart to his girl, and the unfortunate self-contradiction in the final stanza: 'I shall return victorious, and if I die . . .'. Beethoven borrows a word from the first stanza for his performance direction: 'entschlossen' (resolute), and overall the soldier's patriotism is emphasised at the expense of the lover's professions. Fanfares lend a martial backdrop, but the piece does not convince. Musically, it is the neat two-bar introduction, heard again at the end, which is most satisfying.

It is difficult to see this song experiencing a revival. Subject matter as dated as this needs great music and individual characterisation to survive the centuries – something rather like Schubert's glorious setting of Rellstab's *Kriegers Ahnung* (D957/2), in fact.

DIE DREI REITER The three riders
Traditional

Early 1816
F major SV364 sketch

etc.

Es ritten drei Reiter zum Tore hinaus,	Three riders rode out of the town gates,
ade!	farewell!
Feinsliebchen schaute zum Fenster hinaus,	My darling looked out from her window,
ade!	farewell!
Und wenn es denn soll geschieden sein,	And if we must indeed be parted,
So reich mir dein goldenes Ringelein!	Then give me your little gold ring.

Ade, ade, ade!	Farewell, farewell, farewell!
Scheiden und Meiden tut weh!	Parting and living apart is so painful!

This tiny sketch is found in the Scheide sketchbook (Princeton, NJ) amid sketches for some major songs, including the song cycle *An die ferne Geliebte*. It is not an original composition, but a familiar folksong, an early version of which dates back to the sixteenth century. Gustav Nottebohm, who published Beethoven's sketch in his *Zweite Beethoveniana*, p. 340, suggests that the composer copied it from Reichardt's *Kunstmagazin*, although the slight deviation from the traditional words (first stanza quoted above) may indicate that the composer wrote it out from memory.

More interesting is the question why this folksong occurred to the composer at just this time. The text, with its theme of involuntary separation ('Scheiden und Meiden') has a superficial connection with *An die ferne Geliebte*, but it seems more likely that Beethoven was reminded of the song during his work on the group of 'Folksongs of various nationalities' (WoO158), which was starting to occupy him at this time. Perhaps he saw possibilities for musical expansion in the modest folk melody, although these were not realised.

DIE FRÜHEN GRÄBER The early graves
Klopstock

1815
SV327 sketch

Wil kom - en o sil - ber ner Mond

Willkommen, o silberner Mond,	Welcome, o silver moon,
Schöner, stiller Gefährt der Nacht!	Fair, silent companion of the night!
Du entfliehst? Eile nicht, bleib,	You flee? Haste not, stay, friend of my
Gedankenfreund!	thoughts!
Sehet, er bleibt, das Gewölk wallte nur hin.	Behold, she stays, the clouds merely passed over.
Des Mayes Erwachen ist nur	Only May's awakening
Schöner noch, wie die Sommernacht,	Is more beautiful than the summer's night,
Wenn ihm Thau, hell wie Licht, aus der Locke träuft,	When dew, fair as light, drips from his locks,
Und zu dem Hügel herauf röthlich er kommt.	And he ascends to the hills with reddish glow.
Ihr Edleren, ach es bewächst	You nobler ones, already, alas,
Eure Maale schon ernstes Moos!	Sombre moss covers your headstones!
O wie war glücklich ich, als ich noch mit euch	O how happy I was, when with you I could still
Sahe sich röthen der Tag, schimmern die Nacht!	Behold the rosy dawn and shimmering nightfall!

Klopstock's poem, one of his 'Oden auf die toten Freunde' (Odes to my dead friends), was written in 1764 and first published in 1771. Gluck's setting of the poem was composed in 1773 and printed the following year in the *Göttinger Musenalmanach auf das Jahr 1775*. Other settings include those of Reichardt (1779) and Neefe (1785). Schubert set the text in 1815, making his composition closely contemporary with Beethoven's sketch. Clearly Beethoven cannot have known Schubert's setting, published posthumously in 1837, but his familiarity with Gluck's setting is suggested by the opening phrase of his sketch.

The sketch is found on a double-sided sketchleaf in The Hague (Nederlands Musiek Instituut). The sketches are fully discussed by Jos van der Zanden in his article 'A Beethoven sketchleaf in The Hague' (*Bonner Beethoven Studien* 3, 2003 pp. 155–67). Van der Zanden identifies on this sheet sketches for the Finale of the Cello Sonata op. 102/2, which suggests a date of early 1815. He speaks of a '24-bar sketch' for Klopstock's *Die frühen Gräber*', but of the isolated melody fragments, written curiously on the second of four staves, only the first two bars are texted (see example above). The sketch is further evidence of Beethoven's desire to set a Klopstock ode to music, and of the extreme difficulty this entailed. Like *Edone* and *Das Rosenband*, this was to remain the merest fragment. It does at least provide a pretext for printing an influential poem, which was thoroughly familiar to Beethoven and which provided a model for numerous graveside elegies.

DIE LAUTE KLAGE The loud lament
Johann Gottfried Herder   c.1814–15
C minor WoO135 Peters 64 Henle 89 GA XXIII/254

Andante sostenuto

Turteltaube, du klagest so laut und raubest dem Armen	Turtledove, you lament so loudly and rob the poor wretch
Seinen einzigen Trost, süssen vergessenden Schlaf:	Of his only solace, the sweet sleep of forgetfulness:
Turteltaub', ich jammre wie du und berge den Jammer	Turtledove, I sorrow like you and conceal my sorrow
Ins verwundete Herz, in die verschlossene Brust.	Within my wounded heart, within my stifled breast.
Ach, die hart-verteilende Liebe! Sie gab dir die laute	Ah, love, which apportions so cruelly, gave to you that
Jammerklage zum Trost, mir den verstummenden Sinn!	Loud sorrowful lament for solace, and to me silence!

Beethoven found the text to this song in Herder's 1792 collection *Zerstreute Blätter* (Scattered leaves), subtitled 'Blumen, aus morgenländischen Dichtern gesammelt' (Flowers gathered from Eastern poets), from which he had also taken the text for *Der Gesang der Nachtigall* (see that entry for details of Herder's significance to Beethoven). The anonymous Arabian poet, upon whose work this poem is based, compares the turtledove's loud lament, which (insult to injury) has kept him awake all night, with his own inability to express his sorrow in verse. Herder would appreciate this contrast between the creature of nature, who ingenuously and instinctively pours forth his lament, and the creature of civilisation, whose natural instincts have been stifled by social convention and a reliance on reasoned thought. The poet's inhibition is expressed as concealment ('berge'), imprisonment ('verschlossene Brust') and ultimately sterility, as he is condemned to silence.

Beethoven rarely changed the words of his texts – unless one considers in this category his unorthodox orthography! It is, then, all the more striking that he changes the final word of the present poem, 'den verstummenden Gram' (silencing sorrow) becoming 'verstummenden Sinn' (silencing sense). It is unfortunate that the old complete edition (GA), which formed the basis for most subsequent editions, retained Herder's 'Gram'. As 'Sinne' refers to the five senses, this has been taken as a reference to Beethoven's deafness. Boettcher (*Beethoven als Liederkomponist*, pp. 51–2) states this almost as a fact. Although the composer's deafness never, of course, rendered him silent, his deafness increased his sense of isolation and the feeling that he must now bear his troubles alone. There is abundant internal evidence for an autobiographical subtext in the setting, in the full repetition of the final two lines, and the subsequent coda-like repetition of 'mir, mir den verstummenden Sinn'. Beethoven will also have sympathised with the description of 'love which apportions so cruelly', having been so often attracted to women such as Therese Malfatti, Antonie Brentano and Josephine Deym, who were, for one reason or another, unobtainable.

A first version of the song (DSB: Grasnick 6) has been reprinted in the Henle edition (No. 107). Its chief interest lies in the lack of the short 'coda', indicating that this important evidence for a personal subtext (see above) was a deliberate afterthought. The autograph of the final version is in Vienna (GdM: A12). This copy was used by Diabelli, who first published the song in April 1837, together with *Seufzer eines Ungeliebten*. Diabelli added a very short prelude, suggesting a bird's chirping, which, although thoroughly spurious, found its way into the first complete edition and thence into the Peters edition; the Henle edition finally consigns it to oblivion. It is interesting to note that Beethoven's first autograph in Berlin has space left for a possible prelude, although the second autograph shows that Beethoven has decided against this. Any prelude of Beethoven's would have been more in keeping with the mournful tone of the composition and would probably have anticipated the opening melody.

Die laute Klage is the only completed song of Beethoven's written in C minor (the fragment *Que le temps me dure*, a conventionalised lament, is the only other song in that key). Coincidentally, *Seufzer eines Ungeliebten* opens in C minor with the lover's sighing protestations, but the oppressive mood quickly brightens into E flat major, and the song is resolved in a brilliant C major. C minor was a favourite key in instrumental works, although these often resolved, like *Seufzer eines Ungeliebten*, into the relative major (E flat major) or into C major. One thinks of the Fifth Symphony, or the Piano Sonata op. 81a ('Les Adieux'), where a slow movement which matches *Die laute Klage* in mood is placed between two outer movements in E flat major. *Die laute Klage* remains firmly in C minor throughout, and this certainly emphasises the tone of oppression and lament. Barry Cooper points out (*Beethoven*, pp. 83f.) that the eighteenth century had defined C minor as a 'pathetic key', and that it became a 'personal emblem' for Beethoven. Thus, Cooper associates Beethoven's 'intense suffering' with the choice of C minor for the Piano Sonata, op. 13 ('Pathétique'). The use of C minor for the present song certainly supports the view that it contains a poignant auto-biographical subtext. Schubart, in his *Ideen zur Ästhetik der Tonkunst* (see *Der Zufriedene*) includes 'lament of unhappy love' in his decription of the key (see also the Introduction).

Throughout the song, Beethoven pays close attention to expressing nuances of the text through subtle inflections of the vocal line. The first phrase rises to a high, confident appoggiatura on 'laut' (loudly) for the uninhibited lament of the bird, which is set in stark relief by the falling chromatic phrase on 'Armen' (poor wretch) in the very next bar, as the poet considers his own unfortunate lot. The music moves to the relative major at the thought of sleep, but the relaxation is as momentary as sleep is presently elusive. 'Jammer' (sorrow), which occurs three times in the poem, is set melismatically, extending the duration of pain. When the word occurs as 'Jammerklage' (sorrowful lament), in bars 15 and 22, the harmonic dislocation reflects the poet's emotional turmoil. The silencing effect of sorrow is represented by a stuttering effect, where the key word ('verstummenden') is actu-ally split by rests into three isolated parts. This stuttering technique also allows Beethoven to stress 'mir' as an isolated syllable, underlining the deeply personal implications of the text. At bar 26, when the voice should come to quiet repose in C minor (as it did, in fact, in the earlier version), Beethoven interpolates 'mir', unex-pectedly and loudly, in F minor, and again on a German sixth chord, and only then permits the music to respond, *pianissimo*, to the irresistible pull of the home key. The case for interpreting this song as one of Beethoven's most directly personal utterances seems proven.

Whereas, in *Der Gesang der Nachtigall*, the hexameters throughout help-fully defined the shape of the melody, here Herder's alternation of hexameters and pentameters, the latter divided by prominent caesuras, are given no prece-dence. The caesura is ignored in the first two couplets and is allowed musical form only in the final couplet, when it suits the composer's interpretative requirements to add emphasis to 'mir'. Despite the use of rests as a *sospirando* rhetorical device in the latter part of the song, the song as a whole is designed to promote forward movement, with piano interludes designed to dovetail into the next vocal phrase. Just as the poet has created a fine poem while complaining of being struck dumb, so Beethoven has managed to combine the expression of over-whelming sadness with a sophisticated perfection of form in this still neglected masterpiece.

DIE LIEBE (LIED) Love
Gotthold Ephraim Lessing   c.1790

F major Op. 52/6 Peters 14 Henle 9 GA XXIII/218

Allegretto

Oh - ne__ Lie - be le - be,__ wer da__kann. Wenn er auch ein__ Mensch schon blie - be,

Ohne Liebe	Let him who can
Lebe, wer da kann.	Live without love.
Wenn er auch ein Mensch schon bliebe,	Even though he remain human,
Bleibt er doch kein Mann.	He is still no man.
Süsse Liebe,	Sweet love,
Mach mein Leben süss!	Make my life sweet!
Stille nie die regen Triebe	Never quench my passionate desires.
Sonder Hindernis.	Give them free rein.
Schmachten lassen	It is the duty of fair women
Sie der Schönen Pflicht!	To make us languish!
Nur uns ewig schmachten lassen,	But let it not be
Dieses sei sie nicht.	To make us languish for ever.

Lessing's little verses first appeared in a supplement to the *Vossische Zeitung* in Berlin in 1751, and were reprinted in the poet's collected works in 1771. This was Beethoven's source for the text. A texted sketch of the song in the Julius Wegeler Foundation collection in Koblenz (SV329) differs only slightly from the published version, and this has been dated on handwriting evidence to around 1790. *Die Liebe* was first published in June 1805 by the Kunst und Industrie Comptoir in Vienna, as the sixth song of op. 52. The poet is named, but no title is given.

In the first edition of the song, the third line of the second stanza was mis-printed as 'Stille *ein* die regen Triebe' (Put an end to my passionate desires), and this version found its way unchecked into the complete edition and thence into the Peters edition (titled *Lied*). The poem is about a self-indulgent surrender to the feel-ings which love engenders, and Lessing's actual words (see above), reinstated in the Henle edition, make better sense. The poet does not wish his desires ever to be sat-isfied; it is the pulsing emotion itself which is celebrated.

Like the poem itself, the music is slight and without any ambition beyond entertaining a sympathetic domestic audience for little over one minute. It is rather in the manner of a Classical sonatina movement by a minor contemporary of Mozart. Perhaps Lessing's text, which is of a previous generation, the poet having been born a full forty years before Beethoven, led the composer to look backwards rather than forwards as he wrote. Suffice it to say that an 'innocent ear' would not guess that Beethoven was the composer.

DIE SCHWESTERN DES SCHICKSALS The sisters of fate
Johann Gottfried Herder   1790–91

D major Bia 50 / SV185 sketch

Die Schwestern das Schickals   herder

Allegro andante maestoso

Nenne nicht das Schicksal grausam,	Do not call Fate cruel,
Nenne seinen Schluss nicht Neid:	Do not call its judgement envy:
Sein Gesetz ist ewge Wahrheit,	Its law is eternal truth,
Seine Güte Götterklarheit,	Its goodness divine clarity,
Seine Macht Nothwendigkeit.	Its power necessity.
Blick umher, o Freund, und siehe	Glance around, my friend, and observe
Sorgsam wie der Weise sieht.	As attentively as the sage observes.
Was vergehen muss, vergehet:	What must perish, perishes:
Was bestehen kann, bestehet:	What can exist, exists:
Was geschehen will, geschieht.	What needs to happen, happens.
Heiter sind die Schicksals Schwestern,	The sisters of fate are cheerful,
Keine blasse Furien:	No pale furies:
Durch der Sanftverschlungnen Hände	Through their gently entwined hands
Webt ein Faden sonder Ende	A thread without end weaves itself
Sich zum Schmuck der Grazien	For the adornment of the Graces.
(Folgen 3 Strophen)	(3 further stanzas)

Herder's poem was first published in part three of his *Zerstreute Blätter* (Scattered leaves) in 1787. Its six stanzas seek to rehabilitate the sisters of fate, presenting them not as monsters who cut short young lives out of sheer spite but as kindly ladies whose constantly woven thread preserves all life in a gentle equilibrium.

Beethoven's two brief sketches, on paper used in Bonn, date from 1790–91 (London, BL: Add.Ms. 29801, f. 100r) and suggest that the young composer is already seeking to balance Herder's positive view of the fates with the negative stance he himself was to adopt. The first setting displays a brisk tempo, but its chromaticism carries ominous undertones; the second, originally marked *allegro*, opts finally for the solemnity of a philosophical pronouncement. Between the two sketches (above), the composer has written 'nach jedem von den nachfolgenden Versen wird der erste widerholt' (After each of the subsequent stanzas, the first is to be repeated), a procedure which hardly seems necessary, as Herder's final stanza is already an exact repetition of his first stanza. It is possible, as 'Vers' can also mean a line of poetry, that Beethoven intended to use the first sketch (actually two lines) as a kind of chorus after each stanza: the true stanza would then begin with the second sketch. This was, after all, a period when Beethoven wrote a number of songs with chorus. The fact that the bass line is in unison octaves for the first two bars of the first sketch strengthens this possibility. The sketches are transcribed by Kerman in his *Autograph Miscellany*.

Beethoven's Bonn teacher Christian Gottlob Neefe was to set the poem to music in his 1798 collection 'Bilder und Träume von Herder', borrowing the subtitle 'Bilder und Träume' (images and dreams) given by Herder to a group of his poems. His neat, unpretentious setting is reproduced by Friedländer in *Das deutsche Lied im 18. Jahrhundert* (music example No. 175).

DIE TROMMEL GERÜHRET Strike the drum
Johann Wolfgang von Goethe   1809
F minor Op. 84/1 Peters 66 Henle IX/7 GA II/12

Die Trommel gerühret!	Strike the drum!
Das Pfeifchen gespielt!	Sound the fife!
Mein Liebster gewaffnet	My beloved fully armed
Dem Haufen befiehlt,	Commands the troops,
Die Lanze hoch führet,	Bears his lance aloft,
Die Leute regieret.	Rules over the people.
Wie klopft mir das Herze! (B: Herz)	How my heart beats!
Wie wallt mir das Blut!	How my blood seethes!
O hätt' ich ein Wämslein	O, if only I had a little doublet
Und Hosen und Hut!	And breeches and hat!
Ich folgt' ihm zum Tor 'naus	I would follow him out of the city gate
Mit mutigem Schritt,	With doughty gait,
Ging' durch die Provinzen,	Would travel through the provinces,
Ging' überall mit.	Would travel everywhere with him.
Die Feinde schon weichen,	The enemies start to fall back,
Wir schiessen hinterdrein! (B: da drein)	We shoot after them as they retreat!
Welch Glück sondergleichen,	What joy beyond compare
Ein Mannsbild zu sein!	To be a man!

Details of Beethoven's incidental music to Goethe's play *Egmont* are given at the entry for *Freudvoll und leidvoll*, the second of Klärchen's songs. As no authentic piano version of *Die Trommel gerühret* (Klärchen's first song) exists, it falls strictly outside the scope of this book, but it would be pedantic to exclude a fine song which is a familiar feature of the Peters edition and other volumes, such as Pauer's edition for Augener, which offer an identical selection. It must be borne in mind, however, that the piano reduction, however effective in its recreation of drums (oscillating bass octaves) and fife, was not made by the composer.

The song is performed by Klärchen, a girl who is passionately in love with Prince Egmont and with the ideas of heroism and freedom which he embodies, in the final scene of the first act. There is a deliberate contrast between the feminine, domestic task she performs (winding knitting wool) and the impassioned song of masculine, military conquest which she chooses to sing to accompany the task (Gretchen at her spinning wheel offers, of course, a similar instance of simple domesticity allied to raw passion in *Faust*). Klärchen introduces her song as 'ein Soldatenliedchen, mein Leibstück' (a soldier's ditty, my favourite song), although the song is specifically linked to Klärchen and Egmont: it is the city gate of Brussels which she wishes to leave by and the provinces of the Low Countries which she wishes to traverse with her lover and hero. Later in the scene, Klärchen clearly echoes the words of the song: 'If only I were a lad and could accompany him all the time, to court and everywhere! I could follow him into battle carrying his banner!' Her feisty attempts to rouse a cowed populace to rebellion, in order to reclaim their freedom and save the imprisoned Egmont, at the opening of the final act, shows her warlike spirit in action. Her subsequent suicide witnesses her inability to accept the loss not just of her hero but of her ideals, and her refusal to live under a regime which suppresses freedom of every kind.

The music opens in F minor, the key which Christian Schubart, whose *Ideen zu einer Aesthetik der Tonkunst* was familiar to Beethoven, associated with melancholy, funereal lament and 'longing for the grave'. One is entitled to wonder whether the choice of key is a deliberate prefigurement of the play's tragic outcome; in act I, there has, after all, already been discussion of the terrible realities of war as a counterbalance to the celebration of heroism. A drum roll introduces the first line, and a piccolo figure in the treble introduces the second line, and the two figures are combined to excellent effect throughout the song. The drum roll continues throughout the first stanza. The voice is initially simply doubled by the pianist's right hand, until the mention of beating heart and boiling blood calls forth a dissonant motif, which interrupts the remainder of the stanza. The character of the music changes completely with a move to F major for the ensuing interlude, and the new key, with its tone of optimistic heroism, is maintained throughout the second stanza. A postlude in F minor introduces a full repeat, and this is augmented by a coda-like extension after the second hearing.

If the song has a weakness, it is that it is too grand for the context of the play – try singing it while you are winding wool! E. T. A. Hoffmann, in his 1813 review of the *Egmont* music, pointed to the song's unsuitability in the context of the play, pointing out that in an operatic environment it would make an excellent effect, but that in a play a song really must be a song (*Lied*) such as one might sing in real life. He felt that the orchestral accompaniment destroyed the intended effect of the whole, constituting a foreign element wholly outside the action of the play, and that only an accompaniment such as could be performed by the actual characters on stage would be truly appropriate. This clearly implies that Hoffmann favours piano or plucked string accompaniment.

DIE ZUFRIEDENHEIT Contentment
Johann Martin Miller

1816

D major Bia 632 / SV364 sketch

Was frag ich viel nach Geld und Gut, wenn ich zu- frie - den bin! Giebt Gott mir nur ge - sun - des Blut, so

hab ich fro - hen Sinn und sing aus dank-ba - ren Ge-müt mein Mor-gen- und_ mein A-bend-lied.

Was frag ich viel nach Geld und Gut,	Why hanker after property and wealth,
Wenn ich zufrieden bin!	When I am content?
Gibt Gott mir nur gesundes Blut,	So long as God grants me good health,
So hab ich frohen Sinn,	I shall remain cheerful
Und sing aus dankbarem Gemüt	And sing with a thankful spirit
Mein Morgen– und mein Abendlied.	My hymns both morning and evening.
So mancher schwimmt im Überfluss,	Many a man swims in abundance,
Hat Haus und Hof und Geld;	Has house and estate and wealth,
Und ist doch immer voll Verdruss,	And yet is always thoroughly discontent
Und freut sich nicht der Welt.	And takes no pleasure in the world.
Je mehr er hat, je mehr er will;	The more he has, the more he wants;
Nie schweigen seine Klagen still.	His laments are never silent.
Da heisst die Welt ein Jammertal,	Then the world becomes a vale of tears,
Und deucht mir doch so schön;	And yet it seems to me so beautiful;
Hat Freuden ohne Mass und Zahl,	It has joys beyond number and measure,
Lässt keinen leer ausgehn.	Lets nobody leave empty-handed.
Das Käferlein, das Vögelein	The tiny beetle, the little bird,
Darf sich ja auch des Maien freun.	Can also rejoice in Maytime.
Und uns zuliebe schmücken ja	For our benefit meadow, mountain and wood
Sich Wiese, Berg und Wald;	Deck themselves out in their finery;
Und Vögel singen fern und nah,	And birds sing far and near
Dass alles widerhallt. -	So that everything re-echoes the sound;
Bei Arbeit singt die Lerch uns zu,	The lark sings to us as we work,
Die Nachtigall bei süsser Ruh.	The nightingale as we enjoy sweet repose.

Und wenn die goldne Sonn aufgeht,	And when the golden sun rises,
Und golden wird die Welt,	And the world becomes golden,
Und alles in der Blüte steht,	And everything is in blossom
Und Ähren trägt das Feld:	And the fields stand rich with corn:
Dann denk ich, alle diese Pracht	Then I reflect, all this glory
Hat Gott zu meiner Lust gemacht.	God has created for my delight.
Dann preis ich Gott und lob ich Gott,	Then I praise and extol God
Und schweb in hohem Mut;	And my spirit soars boldly,
Und denk, es ist ein lieber Gott,	And I think, He is a kind God
Und meints mit Menschen gut;	And wants the best for people;
Drum will ich immer dankbar sein,	Therefore I shall be ever thankful
Und mich der Güte Gottes freun!	And rejoice in God's loving-kindness.

Miller's poem was first published in the *Ulmisches Intelligenzblatt* on 28 March 1776 and subsequently reprinted in Voss's *Musen-Almanach* for 1777 with a setting by Beethoven's Bonn teacher Christian Gottlob Neefe. Neefe has found a rounded melody in common time, which conveys both the poet's contentment with his lot and his piety; indeed, the homophonic setting of the final line suggests the very act of hymn-singing. Neefe's fine setting achieves the 'Schein des Kunstlosen, des Bekannten' (the appearance of artlessness, of familiarity) which Schulz was to define as the secret of capturing the 'Volkston' in 1785.

Beethoven, like Mozart, opts for 6/8 metre. His setting consists of a complete melody of twelve bars, which a practised musician could harmonise at sight. The melody sketch is in the Scheide sketchbook (Princeton, NJ, p. 58). Had Beethoven prepared the sketch for publication, it seems likely that the structure of his song would have borne a still closer resemblance to that of Mozart's setting (K349), with a brief introduction, and the *fermata* (pause) on the final word replaced by a written-out extension of the phrase, leading to a neater finish on a new final bar.

Like his teacher, Beethoven opts for a simple, rounded melody, redolent of contentment. The simplicity of both Beethoven's and Neefe's settings reflects the consciously naive tone of Miller's text, its folksong tone enhanced by his habitual elision of verb endings (frag(e), hab(e), ausgeh(e)n, etc.) and the lack of sophistication in its grammatical structure (eight lines begin 'Und' in the final two stanzas). Gustav Nottebohm, who published the melody sketch in his *Zweite Beethoveniana* (p. 331), suggests that the song may have been composed for Beethoven's young nephew Karl, who was then nine years old. This would perhaps explain why Beethoven turned to a relatively slight text at a time when he was sketching his great song cycle *An die ferne Geliebte* and even considering a setting of Goethe's quasi-philosophical *Gesang der Geister über den Wassern*. Beethoven would have considered Miller's innocent poem, with its themes of contentment, piety and the beauty of the natural world, ideal material for the calming edification of his nephew's young mind.

DIMMI, BEN MIO, CHE M'AMI Tell me you love me
Unknown   1809

A major Op. 82/1 Peters 23 Henle 46 GA XXIII/220

Dimmi, ben mio, che m'ami,	Tell me, darling, that you love me,
Dimmi che mia tu sei,	Tell me you are mine,
E non invidio ai Dei	And I shall not envy the gods
La lor divinità.	Their divinity.
Con un tuo sguardo solo,	With a single glance,
Cara, con un sorriso	Sweetheart, with one smile
Tu m'apri il paradiso	You open for me the paradise
Di mia felicità.	Of my contentment.

These verses are known only from Beethoven's setting. The exaggerated rhetoric, with references to the gods and a metaphorical paradise on earth, is wholly in line with the conceits which characterise such Italian romantic verse. For the first edition, Härtel commissioned a German translation from Christian Schreiber, who was a personal friend of the publisher, a regular contributor to his *Allgemeine musikalische Zeitung* and an occasional composer of songs. The translation, under the title 'Hoffnung' (Hope), shows little consideration for either literal meaning or correctness of stress. It is added below the Italian text in GA and Peters (and hence other dependent editions), but finally jettisoned by Hess and Henle. The English publisher Clementi considered it unnecessary to include an English translation, clearly expecting purchasers to cope with Italian as they could not with German.

The first sketch which relates to this song is written on the back of *Der Zufriedene*, op. 75/6. This single sheet in Moscow (Central State Archive) has been dated to the autumn of 1809. A heavily corrected autograph in Paris (BN: Ms. 38) represents the first version of the song (Hess 140). There is no other autograph source material for the final version as published. Max Unger, in his article 'Zu Beethovens italienischer Gesangmusik' in *Zeitschrift für Musik* 1938 (pp. 153f.), suggests however that some of the revisions in the earlier autograph were made after publication. It is well known that Beethoven was seldom entirely happy with his first thoughts and continued to chisel away at published works.

The five songs of op. 82, to which this belongs, were published separately in England a full six months before they appeared in a continental edition. The aim was to synchronise publication, but while Clementi in London kept to schedule, issuing the song as 'Dimmi ben mio, an Italian Arietta' in early February 1811,

Gottfried Härtel (of Breitkopf und Härtel) wished to negotiate a lower price for the songs, with the excuse that they had been offered also to Clementi. This delayed publication of the German edition until July 1811, when they appeared as 'Vier Arietten und ein Duett' in Leipzig.

Max Unger (see above) suggests that these Italian songs may have been composed for Therese Malfatti, a young lady of Italian ancestry to whom Beethoven was deeply attracted. There is evidence that the composer contemplated marriage to Therese in 1810, although, when he made his intentions plain, he suddenly became *persona non grata* with the family. It is certainly tempting to attach an autobiographical subtext to the poem. The composer's love for Therese filled him with joyful hope, and the news that he had offended the Malfattis in some way plunged him into despair. In a letter to Baron Ignaz von Gleichenstein, who had communicated the news to the composer, Beethoven writes: 'Deine Nachricht stürzte mich aus den Regionen des höchsten Entzückens wieder tief hinab' (Your news plunged me from the sphere of highest delight down again to the depths). In this letter (EA254 / BB445) the composer complains bitterly that he is, after all, no more than a mere 'Musikus' to the family.

The arietta lacks the expected introduction, but starts in an otherwise conventional manner, the piano providing a bland accompaniment to the vocal line, which is decorated with turns and frequent instances of melisma (the setting of syllables to more than one note). Interestingly, Beethoven writes out the turn in the first bar, but not at the reprise of the introductory melody (at bar 25), indicating that such embellishments were to be taken as read by singers trained predominantly on Italian models. Starting in A major and modulating conventionally to the dominant, E major, Beethoven then surprises his listeners with a turn to C major (bar 12) for the 'paradise of . . . contentment' (a letter of 6 May 1811 (EA306 / BB496) corrects a left-hand chord at the end of bar 12, carelessly misprinted in the German edition). The reprise is prefaced by falling phrases on 'dimmi' (tell me), where the voice echoes the piano, and by a three-bar written-out cadenza with voice and piano in unison. There is variation in the reprise, but no more C major interludes – the surprise would not work a second time.

The first version (Hess 140) is longer by two bars, with more ambitious excursions in the reprise, the voice rising to top A. It was first published by Willy Hess in 1962 (Supp V/14). Henle also includes it (No. 84). For those enthusiasts whose appetite for Italianate Beethoven song is still not sated, Hess also prints a so-called 'Endfassung' (final version), taking Beethoven's manuscript revisions into account, in so far as they are legible! This version varies only slightly from the familiar version; indeed, the most notable difference is the omission of most tempo and expression indications, which Beethoven tended to add as a final stage, immediately prior to publication.

Beethoven's occasional studies with Antonio Salieri, during which he composed a significant number of unaccompanied part songs to Metastasian texts, clearly bore fruit in the fine songs with pianoforte which make up op. 82 (see also *T'intendo sì, L'amante impaziente* and *Odi l'aura*). Peter Clive (*Beethoven and His World*, p. 303) suggests that Beethoven may have been hoping to show the opus to Salieri in 1809, when he called unsuccessfully and left a note reading 'The pupil

Beethoven was here' (the modest composer was 38). If so, was Beethoven hoping to seek Salieri's constructive criticism, or simply to show off proudly to the maestro these fine settings of Italian texts?

EDONE Edone
Friedrich Gottlieb Klopstock

1809

F major SV59 sketch

Dein	süß - es	Bild	E	-	do - ne	schwebt	stets	vor	mei - nem	Blick

Dein süsses Bild, Edone,	Your lovely image, Edone,
Schwebt stets vor meinem Blick;	Hovers constantly before my gaze;
Allein ihn trüben Zähren,	But it is clouded by tears, to think
Dass du es selbst nicht bist.	That it is not you yourself.
Ich seh' es, wenn der Abend	I see it when the evening twilight
Mir dämmert, wenn der Mond	Falls, when the moon
Mir glänzt, seh' ich's, und weine,	Shines, I see it and weep to think
Dass du es selbst nicht bist.	That it is not you yourself.
(Folgen 2 Strophen)	(2 further stanzas)

Following his tiny and tentative sketch of 1803 for Klopstock's *Das Rosenband* (p. 93), Beethoven turned next to *Edone* in 1809 in an attempt to produce a worthy setting of the poet he so much admired. However, this too remained a sketch, situated forlornly at the very end, page 112, of the so-called Landsberg 5 sketchbook in Berlin (DSB); indeed, Clemens Brenneis omitted this final page from his facsimile edition of the sketchbook in 1993, considering that it was interpolated from another source. The sketch, which sets the first two lines of the poem and the first words of the second stanza, is in pencil and has become difficult to read.

Hans Boettcher (*Beethoven als Liederkomponist*) lists the sketch as being in B flat major, without further comment. The melody acquires musical sense and shape, however, only when it is read as being in F major, that is to say in soprano clef and with the B flattened.

This poem has not been a first favourite among composers, although Schubert valued his own setting of the text (D445), copying it out in a neat hand for his beloved Therese Grob in 1816. More interesting in the context of Beethoven's sketch is the fact that a setting of the text by Zumsteeg had appeared in Bossler's *Blumenlese für Klavierliebhaber* in 1783, the selfsame year in which Beethoven's first song had been printed in the same journal (see *Schilderung eines Mädchens*). If this publication first drew the composer's attention to this poem, it must be admitted that the gestation period was excessive and the progeny disappointing.

EIN SELBSTGESPRÄCH A soliloquy
Johann Wilhelm Ludwig Gleim

c.1793

E major WoO114 Not in Peters Henle 77 GA XXV/275

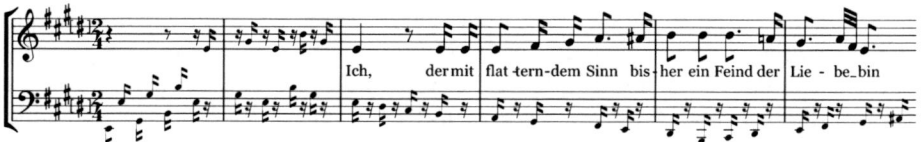

Ich, der mit flatterndem Sinn	I, who with my fickle mind
Bisher ein Feind der Liebe bin	Have hitherto been an enemy of love,
Und es so gern beständig bliebe,	And who would gladly remain so for ever,
Ich! ach! ich glaube, dass ich liebe.	I, ah, I do believe I'm in love!
Der ich sonst Hymen angeschwärzt	I who used to denigrate marriage
Und mit der Liebe nur gescherzt,	And treated love merely as a joke,
Der ich im Wankelmut mich übe,	I, the master of inconstancy,
Ich glaube, dass ich Doris liebe.	I do believe I love Doris.
Denn ach! seitdem ich sie gesehn,	For, ah, since I first saw her,
Ist mir kein' andre Schöne schön.	No other beauty seems beautiful to me.
Ach, die Tyrannin meiner Triebe,	Ah, this tyrant who dictates my desires,
Ich glaube gar, dass ich sie liebe.	I truly believe I love her.

The text of Beethoven's song is from the edition of Gleim's 'Lieder', published in Amsterdam in 1749. Beethoven's only textual change is in the first line, which read: 'Ich, der mit flatterhaftem Sinn'; we presume this to have been an oversight, as Gleim's original 'flatterhaftem', audibly suggesting the casual fickleness of a butterfly flitting from flower to flower, is immeasurably stronger than Beethoven's 'flatterndem' (fluttering), and better suited to the busy rhythm of the song. The poem was frequently reprinted in other collections, in one of which it is aptly entitled 'Der Liebhaber wider seinen Willen' (The reluctant lover). Gleim's title, as above, stresses the dramatic aspect of the poem. The poetic persona is clearly speaking aloud to himself, and the poem cries out to be set as a self-contained *buffo* aria. Friedländer (*Das deutsche Lied im 18. Jahrhundert* II, p. 60) says that 'the long through-composed song offers a kind of dramatic scene' and feels that Beethoven's apprenticeship in the Bonn opera orchestra bears fruit in this song.

Ein Selbstgespräch was possibly conceived in Bonn. There is a sketched fragment in Vienna (GdM: A61), dating from 1792. Although the autograph in Berlin (DSB: Grasnick 28) has been dated to 1793, there are indications (such as two bars which were omitted and inserted later) that this is a fair copy of an earlier manuscript. Another oversight in the copying out is Beethoven's omission of the fourth sharp sign at the start of the song. Although Beethoven included the song in his list of works for sale in 1822 (see Tyson: 'A Beethoven Price List'), it remained unpublished until 1888, when it was included in the Supplementary Volume XXV of the old complete edition. Like the other songs in this supplementary volume, it was not included in the Peters edition, and so has not received the attention it deserves.

The characterisation of the man who has fallen in love despite himself, despite indeed his opposition to the whole idea of love and marriage, is masterful. The use of syncopation for comical agitation is a recognised technique of the *buffo* style, as is the frequent repetition of phrases, which here achieves almost manic proportions, as the singer strives, in broken phrases, to make sense of his unwonted emotions. The *parlando* effect of these broken speech rhythms is again a dramatic technique, as the singer-cum-actor comes to the front of the stage to confide in the audience. As the song was never prepared for publication, all performance directions are lacking, but one can easily imagine an initial 'agitato, ma non troppo allegro', with a quiet opening, but generous use of Beethoven's beloved *sforzandi*, as the poet realises to his horror, and to our amusement, the enormity of his predicament.

EINSAM WALL ICH Lonely I wander
Unknown   1826
SV30 sketch

This sketch in the 'Kullak' desk sketchbook (SPK: Aut.24, f. 50v), which Beethoven used in late 1825 and throughout 1826, is listed by Schmidt (SV) as 'Einsam wall ich im Haus', although Klein can identify only the words 'Einsam wall ich im Haine'. Klein describes the pencilled sketch as 'schwer lesbar' (difficult to read), and the few bars of music are indeed virtually indecipherable. The sketch is mentioned here merely for the sake of completeness.

ELEGIE AUF DEN TOD EINES PUDELS
Elegy on the death of a poodle
Unknown   c.1790
F minor–major WoO110 Not in Peters Henle 29 GA XXV/284

Maestoso

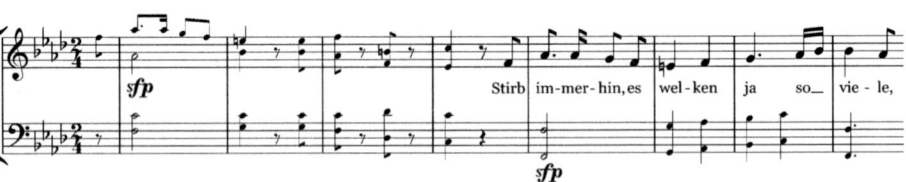

Stirb immerhin, es welken ja so viele	Die you must; so many of our pleasures
Der Freuden auf der Lebensbahn.	Wither away on our path through life.
Oft, eh' sie welken in des Mittags Schwüle,	Often, before they wilt in the heat of the midday sun,
Fängt schon der Tod sie abzumähen an.	Death begins to cull them with his scythe.
Auch meine Freude du! dir fliessen Zähren,	You too, my delight! Tears flow for you,
Wie Freunde selten Freunden weihn;	Such as friends rarely shed for friends;

Der Schmerz um dich kann nicht mein Aug'
  entehren,
Um dich, Geschöpf, geschaffen mich zu freun.

Such grief at your passing cannot shame my
  eyes,
Innocent creature, created to bring me joy.

Allgeber gab dir diese feste Treue,
Dir diesen immer frohen Sinn;
Für Tiere nicht, damit ein Mensch sich freue,
Schuf er dich so, und mein war der Gewinn.

The all-giver gave you this absolute fidelity,
This constantly cheerful disposition;
He created you thus, not for other animals,
But to bring joy to a person, and I it was
  who profited.

Du warst so rein von aller Tück' und Fehle
Als schwarz dein krauses Seidenhaar;
Wie manchen Menschen kannt' ich,
  dessen Seele
So schwarz als deine Aussenseite war.

You were as free from any deceit or failing,
As your curly, glossy coat was black.
How many people have I known whose
  souls
Were as black as your exterior.

Oft, wenn ich des Gewühles satt und müde

Mich gern der eklen Welt entwöhnt,
Hast du, das Aug' voll Munterkeit und
  Friede,
Mit Welt und Menschen wieder mich
  versöhnt.

Often, when I had withdrawn from this
  miserable world,
Tired and fed up with the milling crowds,
You, your eyes sparkling with gaiety and
  peace,
Reconciled me again to the world and its
  people.

Trüb sind die Augenblicke unsers Lebens,
Froh ward mir mancher nur durch dich!
Du lebtest kurz und lebtest nicht
  vergebens;
Das rühmt, ach! selten nur ein Mensch
  von sich.

The moments of our life are gloomy,
Many a one was cheered for me by you alone!
You lived but a short time and did not live
  in vain;
Ah, only seldom can a person make the
  same claim.

Doch soll dein Tod mich nicht zu sehr
  betrüben;
Du warst ja stets des Lachens Freund;
Geliehen ist uns alles, was wir lieben;
Kein Erdenglück bleibt lange unbeweint.

And yet your death must not sadden me
  overmuch;
You were, after all, always fond of laughter;
Everything we love is merely on loan to us;
No earthly joy stays unlamented for long.

Mein Herz soll nicht mit dem Verhängnis
  zanken
Um eine Lust, die es verlor;
Du, lebe fort und gaukle in Gedanken
Mir fröhliche Erinnerungen vor.

My heart must not argue with destiny

Because of a pleasure it has lost;
You, continue to live in my thoughts
And conjure up happy memories for me.

This song remains little known despite having been published in 1888 in Breitkopf
und Härtel's supplementary volume (GA XXV). This is because Peters decided not
to incorporate the songs from volume 25 into their popular edition, rendering the

designation *Sämtliche Lieder* (Complete songs) inappropriate. Henle (1990) rescues the song from oblivion in the new complete edition, indeed promoting the song as a curiosity on the firm's website.

No autograph is known to exist, but two early copies survive, both in Vienna (GdM). The first copy (GdM: Q4251 (VI 3743)) was used as the basis for the modern Henle edition. The keyboard part is designated 'Cembalo' (harpsichord), strengthening the case for an early date of composition. The second copy forms part of the so-called 'Haslinger-Rudophinische' collection, consisting of fine copies of Beethoven's works, commissioned by the publisher Tobias Haslinger between 1817 and 1821, in connection with a projected publication of the composer's complete works. The set of sixty-one volumes was acquired by Beethoven's noble pupil Archduke Rudolph in 1823 and is now in the archives of the Gesellschaft der Musikfreunde in Vienna (GdM: XVII 67000). The elegy occurs just before those published in almanachs and periodicals, inviting the suspicion that it may have been published in a periodical which has not yet been traced. The unknown source for the copies was clearly available in Vienna, which suggests a publication date after 1792, when Beethoven moved to Vienna. The date of composition seems to be earlier, however, and it is quite likely that the song was among the musical material which Beethoven brought with him from Bonn. If Kris Worsley (see below) is correct in hearing the influence of one of Neefe's Klopstock settings of 1776 in the *Elegie*, the argument for an early date of composition is clearly reinforced.

The relationship between humans and pets has ever been a close one. The demise of this man's (or more likely woman's) best friend is lamented in an elegy, probably commissioned from a jobbing poet who no doubt valued his anonymity. That said, there were precedents for such elegies from recognised poets. The Hamburg *Musenalmanach* for 1793, for example, includes a heartfelt elegy for a parrot, written by its editor Johann Heinrich Voss in Classical hexameters 'after Ovid' which begins:

> Wehe! Der Pfittich ist todt, der schönnachahmende Vogel
> Indiens! Häufig zur Gruft folget ihm, Sänger des Hains,
> Folgt, empfindsame Sänger, und schlaget die Brust mit den Flügeln,
> Und mit starrender Klau krazet die Wängelchen wund

> (Alas! The parrot is dead, the Indian bird with its wonderful mimicry! Follow him to his grave in great numbers, sensitive singers, and beat your breasts with your wings, and scratch your cheeks sore with your stiff claws)

Beethoven, who had probably accepted the song's composition as a commission, sets the song strophically, although each verse covers two poetic stanzas. This is a feature of many early songs, such as *Schilderung eines Mädchens* and *Feuerfarb'*. The conventional setting here stays within F minor and its relative major A flat, but its Mozartian fluency and elegance show that Beethoven treats the subject matter with serious respect. The lady's devotion to her lapdog becomes an idealised model for human friendship, held in such esteem at this period. De Curzon (*Les Lieder*, p. 13) comments that Beethoven writes this elegy with the same elevated seriousness which the death of a young girl would merit. A tone of gentle lament is maintained through generous use of melodic appoggiaturas, which occur at the end of each line of the poem. For the final two stanzas, Beethoven turns to the tonic major, as the poet adopts a more optimistic outlook; but neither the jogtrot quaver syncopation which accompanies the first section here nor the semiquaver rippling which dominates the second section serves to lift our spirits overmuch.

With some of the more dated *Lieder* texts, modern listeners must be prepared to accept the outmoded sentiments to enjoy the song, and performers should treat this song as a serious lament rather than a species of parody. Nevertheless, it is best heard as a *Zeitdokument*, a monument to a very specific aspect of social taste and convention towards the end of the eighteenth century. Musically, the song shows Beethoven to be a master of the Classical style and on the threshold of more ambitious developments in the genre.

In a recent dissertation (*Investigating the influence of Christian Gottlob Neefe on the Music of Ludwig van Beethoven*, University of Manchester 2005, pp. 153f.), Kris Worsley points to correspondences between this song and Neefe's ode *An Fanny* of 1776, to a text by Klopstock. The most marked similarity is in Neefe's use of F minor for the first part of the poem with its thoughts of death, with a move to F major for the final two stanzas where the poet's spirits are lifted by thoughts of resurrection and an eternal union of souls. This is one of the very few instances where Neefe's influence of Beethoven's song composition can even be postulated, and is the more important as Beethoven was to use the same major–minor pattern in a much greater song, the Gellert *Busslied*.

It is perhaps worth referring to Haydn's *Der schlaue und dienstfertige Pudel* (The artful and obedient poodle), Hob XXVIa/38c of 1784, a twenty-stanza narrative marathon. Here too the poodle who recovers a lost coin for his master by unexpected artifice is a model of loyalty, but he is very much alive and kicking, and Haydn's brisk but arch setting in B flat major is related to Beethoven's lament only by the breed.

ERHEBT DAS GLAS MIT FROHER HAND (TRINKLIED, BEIM ABSCHIED ZU SINGEN)
Raise your glasses with joyful hand (Drinking song for farewells)
Unknown   1791–92
C major WoO109 Not in Peters Henle 72 GA XXV/282

| Erhebt das Glas mit froher Hand | Raise your glasses with joyful hand |
| Und trinkt euch heitren Mut. | And drink yourselves into good cheer. |

Wenn schon, den Freundschaft euch verband,	Even though fate now parts you from him
Nun das Geschicke trennt,	Who was bound to you by friendship,
So heitert dennoch euren Schmerz	Still let happiness conquer the pain
Und kränket nicht des Freundes Herz.	And do not wound your friend's heart.
Chor: Erheitert, Brüder, euren Schmerz	*All:* Let happiness conquer the pain, brothers,
Und kränket nicht des Freundes Herz.	And do not wound your friend's heart.

Nun trinkt, erhebt den Becher hoch,	Now drink, and raise your goblets high,
Ihr Brüder, hoch und singt	High, my brothers, and sing,
Nach treuer Freunde weisem Brauch	As is the wise custom of faithful friends,
Und singt das frohe Lied.	Sing this merry song.
Uns trennt das Schicksal, doch es bricht	Fate separates us, but cannot destroy
Die Freundschaft treuer Herzen nicht.	The friendship of true hearts.
Chor: Uns trennt das Schicksal, doch es bricht	*All:* Fate separates us, but cannot destroy
Die Freundschaft treuer Herzen nicht.	The friendship of true hearts.

The author of the text is unknown. Paper studies have dated the song, originally considered a product of Beethoven's teenage years, to 1791 or 1792, suggesting that it may have been intended as a song of farewell to Beethoven himself, as he left Bonn to seek fame and fortune in Vienna. The author is likely to have been one of Beethoven's friends, most of whom will, in the manner of the time, have tried their hand at poetry at one time or another. Helga Lühning, in the Critical Report to the Henle edition, suggests that Beethoven may even have written the words himself. The writing of such occasional verse was immensely popular among cliques, for whom friendship was a veritable cult. Here, male bonding has been lavishly reinforced with alcohol. The presence of repeat marks indicate that further stanzas once existed, and we can assume that they were in a very similar vein.

The neat autograph in London (BL: Add.Ms. 29801), part of the Kafka Album, has the appearance of a fair copy. It was not offered for publication, and may have been intended as a keepsake for the original drinking companions. It bears no title, and the accurately descriptive subtitle was added only when the song was first published in the Supplementary Volume XXV of the old complete edition in 1888.

The song is one of a significant group of early songs which include a choral refrain. The jaunty triplets of the introduction and postludes avoid any hint of sorrow at parting, reflecting the positive sentiments of the text. De Curzon (*Les Lieder*, p. 13) finds in the song 'beaucoup d'entrain, de gaîté, de jeunesse et un accompagnement bien amusant en lui-même' (lots of drive, jollity, youth and an accompaniment which is entertaining in itself). The opening of the stanza evokes the simple style of folksong; its rhythm calls to mind the mock-folksong of Mozart's Papageno, 'Ein Mädchen oder Weibchen', which Beethoven was to use as the theme for his variations for cello and piano, op. 66, a few years later.

Having been excluded from the Peters edition, the song is little known, although it still evokes a tradition of which Beethoven was part, and values – friendship, brotherhood, constancy – which he was to uphold throughout his life.

ERLKÖNIG The Erlking
Johann Wolfgang von Goethe

Early 1796

D minor WoO131 Not in Peters Henle102 Not in GA

Wer rei - tet so spät durch nacht__ und Wind es__ ist der Va - ter mit sei - nem sohn

Wer reitet so spät durch Nacht und Wind?	Who rides so late through night and wind?
Es ist der Vater mit seinem Kind;	It is the father with his child;
Er hat den Knaben wohl in dem Arm,	He has the boy firmly in his arms,
Er fasst ihn sicher, er hält ihn warm.	He grasps him safely, he keeps him warm.
Mein Sohn, was birgst du so bang dein	My son, why do you hide your face so
Gesicht? -	fearfully? -
Siehst, Vater, du den Erlkönig nicht?	Can you not see the Erlking, father,
Den Erlenkönig mit Kron und Schweif? -	The Erlking with his crown and tail? -
Mein Sohn, es ist ein Nebelstreif. -	My son, it is just a streak of mist.
'Du liebes Kind, komm, geh mit mir!	'You lovely child, come along with me!
Gar schöne Spiele spiel ich mit dir;	I'll play the most delightful games with you;
Manch bunte Blumen sind an dem Strand,	Many pretty flowers bloom along the shore.
Meine Mutter hat manch gülden Gewand.'	My mother has many golden robes.'
Mein Vater, mein Vater, und hörest du nicht,	My father, my father, can you not hear
Was Erlenkönig mir leise verspricht? -	What the Erlking promises me in his
	whispers?
Sei ruhig, bleibe ruhig, mein Kind;	Be calm, stay calm, my child;
In dürren Blättern säuselt der Wind. -	It is the just wind rustling in the dry leaves. -
'Willst, feiner Knabe, du mit mir gehn?	'Will you not come with me, my fine boy?
Meine Töchter sollen dich warten schön;	My daughters will wait upon you gracefully;
Meine Töchter führen den nächtlichen Reihn,	My daughters lead the nightly dancing,
Und wiegen und tanzen und singen	And will rock you, dance and sing you to
sich ein.'	sleep.'
Mein Vater, mein Vater, und siehst du	My father, my father, can you not see
nicht dort	
Erlkönigs Töchter am düstern Ort? -	The Erlking's daughters over there in the
	gloom? -
Mein Sohn, mein Sohn, ich seh es genau:	My son, my son, I see exactly what you mean:
Es scheinen die alten Weiden so grau. -	It is the grey gleam from those old willows.
'Ich liebe dich, mich reizt deine schöne	'I love you, your beautiful figure arouses
Gestalt;	me;
Und bist du nicht willig, so brauch ich	And if you are unwilling, then I must use
Gewalt.'	force.'

Mein Vater, mein Vater, jetzt fasst er mich an!	My father, my father, now he is seizing me!
Erlkönig hat mir ein Leids getan! -	The Erlking has hurt me!
Dem Vater grausets, er reitet geschwind,	The father is seized with horror, he rides swiftly,
Er hält in Armen das ächzende Kind,	He holds the groaning child in his arms,
Erreicht den Hof mit Müh und Not;	Reaches his home with the greatest difficulty:
In seinen Armen das Kind war tot.	In his arms the child lay dead.

Goethe's poem was first printed in his *Singspiel Die Fischerin* in 1782. The first setting, a bland affair in A major, was by the actress Corona Schröter who took the leading role in the *Singspiel*, and since then it has been set to music innumerable times. Composers are no doubt attracted by the dramatic possibilities inherent in the ballad and by the four sharply differentiated protagonists – narrator, boy, father and Erlking. Beethoven will have been familiar with Reichardt's dramatic setting in G minor (1794) which gallops along in 3/8 time and sets the words of the Erlking on an unsettling monotone, and in later years he will have had the opportunity to study Schubert's celebrated version, which was published in 1821.

Beethoven's sketch is an extended fragment. Although many words and one entire stanza are missing, there are generous clues to Beethoven's intention, with adumbrated accompaniment figures, an interlude notated at a high pitch, and an eight-bar piano postlude, which would serve also as an introduction. It is essentially a shorthand sketch from which Beethoven could quite easily have reconstructed his original intentions, had he returned to the piece. Since Nottebohm first published a transcription of the sketch in 1871 (*Allgemeine musikaliche Zeitung*, Leipzig, reprinted in his *Beethoveniana* 1872), several musicians have tried to second-guess Beethoven. There are completions by Heinrich Zöllner (New York 1898) and Gustave Doret (Paris n.d.). The completion by Reinhold Becker (Leipzig 1897) is of particular interest, as it was adapted and orchestrated by no less a composer than Bela Bartók in the first decade of the twentieth century (see Alexander Ringer: 'The Art of the Third Guess: From Beethoven to Becker to Bartok' in *Musical Quarterly* 52 (1966) for details of this unexpected collaboration). As only the postlude is notated on two staves, it is conceivable that Beethoven was himself considering an orchestral song. This idea is strengthened by the miniature interlude at bars 18–19 at an unusually high pitch, which suggests the flute.

There is disagreement as to the date of the sketch (Vienna, GdM: A67). Nottebohm favoured the first decade of the eighteenth century, and Ringer relates it to Beethoven's preoccupation with Goethe from 1808 to 1810; but Douglas Johnson's paper studies (*Beethoven's Early Sketches*) has revised the date back to 1796, the date already posited by Henri de Curzon in 1905.

A fragmentary sketch in Paris (BN: Ms. 70), probably preceding the familiar sketch by two years, shows that Beethoven was consistent in his choice of key (D minor) and in his 6/8 time signature:

Wer

Notwithstanding attempts at completion, the sketches constitute a musical torso, sad evidence of a grand project which, for whatever reasons, was not seen through.

ES LEBE UNSER TEURER FÜRST Long live our dear prince

Ludwig van Beethoven   April 1822 (or 1823)
E flat major WoO106 Not in Peters Henle 93 GA XXV/274

Es lebe unser teurer Fürst! Er lebe!	Long live our dear prince! Long may he live!
Edel handeln sei sein schönster Beruf!	To act nobly, may that be his fairest occupation!
Dann wird ihm nicht entgehen	Then he will not be denied
Der schönste Lohn.	The fairest of rewards.

This little cantata, the 'Lobkowitz-Kantate', was written for Prince Ferdinand Lobkowitz (1797–1868), son of Beethoven's patron Prince Franz Joseph von Lobkowitz (1772–1816). While visiting the Hofrat Karl Peters, a highly educated man in the service of the Lobkowitz family and Ferdinand's former tutor, Beethoven learned that no celebration was planned for the Prince's forthcoming birthday on 13 April 1823. According to Peters, the composer replied: 'No, that won't do. I'll write a quick cantata for you to perform for him.' The composer had reason to be indebted both to Prince Ferdinand, who continued the payment of his father's annuity until Beethoven's death, and to Karl Peters, who acted as joint guardian to Beethoven's nephew Karl between 1820 and 1825.

Two copies of the lost autograph are preserved in the Lobkowitz Archive in the National Museum in Prague (X.B. f. 1) and both bear the date 'Abends am 12t April 1823', the eve of the Prince's 26th birthday. A lost copy, formerly in the possession of Thayer, is reported to have been dated '1822', corresponding with the eve of the Prince's 25th birthday, and one wonders whether this is the true date, a quarter-century more urgently requiring such celebration. Karl Peters further reported to Thayer that Beethoven himself wrote the words: 'The Cantata consists of a few repeated words of his own; one can hardly talk about poetry' (KH, p. 569). The song was first published in Ludwig Nohl's *Neue Briefe Beethovens* in 1865 (Stuttgart).

The cantata is written for a high-pitched solo voice and a four-part chorus. The direction 'Chor' does not indicate whether only four singers or a full chorus were intended. Both are possible, just as the writing of the upper parts in treble clef would not preclude male voices from these lines. The Gesamtausgabe carelessly states that the Cantata is 'for three voices'. It is possible, as Kinsky suggests (KH, p. 570), that the solo part was taken in the first performance by Karl Peters's wife

Josephine (aptly née 'Hochsinger'!), a fine amateur singer, and that she may also have sung the upper line of the chorus, being joined by three other singers in the twelve bars of choral writing.

The cantata, in ternary form, consists of a short solo aria (*Adagio assai*) framed by two triumphant 'Vivat' sections, where an almost martial air is reinforced by the use of E flat major, the heroic key of the Third Symphony, first performed at the Palais Lobkowitz. The aria is in B flat major, although the key signature is not altered, and the smooth *bel canto* style and florid cadenzas (the second leading back to the home key by way of a decorated dominant seventh) form a meaningful contrast to the outer sections. Indeed, two aspects of the enlightened prince – his nobility by birth, and the nobility of his benevolent actions, the latter truly deserving of respect and reward – are here neatly adumbrated in words and music by the composer. If the cries of 'Long live the Prince!' are rather tritely expressed in alternations of tonic and dominant, the tribute is no less sincerely meant.

FEUERFARB' Colour of flame (final version)
Sophie Mereau   c.1792, revised 1803
G major Op. 52/2 Peters 10 Henle 5 GA XXIII/218

Ich weiss eine Farbe, der bin ich so hold,	I know a colour which is so dear to me,
Die achte ich höher als Silber und Gold;	I value it more highly than silver or gold;
Die trag' ich so gerne um Stirn und Gewand	I love to wear it upon my brow and my clothes
Und habe sie *Farbe der Wahrheit* genannt.	And have christened it the *colour of truth*.
Wohl blühet in lieblicher, sanfter Gestalt	To be sure, the radiant rose blossoms with great
Die glühende Rose, doch bleichet sie bald.	Loveliness and delicacy, and yet it soon fades.
Drum weihte zur Blume der *Liebe* man sie;	That is why it was consecrated the flower of *love*;
Ihr Reiz ist unendlich, doch welket er früh.	Its charm is infinite, but quickly withers.
Die Bläue des Himmels strahlt herrlich und mild;	The blue of the sky radiates gentle splendour;
Drum gab man der *Treue* dies freundliche Bild.	And so this gentle image was granted to *constancy*.
Doch trübet manch Wölkchen den Äther so rein;	And yet many a cloud darkens the pure blue sky;
So schleichen beim Treuen oft Sorgen sich ein.	So cares often steal into the heart of the constant one.

Die Farbe des Schnees, so strahlend und licht,	The colour of snow, so brightly radiant,
Heisst Farbe der *Unschuld*; doch dauert sie nicht.	We call the colour of *innocence*; yet it does not last.
Bald ist es verdunkelt, das blendende Kleid:	Soon the dazzling covering is sullied,
So trübet auch Unschuld Verleumdung und Neid.	Just as lies and jealousy sully innocence.
Und frühlings, von schmeichelnden Lüften entbrannt,	And in the Spring, fanned by amorous breezes,
Trägt Wäldchen und Wiese der *Hoffnung* Gewand.	Meadow and copse wear the mantle of *hope*.
Bald welken die Blätter und sinken hinab;	Soon the leaves wither and fall,
So sinkt oft der Hoffnungen liebste ins Grab.	Just as our dearest hopes sink to their grave.
Nur *Wahrheit* bleibt ewig und wandelt sich nicht:	Only *truth* remains for ever and does not change;
Sie flammt wie der Sonne alleuchtendes Licht.	It blazes like the sun which illuminates everything.
Ihr hab' ich mich ewig zu eigen geweiht.	I have dedicated myself to truth for eternity;
Wohl dem, der ihr blitzendes Auge nicht scheut!	Happy are those who do not fear its blazing eye!
Warum ich, so fragt ihr, der Farbe so hold,	Why, you ask, have I bestowed the hallowed
Den heiligen Namen der *Wahrheit* gezollt? -	Name of *truth* upon this dear colour?
Weil flammender Schimmer von ihr sich ergiesst,	Because a blazing glory radiates from it and
Und ruhige Dauer sie schützend umschliesst.	It is surrounded by a calm permanence.
Ihr schadet der nässende Regenguss nicht,	It is not harmed by downpours,
Noch bleicht sie der Sonne verzehrendes Licht;	Nor bleached by the searing light of the sun;
Drum trag' ich sie so gern sie um Stirn und Gewand	That is why I love to wear it upon my brow and my
Und habe sie *Farbe der Wahrheit* genannt.	Clothes and have christened it the *colour of truth*.

The poem appeared in August 1792 in the *Journal des Luxus und der Moden*. Beethoven found the text here and made his first setting almost immediately, although the song was subject to regular revision before its eventual publication in June 1805, along with the other songs of op. 52, by the Kunst und Industrie Comptoir in Vienna. A fragmentary autograph in London (BL: Add.Ms. 29801) is a neatly written version of the first fifteen bars, with minor corrections to the left-hand part of the accompaniment, which, apart from being untexted, closely resembles the published version. The published version omitted the fifth and sixth stanzas, probably for reasons of space and certainly with little thought as to the meaning of the verses. It was not until 1990 that they were finally reinstated in the Henle complete edition.

Sophie Mereau, also known as Sophie Brentano after her marriage to the Romantic poet Clemens Maria Brentano in 1803, was Beethoven's exact contemporary. She was a regular contributor to monthly journals and to the annual almanacs which were eagerly awaited by the many lovers of literature and music among the educated classes. *Feuerfarb'* was a popular poem with composers; other settings include those by J. C. F. Bach, Zumsteeg and Diabelli. Beethoven's musical verse covers two stanzas, which are set to different, but subtly related music. There is no justification for this process in the text, where each stanza is self-contained. Mereau nails her colours (in this case, one colour only) to the mast in the first stanza, and successive stanzas rule out other chromatic candidates, before the final two stanzas gloriously confirm the rightness of her choice. The verse seems excessively sentimental to modern ears, but in the late eighteenth century wearing one's heart on one's sleeve was tantamount to a fashion accessory, Klopstock having well and truly enabled sentiment.

The song is a product of the eighteenth century and contains a mixture of the thoroughly traditional (which predominates) and the interestingly innovative. It opens with a predictable three-bar prelude and the piano's right hand clings to the vocal melody almost throughout. A short interlude leads directly and neatly into the second stanza, where there is a clear attempt to mirror the words, with a lusher accompaniment for the blossoming of the rose. This is followed by a *calando* marking, requiring the performers to both slow down and become quieter, leading to a pause as the rose fades. The four-bar postlude has a momentary sidestep to the minor mode before the overall tone of bright confidence is restored.

FEUERFARB' Colour of flame (first version)
Sophie Mereau   Autumn 1792

G major   Hess 144   Supp V/2   Henle 76   Not in GA/Peters

See final version (previous entry) for text, translation and details of poetic source.

The first version of *Feuerfarb'* was composed in Bonn in the autumn of 1792, shortly after Beethoven discovered the poem in a journal. An autograph in Vienna (GdM: A11) is a neat copy, with many careful corrections. It is natural for a young creative artist to take great care over early productions, and Beethoven certainly looked after the songs which he wrote during his final years in Bonn, refining and revising them. This, the original version of the song, was first published in 1955 by Willy Hess in *Musik und Unterricht* 46.

This is the song referred to in a letter from Professor Fischenich in a letter to Charlotte von Schiller, wife of the poet, of 26 January 1793. Fischenich, a professor of Law at Bonn university, had known the Schillers well during his time as a student in Jena, and sent a copy (now lost) of *Feuerfarb'* to Frau von Schiller, with a covering letter which sang the praises of the young Beethoven and also promised a setting of the ode *An die Freude*: 'I am enclosing a setting of *Feuerfarbe* and would very much like to hear your opinion of it. It is by a local young man (Beethoven) whose musical talents are universally praised and whom the Prince Elector has now sent to Haydn in Vienna . . . Usually he does not trouble himself with such bagatelles as the enclosed, which he wrote for me at the request of a lady.'

Whether the song or a copy was written for Fischenich remains unknown, as does the identity of the 'lady'. The comment on Beethoven not troubling himself with such a minor form of composition as the solo song has the ring of truth about it, even at this stage of his career, and it is easy to prove that the composer preferred the larger musical forms from his later letters. In December 1822, for example, he writes to Peters (EA1111/1516), employing a weak but untranslatable play on words: 'Wär mein Gehalt nicht gänzlich *ohne Gehalt*, ich schrieb nichts als Opern, Sinfonien, Kirchenmus, höchstens noch Quartetten' (If my income were not entirely *without substance*, I would compose nothing but operas, symphonies, church music, at most some more quartets).

The differences between this setting and the later, published one are found in the accompaniment. During the course of the song, the piano adopts a greater independence from the vocal line, although the figuration is hardly innovative. The principal difference, as with the first version of *Der freie Mann*, lies in the postlude, which here starts with a rushing scale figure in octaves and communicates something of the ingenuous, enthusiastic sentiment of the poem.

FLÜCHTIGKEIT DER ZEIT (VORSATZ)
Fleeting time (Resolution)
Johann Wilhelm Ludwig Gleim   c.1822
                                          D major Bia 762 / SV14 sketch

Den flüch - ti - gen   Ta - gen wehrt kei - ne   Ge - walt

Den flüchtigen Tagen	No force can prevent
Wehrt keine Gewalt;	The rush of fleeting days;
Die Räder am Wagen	The wheels on time's chariot
Entflieh'n nicht so bald.	Do not disappear so easily.
Wie Blitze verfliegen,	Just as lightning disperses,
So sind sie dahin,	So the days are gone.
Ich will mich vergnügen,	I shall enjoy myself
So lang' ich noch bin!	While I am yet alive!

Gleim's poem is subtitled 'Vorsatz zum 20. Geburtstag' (Resolution on his 20th birthday) and is an exhortation not to waste fleeting time, but to enjoy every moment. It was first printed in Gleim's collected poems in Zurich in 1749 and set by C. P. E. Bach in 1753. Hans Boettcher, who is seldom wrong, lists the key of this sketch as G major and the time signature as 2/4, but the opening bars strongly suggest D major, notwithstanding the single-sharp key signature, and 6/8. The compound-time signature would suit this text, as would the breathless syncopations of Beethoven's one completed Gleim setting, *Ein Selbstgespräch*.

In his sketch, Beethoven has changed the last two lines of the second stanza, to read: 'Drum will ich *nutzen*, / So lang ich noch bin' (Therefore I shall use every moment, while I am yet alive). The idea of giving himself over to a life of self-indulgence would have been anathema to the composer, who worked hard throughout his life in the unremitting service of high ideals. 'Nutzen' could also mean to 'be of use' (the modern 'nützen'). Beethoven rarely changed the words of his texts, aside from an inserted 'ja' or simple word repetition, but the rare changes he made clearly aim to personalise the text to his own situation or outlook (see *Die laute Klage*).

The autograph in Berlin (SPK: Artaria 201, p. 124) is very near the end of a sketchbook which Beethoven used throughout 1822 and possibly into 1823. It thus postdates the final completed songs, like several other short song sketches. Songwriting was still in the composer's mind, but frankly he had bigger fish to fry: the sketchbook is dominated by preparatory work on the last piano sonata, the *Missa Solemnis* and the Ninth Symphony. The opening bars of the song were published in Nottebohm's *Zweite Beethoveniana*, p. 474, in 1887.

FREUDVOLL UND LEIDVOLL To be joyful and sorrowful
Johann Wolfgang von Goethe Late 1809/1810

A major Op. 84/4 Peters 67 Henle 94/95 GA II/12

Andante con moto

Andante

Freudvoll	To be joyful
Und leidvoll,	And sorrowful
Gedankenvoll sein,	To be lost in thought,
Langen	To yearn
Und bangen	And be anxious
In schwebender Pein,	In ever-looming torment,
Himmelhoch jauchzend,	Rejoicing to the heavens,
Zum Tode betrübt -	Saddened to death -

Glücklich allein	Happy alone
Ist die Seele, die liebt.	Is the soul which loves.

In 1809, in response to Napoleon's advance on Vienna, the Viennese theatre directors decided to stage two plays about heroes fighting for freedom from foreign occupying forces (see Barry Cooper, *Beethoven*, pp. 195f.). The plays were Schiller's *Wilhelm Tell* and Goethe's *Egmont*. Both required incidental music; Beethoven was allocated *Egmont*, while the Schiller play went to Gyrowetz. Czerny reported that Beethoven would have preferred *Wilhelm Tell*, but there is no doubt that the composer would also have been attracted to Goethe's play with its forceful pleas for physical and intellectual freedom and its condemnation of tyranny. Beethoven's music was first heard at a performance on 15 June 1810 in the Hofburgtheater. In addition to Klärchen's two songs (see also *Die Trommel gerühret*), Beethoven provided the celebrated Overture, four Entr'actes, music for Klärchen's death and a final Victory Symphony. He further provided music to accompany Egmont's spoken address to 'sweet sleep' and his vision of Freedom transfigured in the form of Klärchen, thus creating a melodrama with tableau.

Klärchen sings the present song in act III, scene 2 of Goethe's play, first humming the final two lines and then performing the entire song. Her mother, impatient with her for her devotion to the heroic Egmont, when she should be settling down with the steady Brackenburg (whom she loves only as a substitute for her dead brother), tells Klärchen to stop her 'Heiopopeio'. This term refers to a lullaby, and Klärchen, a fascinating mixture of fragility and feistiness, responds cheekily that she has often used this song to rock a 'big child' to sleep, referring to her affair with Egmont. The poem deliberately contrasts the highs and lows of love, and reflects the extremes of emotion which Klärchen experiences during the play – her proud joy when Egmont, entering shortly after this song is heard, reveals himself magnificently dressed and displaying the order of the Golden Fleece, and the despair which eventually drives her to suicide when she learns of her lover's forthcoming execution.

The song is familiar from its inclusion, with a piano reduction, in the Peters edition, but Beethoven made two authentic piano arrangements himself, both in A major (see above), which are printed in the Henle edition. The autograph to the first and simpler arrangement is in the Floersheim–Koch collection in Basel and was first published by Max Unger in the *Zeitschrift für Musik* in 1935; the autograph to the second version is in the Central State Archive in Moscow and was published in 1962 in the Supplementary Volume V, edited by Willy Hess.

Sketches for the song vacillate between F, G and A majors. Beethoven's earliest sketches for a setting were possibly made before he received the commission for the *Egmont* incidental music in the autumn of 1809, but, once the commission had been received and the singer selected, his ideas were steadily modified according to practical requirements. Henle reproduces (No. 105) a sketch in G major (SPK: Artaria 177/2), bearing the inscription 'one tone lower', and a further version in F major (SPK: Artaria 177/3) reads 'one further tone lower'. We must assume that the final version, restored to A major, was tailored to the voice of the first Klärchen, Antonie Adamsberger, then 18 years of age. Her interesting life included friendship with

Schubert, whose songs she admired, and engagement to the poet-soldier Theodor Körner, curtailed by his early death in the field. Shortly before her death in 1867, Antonie told Thayer of her meeting with Beethoven. She apparently told the composer she could not sing, but he listened to her in an aria by Zingarelli, exclaimed 'Right, now I know' and returned three days later, singing the song to her over and over until she knew it by heart (one of the few reported instances of Beethoven's singing). Then he left, exhorting her to sing it just so, with no embellishments. The simpler first version (above), which has no introduction and is written on two staves only, may have been originally prepared for Antonie to learn from.

The short poem is expanded by Beethoven, in the final version, by means of an introduction, interlude and postlude, and by word repetition which effectively doubles its length. The composer exploits Goethe's dactylic metre (long–short–short) to good effect. The musical devices are perhaps rather predictable. The first three lines of the text are set in the major mode, and the next three in minor mode echo, to reflect changing moods; such sentimental alternation between major and minor was almost *de rigueur* in Vienna at the opening of the nineteenth century (Schubert was to exploit the device with unprecedented subtlety in songs such as *Lachen und Weinen*, D777). To set 'heavens' at a high pitch and 'death' at a low one was also to be expected. But this naive approach to word-setting conveys the essential innocence of Klärchen, just as the manifold repetitions of the final lines reflect her refusal throughout the play to conceal even for a moment the strength of her affection for Egmont.

With orchestral accompaniment, however, the song 'almost degenerates into an aria', as the writer, critic and composer E. T. A. Hoffmann states in his 1813 review of the *Egmont* music (see also *Die Trommel gerühret*, which comes under similar attack). He criticises Beethoven's excessively operatic treatment of the melody ('zu opernmässig behandelt'), preferring the perfectly simple, but deeply felt setting of Reichardt. Hoffmann would no doubt have preferred the simpler melodic sketches, quoted by Nottebohm (*Zweite Beethoveniana*, pp. 270–1) and Biamonti (Bia 491), which probably represent the first stage of the composer's complex preoccupation with this text.

Themes from the song are quoted in the first part of the Entr'acte (Zwischenaktsmusik III) which occurs at the end of the third act.

GEDENKE MEIN! Remember me
unknown (?Beethoven) 1820

E flat major WoO130 Not in Peters Henle 92 GA XXV/281

Gedenke mein!
Ich denke dein!

Remember me!
I shall be thinking of you!

| Ach, der Trennung Schmerzen | Ah, only hope makes bearable |
| Versüsst nur die Hoffnung. | The pain of separation. |

The author of the short text, with its conventional sentiments on parting, is unknown. The autograph is lost, but a faithful copy survives in Bonn (BH: NE 167), which shows close correspondence with a sketch for the accompaniment in Berlin (SPK: Landsberg 10). The Bonn copy is dated 'Mödling, am 11t September 1820' and the inscription translates: 'Prior to the departure of his Imp. Highness, the most serene Archduke Rudolph, an exercise for his Imp. Highness, our well-beloved Archduke Rudolph, from L. v. Beethoven'. The rediscovery of the Bonn copy in the 1980s proves beyond doubt that this song is indeed the work referred to in an inventory of Archduke Rudolph's music collection: 'Aufgabe für S. K. Hoheit den Erhz. Rudolph vor der Abreise. Mödling 11ten Sept. 1820'. Confusion had arisen over the matter, as the publishers Breitkopf und Härtel specifically mentioned a song 'Gedenke mein' among a list of works they were returning to the composer, in a letter of 21 June 1805 (BB226). This cannot have referred to the present song and refers either to a lost song with the identical title or possibly to *Andenken* (which opens 'Ich denke dein'), although such sloppiness in misquoting a song title does not fit with the businesslike tone of the publishers' letter.

The 'exercise' takes the form of a song, upon which His Imperial Highness could compose variations; this has a precedent in 'O Hoffnung' (WoO200), a set of 40 variations by the Archduke, published in 1819. The Archduke was a very important figure in Beethoven's life. The composer instructed his illustrious pupil initially in piano and later in theory and composition. From 1809, the Archduke contributed generously to an annual annuity in order to keep the composer in Vienna. Beethoven expressed his gratitude with a series of dedications, including the 'Archduke' Trio, the *Missa Solemnis* and the last two piano concertos. The Piano Sonata op. 81a ('Les Adieux') was written upon the Archduke's departure from Vienna in the winter of 1809–10, similarly expressing the sorrow of parting and the pain of absence in its first two movements. Although Beethoven's very numerous letters to the Archduke are couched in formal language, reminding us that the gulf between aristocracy and commoners could not ultimately be bridged, there was a genuine warmth in their relationship.

The song was first published by Haslingers in Vienna in April 1844. By this time, Tobias Haslinger had been dead for two years and the firm was continued by his widow and his son Carl. Tobias Haslinger was on good terms with Beethoven and the butt of his coarse humour for many years, particularly during his time as Steiner's assistant.

Gedenke mein! has a biographical significance which outweighs its intrinsic interest. The short song ends in E flat, although the tonality is slow to settle, with a series of chords over a bass moving by close steps in octaves which has an almost Baroque effect. The most remarkable feature of the song is the interpolation of the word 'Ach!' for purely expressive effect, at the opening of the second section and twice in a short coda. This innovation, together with the willingness to experiment with modulation, seems to confirm the now established date of composition.

GELLERT (SECHS LIEDER VON GELLERT)
Six songs by Gellert
Christian Fürchtegott Gellert   Before March 1802
Op. 48/1–6 Peters 3–8 Henle 20–5 GA XXIII/217

Gellert's fifty-four *Geistliche Oden und Lieder* (Spiritual odes and poems) were published in Leipzig in 1757. Gellert stressed in his Preface that they were expected to be sung, as it is melody which gives the text its full power of expression. He even appended some suggestions for existing chorale melodies which would fit specific poems. They were indeed widely set to music. C. P. E. Bach led the way; his settings of the complete anthology were published in 1758, only one year after the publication of the texts. According to Friedländer's listing in *Das deutsche Lied im 18. Jahrhundert*, eighteen sets of musical settings were published between 1758 and 1792. Beethoven's were the last significant settings of Gellert, who was becoming rather old-fashioned by the turn of the century. He probably knew C. P. E. Bach's settings and these may even have furnished his texts, although the poems were available in numerous editions at the time.

Gellert's collection is a compendium of pious texts to be dipped into. Very frequent echoes of scriptural sources give the collection a sense of universality, but also of repetitiveness. It would be no exaggeration to regard the collection as a reworking of the Psalms of David for the eighteenth century, as these are quoted so freely. Later editions of the poems sought to order the poems under five headings: general prayers, church festivals, hymns of praise, moral exhortations, and meditations on illness and death. Beethoven included examples from all groups except church festivals. Two prayers frame his set, with two hymns of praise placed consecutively (4, 5) after a moral admonishment (2) and the *memento mori* meditation on the brevity of life (3).

There are strong reasons for regarding the six Gellert songs as a 'song cycle'. They constitute a themed group of songs to texts by a single poet, taken from a single work of that poet. There are also significant musical links between songs, and devices which are common to several songs, which will be discussed in the notes on individual songs. The thought which went into the ordering of the songs within the set (see next paragraph) also suggests that Beethoven and his publisher anticipated that the songs should always be performed as a set and were concerned to maximise the musical and emotional impact of individual songs within the set.

Beethoven's original ordering of the poems was different, as is clear from a copy of a lost autograph in Vienna (GdM: VI 8819) and two fragmentary autographs in Bonn (BH: Bodmer Mh30/31). Furthermore, in the third edition (Leipzig, end of 1803), the publishers Hoffmeister und Kühnel revised the order of the songs as published in Vienna a few months previously, producing a better degree of tonal and thematic symmetry. This may well have been with Beethoven's approval, as the composer corresponded frequently with Franz Anton Hoffmeister in Leipzig at the time, addressing him as 'friend and brother'. The table shows the ordering of the songs as first published and as in all modern editions; in Beethoven's first conception as indicated by manuscript sources; in Hoffmeister's Leipzig edition; and as they appear in Gellert's *Geistliche Oden und Lieder*.

poem	as published	manuscripts	Hoffmeister	Gellert
Bitten	1	1	1	1
Die Liebe des Nächsten	2	2	3	4
Vom Tode	3	3	4	5
Die Ehre Gottes aus der Natur	4	4	5	2
Gottes Macht und Vorsehung	5	6	2	3
Busslied	6	5	6	6

The six songs were first published by Tranquillo Mollo in Vienna at the beginning of August 1803 and dedicated to Count Johann Georg Browne, one of Beethoven's earliest patrons in Vienna. Two further editions appeared before the end of the year, the edition from Hoffmeister und Kühnel, referred to above, and an edition published by Nikolaus Simrock in Bonn.

It is unclear whether Beethoven intended all stanzas of the first five poems to be sung (the problem does not arise with the sixth song *Busslied*, as it is through-composed). Beethoven texts only the first stanza in the surviving autograph for *Gottes Macht und Vorsehung*, but this is a familiar practice and gives no decisive clue as to his final intention. A full copy in Vienna (GdM: VI 8819), signed by the dedicatee and dated 8 March 1802, includes all the stanzas for all songs, apart from a single stanza which was probably omitted through an oversight, and Simrock's edition similarly includes all stanzas. Simrock's edition was based on Mollo's first edition, which Ferdinand Ries had sent to the Bonn publisher on 6 August 1803, and the inclusion of the full texts may have been authorised or even suggested by Beethoven through Ries.

The poems are printed in full here, as they are in the Henle edition, enabling performers to make their own decisions, but it is improbable that either audience or singer would feel comfortable with all fourteen stanzas of *Die Liebe des Nächsten* or all fifteen of *Gottes Macht und Vorsehung*. Any selection of stanzas must consider the musical balance of the set, as well as the actual sense of the words and how well they fit the melody, as Gellert's occasionally irregular prosody can cause problems in subsequent stanzas. It is interesting that the reviewer of the Leipzig *Allgemeine musikalische Zeitung*, writing in 1804, mentions this problem of fitting the melody to all stanzas, but assumes without question that all stanzas will be performed (see *Kunze, Die Werke im Spiegel*, pp. 45f.).

Performers may also wish to experiment with the ordering of the songs. The opening song *Bitten* seems a suitable bidding prayer to introduce the group, but thereafter Hoffmeister's ordering (see above) deserves serious consideration. By shifting *Gottes Macht und Vorsehung* into second position, he has created a frame within a frame. The first and final songs are fervently personal prayers, while the second and penultimate songs are hymns of praise in the shared key of C major. But Beethoven had his reasons too for placing *Gottes Macht und Vorsehen* after *Busslied*, choosing to finish with a strikingly confident hymn of praise which ends with a bold perfect cadence, rather than an intimate 'song of penitence' which tapers into a subdued expression of assurance on a plagal cadence.

I BITTEN Prayer   E major Op. 48/1 Peters 3 Henle 20

Gott, deine Güte reicht so weit,
So weit die Wolken gehen;
Du krönst uns mit Barmherzigkeit
Und eilst, uns beizustehen.
Herr, meine Burg, mein Fels, mein Hort,
Vernimm mein Flehn, merk auf mein Wort;
Denn ich will vor dir beten!

Ich bitte nicht um Überfluss
Und Schätze dieser Erden.
Lass mir, so viel ich haben muss,
Nach deiner Gnade werden.
Gib mir nur Weisheit und Verstand,
Dich, Gott, und den, den du gesandt,
Und mich selbst zu erkennen.

Ich bitte nicht um Ehr' und Ruhm,
So sehr sie Menschen rühren;
Des guten Namens Eigentum
Lass mich nur nicht verlieren.
Mein wahrer Ruhm sei meine Pflicht,
Der Ruhm vor deinem Angesicht
Und frommer Freunde Liebe.

So bitt' ich dich, Herr Zebaoth,
Auch nicht um langes Leben.
Im Glücke Demut, Mut in Not,
Das wollest du mir geben.
In deiner Hand steht meine Zeit:
Lass du mich nur Barmherzigkeit
Vor dir im Tode finden.

God, your goodness extends so far,
As far as the passing clouds;
You crown us with compassion
And hasten to assist us.
Lord, my fortress, my rock, my refuge,
Hear my pleading, attend to my words;
For I wish to pray before you!

I ask not for abundance
And earthly treaures.
Allow me to receive just what I need
According to your grace.
Give me but wisdom and understanding
To recognise you, O God, and
Him whom you sent, and myself.

I ask not for honour and fame,
However much they mean to people;
Just let me never lose
The possession of a good name.
May my true fame be my duty,
Fame in your eyes
And the love of devout friends.

And so I do not ask you either,
Lord Sabaoth, for a long life.
Be pleased but to give me
Humility in joy, strength in need.
My lifespan is in your hands:
Let me but find compassion
When I stand before you in death.

The opening song of this group sets the general tone in many ways. Gellert's meditational poetry retains overtones of the baroque verse of the previous century, although the poet avoids both the severity of the *memento mori topos* and the recondite utterances of the mystics. His style is akin to personal confession, but intended for all believers to share. It is also coloured by the influence of the Psalms which are quoted freely, here at the end of the first stanza (see Psalm 5, 3).

Beethoven responds with a style which retains aspects of the German chorale and Handelian features, while remaining wholly himself. Handel's influence is evident in the canonic imitation of the keyboard introduction and in the striding bass line. The descending scales which dominate the bass line throughout are a feature common to several songs, as is the use of a repeated melodic note acting as a 'pedal' above changing harmonies (bars 27–32). The constant flow of crotchets in the bass line suddenly stops at bar 35, effectively slowing the tempo and creating a wholly hymn-like tone for the final line, as the poet kneels to pray. Like the last song of the set, this one finishes quietly, but here the plagal cadence is interrupted by a disturbing dissonance in the penultimate chord, anticipating the striking minor second clashes in *Vom Tode*.

Another aspect which this strophic song shares with others is the way the music fits the first stanza very snugly, but feels less comfortable when further stanzas are performed. Beethoven invariably gave greatest consideration to the opening stanza in strophic settings. Occasionally (as in *Das Liedchen von der Ruhe*) a second stanza was printed to accommodate a varying line-length, indicating that Beethoven was well aware of the problem. Here, as elsewhere in the set, it is Gellert's occasionally erratic stresses within an ostensibly regular metre which create problems.

Gellert himself suggested the chorale melody 'Es ist das Heil uns kommen her' as suitable for this poem.

II DIE LIEBE DES NÄCHSTEN Love of one's neighbour

E flat major Op. 48/2 Peters 4 Henle 21

Lebhaft, doch zu sehr

So jemand spricht: Ich liebe Gott!	If anyone announces: I love God!
Und hasst doch seine Brüder,	And yet hates his fellow men,
Der treibt mit Gottes Wahrheit Spott	He makes a mockery of God's truth
Und reisst sie ganz darnieder.	And utterly debases it.
Gott ist die Lieb' und will, dass ich	God is Love and wishes me
Den Nächsten liebe, gleich als mich.	To love my neighbour, even as myself.

Wer dieser Erden Güter hat	Whoever possesses worldly goods
Und sieht den Bruder leiden	And yet watches his brother suffer
Und macht den Hungrigen nicht satt,	And does not satisfy the hungry,
Lässt Nackende nicht kleiden,	Fails to clothe the naked,
Der ist ein Feind der ersten Pflicht	He offends against the first commandment
Und hat die Liebe Gottes nicht.	And does not share God's love.

Wer seines Nächsten Ehre schmäht
Und gern sie schmähen höret,
Sich freut, wenn sich sein Feind vergeht,
Und nichts zum Besten kehret,
Nicht dem Verleumder widerspricht,
Der liebt auch seinen Bruder nicht.

Wer zwar mit Rat, mit Trost und Schutz
Den Nächsten unterstützet,
Doch nur aus Stolz und Eigennutz,
Aus Weichlichkeit ihm nützet,
Nicht aus Gehorsam, nicht aus Pflicht,
Der liebt auch seinen Nächsten nicht.

Wer harret bis, ihn anzuflehn,
Ein Dürft'ger erst erscheinet,
Nicht eilt, dem Frommen beizustehn,
Der im Verborgnen weinet,
Nicht gütig forscht, ob's ihm gebricht,
Der liebt auch seinen Nächsten nicht.

Wer andre, wenn er sie beschirmt,
Mit Härt' und Vorwurf quälet
Und ohne Nachsicht straft und stürmt,
Sobald sein Nächster fehlet;

Wie bleibt bei seinem Ungestüm
Die Liebe Gottes wohl in ihm?

Wer für der Armen Heil und Zucht
Mit Rat und Tat nicht wachet,
Dem Übel nicht zu wehren sucht,
Das oft sie dürftig machet,
Nur sorglos ihnen Gaben gibt,
Der hat sie wenig noch geliebt.

Wahr ist es: du vermagst es nicht,
Stets durch die Tat zu lieben;
Doch bist du nur geneigt, die Pflicht
Getreulich auszuüben,
Und wünschest dir die Kraft dazu
Und sorgst dafür: so liebest du.

Ermattet dieser Trieb in dir,
So such ihn zu beleben.
Sprich oft: Gott ist die Lieb', und mir

Whoever reviles his neighbour's good name
And is pleased to hear it reviled,
Rejoices when his enemy goes astray
And everything goes wrong for him,
Fails to contradict calumny against him,
He does not love his brother either.

Whoever supports his neighbour
With advice, comfort and protection,
And yet acts only from self-seeking pride
And weakness of character,
Not from obedience or a sense of duty,
He does not love his neighbour either.

Whoever waits until a needy man
Comes to beseech his help,
Does not hasten to assist a devout man
Lamenting in secret,
Does not enquire kindly after his needs,
He does not love his neighbour either.

Whoever torments those he protects
With severe reproaches
And rants and raves, making no allowances,
The moment his neighbour makes a
    mistake;
How can God's love reside within him
Amidst all that ranting?

Whoever is not ever alert to advise and act
For the salvation and moral good of the poor,
Does not seek to fight against the evil
Which so often makes them needy,
Simply gives them gifts without a care,
He has loved them but little.

True enough, you cannot always
Demonstrate love through deeds;
But if you are but willing to carry out
Your obligations faithfully
And truly desire the strength to do so
And see that you find it: then you show love.

If this impulse should weaken in you,
Then try to revive it.
Repeat often: God is Love and

Hat er sein Bild gegeben.	Has granted me his own image.
Denk oft: Gott, was ich bin, ist dein;	Think often: God, what I am is yours.
Sollt' ich, gleich dir, nicht gütig sein?	Should I not then be kind like you?

Wir haben einen Gott und Herrn,	We have one God and Lord,
Sind eines Leibes Glieder;	We are members of one body;
Drum diene deinem Nächsten gern,	Therefore serve your neighbour gladly,
Denn wir sind alle Brüder.	For we are all brothers.
Gott schuf die Welt nicht bloss für mich;	God did not create the world for me alone;
Mein Nächster ist sein Kind wie ich.	My neighbour is his child just like me.

Ein Heil ist unser aller Gut.	One salvation belongs to us all.
Ich sollte Brüder hassen,	Should I then hate my fellow men
Die Gott durch seines Sohnes Blut	Whom God has purchased so dear
So hoch erkaufen lassen?	Through the blood of his son?
Dass Gott mich schuf und mich versühnt,	That God created me and removes my sin,
Hab' ich dies mehr als sie verdient?	Have I deserved this more than they?

Du schenkst mir täglich so viel Schuld,	You put me every day so much in your debt,
Du Herr von meinen Tagen!	O Lord of my days!
Ich aber sollte nicht Geduld	Should I not then be tolerant
Mit meinen Brüdern tragen?	Towards my fellow men?
Dem nicht verzeihn, dem du vergibst,	Not forgive him whom you forgive,
Und den nicht lieben, den du liebst?	And not love him whom you love?

Was ich den Frommen hier getan,	Whatever I have done for fellow believers,
Dem Kleinsten auch von diesen,	Even the lowliest among them,
Das sieht er, mein Erlöser, an,	He, my Saviour, regards this
Als hätt' ich's ihm erwiesen.	As though I had done it for him.
Und ich, ich sollt' ein Mensch noch sein	And I, I should continue a man
Und Gott in Brüdern nicht erfreun?	And not please God in my fellow men?

Ein unbarmherziges Gericht	An unmerciful judgement
Wird über den ergehen,	Will befall him
Der nicht barmherzig ist, der nicht	Who is not merciful, who does not
Die rettet, die ihn flehen.	Rescue them who plead to him.
Drum gib mir, Gott, durch deinen Geist	Then give me, God, through your Spirit,
Ein Herz, das dich durch Liebe preist.	A heart which praises you through love.

Gellert suggested the chorale melody 'Machs mit mir, Gott, nach deiner Güt' for this poem. In Beethoven's setting, the music is tailored very closely and aptly to the words and sentiment of the first stanza, with other stanzas left to fend for themselves as a 'best fit'. The process is especially problematic in this song, as Gellert runs the final two lines of his first stanza together ('dass ich / den Nächsten liebe') in a way not mirrored in the remaining thirteen stanzas. While this musical dilemma may discourage singers from performing extra stanzas, the setting of the first stanza is such a finely crafted miniature masterpiece that we are inclined to forgive the composer for his cavalier attitude to the demands of strophic repetition.

The first two bars, with voice and piano in unison, introduce the hypocrite's profession of his love of God; we almost hear the colon before the direct speech. The bubble is pricked at once, with dissonant staccato chords relating a hatred of one's fellow men to the undermining of God's truth. The quiet, legato second section, where homophony yields to true counterpoint, forms a complete contrast and describes the true, loving nature of God and his commandment that we love others as ourselves. It is perhaps not too fanciful to see in the falling broken triad which opens this phrase ('Gott ist die Lieb') a symbolic representation of the Trinity; indeed, E flat major was considered by contemporary theorists to symbolise the Trinity in itself, through its three-flat key signature. The music of this second section is incorporated into the bass line of the polyphonic postlude, rounding off and unifying the composition.

Gellert's emphasis here on true feelings and charity, as opposed to empty ritual, are characteristic of his strict but essentially sentimental approach to religion. The poem, judiciously cropped, survives today in Protestant hymnbooks, but not, of course, in Beethoven's sophisticated *Kunstlied* setting.

III VOM TODE   Death   F sharp minor Op. 48/3 Peters 5 Henle 22

Mäßig und eher langsam als geschwind

Meine Lebenszeit verstreicht,	My lifespan is passing,
Stündlich eil' ich zu dem Grabe;	With each hour I race towards the grave;
Und was ist's, das ich vielleicht,	And what is it that I still
Das ich noch zu leben habe?	Have to achieve in life?
Denk, o Mensch! an deinen Tod;	Think, O man, upon your death;
Säume nicht, denn eins ist not.	Do not delay, for one thing is essential.
Lebe, wie du, wenn du stirbst,	Live as you will wish to have lived
Wünschen wirst, gelebt zu haben.	When you die.
Güter, die du hier erwirbst,	Possessions that you acquire here,
Würden, die dir Menschen gaben:	Honours which men granted you:
Nichts wird dich im Tod erfreun;	Nothing will cheer you in death;
Diese Güter sind nicht dein.	These possessions are not yours.
Nur ein Herz, das Gutes liebt,	Only a heart that loves what is good,
Nur ein ruhiges Gewissen,	Only a quiet conscience
Das vor Gott dir Zeugnis gibt,	That bears witness for you before God
Wird dir deinen Tod versüssen.	Will make death more bearable for you.

Dieses Herz, vor Gott erneut,
Ist des Todes Freudigkeit.

This heart, renewed before God,
Is the joyfulness of death.

Wenn in deiner letzten Not
Freunde hilflos um dich beben,
Dann wird über Welt und Tod
Dich dies reine Herz erheben;
Dann erschreckt dich kein Gericht;
Gott ist deine Zuversicht.

When in your final hour of need
Friends tremble helplessly around you,
Then this pure heart will rise
Above the world and death;
Then no judgement will afright you,
God is your assurance.

Dass du dieses Herz erwirbst,
Fürchte Gott und bet und wache.
Sorge nicht, wie früh du stribst;
Deine Zeit ist Gottes Sache.
Lern nicht nur den Tod nicht scheun,
Lern auch seiner dich erfreun.

So that you might acquire this heart,
Fear God, watch and pray.
Give no thought for how early you die;
You lifespan is God's decision.
Learn not only not to fear death,
Learn also to take pleasure in it.

Überwind ihn durch Vertraun;
Sprich: Ich weiss, an wen ich glaube,
Und ich weiss, ich werd' ihn schaun
Einst in diesem, meinem Leibe.
Er, der rief: Es ist vollbracht!
Nahm dem Tode seine Macht.

Conquer it through trust;
Say: I know in whom I believe,
And I know that I shall behold him
One day in this my body.
He who cried out: It is finished!
Took from death its power.

Tritt im Geist zum Grab oft hin,
Siehe dein Gebein versenken;
Sprich: Herr, dass ich Erde bin,
Lehre du mich selbst bedenken;
Lehre du mich's jeden Tag,
Dass ich weiser werden mag!

Visit the grave often in your mind,
Imagine your bones being lowered;
Say: Lord, teach me myself to consider
That I am but earth;
Teach me this every day,
So that I might grow in wisdom.

This severe baroque meditation on death occupied Beethoven at least from the end of 1798 until mid-1803. In addition to the familiar setting from op. 48, there is an extended sketch in D minor from the end of 1798 in Berlin (DSB: Grasnick 1), discussed below. A few sketches in E minor in Krakow (BJ: Landberg 6) which date from no earlier than June 1803 demonstrate that Beethoven's interest in this poem continued after the completion of op. 48 the previous year. A price list compiled by Beethoven in 1822 (see Alan Tyson: 'A Beethoven Price List of 1822') intriguingly mentions a setting of the same text in G minor, but no such setting survives.

The familiar setting is, uniquely among Beethoven's songs, in F sharp minor. The opening unisons toll in slow triple time, minim followed by crotchet, and this musical metre underlies the entire setting; in the postlude, the passing bell will toll three octaves lower in the furthest depths of the keyboard. The unisons become disturbing minor seconds, and even when the harmony opens out a little, slow appoggiaturas prevent the music from settling until the dominant is reached at bar 17. The piano accompaniment then prefigures the singer's *memento mori* utterance, where the inexorable advent of death is suggested not only by the doubled octaves but by the persistent C sharps in the bass, which are not shaken off for ten bars. The admonition to avoid procrastination ('Säume nicht') is heard three times, the final repetition engineered by a false cadence to D major. The doubled bass D finally emerges from pedalled dissonances as the flattened submediant of the home key. An eight-bar postlude gives time for reflection, diminished sevenths yielding each time to the inevitability of the tonic key, and the tolling F sharp in the depths of the keyboard rising only to descend whence it came. A clearer tonal analogue for death and burial would be difficult to imagine.

The extended sketch in D minor is deservedly reprinted in the Henle edition (No. 103). The introduction and opening of the melody are given here:

The sketch is almost fully harmonised. Following its transcription, published in *Die Musik* IX (1909/10) by A. Ebert, a completion was made by G. Massenkeil and printed in *Studien zur Musikgeschichte des 19. Jahrhunderts* 51 (Regensburg 1978). The bold introduction quoted above survives as melody alone, although Beethoven may well have meant it to stand alone. Also of interest are the chromatically descending minor thirds at 'Stündlich eil' ich zu dem Grabe', suggesting the 'slippery slope' down to the grave. Elsewhere Beethoven's second thoughts are preferable. For example, the third repetition of 'Säume nicht', so effective in the final version, is here just an extra idea added after a full close and consists simply of repeated diminished sevenths in various positions. Nevertheless, a performance of this virtually complete fragment would create a talking point at any *Lieder* recital.

It should be added that Gellert himself looked to the past in recommending the chorale melody 'Jesus, meine Zuversicht' as a suitable one for this poem. In 1757 he could not possibly have envisaged the intensity with which his poems would be revisited forty-five years later.

IV DIE EHRE GOTTES AUS DER NATUR

The glory of God in Nature   C major Op. 48/4 Peters 6 Henle 23

Majestätisch und erhaben

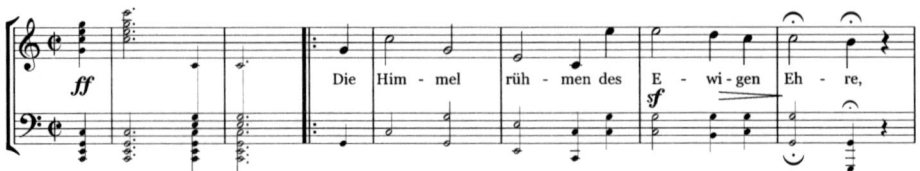

Die Himmel rühmen des Ewigen Ehre,   The heavens proclaim the glory of the
                                                                           Eternal One,

Ihr Schall pflanzt seinen Namen fort.	Their sound propagates his name.
Ihn rühmt der Erdkreis, ihn preisen die Meere;	The round earth and the seas praise him;
Vernimm, o Mensch, ihr göttlich Wort!	Hear, O man, their divine message!

Wer trägt der Himmel unzählbare Sterne?	Who bears up the countless stars of the firmament?
Wer führt die Sonn' aus ihrem Zelt?	Who leads forth the sun from its resting place?
Sie kommt und leuchtet und lacht uns von ferne	It comes and beams and laughs to us from afar
Und läuft den Weg gleich als ein Held.	And runs its course just like a hero.

Vernimm's und siehe die Wunder der Werke,	Hear it and behold the wonders of those works
Die die Natur dir aufgestellt!	Which Nature has assembled for you!
Verkündigt Weisheit und Ordnung und Stärke	Do not wisdom and order and strength
Die nicht den Herrn, den Herrn der Welt?	Proclaim to you the Lord, Lord of the world?

Kannst du der Wesen unzählbare Heere,	Can you observe the innumerable armies of beings,
Den kleinsten Staub fühllos beschaun?	Or the smallest speck, without feeling?
Durch wen ist alles? Oh, gib ihm die Ehre!	Who is responsible for it all? O, give him the glory!
Mir, ruft der Herr, sollst du vertraun.	You shall put your trust in me, cries the Lord.

Mein ist die Kraft, mein ist Himmel und Erde;	Mine is the power, mine is heaven and earth;
An meinen Werken kennst du mich.	You know me through my works.
Ich bin's und werde sein, der ich sein werde:	I am and shall ever be what I shall be:
Dein Gott und Vater ewiglich.	Your God and Father through all eternity.

Ich bin dein Schöpfer, bin Weisheit und Güte,	I am your creator, am wisdom and kindness,
Ein Gott der Ordnung und dein Heil;	A God of order and your salvation;
Ich bin's! Mich liebe von ganzem Gemüte	It is I! Love me with your whole heart
Und nimm an meiner Gnade teil.	And partake of my grace.

Gellert's text begins with a paraphrase of the opening of Psalm 19, familiar from the chorus which ends the first part of Haydn's *Creation*: 'The Heavens are telling the glory of God'. Beethoven's hymn of praise to the Creator whose wonders are seen in all his works is cast brightly and majestically in C major. The descent through F sharp minor to the darkest depths of the keyboard, with which the last song ended, becomes here a controlled C major fall in open octaves, serving as a springboard to launch the high-lying phrase on 'des Ewigen Ehre' which follows. There is scarcely a hint of dissonance in this song. Apart from a twice-heard augmented sixth (bars 9 and 26) and dominant sevenths, all is purely triadic. Beethoven sets two poetic stanzas successively. The first section is essentially homophonic and hymn-like, but the second section opens with throbbing repeated chords, a tonal analogue for the 'countless stars of the firmament'. It is no coincidence that a similar musical figure is used in *Adelaide* ('im Gefilde der Sterne') and in *Abendlied unterm gestirnten Himmel* ('Wenn die Sterne prächtig schimmern'). The association of this repeated chord figure with stars, and in turn with a sense of joyful exaltation at a sudden realisation of the wonder of creation, is inescapable.

The final line, describing the sun blazing across the sky, an exultant hero, is set twice, to massive chords which effectively represent the glory of God in all creation, but this same music is less well suited to subsequent stanzas. This illustrates well the difficulties composers face in a strophic setting. We cannot begrudge Beethoven the grand gesture of eight-note fortissimo chords, as they suit the words of the first verse (second poetic stanza) so well, but subsequent stanzas can too often be left to fend for themselves as a 'best fit', both metrically and sentimentally. Here, the metrical pattern of the music does not cater for the important stress on 'Mir' in the fourth stanza, and the music is too grand altogether for the final line of the sixth stanza where God offers compassion.

Precise performance indications are given throughout the song; as in all of Beethoven's works, their careful observance will give much greater force to the overall performance. The song is marked 'majestic and sublime' ('erhaben' is a term unique to this song), dynamics and accents are indicated, and the use of *fermata* pauses at four points in the verse reminds us irresistibly and appropriately of a Bach chorale.

Despite the demanding vocal tessitura (low C to high G), this great hymn of praise has always been one of Beethoven's most popular songs. Nottebohm, in his thematic catalogue of 1868, listed arrangements for male chorus with orchestra, piano or brass band, and arrangements continue to appear at regular intervals today.

V GOTTES MACHT UND VORSEHUNG

God's power and providence   C major Op. 48/5 Peters 7 Henle 24

Mit Kraft und Feuer

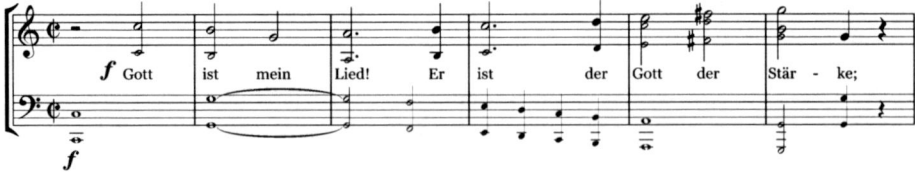

Gott ist mein Lied!
Er ist ein Gott der Stärke;
Hehr ist sein Nam', und gross sind seine
    Werke
Und alle Himmel sein Gebiet.

Er will und spricht's:
So sind und leben Welten.

God is my song!
He is a God of strength;
Exalted is his name and great are his
    works
And all the heavens are his realm.

He wills it and speaks:
And thus worlds come into being.

Und er gebeut: so fallen durch sein Schelten
Die Himmel wieder in ihr Nichts.

Licht ist sein Kleid
Und seine Wahl das Beste;
Er herrscht als Gott, und seines Thrones
   Feste
Ist Wahrheit und Gerechtigkeit.

Unendlich reich,
Ein Meer von Seligkeiten,
Ohn' Anfang Gott und Gott in ewigen
   Zeiten!
Herr aller Welt, wer ist dir gleich?

Was ist und war
In Himmel, Erd' und Meere,
Das kennet Gott, und seiner Werke Heere
Sind ewig vor ihm offenbar.

Er ist um mich,
Schafft, dass ich sicher ruhe;
Er schafft, was ich vor – oder nachmals tue,
Und er erforschet mich und dich.

Er ist dir nah,
Du sitzest oder gehest;
Ob du ans Meer, ob du gen Himmel
   flöhest,
So ist er allenthalben da.

Er kennt mein Flehn
Und allen Rat der Seele.
Er weiss, wie oft ich Gutes tu' und fehle,
Und eilt, mir gnädig beizustehn.

Er wog mir dar,
Was er mir geben wollte,
Schrieb auf sein Buch, wie lang ich leben
   sollte,
Da ich noch unbereitet war.

Nichts, nichts ist mein,
Das Gott nicht angehöre.
Herr, immerdar soll deines Namens Ehre,
Dein Lob in meinem Munde sein!

And he commands: upon his pronouncement
The heavens fall back into the void.

Light is his garment
And his decision the best;
He reigns as God, and his throne's
   support
Is truth and justice.

Infinitely rich,
An ocean of blisses,
God with no beginning and in all
   eternity!
Lord of all things, who is your equal?

What is and was
In sky and earth and sea,
Knows God, and the legions of his works
Stand revealed before Him.

He is around me,
Makes me to rest in safety;
He directs what I have done, or shall do,
He knows the secrets of all our hearts.

He is close to you,
Whether you sit or walk;
If you flee to the sea or upwards to the
   sky,
He is everywhere present.

He knows my pleading
And all the council of my heart.
He knows how often I do good or fall short,
And hastens mercifully to my aid.

He has weighed out my lot,
That which he chose to grant me,
Has written in his book how long I am to
   live,
When I was yet unmade.

Nothing, nothing is mine
Which does not belong to God.
Lord, the glory of your name, your praise
Shall be for ever in my mouth!

Wer kann die Pracht	Who can comprehend
Von deinen Wundern fassen?	The splendour of your wonders?
Ein jeder Staub, den du hast werden lassen,	Each tiny speck which you have called into being
Verkündigt seines Schöpfers Macht.	Proclaims the power of its creator.
Der kleinste Halm	The smallest blade of grass
Ist deiner Weisheit Spiegel.	Is the mirror of your wisdom.
Du, Luft und Meer, ihr, Auen, Tal und Hügel,	You, air and sea, you, meadows, valley and hills,
Ihr seid sein Loblied und sein Psalm!	You are his song of praise and his psalm!
Du tränkst das Land,	You water the land,
Führst uns auf grüne Weiden;	Lead us into green pastures;
Und Nacht und Tag und Korn und Wein und Freuden	And night and day, corn and wine and joys
Empfangen wir aus deiner Hand.	We receive from your hands.
Kein Sperling fällt,	Not even a sparrow falls,
Herr, ohne deinen Willen;	Lord, unless it be your will;
Sollt' ich mein Herz nicht mit dem Troste stillen,	Should I not comfort my heart with the thought
Dass deine Hand mein Leben hält?	That you hold my life in your hands?
Ist Gott mein Schutz,	If God is my shield,
Will Gott mein Retter werden,	If God desires to be my saviour,
So frag' ich nichts nach Himmel und nach Erden	Then I ask not after heaven nor earth
Und biete selbst der Hölle Trutz.	And can defy hell itself.

Nowhere is Beethoven closer to Handel than in this song. Despite its brevity, it exhibits some delightful contrapuntal effects on a miniature scale. This is evident in the opening six bars, where the treble rises through an octave from G to G, while the bass descends from G to G in contrasting note values. The boldness of the postlude, with its imitative rhythmic figures in octaves, also lifts this very short song out of the ordinary. We encounter pure Beethoven, however, in his use of massive chords at the words 'All the heavens are his realm'. The music merits more than one hearing. To sing all fifteen stanzas would perhaps be to gild the lily; to perform the odd-numbered stanzas would work very well in this case. The seventh stanza ('Er ist dir nah . . .') was omitted in Browne's copy of March 1802 (see introductory remarks), almost certainly through an oversight.

VI BUSSLIED Song of repentance

A minor–A major Op. 48/6 Peters 8 Henle 25

Poco adagio

An dir al-lein, an dir hab' ich ge - sün - digt und übel - oft vor dir ge - tan.

An dir, an dir allein hab' ich gesündigt	Against you, you only have I sinned
Und übel oft vor dir getan.	And often done evil in your sight.
Du siehst die Schuld, die mir den Fluch verkündigt;	You see the guilt which proclaims a curse upon me;
Sieh, Gott, auch meinen Jammer an.	God, behold also my misery.
Dir ist mein Flehn, mein Seufzen nicht verborgen,	My pleading, my sighing is not hidden from you,
Und meine Tränen sind vor dir.	And my tears are before you.
Ach Gott, mein Gott, will lange soll ich sorgen?	Oh God, my God, how long must I agonise?
Wie lang entfernst du dich von mir?	How long will you withdraw yourself from me?
Herr, handle nicht mit mir nach meinen Sünden,	Lord, treat me not according to my wickedness,
Vergilt mir nicht nach meiner Schuld.	Repay me not according to my guilt.
Ich suche dich; lass mich dein Antlitz finden,	I seek you; let me discover your face,
Du Gott der Langmut und Geduld.	You, God of patience and forbearance.
Früh woll'st du mich mit deiner Gnade füllen,	Be pleased to fill me soon with your grace,
Gott, Vater der Barmherzigkeit.	God, father of compassion.
Erfreue mich um deines Namens Willen;	Restore my happiness for your name's sake;
Du bist ein Gott, der gern erfreut.	You are a God who likes to restore happiness.
Lass deinen Weg mich wieder freudig wallen	Let me again walk joyfully in your paths
Und lehre mich dein heilig Recht,	And teach me your holy law,
Mich täglich tun nach deinem Wohlgefallen;	To do daily what is well-pleasing in your sight;
Du bist mein Gott, ich bin dein Knecht.	You are my God, I am your servant.
Herr, eile du, mein Schutz, mir beizustehen	Lord, my refuge, hasten to my aid
Und leite mich auf ebner Bahn.	And direct me on the even path.
Er hört mein Schrein, der Herr erhört mein Flehen	He hears my cry, the Lord heeds my pleading
Und nimmt sich meiner Seele an.	And accepts my soul into his keeping.

The text to this hymn of repentance borrows heavily from the Psalms: the opening lines are quoted directly from the penitential Psalm 51 ('Miserere mei'), and there are clear echoes from Psalm 13 ('How long wilt thou hide thy face from me?') and Psalm 6 ('The Lord hath heard my petition'). Nowhere is Gellert's reworking and updating of his scriptural sources more evident.

Even before we realise that this final song is through-composed, it is marked out as different by the use of Italian for the tempo indication. All the other songs have indications of tempo or style in German. The use of Italian immediately suggests a more extended work, more aria-like, with more operatic features perhaps, possibly more instrumentally conceived. Our initial prejudices are indeed confirmed in the course of the work.

The song opens in A minor with a personal confession of guilt. There are dramatic alternations of dynamics and generous use of the expressive appoggiatura. When the word 'Fluch' (curse) is uttered, the rising interval of a diminished seventh expresses anguish with the selfsame notes we heard in *Vom Tode*, bars 10–13 (A sharp to high G). The aria-like writing, with delicate ornamentation is well suited to the poet's impassioned plea for mercy. Hans Boettcher (*Beethoven als Liederkomponist*, p. 165) convincingly illustrates Beethoven's indebtedness to Italian opera in his arioso sections with a quotation from Cherubini's opera 'Demophoon', which parallels features of both the voice and accompaniment in *Busslied*. The first section of the song culminates with a long pause (meaningfully, if predictably, placed on the 'Lang-' of 'Langmut'), suspended above an augmented sixth and leading to a resolution in E major, preparing the return to the home key.

The final section begins with a phrase in A major, clearly derived from the A minor theme of the opening section, but quite different in its effect. After a perky introduction, spiced with imaginative use of arpeggiated figures in the pianist's left hand, the singer proceeds to tell of God's grace, the return to the right paths of joy and God's acceptance of the sinner, in a melodic line which remains unvaried throughout three stanzas. It is the pianist who takes centre stage, as the accompaniment becomes ever more intricate and exciting, giving almost the impression of a short set of variations. Rare indeed is the song composer who is not also a competent pianist and who can resist putting his own instrument first at times. A codetta which begins boisterously, describing the sinner's incredulous realisation that he is forgiven, tails off to a quiet close on a plagal cadence, as God receives the errant soul back into his safe keeping.

This ending must be well managed. It should seem not an anti-climax, but a culmination of the whole song set. Prayers have been answered; we are cleansed. A fine performance of these Gellert songs should be ultimately a cathartic experience.

Mention should be made here of an autograph fragment in Bonn (BH: Bodmer Mh31), which consists of the final twelve bars of *Busslied*. This fragment has its own number in the Hess catalogue (Hess 141). It was first transcribed by A. Ebert and published in *Die Musik* IX (1909/10) in his article 'Das Autograph der Gellert Lieder op. 48, Nos. 5 und 6 von Beethoven'. The fragment has no clef, key signature or time signature, although it is clearly in A major and in 3/4. The vocal part is in the soprano clef, in common with the very first published edition from Mollo and the Browne copy (see introductory notes). There are few significant differences from the final version, but clear corrections in Beethoven's hand. The absence of dynamic markings indicates that the song was still in a draft state and by no means ready for publication.

The fragment is available in two modern editions. Willy Hess (Supp V, 1962) transfers the vocal part to treble clef and adds clefs and key signature without comment. Helga Lühning, in true Henle *Urtext* style (1990), prints the fragment as seen (No. 104), but adds clefs, key and time signatures in square brackets.

GESANG (LIED) AUS DER FERNE Song from far away
Christian Ludwig Reissig   1809

B flat major WoO137 Peters 46 Henle 38 GA XXIII/236

Als mir noch die Träne	Before my tears of longing
Der Sehnsucht nicht floss	Had started to flow
Und neidisch die Ferne	And distance had enviously
Nicht Liebchen verschloss,	Locked away my sweetheart,
Wie glich da mein Leben	How my life then resembled
Dem blühenden Kranz,	A garland of flowers,
Dem Nachtigallwäldchen	A nightingale copse
Voll Spiel und voll Tanz!	Filled with games and dancing!

Nun treibt mich oft Sehnsucht	Now longing often drives me
Hinaus auf die Höhn,	Out into the hills,
Den Wunsch meines Herzens	Somewhere perchance to glimpse
Wo lächeln zu sehn!	The smile of my heart's desire!
Hier sucht in der Gegend	My languishing gaze
Mein schmachtender Blick;	Searches every corner;
Doch kehret er nimmer	And yet it never
Befriedigt zurück.	Returns satisfied.

Wie klopft es im Busen,	How my heart beats within me,
Als wärst du mir nah;	As though you were near;
O komm, meine Holde,	O come, my fair one,
Dein Jüngling ist da!	Your young man is here!
Ich opfre dir alles,	I offer up to you everything
Was Gott mir verlieh,	God has blessed me with,

Denn wie ich dich liebe,	For I never before loved
So liebt' ich noch nie!	As I love you!
O Teure, komm eilig	Come swiftly, my dearest,
Zum bräutlichen Tanz;	To the wedding dance;
Ich pflege schon Rosen	I am already tending roses
Und Myrten zum Kranz.	And myrtle for our garlands.
Komm, zaubre mein Hüttchen	Come, transform my humble cottage
Zum Tempel der Ruh',	Into an enchanted temple of peace,
Zum Tempel der Wonne;	A temple of ecstasy;
Die Göttin sei du!	And may you be its goddess!

The text does not appear in Reissig's first collection of poems published in 1809 under the title *Blümchen der Einsamkeit* (Flowers of solitude), but only in a later edition of 1815. Reissig must then have given the poem to Beethoven in manuscript form. Reissig, who had been seriously wounded in battle in May 1809, played on the sympathy of composers in asking them to set his poems without fee. Beethoven was happy to do this, but furious when he discovered that Reissig was having the present song engraved by Artaria in Vienna without his permission. On 4 February 1810 he wrote to Breitkopf und Härtel in Leipzig (EA245 / BB423): 'Der Gesang in der ferne, den ihnen mein Bruder neulich schickte, ist von einem Dilettanten wie sie ohnehin werden gemerkt haben, welcher mich dringend ersuchte, ihm Musik dazu zu sezen, nimmt sich aber auch die Freyheit diese A(rie) stechen zu lassen' (The *Gesang in der Ferne*, which my brother sent you recently, is by a dilettante poet, as you will have noticed anyway, who urgently requested me to set it to music, but is now taking the liberty of having this aria engraved).

Beethoven continued by urging Breitkopf to publish the song immediately, so that copies would reach Vienna before Artaria could issue their unauthorised edition. The song was indeed engraved at top speed and the first edition appeared from Breitkopf und Härtel in Leipzig the same month, February 1810, although Beethoven had not seen a copy by October, when he reminded the publishers again of the urgent need to publish the song if they had not already done so (EA281 / BB474). The English edition, published by Clementi in London according to an agreement reached between the Leipzig publishers, the London publisher Muzio Clementi and Beethoven, was not rushed and appeared in October 1810 as 'Anxiety of Absence. A favorite Arietta'. Meanwhile the song had been published in Vienna by Artaria in the first part of 'Achtzehn deutsche Gedichte', a collection of eighteen Reissig poems in musical settings by various composers, dedicated by the poet to Archduke Rudolph, which included settings by Weigl, Salieri, Reichardt and Amadè, as well as Beethoven's *Der Liebende*.

An autograph in London (BL: Add.Ms. 47852) includes the latter song together with *Gesang aus der Ferne*. Beethoven has written 'Lied aus der Ferne', then crossed out 'Lied' to replace it with 'Gesang'. This designation is confirmed by his reference to 'Gesang' in the letter quoted above, where he also refers to the song as an 'Aria'. The reinstatement of Beethoven's title in the Henle edition, reserving *Lied aus der Ferne* for the composer's original conception (p. 204), is to be applauded and is followed here. The Peters edition has *Lied aus der Ferne*.

This large-scale composition certainly has more in common with the aria than with the home-grown *Lied*; 'Gesang' is an appropriate catch-all term for a longer song, which avoids categorisation. Hans Boettcher calls it a 'Da-capo-Arienlied' (*Beethoven als Liederkomponist*, p. 61), and both Boettcher (p. 106) and Leslie Orrey (*The Beethoven Companion*, p. 421) refer to the instrumental conception of the work, with purely musical considerations overriding consideration of the poetic content. The opening *ritornello* occupies no fewer than twenty-three bars and is virtually a full exposition of the singer's first stanza, and indeed of his final stanza, as the song is in ternary (ABA) form.

It is possible, of course, to put a positive slant on the instrumental feel of the song and suggest that Beethoven was actually expanding the expressive range of the solo song with piano by introducing styles more commonly associated with non-vocal works. The problematic aspect of the opening *ritornello* is that is disturbs the song's formal symmetry, which in other respects corresponds closely to the contours of the poem. The dancing 6/8 metre of the outer sections mirrors the poet's recollection of past happiness in the first stanza and his dream of future happiness in the fourth stanza, while the syncopated 2/4 metre of the central section evokes the poet's restlessness in the second stanza and (with accelerated syncopation in the piano) his wildly beating heart in the third stanza.

A wealth of detail adds picturesque cameos to this overall picture. Each time 'voll Spiel und voll Tanz' is heard at the end of the first stanza, the piano responds immediately with ever fancier interludes; the trill heard at the end of the ritornello and at the end of the first stanza is a stylised response to the image of the 'nightingale copse'. The syncopation of the central section, in alternating quavers in the second stanza and jumpy semiquavers in the third stanza, vividly suggests the physical effect upon the poet's heart of his rising hope and love.

The vocal cadenza at the end of the third stanza, on the other hand, is a purely musical device which bows to a singing tradition of the previous century and is not confined to the formal aria. Barry Cooper (*Beethoven's Folksong Settings*, p. 130) lists 26 folksong arrangements where Beethoven was tempted, and occasionally encouraged by his publisher, to embellish a pause with a written-out cadenza.

The fourth stanza offers a varied and lengthened recapitulation of the music to the first stanza. Not only is the accompaniment figuration much 'blacker' on the page, with a constant flow of semiquavers for 34 bars, but the performers are instructed to adopt a livelier speed than in the first section ('Man nimmt jetzt die Bewegung lebhafter als das erste Mal'). The composer translates the exhortation to the beloved to 'come quickly' into the clearest musical terms. It is clear that this final stanza is nothing less than a proposal of marriage (roses, myrtle and all) and Beethoven certainly shares the poet's enthusiasm. His insertion of the expressive 'ja' to heighten the climax of his closing phrases is a much-used trick which threatens to become a mannerism, but which works well here.

GESANG DER GEISTER ÜBER DEN WASSERN
Song of the spirits over the waters
Johann Wolfgang von Goethe   1816

C major Bia 625 sketch

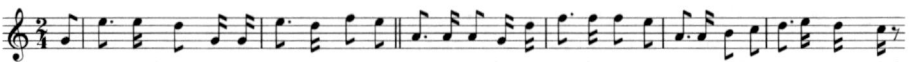

Vom Him-mel kommt es, zum Him-mel steigt es wie-der nie-der und wie-der nie-der er-de muß es e-wig wech-selnd

Des Menschen Seele	The human soul
Gleicht dem Wasser:	Is like water:
Vom Himmel kommt es,	It comes from Heaven,
Zum Himmel steigt es,	It rises to Heaven,
Und wieder nieder	And must again
Zur Erde muss es,	Descend to earth,
Ewig wechselnd.	Eternally changing.
(Es folgen 5 freie Strophen)	(5 further irregular stanzas)

The Scheide sketchbook, named after its owner William Scheide of Princeton, New Jersey, dates from March 1815 to May 1816 approximately and demonstrates Beethoven's revived interest in song at this time. Aside from several fragmentary jottings for vocal works, the book contains extensive sketches for Reissig's *Sehnsucht* (WoO146) and for the song cycle *An die ferne Geliebte*. Sadly, the pencilled sketch for *Gesang der Geister* (Scheide, NJ, p. 49) has become increasingly illegible over the years. We are fortunate that Gustav Nottebohm (1817–82) studied and described the sketchbook, then in the possession of Eugen von Miller in Vienna, in 1876. Nottebohm's description was reprinted in *Zweite Beethoveniana*, a posthumous collection of essays, in 1887, and the musical examples above are quoted from this book (p. 328). They represent the entire sketches.

Goethe's poem was written in October 1779 after a visit to the waterfall at Lauterbrunnen and compares the human soul to water as it condenses, falls as rain, tumbles over cliffs and finally flows smoothly through gentle meadows. The metaphor becomes increasingly strained as the poem progresses, and Beethoven did not get far in his desire to set Goethe's rather grandiose verse. Schubert, incidentally, also struggled with this grandiose text, but won the battle in the end with two very fine settings for male voice chorus (D538 and D714).

GOTT ALLEIN IST UNSER HERR
God alone is our Master
unknown   summer 1818

E flat major Hess 322 sketch

Auf dem Wege Abends zwischen und auf den Bergen

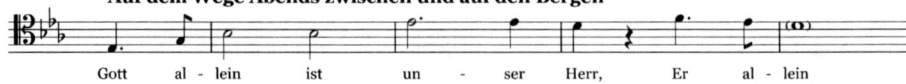

Gott al - lein ist un - ser Herr, Er al - lein

This four-bar sketch, notated in tenor clef, appears in a pocket sketchbook (Vienna, GdM: A45, f. 20v–21r), across the top of the two centre pages. The pocket sketchbooks were intended for use as inspiration occurred, not least out of doors, and Nottebohm suggests that the present sketch was written during a walk near Mödling, south of Vienna, as the sheet is headed 'In the evening on the path between and on the mountains'. It seems to have more the style of a canon than a solo song, but is included here not only for the sake of completeness but because it gives an insight into Beethoven's use of his sketchbooks and his instinctive response to natural wonders. The sketch gives every impression of arising from an acute religious impulse, inspired by the spectacle of the glorious sunset to which the companion sketch refers (see *An die Abendsonne*).

The sketch was quoted by Nottebohm (*Zweite Beethoveniana*, p. 137) and the sheet is reproduced in *The Beethoven Sketchbooks*, p. 352.

GRAZIE AGL'INGANNI TUOI Thanks to your deceits
Pietro Metastasio 1802

C major / G major SV263 sketches

gra-zie al in.. gan.. ni tuo... i al fin__ re.. spi...__ ro o ni - ce al fin d'un in - fe

gra - zie__ agl' in.. gan.. ni tuo.. i al fin re.. spi...__ ro o Ni - ce al

Grazie agl'inganni tuoi,	Thanks to your deceits
Al fin respiro, o Nice,	I can breathe at last, O Nice,
Al fin d'un infelice	At last the gods have taken pity
Ebber gli dei pietà:	On a wretched man.
Sento da' lacci suoi,	I feel that my soul is now
Sento che l'alma è sciolta;	Released from your bonds.
Non sogno questa volta,	I am not dreaming this time,
Non sogno libertà.	Not just dreaming of freedom.

Beethoven sets the opening lines of Metastasio's long canzonetta *La Libertà* (Freedom), subtitled 'A Nice' (To Nice) and 'written in Vienna in the year 1733'. Beethoven's sketches for the song are in the Kessler sketchbook in Vienna (GdM: A34, f. 81r/f. 93r). As this sketchbook also contains extended sketches for *No, non Turbati* (WoO92a) and *Tremate, empi tremate* (op. 116), both works with orchestral accompaniment, the present sketches too may be an orchestral work in embryo. However, the simple vocal line, lyrical rather than dramatic in style, and the clearly designated *ritornello* suggest a work for voice and keyboard, although there is no trace of an actual accompaniment to help decide the matter in either sketch.

Grazie agl'inganni seems to represent one of the last tasks that Beethoven completed for Salieri, who was apt to use extracts from the works of his late friend Metastasio for exercises in word-setting. Beethoven's modesty and self-discipline in seeking tuition from Salieri, despite being already a published composer of songs (*Adelaide* had appeared as early as 1797), is indicative of his self-doubts concerning his ability to set Italian texts in particular. Studies of the paper used for Beethoven's known exercises for Salieri, principally the unaccompanied partsongs (WoO99), suggest a date of around 1800. As *Grazie agl'inganni* occurs late in the Kessler sketchbook, used from about December 1801 until around July 1802, a date of 1802 can be reliably posited.

The melodies clearly aim at elegance combined with correctness of declamation, rather than originality of style. A correction in the very first bar of the C major sketch is evidence of Beethoven's insecurity with Italian metre. It is evident that Beethoven's studies with Salieri, which the maestro corrected conscientiously, helped him with the composition of Italian songs such as those of op. 82. Indeed, Peter Clive (*Beethoven and His World*, p. 303) suggests that Beethoven may have been hoping to show these later songs to Salieri in 1809, when he called and found him absent. The note he left on this occasion, reading 'The pupil Beethoven was here', indicates that even at the age of 38 Beethoven was humble enough to remember his debt to the Italian master.

GRETCHEN AM SPINNRADE
Gretchen at her spinning wheel
Johann Wolfgang von Goethe   c.1803
G major / G minor Bia 260 sketch

Meine Ruh' ist hin,	My peace is gone,
Mein Herz ist schwer;	My heart is heavy;
Ich finde sie nimmer	I shall never ever
Und nimmermehr.	Find it again.
Wo ich ihn nicht hab',	Wherever I cannot have him
Ist mir das Grab	Is for me the grave,
Die ganze Welt	The entire world
Ist mit vergällt.	Is soured for me.
Mein armer Kopf	My poor head
Ist mir verrückt,	Is turned crazy,
Mein armer Sinn	My poor mind
Ist mir zerstückt.	Is in tatters.
Meine Ruh' ist hin,	My peace is gone,
Mein Herz ist schwer;	My heart is heavy;

Ich finde sie nimmer	I shall never ever
Und nimmermehr.	Find it again.
Nach ihm nur schau' ich	I look from the window
Zum Fenster hinaus,	Only to espy him,
Nach ihm nur geh' ich	I leave the house
Aus dem Haus.	Only to seek him.
Sein hoher Gang,	His upright gait,
Sein' edle Gestalt,	His noble figure,
Senes Mundes Lächeln,	The smile on his lips,
Seiner Augen Gewalt,	The power of his eyes,
Und seiner Rede	And the magic flow
Zauberfluss,	Of his speech,
Sein Händedruck,	The touch of his hand,
Und ach sein Kuss!	And ah, his kiss!
Meine Ruh' ist hin,	My peace is gone,
Mein Herz ist schwer;	My heart is heavy;
Ich finde sie nimmer	I shall never ever
Und nimmermehr.	Find it again.
Mein Busen drängt	My bosom aches
Sich nach ihm hin.	With longing for him.
Ach dürft' ich fassen	Ah, if I might but
Und halten ihn,	Grasp and hold him,
Und küssen ihn,	And kiss him
So wie ich wollt',	As I would like to,
An seinen Küssen	And should I perish
Vergehen sollt'!	Under his kisses!

The poem was first published in Goethe's *Faust. Ein Fragment*, which appeared in 1790, although it was written in 1774 or 1775 at the height of the *Sturm und Drang* period. Gretchen expresses not only her love for Faust but also her intense desire for sexual union, with unabashed passion. She realises that she is losing her mind, but cannot resist her feelings (the 'magic flow' of Faust's speech was enabled by a love potion provided by Mephistopheles). Earlier in the play Gretchen's *Der König in Thule* was clearly designated to be sung; there is no such indication for the present soliloquy.

Fragmentary sketches for a setting are found consecutively on a single leaf in Vienna (GdM: A83, SV306): starting in G major in *alla breve*, and continuing in G minor in 6/8 time. Both time signatures suggest a brisk speed, reflecting Gretchen's disquiet – not only has her head been turned but her whole psychological balance has been upset by her passionate attraction to Faust. The sketches are only erratically texted, but the two sections seem to form parts of one continuous setting. After the 6/8 section, a passage in 4/4 time, setting the words 'Und seiner Rede Zauberfluss', builds up stepwise to four *fermata* pauses, clearly intended for the words 'Und ach sein Kuss!' before a marginal note indicates the return of the opening phrase. Here Beethoven is closest to Schubert's celebrated setting.

The sketch is interesting principally as further evidence of Beethoven's attraction to *Faust*. A conversation book entry of April 1823 reads: 'So hoffe ich endlich zu schreiben, was mir und der Kunst das Höchste ist – Faust' (And so I hope finally to compose what for me and for art represents the pinnacle – *Faust*). This project was never achieved, of course, and the fine early setting of Mephistopheles' 'Flea Song' (see *Aus Goethes Faust*) is the only part of the grand plan which was fully realised.

On the basis of these fragmentary sketches, musical ideas were not flowing in response to the celebrated text. It is generally true that lyric verse of high quality often caused Beethoven the greatest problems as a song composer. The 17-year-old Schubert, who was never intimidated by his texts, was to find his true voice as a Romantic song composer through his setting of this poem in 1814. Schubert would never have considered mapping out independent melody sketches, when the spinning wheel is a 'given' as a basis for the accompaniment. For Schubert the accompaniment is of crucial significance, both in establishing overall mood and in underpinning the text with subtle tonal analogues (in this case the erratic spinning, stopping and restarting of the wheel, reflecting Gretchen's lovesick distraction and despair), and voice and piano were inseparable in his mind from the outset. Beethoven's only indications of accompaniment (marked 'Cembalo'(harpsichord)) are a few bars in the rather jaunty 6/8 metre of the second section.

GRETELS WARNUNG   Gretel's warning
Gerhard Anton von Halem   1809, sketched 1795
A major Op. 75/4 Peters 20 Henle 43/80 GA XXIII/219

Etwas lebhaft mit leidenschaftlicher Empfindung, doch nicht zu geschwind

Mit Liebesblick und Spiel und Sang	With loving glances, singing and playing,
Warb Christel, jung und schön.	Christel, young and handsome, went courting.
So lieblich war, so frisch und schlank,	No other lad could be seen anywhere
Kein Jüngling rings zu sehn.	Who was as charming, clean-cut and slim.
Nein, keiner war	No, there was nobody
In ihrer Schar,	In their group
Für den ich das gefühlt.	About whom I felt the same.
Das merkt' er, ach!	He spotted that, alas,

Und liess nicht nach,	And did not let up
Bis er es all, bis er es all,	Until he had got everything,
Bis er es all erhielt.	Everything, everything.
Wohl war im Dorfe mancher Mann	There must have been in the village
So jung und schön wie er;	Many men as young and handsome as he
Doch sahn nur ihn die Mädchen an	But the girls had eyes for him alone
Und kosten um ihn her.	And mooned lovingly around him.
Bald riss ihr Wort	Soon their flattering words
Ihn schmeichelnd fort;	Won him over;
Gewonnen war sein Herz.	His heart was enthralled.
Mir ward er kalt,	He became cold towards me,
Dann floh er bald	Then soon was off,
Und liess mich hier, und liess mich hier,	Leaving me here, leaving me here,
Und liess mich hier im Schmerz.	Leaving me here with my heartache.
Sein Liebesblick und Spiel und Sang,	His lovelorn glances, singing and playing,
So süss und wonniglich,	So sweet and charming,
Sein Kuss, der tief zur Seele drang,	His kiss, which reached to my very soul,
Erfreut nicht fürder mich.	No longer bring me any pleasure.
Schaut meinen Fall,	Behold my downfall,
Ihr Schwestern all,	All you other girls
Für die der Falsche glüht,	After whom the traitor now lusts,
Und trauet nicht	And do not trust
Dem, was er spricht,	A word he says.
O seht mich an, mich Arme an,	Oh, look at me, poor me,
O seht mich an und flieht.	Look at me and flee.

For the fourth song in his op. 75 collection, Beethoven returned to a trifle composed fifteen years earlier. A copy of the song's first version in Vienna (GdM: A29), with corrections in Beethoven's hand in several stages, has been dated to 1795. Beethoven first corrected literal errors by the copyist and then turned his attention to revisions and the incorporation of dynamic markings.

It is uncertain where Beethoven found this poem, which was very popular in its day, although it is hardly to modern tastes with its pathetic, moralising tone. We know that Beethoven turned often to the annual almanacs, which consisted almost entirely of recent poetry, with occasional musical supplements, and the *Musenalmanach* for 1793, edited by Voss, is a likely source of Halem's text. By the time the song was revised for publication, probably in 1809, the poem had appeared in Matthisson's influential *Lyrische Anthologie* (Vienna 1806) and Beethoven or his publisher may well have turned to this accessible collection for the words of the second and third stanzas. The copy of the song has only one stanza written out and no repeat signs.

Gretels Warnung first appeared in London in August 1810, published by Clementi under the title 'Mary's Warning, a Favorite Arietta'. As was then customary, the translation sacrifices literal accuracy to poetic appeal; not only does

Gretel become Mary, but the seducer Christel is renamed Edwin, with the song opening: 'Of all the youth that grac'd the plain / Young Edwin pleas'd my eye'. The song was published in its original form in October 1810 by Breitkopf und Härtel in Leipzig as the fourth song of op. 75.

However, it had been pre-printed at the beginning of the month in the same publishers' *Allgemeine musikalische Zeitung* (3 October 1810) by way of an advertisement for the series of works appearing from Breitkopf und Härtel around this time. It was an odd choice, and hardly improved by the false attribution of the poem to Goethe, confusing Gretel with Gretchen of *Faust* fame. A note advertised op. 75 as a collection of 'meistens höchst origineller und treffliche Lieder' (generally highly original and fine songs), but apologised for printing the present one, which was 'not one of the best', but 'one of the shortest'. We shall never know whether this frank admission actually depressed potential sales of the opus!

Despite Beethoven's performance indication (Fairly lively with passionate feeling, but not too fast), which strains for expression, this song, in a delicate 6/8 metre, is essentially an insipid affair, and the guileless girl who has learned too late to say 'No' elicits no trace of sympathy. Friedländer (*Das deutsche Lied*, p. 340) sums up as positively as he can, describing the song as 'a pleasant, not exactly significant youthful work'.

The Henle edition additionally includes the first version of the song (No. 80), from the copy in Vienna (see above). There are significant differences in the accompaniment, including held chords in the opening two bars and a fairly extended postlude, which echoes the chromatic rise of the melody in the second half of the vocal part. Longer note values on 'bis er es all', heard three times to stress the totality of the girl's loss of innocence, add a little drama to the proceedings, aided by incidental dissonances, and in all the song extends to 30 bars. It is interesting that for publication Beethoven chose to impose cuts and create a more satisfying, but blander song of 24 bars.

HEIDENRÖSLEIN Heath rose
Johann Wolfgang von Goethe   1796–1822
                                                 Various keys Hess 150 sketches

Sah ein Knab ein Röslein stehn,	A lad saw a little rose growing,
Röslein auf der Heiden,	Little rose upon the heath.
War so jung und morgenschön,	It was so young, and fair as morning,
Lief er schnell, es nah zu sehn,	He rushed to look at it more closely.
Sahs mit vielen Freudcn.	He beheld it with great delight.
Röslein, Röslein, Röslein rot,	Little rose, little rose, little red rose,
Röslein auf der Heiden.	Little rose upon the heath.
Knabe sprach: Ich breche dich,	Said the lad: I shall pluck you,
Röslein auf der Heiden!	Little rose upon the heath!
Röslein sprach: Ich steche dich,	Said the little rose: I shall prick you
Dass du ewig denkst an mich,	So that you remember me for ever,

Und ich wills nicht leiden.	And I shall not suffer it.
Röslein, Röslein, Röslein rot,	Little rose, little rose, little red rose,
Röslein auf der Heiden.	Little rose upon the heath.
Und der wilde Knabe brach	And the wayward lad plucked
's Röslein auf der Heiden;	The little rose upon the heath;
Röslein wehrte sich und stach,	The little rose resisted and pricked him,
Half ihm doch kein Weh und Ach,	But her woe and alack were to no avail.
Musst es eben leiden.	She simply had to suffer it.
Röslein, Röslein, Röslein rot,	Little rose, little rose, little red rose,
Röslein auf der Heiden.	Little rose upon the heath.

Goethe's celebrated poem was written in 1771. It was first published by Herder as *Fabelliedchen* in 1773 and then in Herder's second collection of *Volkslieder* in 1779 as *Röschen auf der Heide*, confirming the folksong status which it has maintained ever since. The version we know today, under its familiar title, appeared only in 1789 in volume VIII of Goethe's works. The text was ever a favourite with composers; indeed, it is difficult to find a composer between Friedrich von Dalberg (1793) and Johannes Brahms (1858) who did not turn to the text at some point.

Beethoven made at least four sketches for a setting of 'Haidenröslein', as he knew it. The first was made in 1796, and Beethoven returned to the poem between 1818 and 1822. This was a period when few new songs were completed and the composer revisited earlier sketches: *Der Kuss* (1798/1822) is a prime example. In the case of *Heidenröslein*, we are dealing on the whole with new sketches rather than the revision of earlier ideas.

The earliest sketches (SV231) from 1796 are in Paris (BN: Ms. 79). One side of the sheet, which once belonged to the Beethoven biographer Alexander Wheelock Thayer, has the sketch (Hess 150) upon which Henry Holden Huss based his completion of the song. This was published with a commentary by Henry Krehbiel in the *New York Tribune: Illustrated Supplement* of 6 March 1898, and in a separate edition from Schirmer, together with a facsimile:

Huss's completion flows pleasantly and deserves to be better known, but he ignores the *ritornello* which follows the melody sketch. This version is in B minor, a key which Beethoven generally shunned, dismissing it as a 'black key'. The minor mode certainly emphasises the tragic aspect of this parable, which culminates in the withering of the little rose (or whatever the rose may be taken to represent).

On the other side of the same sheet (BN: Ms. 79) are further sketches, which have been tentatively identified as sketches for the same text. Willem Holsbergen's recent completion, privately published under the aegis of the Unheard Beethoven project, is based on these sketches. The opening bar, with a minim followed by four descending semiquavers, is echoed in two of the later sketches (see below), and Krehbiel argues convincingly that this figure was self-borrowed from an accompaniment figure in the concert aria *Ah! perfido*. The song sketch is, in fact, written on unused staves of an autograph score fragment of the concert aria, which dates it firmly to 1796:

A sketch of 1818 (SV275) appears to be in G major and is in Vienna (GdM: A45). Robert Winter (Johnson et al., *The Beethoven Sketchbooks*, p. 354) sounds a sensible note of caution: '(These) are short, fragmentary items of the kind that Beethoven made often without pursuing them further; the Hess numbers should not tempt one into conferring upon them the status of independent pieces'. The faux-folksong style is immediately apparent:

A sketch of 1820 (SV293) is in A minor and is the longest (Vienna, GdM: A63, pp. 2–4):

Further fragments from 1822 (SV14) are in Berlin (SPK: Artaria 201, pp. 77, 115). Beethoven states (p. 115) that the text 'comes from the middle' of the poem:

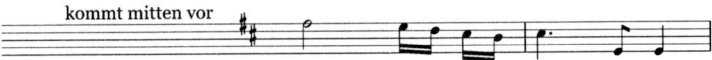

The brief, pencilled sketch on p. 77 is not texted, but the composer writes 'Göthe' above the sketch:

Beethoven may never have achieved his ambition to set Goethe's poem in a worthy manner, but his preoccupation with the text is well documented and constitutes a fascinating study in itself.

HOMER

1816
G minor Bia 624 sketch

This sketch is found in the Scheide sketchbook (Princeton NJ, p. 49) just before the sketches for *Gesang der Geister über den Wassern*. Beethoven has written 'Hexameter' prominently above the stave, indicating that this was intended as a metrical study at a time when he was experiencing a renewed interest in song composition. The words 'Wär es ein anderer nun, den wir Danaer ehrten mit Wettkampf' (Were it anyone else whom we Greeks were honouring with our contest) come from the *Iliad* (xxiii/274) in Voss's translation and refer to a chariot race, part of the funeral games held in honour of the dead Patroclus, cousin and bosom friend of Achilles, who speaks these lines. Achilles says that were it anyone else but his friend Patroclus who was being honoured, he would race and would win as he has immortal horses, a gift from the god Poseidon. Why Beethoven should have set just this one line from a long narrative passage remains a mystery, as he was wont to isolate lines which summarised a philosophical truth or a motto for life (see below). Perhaps the five successive dactyls interested him, and he certainly grasped the metre in this instance. The lines comes from the very canto which Schiller is reported to have valued above all else. Frau K. von Wolzogen (*Schillers Leben*, Stuttgart 1845, p. 335), quotes the poet as saying: 'Wenn man auch nur gelebt hätte um den dreiundzwanzigsten Gesang der Ilias zu lesen, so könnte man sich über sein Dasein nicht beschweren' (If one had lived only to read the 23rd canto of the *Iliad*, then one could not complain about one's existence).

Beethoven had a lifelong fascination with great and epic literature, and Homer, in the celebrated translations by Johann Heinrich Voss in German hexameters (*Odyssey* 1781, *Iliad* 1793), was a favourite author. He is mentioned as such in a letter of 8 August 1809 (EA224 / BB395) to Breitkopf and Härtel, where his name is linked with Schiller and Goethe, but also with Ossian, indicating that Beethoven, like Herder and Goethe before him, was completely fooled by these forged tales of Celtic lore and Gaelic warriors:

> vieleicht könnten sie mir eine ausgabe von Göthe's und Schillers Vollständigen Werken zukommen lassen . . . Die zwei Dichter sind meine Lieblings Dichter so wie Ossian, Homer (den) welchen Letzern ich leider nur in übersezungen lesen kann.

> (Perhaps you could let me have an edition of Goethe's and Schiller's complete works . . . Those two poets are my favourite poets along with Ossian and Homer, the latter of whom I can sadly read only in translations.)

Perhaps this last comment gives us a clue as to why Beethoven never completed a song to a text by Homer despite his predilection for the poet. As a rule, he set only original German or Italian texts, although Herder's fine translations of oriental poetry are a distinguished exception. A letter to Raphael Georg Kiesewetter of January 1822 (EA1260 / BB1773) indicates that Beethoven hoped to produce worthy settings of the 'immortal poets' Homer, Klopstock and Schiller 'even if one has problems to overcome', but the only result of this intention was the choral setting of Schiller's *An die Freude* in the Ninth Symphony.

Beethoven's preoccupation with Homer is well documented. In London (BL: Egerton 2795) there are sketches for a canon on lines from the *Odyssey* (xiv/83f.):

'Alle gewaltsame Tat missfällt ja den Göttern, Tugend ehren sie nur und Gerechtigkeit' (All violent deeds displease the gods, they honour only virtue and justice). Printed copies of the choral work *Meeresstille und glückliche Fahrt* (op. 112), dedicated to Goethe, bore an inscription from the *Odyssey* (viii/479f.): 'Alle sterblichen Menschen nehmen die Sänger / Billig mit Achtung auf und Ehrfurcht; selber die Muse / Lehrt sie den hohen Gesang, und waltet über die Sänger' (All mortals receive singers with respect and reverence; the muse herself teaches them exalted song and rules over the singers). The quotation was clearly intended as homage to Goethe, worthy successor to the Classical poets of antiquity.

There are over fifty underlinings in the well-thumbed copy of Voss's *Odyssey* found among Beethoven's effects after his death, and the diary he kept between 1812 and 1818 (see Solomon: 'Beethoven's Tagebuch') also illustrates how Beethoven found motto-like quotations of deep personal significance among Homer's writings. Entry T26 from the *Iliad* (xxiv/49) reads: 'Den(n) ausduldenden Muth verlieh den Menschen das Schiksal' (For fate granted man the courage to endure all things to the end). T49, also from the *Iliad* (xxii/303f.), reflects Beethoven's active sense of his vocation: 'nun aber erhascht mich das Schicksal, / dass nicht arbeitslos in den Staub ich sinke, noch ruhmlos, / Nein erst grosses vollendet, wovon auch Künftige hören' (But now fate seizes me up, that I should not lie in the dust, idle and bereft of fame; no, first great things to be achieved, which future generations will hear of). These entries actually echo, sentimentally and linguistically, parts of Beethoven's own Heiligenstadt Testament of October 1802, where the composer, depressed by his deafness, rejects thoughts of suicide and decides to endure life for the sake of his art. The second entry is interesting also because Beethoven has attempted to scan the lines and has made at least three mistakes in his scansion (T49, p. 232). His failure to sense correctly the metre of the Classical hexameter is no doubt a further reason why attempts to set Homer to music came to nothing.

ICH DENKE DEIN I think of you
Johann Wolfgang von Goethe

1799/1803–4
D major WoO74 GA X V/123

Ich denke dein, wenn mir der Sonne Schimmer
Vom Meere strahlt,
Ich denke dein, wenn sich des Mondes Flimmer
In Quellen malt.

I think of you, when the sun's shimmering rays
Are reflected on the sea,
I think of you when the moon's gleam
Colours the springs.

Goethe's poem *Nähe des Geliebten* was ever popular with song composers. Beethoven sketched a solo setting of the text (Bia 176) in 1799. Here, Beethoven's setting of the first stanza only forms the theme for a set of six variations for piano duet. The song's melody is doubled by the piano throughout, ostensibly rendering the words dispensable, but the fact that the melody and words are written out on their own staff above both *primo* and *secondo* parts suggests that the two pianists could sing along during the playing of the theme, or at least consider the meaning of the words as they play. When one learns that the dedicatees were the two Brunsvik sisters, Josephine and Therese, to whom Beethoven was devoted throughout his life, the text acquires significant personal overtones.

Variations 1, 2, 5 and 6 were composed in May 1799 and written out in the sisters' album on 23 May. Beethoven asked to borrow the album version when he prepared the work for publication in 1803. Two further variations were composed at this time or early in 1804. The Brunsvik album is lost, but an autograph in Berlin (SPK: Grasnick 23) contains the same four variations (1, 2, 5, 6), although the title page and theme are missing. The variations were published by the Kunst und Industrie Comptoir in Vienna in January 1805.

See *Nähe des Geliebten* for details of Goethe's text, the solo song sketches and their relationship to the present composition.

ICH LIEBE DICH I love you
Karl Friedrich Wilhelm Herrosee 1795

G major WoO123 Peters 59 Henle 12 GA XXIII/249

Andante

Ich liebe dich, so wie du mich, | I love you as you love me,
Am Abend und am Morgen. | Evening and morning.
Noch war kein Tag, wo du und ich | There was never yet a day when you and I
Nicht teilten unsre Sorgen. | Did not share our troubles.

Auch waren sie für dich und mich | They were easier to bear, too,
Geteilt leicht zu ertragen. | When we shared them.
Du tröstetest im Kummer mich, | You consoled me in my grief;
Ich weint' in deine Klagen. | I wept with you over your worries.

Drum Gottes Segen über dir, | And so may God's blessing rest upon you,
Du meines Lebens Freude. | You the joy of my life.
Gott schütze dich erhalt' dich mir, | May God protect you, keep you for me,
Schütz' und erhalt uns beide. | Protect and preserve us both.

The poem by Herrosee, originally entitled 'Duett eines sich zärtlich liebenden Ehepaares' (Duet of a married couple who love each other tenderly), first appeared in the Leipzig literary journal *Für ältere Literatur und neuere Lectüre* in 1784. The poem contains ten stanzas, of which only the third, fourth and sixth are set by Beethoven. Helga Lühning, in the Critical Report to the Henle edition, suggests that Beethoven found the poem in this cropped form. An earlier composer, Gottfried von Jacquin (1767–92), set precisely these stanzas, indicating that the poem was indeed current in this form, although there are sufficient textual differences to rule out Jacquin's setting as the source for Beethoven's text. Max Friedländer, on the other hand, praises Beethoven's unerring artistic instinct in omitting the other overly sentimental verses of the long poem (*Jahrbuch Peters* 1899). A copy of the song in Vienna (GdM: XVII 67000) unconvincingly underlays the first two stanzas of the original poem, repeating the second stanza as the reprise, and texts the other eight stanzas below. It seems certain that this copy, which carries the title 'Zärtliche Liebe' (Tender love), was made without Beethoven's authority.

Beethoven's autograph, also in Vienna (GdM: A13) bears no title. There are some interesting differences from the printed version, notably in the inclusion of semiquaver passing notes in the melody, which Beethoven chose to expunge in the interests of simplicity of expression, and in a more extended rising scale in the postlude. The manuscript occupies the middle pages of a double sheet. The outer pages contain a Schubert autograph: the first version of the slow movement of his Piano Sonata D568 of 1817. It is unexplained how this remarkable double autograph came about. Kinsky surmises that Salieri may have given the Beethoven autograph to Schubert in 1817. Schubert, always desperate for manuscript paper, would then have filled the unused outer leaves without thinking. What is certain is that Schubert gave one half of the folded sheet to his friend Anselm Hüttenbrenner (later purchased by the collector Johann Kafka) and that the other half went to Schubert's nephew Edward Schneider after the composer's death. In 1872, Brahms obtained both sheets and reunited them. He donated the unique object, now effectively a triple composer autograph (or quadruple if one counts the additional signature of Hüttenbrenner) to the Gesellschaft der Musikfreunde in 1893.

The cropped poem still gives a sufficient flavour of the whole poem and probably contains the best writing. The poem tells of a married couple's mutual love and support through happy and sad times, and their conviction that they will rise united again from their graves on the day of resurrection. Herrosee, a private tutor and Protestant rector, has been saved from oblivion by Beethoven's interest in three of his sentimental, but sincerely meant stanzas.

The subject of the poem was hardly novel. From at least of the middle of the eighteenth century, marriage had come to be regarded as an equal partnership and its basis of emotional sharing was often celebrated in verse. Nikolaus Giseke (1724–65), a close friend of Klopstock and like Herrosee a Protestant cleric, wrote a poem addressed to his wife which included the lines: 'Geteilt wächst unsere Freude / Geteilt weicht unser Kummer' (Shared our joy grows / Shared our anxiety fades), and Klopstock's wife Meta referred to such rather self-satisfied glorification of the married state as 'Modesentiment' (fashionable sentiment). But the recognition of marriage as an equal partnership was a social breakthrough and led directly to improved educational opportunities for women throughout the second half of the century.

Beethoven's song was published in June 1803 in Vienna by Traeg, together with *La Partenza*. The two songs, one about the bliss of married love (in German) and one about the distress of parting (in Italian), may be thought at first to be odd bedfellows. But they are related musically. Both move with a quiet confidence, enabled by flowing semiquavers in the accompaniment; the first interlude bears an identical shape in each song (bars 9–10 in both cases). This gives both settings a superficial blandness, and Lesley Orrey (*The Beethoven Companion*, p. 436) criticises their lack of feeling: the absence of real ardour in the present song, and the painlessness of the parting in *La Partenza*.

This criticism may be valid for the Italianate conceit which is *La Partenza*, but the lack of ardour is quite deliberate in the present song. It celebrates, after all, not youthful passion but the reflective pleasure of a happily married couple, who, as the first stanza of the original poem states, need nobody but each other to enjoy perfect happiness. The final stanza, where one partner confers God's blessing upon the other and prays for their joint protection and preservation, is in effect a religious confirmation of marriage vows.

Beethoven's setting has a somewhat Italianate feel to it in the smoothness of the vocal line, the correctness of the prosody, the simple flowing accompaniment and the emphatic pause at the end of the second verse, which under different circumstances would call for improvised vocal embellishment. But here it is the apparent and transparent simplicity of the setting which gives it a universality, rendering it one of Beethoven's most personal and endearing utterances. From the rising sequence of the opening bars, by way of the contrasting second verse, pause, reprise and false cadence, to the extended coda and short postlude, this song exudes a quiet mastery which exemplifies the art which conceals art.

ICH SAH SIE HEUT I saw her today
unknown

1793–96
G major Bia 261 sketch

Ich sah sieheuto | Lie- be! Wie | war das Mäd chen | schön da | wollt ich was ich | Füh-le ihr | oh-ne scham ge-|steh en

Ich sah sie heut, o Liebe,	I saw her today, O dear one,
Wie war das Mädchen schön!	How pretty the girl was!
Da wollt ich, was ich fühle	Then I wanted to confess to her
Ihr ohne Scham gestehn.	Without shame just what I feel.

Beethoven's sketch, in the Kafka Album in London (BL: Add.Ms. 29801, f. 39r), has been dated by watermark studies to Beethoven's early years in Vienna. It consists of eight bars of melody with a bass line accompaniment following, which extends to 20 bars in total. The first eight bars of the accompaniment dovetail perfectly with the melody (see above), although the end product is disappointing. It is the opening of a conventional eighteenth-century song on two staves, standard almanac supplement material.

The Kafka Album has been made accessible by Joseph Kerman, whose *Autograph Miscellany* includes not only a full facsimile but a volume of transcriptions, in which Kerman has sought to piece together discontinuous sketches. Sadly, in the present instance any idea of completing the song is frustrated by the fact that the text has not been identified. As with other fragmentary sketches to unidentified texts, the question briefly arises whether Beethoven himself devised the words. This will always remain the merest hypothesis, and any search for an autobiographical subtext must remain equally futile.

ICH WIEGE DICH IN MEINEM ARM
I cradle you in my arms
unknown

date unknown

Hess 137 lost

This song was included in a scribbled list of works with target prices, prepared by Beethoven with a view to sales and later offered to Peters. (EA1079 / BB1468). Alan Tyson ('Beethoven Price List of 1822') gives an accurate transcription of the list, which includes a song with this title. There is no trace of the song beyond the reference in the composer's list. Hess, who had not seen the list (now in Berlin, DSB), rendered the title of the song incorrectly as 'Schwinge dich in meinen Dom' (Swing yourself into my cathedral), which makes no sense at all and should have raised instant doubts.

The composer Ludwig Abeille (1761–1838) set a poem which begins with these words, which is attributed to an author named Schmidt. More entertainingly, an internet search reveals that two modern popular songs have begun with similar words, although it is unlikely that even Beethoven was enough of a trendsetter to anticipate 'Austro-Pop' by two centuries!

IN QUESTA TOMBA OSCURA   In this dark tomb
Giuseppe Carpani

1806

A flat major Wo133 Peters 62 Henle 31 GA XXIII/252

In questa tomba oscura	In this sombre grave
Lasciami riposar!	Leave me to rest!
Quando vivevo, ingrata,	You should have thought of me
Dovevi a me pensar.	When I was alive, ungrateful one,

Lascia che l'ombre ignude	Let this naked shade
Godansi pace almen,	Enjoy peace at least,
E non bagnar mie ceneri	And do not bathe my ashes
D'inutile velen.	With the idle venom of your tears.

Carpani's poem was written during a stay in Baden in 1805. The *Journal des Luxus und der Moden* reported in November 1805 how Countess Rzewuska improvised an air on the piano, whereupon Carpani improvised a text to the air. Carpani imagined a lover who had died from the grief of unrequited love; his beloved, filled with remorse, wets his grave with her tears, and the lover's ghost responds with the words of the poem.

The song was first published by Mollo in Vienna as the final contribution to a collection of 63 settings of the text by a total of 46 different composers, sponsored by the Countess and dedicated to Prince Lobkowitz. The publication was announced in November 1806, but a delay followed, possibly because the publisher was hoping for a late contribution from Haydn, and the edition did not become generally available until the end of 1808. An editor's preface contained a poeticised and extended version of the story of the poem's conception, in Italian. The final page illustrated the poem in a less than serious manner, and this parody caused some bad feeling among the composers who had contributed serious settings of the text.

Beethoven probably composed his first setting of the text (see below) in 1806, but this final version was handed to the publisher at a late stage, since Mollo's Preface stated that the settings had been printed in the order in which they had been received from the composers. Beethoven's was the last. The autograph manuscript, now in New York (Pierpont Morgan Library: Lehmann collection), was returned to Beethoven during the publication process for further revision, as he had requested in a note in Italian, together with a proof offprint. It was at this point that Beethoven noticed an error: 'alma' for 'almen' at bar 17. The error was not corrected in the first version.

In comparison with other settings in this collection, Beethoven's is a very controlled and restrained affair. It avoids the mannerisms associated with Italian aria, such as the overuse of expressive melisma, sighing appoggiaturas and frequent word repetition. Word repetition is restricted to a simple echo of the final phrase 'a me pensar' both times it occurs, the expressive repetition of 'e non', an introductory 'In questa' which eases into the repeat of the first verse, and a twice-heard 'ingrata!' which is incorporated into the final cadence.

The first section, moving slowly in A flat major, suggests the utter stillness of the dark grave; the mood is set by the four simple chords which are heard before the voice enters. A flat major was regarded by eighteenth-century theorists as the key of death and the grave. In the middle section, A flat is enharmonically altered to G sharp, and the key to E major, as the lover's bitter plea to be left alone rises through a slow *crescendo* to climax at the resentful reference to the 'idle venom' of the beloved's belated tears. Expression is achieved here principally through the densely black figuration of the piano accompaniment, which even on the printed page suggests physical and spiritual unrest. The song ends quietly with a recapitulation of the opening verse. Only the final loud cry of 'Ingrata!' disturbs the even temper of the utterance, but even here the final syllable of the word is hushed (compare the opening cry of 'Kyrie' in the Missa Solemnis), as the shade slips back into the rest he has been seeking, 'all passion spent'.

In questa tomba is a miniature masterpiece. The transparency of its form and modulations reveal fine craftsmanship, but manage to preserve the veil of art which conceals art.

The Henle edition has the Italian text only. The Peters edition, following GA, includes a clumsy German translation ('In dieses Grabes Dunkel') which singers must avoid at all cost. The extraordinary decision to offer a differing translation for the repeated first stanza does nothing to redeem the consistent mismatch between the metre of words and music. The better translation which Schindler includes in his biography of the composer is offered here for the rare singer who wishes to avoid the Italian text:

> Lass ruhen mich in Frieden / In dunkler Grabesnacht!
> O hätt'st du, Undankbare / Des Lebenden gedacht!

> Entweiche, dass mein Schatten / In Frieden endlich ruht,
> Nicht weckt die kalte Asche / Der gift'gen Thränen Fluth.

Stanford University, California (Memorial Library of Music) possesses the autograph of an earlier version of the song. Paper studies have dated this version to the summer or autumn of 1806. There are numerous corrections and revisions, but Helga Lühning has based her edition for Henle (No. 83) on the first stage of revisions, which alone are in ink and fully legible.

The differences in the setting of the first stanza principally concern the more abrupt opening. The two bars of introduction are missing here, and at the recapitulation of the same stanza, two anticipatory bars are again absent. In the central section, the piano figuration is altered to setxuplets, but the main difference is in the setting of 'godansi pace alma' (bar 15). The unexpected rise through a perfect sixth on 'pace', in a song where it is the fourth which dominates melodic proceedings, only serves to draw attention to the incorrect declamation which follows, even ignoring the fact that Beethoven wrongly gives the next word as 'alma' (recte: 'almen'). Beethoven admits his mistakes in setting the wrong word and in failing to recognise a vocal elision, in a letter in French to the poet Carpani (EA171 / BB301), asking him to return the autograph for immediate correction.

This letter of 1808 must have been written as a matter of urgency at a time when the publisher was waiting impatiently for Beethoven's contribution to the collection of 63 settings of Carpani's text, in which the final version appeared. Such musical celebrities as Gyrowetz, Kozeluch, Salieri, Tomášek, Mozart junior, Weigl and Zelter had, after all, managed to meet the deadline, not to mention Carpani himself and Countess Rzewuska, financial sponsor of the work, who had also delivered musical settings for this lavish publication.

KENNST DU DAS LAND Do you know the land
Johann Wolfgang von Goethe   1809

A major Op. 75/1 Peters 17 Henle 40 GA XXIII/219

Kennst du das Land, wo die Zitronen blühn,	Do you know the land where lemon trees bloom,
Im dunklen Laub die Gold-Orangen glühn,	Golden oranges glow amid dark foliage,
Ein sanfter Wind vom blauen Himmel weht,	A gentle breeze wafts from the clear blue sky,
Die Myrte still und hoch der Lorbeer steht,	The myrtle stands silent, the laurel grows tall?
Kennst du es wohl?	Do you perhaps know it?
Dahin! Dahin!	Thither! Thither!
Möcht ich mit dir, o mein Geliebter, ziehn.	I wish to go with you, O my beloved.

Kennst du das Haus? Auf Säulen ruht sein Dach,	Do you know the house? Its roof rests on columns,
Es glänzt der Saal, es schimmert das Gemach,	The hall sparkles, the chambers gleam,
Und Marmorbilder stehn und sehn mich an:	And marble statues stand and look at me:
Was hat man dir, du armes Kind, getan?	What have they done to you, poor child?
Kennst du es wohl?	Do you perhaps know it?
Dahin! Dahin!	Thither! Thither!
Möcht ich mit dir, o mein Beschützer, ziehn.	I wish to go with you, O my protector.

Kennst du den Berg und seinen Wolkensteg?	Do you know the mountain and its track up in the clouds?
Das Maultier sucht im Nebel seinen Weg,	The mule struggles to find his path in the mists,
In Höhlen wohnt der Drachen alte Brut,	An age-old race of dragons dwells in the caverns,
Es stürzt der Fels und über ihn die Flut.	The rock face tumbles and with it the torrent.
Kennst du ihn wohl?	Do you perhaps know it?
Dahin! Dahin!	Thither! Thither!
Geht unser Weg, o Vater, lass uns ziehn!	Our path leads. O father, let us go now!

Goethe's poem, surely the most celebrated expression of the recurring German literary theme of longing for southern climes, is taken from his novel *Wilhelm Meisters Lehrjahre*, where it opens the Third Book. It is sung by the mysterious waif Mignon:

After a few hours had passed, Wilhelm heard music outside his door. He thought at first that the Harper must be there again, but he soon made out the sound of a zither, and the voice which began to sing was Mignon's. Wilhelm opened the door, the child entered and sang the song we have just printed.

Melody and expression pleased our friend exceedingly, although he could not understand all the words. He got Mignon to repeat and explain the verses, wrote them down and translated them into German. But he could achieve only a poor imitation of the highly original turns of phrase. The childlike innocence of expression evaporated as the broken language was harmonised and disconnected phrases welded together. There was also nothing to compare with the charming appeal of the melody.

She began every line with an air of solemnity and magnificence, as though she wished to draw his attention to something extraordinary and perform something of importance. The voice became duller and darker at the third line; she expressed the 'Kennst du es wohl?' with secrecy and deliberation; there was an irresistible longing in her 'Dahin! Dahin!'; she managed to vary the 'Lass uns ziehn!' at every repetition so that it was now an urgent entreaty, now a dynamic anticipation.

. . . Italy! said Mignon significantly. If ever you go to Italy, take me with you, I'm freezing here. – Have you ever been there, little treasure?, asked Wilhelm. – The child was silent and it was impossible to get any more out of her.

The passage has been quoted at length, as the context is generally forgotten today, but was fully familiar to Beethoven, who owned a copy of *Wilhelm Meisters Lehrjahre*. Indeed, he recommended the work to Therese Malfatti in a letter of 1810, offering to send her the book (EA258 / BB442). To what extent Beethoven responded to the performance indications given in Goethe's account of Mignon's rendering and whether his setting was informed by his knowledge of the true history of Mignon (who had indeed been to Italy) are issues which cannot but arouse our curiosity.

The original song was first published in October 1810 by Breitkopf und Härtel in Leipzig as the first of the six songs of op. 75. The first English edition, comprising only the first two stanzas, had actually appeared two months previously, in August 1810, issued by Clementi in London with the title 'Know'st thou the land'. An agreement had been reached to synchronise publication of several works on the continent and in England, although many factors, including communication difficulties during the Napoleonic era, made it impossible to synchronise dates exactly. Alan Tyson gives precise information in *The Authentic English Editions of Beethoven* (London 1963).

There is no autograph, but a copy in Bonn (BH: NE158) has been corrected by the composer and was clearly used as the basis for the engraving of the German edition. A second copy, also in Bonn (BH: Bodmer Mh41), was probably made by Therese Malfatti, with some corrections and the second half of the voice part in Beethoven's hand. There are numerous mistakes, not least in the underlay of the text, suggesting that Therese was working from an untexted original manuscript, now lost. Sketches in Vienna (GdM: A41) and Bonn (BH: Mh79, BH102) are identifiable only from the text, although the Viennese sketches do suggest that Beethoven once considered a minor key for the song.

Beethoven does indeed take notice of the hints given by Goethe in his description of Mignon's performance. The song starts in a solemn and stately manner, and at the third line the music darkens slightly with a brief move to the minor mode. At this point the accompanying triplet figure fits the 'gentle wind' well, but becomes less appropriate for the staring marble statues at the identical point in the second stanza. The questioning 'Kennst du es wohl?' is delivered with deliberation, as indicated by the author. The final section at 'Dahin', turning to 6/8 metre and marked 'faster' is perhaps too jaunty to suggest the 'irresistible longing' mentioned in Goethe's text. The second stanza is a repetition of the first, and variation in the final stanza concerns only some word-painting; at the mention of dragons, Beethoven feels it *de rigueur* to double the treble line with octaves and have some associative growling in the bass. The lengthening of the final 'Lass uns ziehn!' is probably determined by musical considerations rather than fidelity to Goethe's performance indications.

Despite Beethoven's clear attempt to take the performing context into consideration, Goethe did not warm to his setting. Writing in *Libussa, Jahrbuch für 1850*, the Prague composer Tomášek recalls Goethe as saying: 'I cannot understand how Beethoven and Spohr could misunderstand the song so completely when they through-composed it . . . Mignon by her very nature can sing only a *Lied*, not an aria.' We in turn cannot understand how Goethe could have regarded this mildly modified strophic song as 'through-composed'. It is known, however, that the poet admired the strictly strophic setting by Reichardt, published in the first edition of the novel. This latter is a well crafted song in D major, but makes no attempt to convey the developing emotions of the poem.

Beethoven himself clearly thought highly of his own song. In June 1810 wrote to Breitkopf und Härtel (EA261 / BB446): '*Nb*: unter den liedern, die ich ihnen angetragen, sind mehrere von Goethe, auch "Kennst du das Land?" welches viel Eindruck auf die Menschen macht' (NB: Among the songs I offered you are several by Goethe, including 'Kennst du das Land?', which is making a big impression on people). Robert Schumann, most literary of composers, who estimated (*Allgemeine Musikalische Zeitung*, April 1827) that there were already a hundred different settings of the text, praised Beethoven's setting as the only one which came close to achieving the same effect that the poem makes without music.

Mention should be made of the unusual marking 'mit Nachdruck' (with emphasis), occurring at bar 34 and reinforced in the Henle edition by *staccato* markings to the voice part, and the similar markings at bar 75 (*staccatissimo* wedges in the Peters edition). The intention is clearly a vocal marcato effect, although the reason for the marking is less clear. In the second stanza the child Mignon is perhaps recalling the wondrous impression which the glittering Italian palazzo made on her when she was even tinier.

The song throws light on the fascinating and still unsettled issue of Beethoven's influence on Schubert. Schubert composed his setting of *Kennst du das Land* (D321) on 23 October 1815, and on the same day set a further text which Beethoven had included in his op. 75 collection: Reissig's *Der Zufriedene* (D320). Both Schubert songs show similarities in outline to Beethoven's settings. The suspicion that Schubert was modelling his settings on Beethoven's is inescapable. The influence of the senior composer is self-evident in *Der Zufriedene* (p. 120), and in his Mignon song too Schubert follows Beethoven in his choice of key, the solemn metre of the opening phrases and a faster movement at 'Dahin'. Like Beethoven, Schubert sets the first two stanzas to identical music, using repeat markings. Schubert's third stanza is set in A minor. A strong reminiscence occurs at 'es stürzt der Fels', where Schubert inserts *staccatissimo* wedges, here in the piano part. Beethoven marks the relevant notes *staccato*, but he habitually used wedges or strokes for normal *staccato*, and one wonders whether Schubert had imitated an autograph which is now lost (the Peters edition reinstates wedges in Beethoven's song at this point). Schubert, at 18, does not seem to grasp the emotional subtlety of the poem and relies heavily on his exemplar. Sadly, Schubert did not return to this poem in January 1826 when he plumbed the psychological depths of the other Mignon poems in his D877 settings.

KLAGE Lament
Ludwig Christoph Heinrich Hölty 1790
E major–E minor WoO113 Not in Peters Henle 70/71 GA XXV/283

Dein Silber schien durch Eichengrün,	Your silvery light shone down on me, O moon,
Das Kühlung gab, auf mich herab,	Through the green leaves of the oak,
O Mond, und lachte Ruh'	Which offered coolness, and smiled,
Mir frohem Knaben zu.	Bringing peace to me, the happy boy.
Wenn jetzt dein Licht durchs Fenster bricht,	Now, when your light breaks through the window,
Lacht's keine Ruh' mir Jüngling zu,	It brings no peace to me, the youth,
Sieht's meine Wange blass,	It sees my cheek pallid,
Mein Auge Tränennass.	My eyes filled with tears.
Bald, lieber Freund, ach bald bescheint	Soon, dearest friend, soon alas, your silvery light
Dein Silberschein den Leichenstein,	Will illuminate the tombstone
Der meine Asche birgt,	That marks my ashes,
Des Jünglings Asche birgt.	The youth's ashes.

Hölty's fine poem, apostrophising the moon and also known as 'An den Mond' or 'Klage an den Mond', addresses mortality in a manner which is both economical and poignant, the more so when one learns of the poet's death from tuberculosis at the early age of 27. It is important to remind ourselves from time to time that, in an age when candlelight was the only artificial source of illumination, the moon and the stars were much more part of people's lives. In the first stanza, the poet is still a young boy ('Knabe') without a care, playing out late on a summer's evening; in the second stanza, he has grown into a youth ('Jüngling'), his peace has gone and he is plagued by sadness and illness; in the final stanza he anticipates an early death. It is a miniature drama in three vivid scenes – referring to past, present and future – featuring poet and moon. One might (anachronistically) refer to cinematographic effects in the moon's changing perspectives.

It is of interest that both Beethoven and Schubert set the poem when they were 19 years old. Beethoven's two similar versions both date from the earlier part of 1790, well before the composer's 20th birthday, and Schubert, always more helpful in the matter of dating manuscripts, composed his setting (D436) on 12 May 1816. Schubert's song is an early masterpiece, beginning with a simple first stanza, varying the accompaniment chromatically for the changed mood of the second stanza, and switching abruptly to the relative minor for the poignant final stanza. Sadly, it is rarely performed, although, unlike Beethoven's setting, it was at least included in the Peters edition, albeit in volume 6.

After his early death, Hölty's poems were edited for publication by his friend Johann Heinrich Voss. The present poem first appeared in Voss's *Poetische Blumenlese für das Jahr 1779* and again in Hölty's collected poems, published in Hamburg in 1783. Voss has been criticised for altering words and even whole lines in Hölty's verse, but his alterations tend to be improvements. For example, at the start of the third stanza, Hölty wrote 'wann . . . wann' (when), whereas 'bald' (soon) adds poignancy and avoids overtones of a sentimental yearning for death.

There are two autographs, representing two similar versions of the song. The first is in Vienna (GdM: A9) and is the version reproduced in the Henle edition (only) as No. 70. Beethoven's remarks on this autograph concerning tempi, speed and notation are of interest, especially in view of his predilection for the 2/4 time signature in his songs:

> *Andante* muss im 2/4tel Takt viel geschwinder genommen werden wie hier im lied das *tempo* ist. wie es scheint, kan das lezte ohnmöglich in 2/4tel takt bleiben, weil es viel zu langsam dafür ist. am besten scheint's, beide in ₵ takt zu sezen . . . das erste in E-*dur* muss im 2/4tel T:(akt) bleiben, weil man es sonst zu langsam singen würde. man wird eher immer bey langen Noten das tempo langsam nehme(n) als bey kurzen z.B. bey vierteln langsamer als bey 8tel.

> (*Andante* has to be taken much faster in 2/4 time than the *tempo* in this song. It seems the last section cannot possibly remain in 2/4 because it is much too slow for it. The best solution seems to be to put both into ₵ time . . . The first section in E *major* must stay in 2/4 time, as people would sing it too slowly otherwise. People are more inclined to take the tempo slowly with long notes rather than with short notes, e.g. with crotchets rather than quavers.)

The second autograph in Vienna (GdM: A66) is clearly the later one. It includes performance directions, but lacks text and dynamics, which Beethoven generally added as a final stage. With text added from the first manuscript, this is the version first published in 1888 in the supplementary volume XXV of the old complete edition and reprinted in 1990 by Henle as No. 71. The thoughts on time signatures (see above) have borne fruit in the marking of the E minor section in ₵ in this second version, and, with quaver triplets replacing the semiquaver triplets of the first version, this certainly encourages a more leisurely and expansive interpretation. There is a general smoothing out of the vocal line. See, for example, bar 28, where the inaptly elaborate setting of 'meine Asche' has yielded to a gently descending line, incorporating sighing minor seconds.

The performance directions are in German throughout, unusual in itself at this early stage of Beethoven's songwriting career, and aim at maximum expressiveness in keeping with the title: 'Lament'. In addition to the initial 'slow and gentle' direction, there is a long opening instruction to the pianist, which essentially asks for *legato* in three different ways: 'Durchaus müssen die Töne geschliffen und so sehr als möglich ausgehalten und zusammengebunden werden' (Throughout the notes must be legato, and as far as possible sustained and joined together). The pianist is later instructed to slow gradually into the E minor section, which is then marked 'very slow and sad' for the singer.

This early song is a distinguished and forward-looking contribution to the Romantic *Lied* repertoire. The first section, in E major, flows smoothly, describing a carefree boyhood. The falling thirds at 'lachte Ruh' (bar 12) are here evocative of the joys of childhood. Of musical interest are Beethoven's experiments in the integration of voice and piano between bars 9 and 14, where closure is avoided at the end of three successive vocal phrases; this 'hovering between openness and closure' is discussed by Amanda Glauert (*Cambridge Companion to Beethoven*, pp. 195–6). In the confident transitional bars (14–15) to the E minor section, Hans Boettcher hears a pre-echo of the Piano Sonata op. 101 (*Beethoven als Liederkomponist*, p. 158).

The E minor section opens with an almost operatic lament, although it is marked 'very slow and sad' and it is probable that Beethoven would have added *pp* as the dynamic indication. The placing of 'Jüngling' (youth) on the highest note suggests that Beethoven fully understands the importance of the word in context: boyhood is past, and the youth finds his growing pains intolerable. The third stanza, introduced by the slowly tolling bell, starts homophonically, suggesting not so much a longing for death as a tired resignation to fate; after the tribulations of his youth, quiet rest beneath a tombstone lit by his dear friend, the moon, does not seem too fearsome. The motif of the passing bell is now heard in octaves, high in the piano.

In the quiet postlude, the high octaves fall and gradually fade, leading into a succession of A minor and diminished seventh chords above a low E pedal note (the final tolling of the passing bell), before closing firmly in the tonic E minor. The whole is reminiscent of Schubert in its confident and meaningful manipulation of musical material, although, in assessing the significance of this song and in considering Beethoven's crucial role in the development of the *Lied*, it is important to recall that Schubert was not born until some seven years after its composition. Barry Cooper (*Beethoven*, p. 38) calls the song 'in many ways fifty years ahead of its time', even though this would take us up to 1840, Schumann's 'Year of Song'.

KRIEGSLIED DER ÖSTERREICHER
War song of the Austrians
Josef Friedelberg   early 1797
C major WoO122 Peters 40 Henle 16 GA XXIII/231

Ein grosses deutsches Volk sind wir,
Sind mächtig und gerecht.
Ihr Franken, das bezweifelt ihr?
Ihr Franken kennt uns schlecht.
Denn unser Fürst ist gut,
Erhaben unser Mut!
Süss unsrer Trauben Blut
Und unsre Weiber schön;
Wie kann's uns besser gehn?

We are one great German people,
Powerful and just.
You Frenchmen, you doubt this?
You do not know us very well.
For our prince is good
Our valour exalted!
The blood of our grapes is sweet
And our women beautiful.
How could things be better for us?

Wir streiten nicht für Ruhm und Sold,
Nur für des Friedens Glück!
Wir kehren, arm an fremdem Gold,
Zu unsrem Herd zurück.
Denn guten Bürgern nur
Blüht Segen der Natur
Auf Weinberg, Wald und Flur.
Gerecht ist unser Krieg;
Uns, uns gehört der Sieg.

We do not fight for fame and money,
Only for the joy of peace!
We shall return to home and hearth,
Without plundered gold.
For only good citizens
Enjoy nature's blessing
On their vineyards, forests and fields.
Our war is just,
The victory belongs to us.

Mit Picken, Sensen und Geschoss
Eilt klein und gross herbei!
Fürs Vaterland! Stimmt, klein und gross,
Stimmt an das Feldgeschrei!
Da stehn wir unverwandt
Für Haus und Hof und Land
Mit Waffen in der Hand
Und schlagen mutig drein,
Wie viel auch ihrer sein!

Come, great and small, rush to join us
With pickaxe, scythe or firearm!
For the fatherland! Great and small,
Strike up the battle-cry!
Here we stand unwavering,
Weapon in hand,
For house, home and country
And join in the battle valiantly,
However many of them there may be!

Mann, Weib und Kind in Österreich
Fühlt tief den eignen Wert.

Man, woman and child in Austria,
Have a deep sense of your own worth.

Nie, Franken, werden wir von euch	Never, Frenchmen, will we be
Besieget, nie betört.	Conquered or led astray by you.
Denn unser Fürst ist gut,	For our prince is good
Erhaben unser Mut!	Our valour exalted!
Süss unsrer Trauben Blut	The blood of our grapes is sweet
Und unsre Weiber schön;	And our women beautiful.
Wie kann's uns besser gehn?	How could things be better for us?

This poem, like its companion piece *Abschiedsgesang an Wiens Bürger*, was written by Joseph Friedelberg for his companions in the Viennese volunteer force. It was written to celebrate the departure of the volunteers to a fortified position on the Wiener Berg. Beethoven's setting was published in April 1797 by Artaria in Vienna. No autograph survives, but we can fairly assume that there was a very small gap between composition and publication in an occasional piece like this one.

Despite being shored up by a whole series of defiant patriotic war songs and rallied by Haydn's new hymn in honour of Emperor Franz II, which had first been sung on 12 February 1797, Austrian national confidence had taken a battering in the months since the *Abschiedsgesang* the previous November. The Austrians had to accept the preliminary Peace of Leoben in the very month this song appeared, and this was to lead to the Peace of Campo Formio in October 1797, which was relatively lenient towards the Austrians, but which still dented national pride and irrevocably undermined the position of Franz II as Holy Roman Emperor.

The defiance of the poem is sincerely meant, but rings hollow. The poem is less inspired than *Abschiedsgesang*, relying on bravado alone. The weakest lines of the poem ('Our prince is good', etc.) are heard twice. Beethovens seems, in contrast to the earlier song, half-hearted and inconsistent. He opens with a suitably martial fanfare, but this leads to a rather limp middle section, significantly setting the weakest lines referred to above, where quiet bars alternate with loud bars, two by two. There is scant regard for the text here: why should the good prince be quiet and the beautiful women loud? The repetition of the refrain is marked for chorus. This song may have raised spirits briefly on a particular occasion in Austrian history, but it is unlikely to be heard now except in the context of a complete survey of the songs.

LA PARTENZA The parting
Pietro Metastasio

1795–96

A major WoO124 Peters 61 Henle 13 GA XXIII/251

Affetuoso

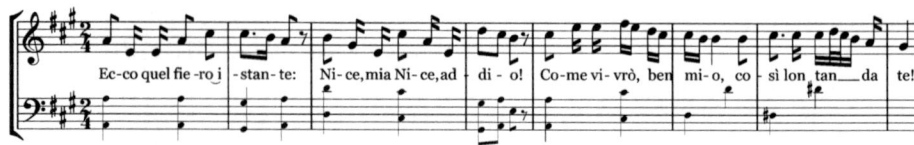

Ec-co quel fie-ro i-stan-te: Ni-ce, mia Ni-ce, ad di - o! Co-me vi-vrò, ben mi-o, co-sì lon_tan__da te!

Ecco quel fiero istante:	Behold that cruel moment:
Nice, mia Nice, addio!	Nice, my Nice, farewell!
Come vivrò, ben mio,	How shall I live, my dearest,
Così lontan da te!	So far from you?
Io vivrò sempre in pene;	I shall live always in torment;
Io non avrò più bene;	I shall never again know happiness;
E tu chi sa se mai	And who knows whether
Ti sovverai di me!	You will ever remember me!

The song sets the first two stanzas of Metastasio's *Canzonetta V*, written in 1746. It seems unlikely that Beethoven knew the other twelve stanzas. These first two stanzas had been set by many composers, both in their original form and in a free German translation by Johann Joachim Eschenburg (1743–1820) under the title 'Die Trennung' (Separation). It was this translation, where Nice becomes Germanised as Daphne, which Beethoven's teacher Neefe had set in 1776. When Beethoven's song was reprinted by Kühnel in 1806, a new German translation by an unknown author was used, with the title 'Der Abschied' (Parting), with Nice reinstated as the catalytic heroine. The GA and Peters print this text below the Italian original; Henle opts for Italian only.

Beethoven's autograph in Vienna (GdM: A29) shows Beethoven busily correcting details prior to publication. An earlier fragmentary sketch (SPK: Artaria 149), dated by paper studies to 1795, shows Beethoven struggling with Italian prosody at the opening of the second stanza. The fact that he altered his original thoughts successfully has been interpreted as evidence that he received useful advice from a native Italian composer, Salieri being the most likely candidate. The song was published in June 1803 in Vienna by Traeg, together with *Ich liebe dich*. In this first edition, the title of the present song was wrongly printed as *L'Apparenza*, presumably a misreading of Beethoven's handwriting (to be fair to the printers, the composer was never celebrated for his calligraphy nor for his orthography).

La Partenza will never be a first-favourite among Beethoven's songs. It lacks the personal intensity of utterance which is the hallmark of his best work, and is merely an exercise, albeit a successful one, in the Italian manner. This may give it some appeal to singers as a curiosity, as the name of Beethoven will always carry a special cachet. The German translation should, however, be avoided at all costs, as it produces a mismatch which serves only to point the remoteness of the music from Beethoven's authentic German song style.

The theme of enforced separation recurs frequently in poems, and hence songs, of the late eighteenth century; indeed, the *Abschieds-Elegie* forms a distinct genus in the taxonomy of the Lied at this period. Mozart's *Das Lied der Trennung* (K519), which begins 'Auch Engel Gottes weinen, / Wo Liebende sich trennen!' (Even God's angels weep when lovers part), sets a poem which imitates Eschenburg's *Die Trennung* (see above) in a blatantly transparent fashion, and thus derives ultimately from Metastasio's Canzonetta.

LA TIRANNA

William Wennington

End of 1798

E flat major WoO125 Supp V/7 Henle 19 Not in GA/Peters

Ah grief to think! Ah woe to name,
The doom that fate has destin'd mine!
Forbid to fan my wayward flame,
And, slave to silence, hopeless pine!

Imperious fair! In fatal hour,
I mark'd the vivid lightnings roll,
That gave to know thy ruthless pow'r,
And gleam'd destruction on my soul!

La Tiranna was published in London in December 1799 by Broderip & Wilkinson as 'A Favourite CANZONETTA for the Pianoforte, composed by L. van Beethoven of Vienna . . .'. The edition claimed to be also 'Published in Vienna by the Principal Music Shops', although no trace of any other edition has been found. When the song was rediscovered and announced by J. H. Blaxland ('Eine unbekannte Canzonetta Beethovens', *Zeitschrift für Musikwisseschaft* XIV) in 1931, there were doubts about its authenticity, but these were dispelled when sketches for the song were found in a sketchbook in Berlin (DSB: Grasnick 1). These sketches showed furthermore that the text was not, as had been reasonably assumed from the title, a free translation from an Italian source, but an authentic English text. In some of the earlier sketches, Beethoven had even used an approximate phonetic transcription of the English text before reverting to the correct spelling. The story is told in an article by Alan Tyson ('Beethoven's English Canzonetta', *Musical Times* CXII, 1971), whose edition of the song for Novello was published the same year.

The possibility remains, of course, that Wennington's inflated verse is loosely based on an Italian poem which has not been traced. William Wennington was a minor man of letters and dabbled in musical composition. He was in Vienna in or around 1798 and may well have been introduced to Beethoven at the home of Prince Lichnowsky; one of Wennington's works has a Preface dated 'Vienna 1798' and mentions Lichnowsky as a subscriber.

It is not known whether Beethoven received a fee from Wennington, but he certainly gave the poem his full attention at the time. The music is essentially conventional, in the form ABA–codetta, and florid in an Italianate way. The smooth vocal line, with generous use of the expressive appoggiatura, is given emotional impetus by the piano figurations. In the central section particularly, the busy piano writing causes the staves to blacken as the 'vivid light'nings' draw near. The picturesqueness of the accompaniment here and in the descending scales and diminished sevenths which introduce the 'wayward flame' are sufficient evidence that Beethoven understood the words he was setting. The song is framed by a neatly rounded eight-bar introduction and the eight bars formed by the codetta and the short postlude. It would make an attractive exhibition piece and a curiosity for an English-speaking audience.

L'AMANTE IMPAZIENTE
The impatient lover (Arietta buffa)
Pietro Metastasio c.1809

E flat major Op. 82/3 Peters 25 Henle 48 GA XXIII/220

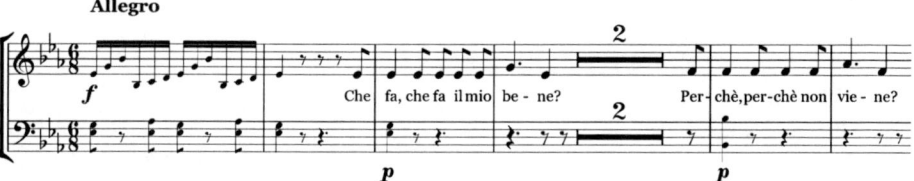

Che fa il mio bene?	What is my sweetheart doing?
Perchè non viene?	Why does she not come?
Veder mi vuole	Does she desire to see me
Languir così?	Languish thus?
Oh come è lento	Oh, how slow the sun is
Nel corso il sole!	In its course!
Ogni momento	Each moment
Mi sembra un di.	Seems like a day to me.

The text is taken from the second version of Metastasio's musical drama *Adriano in Siria*, although it stands happily alone as a general expression of a lover's impatience as he or she waits to see the beloved once again. Beethoven's text varies from Metastasio's, notably in the fifth line, where the original reads 'Oggi è pur lento'. This encourages one to wonder whether Beethoven borrowed the text from a setting by another composer, which was not an unusual practice at a time when popular texts were set by a multitude of minor lights who have since faded.

Beethoven set the text twice in two contrasting styles: this 'Arietta buffa', and the 'Arietta assai seriosa' which follows. There are no surviving manuscript sources for the present version. Both versions were published in Leipzig in July 1811 by Breitkopf und Härtel as the third and fourth songs of op. 82. This version included a two-stanza German translation by Christian Schreiber, under the title 'Stille Frage' (Silent question), which, as well as being metrically unsound, utterly undermines the lightness of Beethoven's *buffo* style. Clementi had already published the song in London as a 'Comic Arietta' in February 1811, offering only the Italian text.

In setting the same text in two contrasting manners, Beethoven is not only demonstrating his mastery of Italian song style, but displaying a slightly ironical stance vis-à-vis rather stylised texts, which by this time were already becoming rather hackneyed. This self-proclaimed comic arietta would not be out of place in a light opera and is a fine piece of dramatic caricature. The impatience takes on a rather manic form, characterised by the galloping semiquavers of the first introductory bar. The self-pitying tone of 'così', first heard three times on a mock-pathetic falling figure, the frequent interpolation of 'sì'and 'ah', the sharply contrasted dynamics and the ironical commentary of the perky accompaniment (see especially bars 44–50, where the piano dances as the singer laments), all contribute to the humorous effect of this song. Beethoven, to borrow W. S. Gilbert's phrase, 'just bubbles with wit and good humour'.

L'AMANTE IMPAZIENTE
The impatient lover (Arietta assai seriosa)
Pietro Metastasio   c.1809
B flat major Op. 82/4 Peters 26 Henle 49 GA XXIII/220

Andante con espressione

See previous entry for text and translation.

This second setting of Metastasio's text was published in Leipzig by Breitkopf und Härtel in July 1811 as the fourth song of op. 82 and included a German text by Christian Schreiber, under the title 'Liebes-Ungeduld' (Love's impatience). As with the other songs of op. 82, Schreiber's translation did scant justice to the metre, tone or content of the original text. Whereas Metastasio expresses his lover's impatience with great economy, Schreiber offers a three-stanza concoction which strains painfully for expression. Above all, the translation is a completely different poem from that used for the first version of L'amante impaziente, whereas the point of the exercise was to hear how different musical styles work with identical words!

Clementi had published the song in London in February 1811 as a 'Serious Arietta', with the slightly corrupt title 'L'amante impazienta', printing the Italian text only. His earlier publication was due to the fact that he kept to an agreed deadline for parallel publication, whereas Härtel's edition was delayed by haggling with Beethoven over the fee for the work. Essentially, the publisher tried to persuade the composer to accept a lower fee per song because of the simultaneous English publication.

The autograph in Bonn (BH: BMh4) was clearly the source for Härtel's engravers, displaying a page-break mark. The date '1809' helps to date the whole of op. 82. Otherwise the most interesting aspect is the indecision over the designation of the Arietta, which shows that 'seria', 'poco seriosa' and 'un poco più seriosa' were considered, before 'assai seriosa' (very serious) emerged triumphant.

Judging by the relative success of Beethoven's two settings, the text lends itself better to a comic approach. After the exuberant first *buffo* setting, the composer here seems to be trying hard to make his setting sound serious, and the slower sections need sensitive treatment if they are not to become ponderous. Although the key is B flat major, the song ranges harmonically in its search for passionate expression, with an attractive interlude in E flat major (at bar 15) and predominantly minor modes in the final reprise, to underline the melancholy of the drooping vocal phrases. There are two faster interludes, in which the lover complains that the sun is moving too slowly, but each time the voice, after a pause, falls back into the deliberate tone of self-indulgent sorrow and resignation.

LANGUISCO E MORO
I languish and die
unknown   1802–3
A minor Hess 229 Supp V/10 Not in GA/Peters/Henle

Adagio

Languisco e moro	I languish and die
Per te mio ben ch' adoro,	For you my love whom I adore
Languisco e moro.	I languish and die.

Richard Kramer in his 'Notes to Beethoven's Education' (*Journal of the American Musicological Society*, 28, 1975) identifies Johann Mattheson (1681–1764) as the source of the text and music. Beethoven simply copied the song into his sketchbook from Mattheson's *Der vollkommene Capellmeister* of 1739 and then attempted a canonic version himself (see Hess2, p. 122, where however Mattheson seems to be confused with the poet Friedrich Matthisson). The sketches in Moscow (CMMC: Wielhorsky, pp. 88–9), comprise this text set as a canon for two voices and the present sketch for a solo setting.

The solo version is notated on two staves. The introduction is in the treble clef, but this changes to soprano clef when the voice enters. The piano accompaniment is indicated by a single bass line; the use of the tenor clef in two bars of the accompaniment is due to space restrictions. The solo song has been realised by Willy Hess, with the insertion of missing rests and harmonic fleshing out, and was published in this form in 1980 (Supp V/10).

The Wielhorsky sketchbook has been published in facsimile and transcription, edited by Natan Fishman (Moscow 1962).

LEBENSGLÜCK (DAS GLÜCK DER FREUNDSCHAFT) A happy life
(The Joy of friendship)

unknown   1803

A major Op. 88 Peters 31* Henle 26 GA XXIII/222

Der lebt ein Leben wonniglich,	He lives a blissful life
Des Herz ein Herz gewinnt!	Whose heart wins another's heart.
Geteilte Lust verdoppelt sich,	Shared joy is doubled joy,
Geteilter Gram zerrinnt.	Shared sadness fades away.

Der lebt ein Leben wonniglich,
Des Herz ein Herz gewinnt!
Geteilte Lust verdoppelt sich,
Geteilter Gram zerrinnt.

Beblümte Wege wandelt ab,
Wem trauliches Geleit,
Den Arm die goldne Freundschaft gab
In dieser ehrnen Zeit.

Sie weckt die Kraft und spornt den Mut
Zu schönen Taten nur
Und nährt in uns die heil'ge Glut
Für Wahrheit und Natur.

Erflogen hat des Glückes Ziel,
Wer sich ein Mädchen fand,
Mit dem der Liebe Zartgefühl
Ihn inniglich verband.

Entzückt von ihr, mit ihr gesellt,
Verschönert sich die Bahn,
Mit ihr, durch sie blüht ihm die Welt,
Und alles lacht ihn an.

He lives a blissful life
Whose heart wins another's heart.
Shared joy is doubled joy,
Shared sadness fades away.

He wanders along flowery paths
To whom golden friendship has offered
its arm as a warm-hearted escort
In this cold age of bronze.

Friendship rouses our strength and spurs
Us on to beautiful deeds alone
And nourishes within us a holy passion
For truth and nature.

He has truly attained happiness
Who has found himself a girl
To whom he is intimately bound
By tender feelings of love.

Delighted by her, joined by her,
His path through life is beautified.
With her, through her the world blossoms
And everything smiles at him.

The author and source of the poem are unknown (the attribution to Tiedge in a later edition from Schott is incorrect). The first edition, published by Löschenkohl in Vienna in October 1803, has several differences in the text, suggesting that the publisher had access to another version of the poem. Ferdinand Ries wrote to Simrock on 22 October 1803, pointing out that Löschenkohl had changed the text and forwarding a copy of the correct text which Beethoven had given him. Simrock's edition, which appeared in Bonn the following month, duly reinstated the correct text, although the changed title 'Das Glück der Freundschaft' was retained. (The Peters edition uses the latter title) The third edition, published by Hoffmeister und Kühnel in Leipzig at the end of 1803, carried the correct title 'Lebensglück', and also included an Italian translation, entitled 'Vita felice'.

The Eroica sketchbook of 1803 (BJ: Landsberg 6) contains a complete melody sketch, which corresponds closely to the published version and is almost fully texted. It lacks an appropriate ending, but the postlude is already outlined.

The song was advertised by Löschenkohl in the *Wiener Zeitung* of 8 October 1803, offering it on special sunflower paper, together with songs by Wanhal and Vogler, as an appropriate keepsake for a young lady on St Theresa's Day (15 October). No copy exists, however, with the advertised title: 'Das Glück der Freundschaft am Theresientage'.

The first two verses, each setting two poetic stanzas, flow along smoothly, enabled by a constant and gentle flow of semiquavers in the accompaniment. Having set two poetic stanzas to a musical verse, Beethoven now has one stanza left over. His solution is to repeat the second (E major) section of his verse for the fifth stanza. Here, at 'Entzückt von ihr' the accompaniment springs to life in triplets to express delight and anticipate the world's laughing with the poet. This justifies Henri de Curzon's evocative description of the song (*Les Lieder*, p. 25) as 'un gazouillis gracieux' (a delicate warbling).

With no words left, however, Beethoven decides to continue the musical setting for a further twenty-three bars, and these bars, which return to the words of the first stanza, change the character of the song beyond redemption. A vocal cadenza marking the return to the first stanza and promising a musical recapitulation, gives the whole song an Italianate feel. This is strengthened by three bars of semiquavers in the voice, where passing notes occur on every beat, suggesting operatic aria. The coda, with dramatic contrasts of dynamic and tempo, is just too much for the song to bear, and even the composer's light touch in the postlude cannot restore balance. The song is neither German *Lied* nor Italian aria, but it has now approached more nearly to the latter. It is unsurprising then that, unlike the Italian translation which Hoffmeister had commissioned for *Adelaide*, this one (entitled *Vita felice* and printed in all editions except Henle) has gained a foothold among singers. It is the version chosen by Dietrich Fischer-Dieskau, for example, for Deutsche Grammophon.

It must be mentioned in all fairness that this negative view of the coda is not universal. Barry Cooper feels that this is the point where the music takes off and adds considerably to the musical interest of the whole, as indeed happens in the Piano Sonata op. 90 (see below). I suspect that the necessity of our differing on this point (a rare instance) arises because we are approaching the work from differing standpoints. Word-setting is rather like translation: the translator struggles with the competing demands of preserving the literal meaning of the original text and observing the stylistic etiquette of his or her own language; the song composer must balance respect for the formal and emotional aspects of a chosen text with the need to produce a neatly structured and musically satisfying whole. To what extent meaning may be reasonably sacrificed to the demands of style, or poetry to pure music, will always be a matter for debate.

The opening vocal line, with its gently oscillating accompaniment, looks forward to the second movement of the Piano Sonata op. 90 of 1814, in the related key of E major, which is interestingly marked 'sehr singbar vorgetragen' (to be performed very singably). Harry Goldschmidt, in his dogged search for meaningful correspondences within Beethoven's music, also points to a close similarity of line and movement in a brief passage (bars 8–13) in the first movement of the Cello Sonata op. 102/2 (*Um die unsterbliche Geliebte*, Leipzig 1977, p. 277).

LIED AUS DER FERNE Song from far away
Christian Ludwig Reissig   1809
B flat major (WoO138) Supp V/12 Henle 37b Not in GA/Peters

Etwas lebhaft, jedoch in einer mäßig geschwinden Bewegung

Als mir noch die Trä - ne der Sehn - sucht nicht floß__ und nei - disch die Fer - ne

Als mir noch die Träne	Before my tears of longing
Der Sehnsucht nicht floss	Had started to flow
Und neidisch die Ferne	And distance had enviously
Nicht Liebchen verschloss,	Locked away my sweetheart,
Wie glich da mein Leben	How my life then resembled
Dem blühenden Kranz,	A garland of flowers,
Dem Nachtigallwäldchen	A nightingale copse
Voll Spiel und voll Tanz! usw.	Filled with games and dancing! etc.

See *Gesang aus der Ferne* for remainder of text and translation.

The music to the song *Der Jüngling in der Fremde* was originally intended for the poem 'Lied aus der Ferne'. In the autograph in Washington (Library of Congress: Whittall Foundation), the first stanza (as above) is written out under the voice part, with space left blank for the remaining three stanzas. Beethoven or his publisher later decided to use the music for the poem 'Der Jüngling in der Fremde', probably after completing a new setting of the poem 'Lied aus der Ferne' (see *Gesang aus der Ferne*).

Willy Hess prints the words and music as originally conceived in volume V of his supplementary volumes. The Henle edition prints just the melody of *Der Jüngling in der Fremde* with the words to 'Lied aus der Ferne' to illustrate Beethoven's first thoughts. The familiar setting of the text is entitled 'Gesang aus der Ferne' in Henle, which honours Beethoven's title in the manuscript to WoO137 and serves to differentiate appropriately between the two settings, 'Gesang' suggesting a rather more ambitious and extended vocal composition than 'Lied'.

All other editions, following GA, ignore the present combination of words and music, and use the title 'Lied aus der Ferne' for WoO137.

MAIGESANG May song
Johann Wolfgang von Goethe   c.1795
E flat major Op. 52/4 Peters 12 Henle 7 GA XXIII/218

Wie herrlich leuchtet	How gloriously
Mir die Natur!	Nature shines out to me!
Wie glänzt die Sonne!	How the sun beams!
Wie lacht die Flur!	How the meadows laugh!

Es dringen Blüten	Buds burst forth
Aus jedem Zweig	From every twig
Und tausend Stimmen	And a thousand voices
Aus dem Gesträuch	From the bushes,

Und Freud und Wonne	And joy and bliss
Aus jeder Brust.	From every heart.
O Erd, o Sonne,	O earth, O sun,
O Glück, o Lust,	O happiness, O delight,

O Lieb, o Liebe,	O love, O love,
So goldenschön,	So golden fair,
Wie Morgenwolken	Like morning clouds
Auf jenen Höhn,	Upon those mountains!

Du segnest herrlich	You shed your glorious
Das frische Feld,	Blessing on the fresh fields,
Im Blütendampfe	On the luxuriant world
Die volle Welt!	In a haze of blossoms.

O Mädchen, Mädchen,	O maiden, O maiden,
Wie lieb ich dich!	How I love you!
Wie blickt dein Auge!	How your eye darts!
Wie liebst du mich!	How you love me!

So liebt die Lerche	As the lark loves
Gesang und Luft,	Song and air
Und Morgenblumen	And as morning flowers
Den Himmelsduft,	Love the scent of heaven,

| Wie ich dich liebe | Just so do I love you |
| Mit warmem Blut, | With a throbbing heart; |

Die du mir Jugend	You who give me youth
Und Freud und Mut	And joy and strength

Zu neuen Liedern	For new songs
Und Tänzen gibst.	And dances.
Sei ewig glücklich,	Be happy for ever,
Wie du mich liebst!	As long as you love me!

Goethe's poem was first published, as 'Maifest', in 1775 in Jacobi's journal *Iris*, and subsequently in Goethe's works (*Schriften*) in 1789, with the title 'Maylied'. It seems to have been Beethoven, whether intentionally or through an oversight, who entitled his setting 'May-Gesang' upon its publication within op. 52 in June 1805 by the Kunst und Industrie Comptoir in Vienna. No autograph survives, and a copy from Goethe's personal library in the Goethe–Schiller Archive in Weimar is based on a published edition, although it does indicate that Goethe both knew and approved of Beethoven's setting. The composer adapted and orchestrated the song for inclusion in Ignaz Umlauf's *Singspiel Die schöne Schusterin*, with new words, beginning 'O welch ein Leben' (What a wonderful life) (WoO91/1). The Baron sings in a mood of romantic euphoria, nature mirroring his mood as in the present song. The *Singspiel* had been revived in Vienna in April 1795, although it is not clear how soon Beethoven's aria was included. It seems probable that *Maigesang* was composed only shortly before the *Singspiel* arrangement.

Goethe's poem was written in May 1771, when the impulsive 21-year-old poet was madly in love with Friederike Brion, a parson's daughter from the village of Sesenheim near Strasbourg. This is not poetry based on the recollection of emotion in tranquillity, as recommended by Wordsworth in his 1800 Preface to the *Lyrical Ballads*; rather, one has the impression of raw emotion pouring forth in the heat of the moment. Many a poet has associated May with love, but few have succeeded so gloriously in fusing love and Nature completely, nor in expressing their emotions with such a total lack of inhibition. It is hardly surprising after this flood of inspiration that Goethe associates being in love with his newfound creativity ('new songs and dances'). It was the young Goethe's achievement to breathe new life into German poetry, in the process enriching the German language itself. The breathless enthusiasm of his short lines, on the one hand interrupted by ecstatic exclamations, on the other running on in an unbroken flow from stanza to stanza, is matched by the energy of his diction; the buds burst ('dringen') from the twigs, the world is luxuriant, saturated ('die volle Welt') with a 'haze of blossom' ('Blütendampfe' is a typically bold coinage).

Beethoven responds to all this with music which is as onrushing as the poem. A neatly rounded fourteen-bar piano introduction prefigures the vocal line, with busy quavers in both hands. The vocal melody encompasses three short stanzas in each section, and these are punctuated by excited interludes with a running quaver bass line accompanied by bouncing semiquaver couplets, which echo in musical form the exclamation marks of the poem. These swift semiquaver couplets in falling thirds hint at birdsong, recalling the 'thousand voices' in the bushes and anticipating the song of the lark in the final section of the poem, although the musical figure is actually more suggestive of a manic cuckoo. They also prefigure the 'Pastoral' Symphony, where they will form part of the woodwind birdsong chorus in the second movement of that work, along with the song of the nightingale and the quail (see *Der Wachtelschlag*).

A short, but exaltant postlude brings the piece to a strong close. This is the first song by Beethoven where the composer does not make the piano's right hand adhere closely to the vocal melody. He seems, like the Schubert of *Gretchen am Spinnrade*, to have found inspiration and a new confidence in response to his first encounter with the greatest of German poets. Indeed, the composer too has found 'joy and strength for new songs and dances'. We must be doubly grateful to the simple parson's daughter from Sesenheim.

MAN STREBT, DIE FLAMME ZU VERHEHLEN
One strives to conceal the flame
unknown   c.1800
F major WoO120 Not in Peters Henle 82 GA XXV/278

Man strebt, die Flamme zu verhehlen,	One strives to conceal the flame
Die bei gefühlvoll edlen Seelen	That steals unnoticed into the hearts
Sich unbemerkt ins Herze stiehlt;	Of those with sensitive noble souls.
Geheimnisvoll schliesst man die Lippen,	One seals one's lips in secrecy,
Jedoch verrät sich bald mit Blicken,	But soon glances betray, alas,
Wie sehr man, ach, die Liebe fühlt.	How much one feels the power of love.
Ein Blick sagt mehr als tausend Worte,	A glance says more than a thousand words.
Ein Blick entriegelt oft die Pforte	A glance often unbolts the door
Der lang verhehlten Leidenschaft.	Of a long concealed passion.
Er zeigt dem Teuren, den ich liebe,	It shows the dear man whom I love
Des Herzens reine, zarte Triebe	My heart's pure and tender impulses
Und gibt ihm auszuharren Kraft.	And gives him the strength to persevere.

The author of the poem is not known, but the quality of the verse, which flows smoothly and expresses with considerable sensitivity the impossibility of concealing the impulse of love, suggests that this is a practised poet. The verses are put in the mouth of a female speaker, as the final line makes clear. As the song was dedicated to an actress and playwright, Johanna Franul von Weissenthurn (1773–1847), one wonders whether the poem was written specifically for her, or whether she was in fact the author of these lines.

Although the autograph in Vienna (GdM: A8) bears at the top the clear dedication 'pour Madame weissenthurn par louis van Beethoven' (capitalisation was never the composer's strongest suit), it was apparently never delivered, and the song was not published in Beethoven's lifetime, nor yet within the longer lifespan of the dedicatee. It first appeared in the Supplementary Volume XXV of the GA in 1888, and, like other posthumously published songs, was not included in the Peters edition.

The song opens with a six-bar introduction, which prefigures in an embellished form the opening bars of the vocal melody. There is something in the Classical poise of the whole song which suggests that Beethoven remembers at all times that he is writing for a lady; passion is certainly not on the agenda in this song. The authentic spirit of Mozart is ever-present, particularly in those episodes where the piano plays alone. The opening phrase bears a marked similarity of outline to the opening of a later song *Als die Geliebte sich trennen wollte*, but the interest lies in the very different ways in which Beethoven employs a similar melodic phrase: in the present song, marked *Andante*, the mood is calm; in the later song, marked 'sehr bewegt', the mood is immediately 'very agitated'.

There are few dynamic indications in the song. It is almost certain that Beethoven would have added many more prior to publication, as was his consistent habit, although here their absence enhances the placid tone of the whole.

Eusebius Mandyczewski, its first editor, dated this song to Beethoven's early years in Vienna (1792–95). While modern paper studies (which compare the paper used for one autograph with identical paper used for works of known date) suggest a date of 1800–1, the earlier date seems stylistically and sentimentally correct. With a little imagination, the song can then be regarded as a homage to Mozart, who had died as recently as 1791, with the young Beethoven consciously picking up the master's fallen baton and paying his tribute to the Classical style, before moving on to bolder enterprises.

MARMOTTE Marmotte
Johann Wolfgang von Goethe c.1790–92
A minor Op. 52/7 Peters 15 Henle 10 GA XXIII/218

Allegretto

Ich komme schon durch manche Land', a-vec - que la mar-mot - te, und im - mer was zu es - sen fand,

Ich komme schon durch manche Land,	I have already travelled through many a land,
Avecque la marmotte,	With my marmot,
Und immer was zu essen fand,	And always found something to eat,
Avecque la marmotte,	With my marmot.
Avecque si, avecque la,	With o yes, with the,
Avecque la marmotte.	With the marmot.
Ich hab' gesehn gar manchen Herrn,	I've seen many a gentleman,
Avecque la marmotte,	With my marmot,

Der hätt' die Jungfern gar zu gern,	Who was far too fond of the girls,
Avecque la marmotte . . .	With my marmot . . .
Hab' auch gesehn die Jungfer schön,	I've also seen a beautiful girl,
Avecque la marmotte,	With my marmot,
Die täte nach mir Kleinem sehn,	Who had an eye for my small stature,
Avecque la marmotte . . .	With my marmot . . .
Nun lasst mich nicht so gehn, ihr Herrn,	Now don't let me leave empty-handed, sirs,
Avecque la marmotte,	With my marmot,
Die Burschen essen und trinken gern,	We fellows like to eat and drink,
Avecque la marmotte . . .	With my marmot . . .

Goethe's little song comes from his Carnival play *Das Jahrmarktsfest von Plundersweilern*, concerning a travelling fair. Max Friedländer (*Das deutsche Lied im 18. Jahrhundert* II, p. 546) suggests that both Beethoven and Andreas Romberg may have composed their settings of this text when the play came to Bonn around 1790–92, if indeed it did. At that time Beethoven and Romberg were both in the orchestra of the Prince Elector's theatre in Bonn – Romberg on violin and Beethoven, like so many composers, playing the viola. Friedländer concedes that the play is not included by Neefe in reviews of the Bonn theatre repertoire, but then these tended to refer only to operas. In the absence of an autograph, all this must remain conjecture. The song was first published in June 1805 (Vienna, Kunst und Industrie Comptoir) as part of op. 52, which consisted entirely of works from the last decade of the previous century.

Only one stanza was included in the first edition of the song, although it is clearly too short in that form. The Henle edition reinstates the missing stanzas, giving a much clearer context to the poem. The song, although attributed to a character called Marmotte, seems to be sung by a lad, or more likely an adult dwarf, who travels around with the fair. The English think of the monkey and the organ-grinder, and the dwarf with his marmot would almost certainly have provided his own musical accompaniment. In successive verses, he introduces himself, has a private joke about men's flirtations, suggests one particular conquest of his own, and finally passes the hat round for donations.

Beethoven simply and amusingly suggests either the droning of the hurdy-gurdy or (as Friedländer suggests) the bagpipes in the first eight bars, where the bass refuses to be drawn away from A to the E which the harmony would dictate. Thereafter, the composer does allow himself to depart from the drone, but the comic effect continues with *sforzando* accents, mid-bar, on the inconsequential words 'si' and 'la'. A perky four-bar postlude, with semiquaver leaps, completes this original variation on the established drone-bass form.

In its full, four-stanza version, the song would provide an apt encore to a *Lieder* recital. While the singer may not actually pass round the hat, the humour would allow the audience to wind down after the intense concentration which the full enjoyment of such an evening entails.

MERKENSTEIN Merkenstein (first setting)
Johann Baptist Rupprecht   Nov./Dec.1814
E flat major WoO144 Not in Peters Henle 58 GA XXV/276

Merkenstein, Merkenstein!
Wo ich wandle, denk' ich dein.
Wenn Aurora Felsen rötet,
Hell im Busch die Amsel flötet,
Weidend Herden sich zerstreun,
Denk' ich dein, Merkenstein!

Merkenstein, Merkenstein!
Bei der schwülen Mittagspein
Sehn' ich mich nach deinen Gängen,
Deinen Grotten, Felsenhängen,
Deiner Kühlung mich zu freun,
Merkenstein, Merkenstein!

Merkenstein, Merkenstein!
Dich erhellt mir Hespers Schein,
Duftend rings von Florens Kränzen,
Seh' ich die Gemächer glänzen,
Traulich blickt der Mond hinein,
Merkenstein, Merkenstein!

Merkenstein, Merkenstein!
Dir nur hüllt die Nacht mich ein.
Ewig möcht' ich wonnig träumen,
Unter deinen Schwesterbäumen
Deinen Frieden mir verleihn,
Merkenstein, Merkenstein!

Merkenstein, Merkenstein!
Weckend soll der Morgen sein.
Lass uns dort von Ritterhöhen
Nach der Vorzeit Bildern spähen:
Sie so gross und wir – so klein,
Merkenstein, Merkenstein!

Merkenstein, Merkenstein!
Höchster Anmut Lustverein!

Merkenstein, Merkenstein!
Wherever I wander, I think of you.
When dawn's rays redden the rocks,
When the blackbird pipes in the bushes,
And flocks of sheep seek the best grazing,
I think of you, Merkenstein!

Merkenstein, Merkenstein!
In the oppressive sultry midday heat
I long for your sheltered walks,
Your grottos, your rocky slopes,
To enjoy the coolness you offer,
Merkenstein, Merkenstein!

Merkenstein, Merkenstein!
The evening star illuminates you for me.
Surrounded by Flora's sweet garlands,
I see the rooms gleaming.
The moon looks in like an old friend.
Merkenstein, Merkenstein!

Merkenstein, Merkenstein!
For your sake alone does night enfold me.
I wish I could enjoy these blissful dreams
For ever, and ever partake of your peace
Under your sister-trees,
Merkenstein, Merkenstein!

Merkenstein, Merkenstein!
May the morning wake me betimes.
Let us, from those heroic prominences,
Seek out images of times long past:
They so great and we – so small,
Merkenstein, Merkenstein!

Merkenstein, Merkenstein!
Where the greatest charm and joy unite!

Ewig jung ist in Ruinen	Nature has come to appear to me
Mir Natur in dir erschienen;	Eternally youthful amid your ruins.
Ihr, nur ihr mich stets zu weihn,	Dedicating myself to her and her alone,
Denk' ich dein, Merkenstein!	I think of you, Merkenstein!

Rupprecht, at the time a successful horticulturalist and freelance writer, clearly sent this poem to Beethoven, suggesting in flattering terms that he might like to set it to his 'heavenly' music. Although the poet's letter is lost, that much is clear from Beethoven's reply (EA506 / BB759): 'Mit größtem Vergnügen Mein verehrter R werde ich ihr gedicht in Töne bringen und ihnen nächstens auch selbst über-bringen – ob himmlisch dass weiss ich nicht, da ich ja nur yrdisch bin, doch will ich alles anwenden ihrem übertriebenem Vorurtheil in Ansehung meiner so gleich zu kommen als möglich' (I shall set your poem to music with the greatest of pleas-ure, my dear R, and deliver it in person very soon. Whether heavenly, I cannot say, as I am only earthly after all, but I intend to try my very hardest to live up to your excessively generous assessment of myself).

Rupprecht's poem is ostensibly about an ancient ruined castle near Baden, set on a hillside; but the castle, which was indeed famed for its outstanding views, is a pretext for a poem about the beauties of nature and the feelings they evoke in the poet. Successive stanzas concern birds and grazing animals, caverns and rocks, flowers, trees, fabulous views which recall times of yore, and the renewal of Nature itself. It is perhaps this celebration of natural beauty which particularly appealed to Beethoven, who not only made two settings of the text but later asked Rupprecht for a further six poems which he might set to music (EA553 / BB870), although these were not forthcoming. Beethoven's love of the countryside is well docu-mented, as in his celebrated letter to Therese Malfatti (EA258 / BB442): 'kein Mensch kann das land so lieben wie ich – geben doch Wälder Bäume Felsen den Widerhall, den der Mensch wünscht' (No one can love the country as I do – for forests trees rocks give back the echo which man delights to hear).

Sketches for both settings of the text survive in Krakow (BJ: Mendelssohn 6), which date the song to the end of 1814, although it seems to have been lost under a pile of papers (see EA553 / BB870) and was not delivered to Rupprecht until the following year. It was published at the end of 1815 as a music supplement to the almanach *Selam*, edited by Ignaz Castelli and printed in Vienna by Anton Strauss. It was marked for 'Singstimme / Cembalo', but, although 'cembalo' now means harpsichord, it was no doubt intended to designate a 'keyboard instrument' at a time when the new pianoforte had not quite superseded other varieties.

In this first setting Beethoven seems to be attempting to create a folksong-like tone, appropriate to the local patriotism and pastoralism of the sentiment. Unfortunately the first vocal statement, twice declaiming 'Merkenstein' is more reminiscent of a military reveille, particularly in the chosen key of E flat, used in the contemporary song *Des Kriegers Abschied* with its deliberate martial over-tones. The intended pastoral effect is better achieved in the repetition of 'Merkenstein' at the very end of the song, where an instrumental echo evokes horns or a shepherd's pipes. In the main body of the song, the undulating movement in 6/8 time recalls the metre of *Andenken* (WoO136). The verbal correspondence of

'Ich denke dein' – 'Denk' ich dein' seems to have engendered a more or less conscious similarity of response in Beethoven's mind.

MERKENSTEIN Merkenstein (second setting)
Johann Baptist Rupprecht

F major Op. 100 Peters 35 Henle 59 GA XXIII/226

Mäßig, jedoch nicht schleppend

For text and translation see first version (previous entry).

The German-speaking nations seem to have a love-affair with ruined castles, which seem to be found at the top of every significant rise throughout Germany and Austria and are the favoured destination for Sunday walks. A leisurely glass of beer at the 'Schenke', whilst enjoying glorious views, and one is ready to return again to the real world, physically and spiritually refreshed. Beethoven may not have found an inn at Merkenstein, but his love of countryside excursions still led him to respond to Rupprecht's idyll with two settings.

One of Beethoven's earliest sketches for these settings (BJ: Mendelssohn 6) shows the composer already considering a setting for vocal duet. Having composed the solo version (WoO144), he returned to the duet idea early in 1815, as texted sketches in a pocket sketchbook in Krakow (BJ: Mendelssohn 1) indicate. The duet version was published by Steiner in Vienna in September 1816 as Beethoven's op. 100. The title page included a description of the castle as a picturesque ruin in a romantic mountainous landscape, affording splendid views. Beethoven was amused when he thought that the song was to be published in the winter season and wrote to Steiner (EA 553 / BB870) in ironical vein: 'Ich höre, das lied auf Merkenstein erscheint zur Zeit des Schlittschuhlaufens, d.h. veni, vidi, vinci!!!' (I hear, the Merkenstein song is to appear in the ice-skating season, i.e.: veni, vidi, vinci!!!).

The poem, with its references to the sultry midday heat and sleeping under the trees to await sunrise, certainly reflects a summer scene, and this is captured better in this unpretentious second setting. The pastoral key of F major is apt, and the duet endearingly suggests shared pleasure in contemplation of the natural setting. Beethoven comes much closer to achieving the feel of genuine folksong in this setting, where the deliberate simplicity of the harmonic underlay sets the tone. The two matched voices move closely together, predominantly in thirds, and the printed vocal part, with a mass of paired semiquavers, looks almost like fluttering birds on the page. This simple homage to Germanic folksong anticipates Dvořák's *Moravian Duets* (although the pianist is kept busier in the Czech works) and like them could be effectively performed by a choir.

Beethoven clearly preferred this setting of the poem, as a letter to Rupprecht (EA553 / BB870) makes clear: 'Die andere ist zweistimmig und scheint mir besser gerathen zu sejn' (The other one is for two voices and seems to me to have turned out better).

MINNELIED Love song
Johann Heinrich Voss

c.1795

A major Bia 259 / SV294 sketch

Der Hold-se-li-gen son - der Wank sing ich fröh li-chen Min - ne-sang, denn die Rei - ne,

die ich mei - ne, winkt mir lieb - li-chen Ha - be-dank. Ha - be - dank.

Der Holdseligen	To my charming girl
Sonder Wank	Without wavering
Sing ich fröhlichen	I sing my cheerful
Minnesang;	Song of love;
Denn die Reine,	For the pure one,
Die ich meine,	Whom I adore,
Gibt mir lieblichen Habedank.	Will give me delightful thanks,
Ach! Bin inniglich	Alas, I am inwardly
Minnewund!	Wounded by love!
Gar zu minniglich	Her mouth thanks me
Dankt ihr Mund;	Just too lovingly;
Lacht so grusslich,	She laughs so welcomingly,
Und so kusslich,	And so kissworthily,
Dass mirs bebt in des Herzens Grund!	That my heart quakes to its depths!
Gleich der sonnigen	Like the sunny
Veilchenau,	Meadow of violets
Glänzt der wonnigen	The blissful blue of
Augen Blau;	Her eyes glistens;
Frisch und ründchen	Fresh and sweetly rounded
Ist ihr Mündchen,	Is her delicate mouth,
Wie die knospende Ros im Tau.	Like the budding rose in the dew.
Ihrer Wängelein	No heavenly cherub,
Lichtes Rot	As God is my witness,
Hat kein Engelein,	Has the lucid redness
So mir Gott!	Of her little cheeks!
Eia! Säss ich	Oh, could I but sit
Unablässig	Constantly
Bei der Preislichen bis zum Tod!	Beside my precious one until death!

The poem was first printed in the Göttingen *Musen-Almanach* for 1774. The title refers back to the Middle High German love poetry (Minnesang) upon which the poem is modelled. 'Minne' was the old term for 'courtly love' and was revived by the youthful poets of the Göttinger Hainbund in the 1770s. Voss is actually better known as editor of annual almanacs, the famed translator of Homer, and as the benevolently interventionist editor of Hölty's collected poetry. Voss knew that his strength did not lie in lyric poetry and explained this atypical outpouring in a letter to his friend Brückner in April 1773: 'I hope you will like my *Minnelied*. I am well aware that I shall actually never be a lyric poet, but this was a sudden idea, my enthusiasm having just been kindled by those truly delightful *Minnelieder* of Vogelweide and Lichtenstein . . . The unusual words are all *minnesingerisch*, except 'sonnigen', 'wonnigen' and 'ründlichen', which I decided to risk' (quoted in *Der Göttinger Hain*, ed. Alfred Kelletat, Stuttgart 1967, p. 339).

Beethoven's melody sketch, first transcribed by Nottebohm (*Zweite Beethoveniana*, p. 574) could easily be realised with basic harmonic support. The shapely melody flows easily in the bright key of A major. Beethoven's provision of an altered final bar for the final stanza simply confirms that he intended a strophic setting. A further brief sketch shows how the Beethoven considered the use of 2/4 time:

This second sketch is cancelled, the composer correctly preferring the pastoral lilt of the first version in 6/8. Beside the sketches Beethoven has written: 'Titel: leichte Lieder' (title: easy songs), suggesting that he envisaged a collection of such trifles.

The single autograph sheet in Vienna (GdM: A64) also contains an early sketch for *Bundeslied* (op. 122) and a sketch for part of the piano variations WoO 72, by which the sheet can be dated to 1795 or 1796. It was formerly in the possession of Johannes Brahms who always demonstrated an avid interest in the relicts of his musical predecessors. Brahms's own *Minnelied* ('Holder klingt der Vogelsang') sets a text by Hölty.

MINNESOLD VON BÜRGER, IN TÖNEN AN AMENDEN AUSBEZAHLT The wages of love by Bürger, paid out to Amenda in musical notes
Gottfried August Bürger   c.1798

Hess 139 lost

Wem der Minne Dienst gelinget,	Whosoever succeeds in love's service,
O wie hoch wird der belohnt!	How richly is he rewarded!
Keinen bessern Lohn erringet,	Not even he who serves a great emperor
Wer den grossen Kaiser front.	Will achieve a higher reward.
Denn, mit Szepter, Kron' und Gold,	For, despite sceptre, crown and gold,
Front er selbst um Minnesold. usw.	Even he does service for love's wages. etc.

Beethoven is known to have composed this text, but the song is lost. The autograph, bearing the title cum dedication given above, was sent to Dr Hermann Härtel in Leipzig by the son of the dedicatee Karl Amenda in 1852, and passed on to a Professor Lobe. Since then it has disappeared without trace. Sadly, its rediscovery after more than 150 years would be implausibly serendipitous.

Karl Amenda (1771–1836) was a young theology student who came to Vienna in 1798, where he worked as a reader for Prince Lobkowitz. He was also a violinist and it was in this role that he met Beethoven. They established an immediate rapport and, despite the brevity of Amenda's sojourn in Vienna (1798–99), he became a close friend and confidant to the composer. Amenda was one of the first to find out about the composer's increasing deafness. The humorous dedication of the song, in which the composer develops Bürger's metaphor of love's wages, is reflected in a letter which Beethoven wrote to Nikolaus Zmeskall von Domanovecz in 1798. The composer could seldom resist even the most obvious pun: 'der *Amenda* soll statt einer *Amende*, (die er zuw)eilen für sein schlechtes pausiren verdient, mir diesen . . . Guitarist besorgen' (*Amenda*, instead of making *amends*, which he sometimes deserves for his scant attention to rests, is to procure this . . . guitarist for me) (EA29 / BB39).

Bürger's poem develops the metaphor of love as a form of military service, requiring an oath of fealty to the beloved in exchange for rich rewards, over eight stanzas. It is fascinating to speculate whether Beethoven was drawn to through-composition for this long poem. Of his other Bürger settings, two are simple strophic affairs (*Mollys Abschied* and *Das Blümchen Wunderhold*), while the third is the highly developed 'Doppellied' *Seufzer eines Ungeliebten / Gegenliebe*. The lost song provides further evidence of Beethoven's interest in Bürger's poetry in the final years of the eighteenth century. It can be dated with confidence to 1798 or 1799, the period of Amenda's residence in Vienna.

MIT EINEM GEMALTEN BAND   With a decorated ribbon
Johann Wolfgang von Goethe   1810
F major Op. 83/3 Peters 30 Henle 53 GA XXIII/221

Leichtlich und mit Grazie vorgetragen

Klei - ne_ Blu- men, klei - ne Blät - ter streu - en mir mit leich- ter_ Hand_

p Leichtlich, nicht geschliffen   *sempre* **pp**

Kleine Blumen, kleine Blätter	The good, young gods of Spring
Streuen mir mit leichter Hand	Have playfully scattered for me
Gute junge Frühlingsgötter	Little flowers and petals
Tändelnd um ein luftig Band.	Around a delicate ribbon.
Zephir, nimm's auf deine Flügel,	Zephyr, take it up on your wings,
Schling's um meiner Liebsten Kleid;	Twine it around my beloved's dress;
Und so tritt sie vor den Spiegel	Then she will step in front of the mirror,
All in ihrer Munterkeit,	In all her carefree gaiety,

Sieht mit Rosen sich umgeben,	See herself girdled with roses,
Selbst wie eine Rose jung.	Fresh as a rose herself.
Einen Blick, geliebtes Leben,	Just one glance, beloved creature,
Und ich bin belohnt genung.	And I have sufficient reward.
Fühle, was dies Herz empfindet,	May you sense what I feel in my heart,
Reiche frei mir deine Hand,	Give me your hand freely,
Und das Band, das uns verbindet,	And may the ribbon which unites us
Sei kein schwaches Rosenband!	Be not just a fragile ribbon of roses!

Goethe's poem is an occasional poem (*Gelegenheitsgedicht*). The poet tells in his autobiography *Dichtung und Wahrheit* how he hit upon the idea of sending a gift to his beloved Friederike Brion during a time when they were briefly separated: 'Painted ribbons had just then become fashionable; I painted a few for her at once and sent them ahead with a little poem, since I had to stay away longer than anticipated this time.' One of the ribbons showed amoretti scattering roses, which were then all the rage. The rococo style of the gift is reflected in the anacreontic diction of the poem, with its mention of zephyrs, gods of spring, rose ribbons and playfulness ('tändelnd'). The very mention of 'little flowers and petals' suggest the decorative 'rocaille' after which the period is named.

The poem was written in 1771 and first printed in Jacobi's almanach *Iris* in 1775. When it was reprinted as part of a collected edition in 1789 (the version set by Beethoven), it was radically revised and effectively sanitised for public consumption. The original version had become embarrassing partly because the rococo had passed out of fashion and partly because the poem had been addressed too intimately to a particular ex-girlfriend. The eleventh line, for example, originally read 'Einen Kuss, geliebtes Leben' (Just one kiss, beloved creature) and a further suppressed stanza made it clear that more than a kiss was expected! The later version is in a way a monument to a bygone age, although given a glorious new lease of life in Beethoven's setting.

A sketch for the song survives in Krakau (BJ) at the very end of the Landsberg 11 sketchbook and can be dated with some certainty to November 1810. An autograph in Paris (BN: Ms. 21) contains corrected versions of the three songs of op. 83, although the final page, with the last seven bars, is missing. *Mit einem gemalten Band* was eventually published as the third of the three Goethe songs of op. 83 in October 1811 by Breitkopf and Härtel in Leipzig. The delays between the conception, completion and publication of these songs suggest that Beethoven was at pains to produce something worthy of Goethe in this opus devoted entirely to the celebrated poet.

Beethoven's intentions are made clear by his performance directions. The song is to begin quietly and performed 'lightly and gracefully'; a simultaneous direction to the pianist indicates that the racing triplets are to be played 'lightly and not in a polished legato' ('nicht geschliffen'). The airiness of the conception is achieved by the setting of quavers in the voice against triplets in the piano. This is never felt as in any way a dislocation, but rather enhances the keen sense of excitement. Quavers plus rests in the bass line further aid the onward rush of the music.

There is an elaborate vocal cadenza, which rises to top A, before the music scampers to a close as fleetingly as it had begun.

The first notes of the vocal line prefigure the opening notes of the 'Ode to Joy' from the Ninth Symphony. This is probably coincidence, although it is unlikely that Beethoven would have failed to notice the correspondence.

MOLLYS ABSCHIED Molly's farewell
Gottfried August Bürger   c.1795

G major Op. 52/5 Peters 13 Henle 8 GA XXIII/218

Lebe wohl, du Mann der Lust und Schmerzen!
Mann der Liebe, meines Lebens Stab!
Gott mit dir, Geliebter! Tief zu Herzen
Halle dir mein Segensruf hinab!

Zum Gedächtnis biet' ich dir statt Goldes -

Was ist Gold und goldeswerter Tand? -
Biet' ich lieber, was dein Auge Holdes,
Was dein Herz an Molly Liebes fand.

Nimm, du süsser Schmeichler, von den Locken,
Die du oft zerwühltest und verschobst,
Wann du über Flachs an Pallas Rocken,
Über Gold und Seide sie erhobst!

Vom Gesicht, der Wahlstatt deiner Küsse,
Nimm, so lang' ich ferne von dir bin,
Halb zum mindesten im Schattenrisse
Für die Phantasie die Abschrift hin!

Meiner Augen Denkmal sei dies blaue
Kränzchen flehender Vergissmeinnicht,
Oft beträufelt von der Wehmut Taue,
Der hervor durch sie vom Herzen bricht!

Diese Schleife, welche deinem Triebe
Oft des Busens Heiligtum verschloss,

Farewell, o man of pleasure and pain!
Man of love, my life's support!
God be with you, my beloved!
May my blessing echo deep into your heart!

As a remembrance I offer you instead of gold

(What is gold and gilded frippery worth?)
Everything which your eyes found fair
And your heart found dear in your Molly.

Take, sweet flatterer, some of my tresses
Which you so often tousled and displaced,
When you praised them high above the flax
On Pallas' distaff, above gold and silk!

For the time I am separated from you,
Take at least a silhouette of my face,
Where you loved to place your kisses,
To aid your imagination.

Let this little blue wreath of forget-me-nots,
Oft bedewed with tears of melancholy,
Bursting forth from my very heart,
Be a remembrance of my eyes.

This ribbon, which often revealed
The sanctity of my bosom to your passion,

Hegt die Kraft des Hauches meiner Liebe,	Cherishes the essence of my love's breath
Der hinein mit tausend Küssen floss.	Which flowed into it amid a thousand kisses.
Mann der Liebe! Mann der Lust und Schmerzen!	Man of love! Man of pleasure and pain!
Du, für den ich alles tat und litt,	You, for whom I did and endured everything.
Nimm von allem! Nimm von meinem Herzen -	Partake of everything! Take part of my heart, yet
Doch – du nimmst ja selbst das ganze mit!	You are of course taking my whole heart with you!

The date of composition of this song is unknown. Sketches for *Seufzer eines Ungeliebten – Gegenliebe*, also to a text by Bürger, have been dated to the end of 1794 or early 1795. As no direct evidence exists, a similar date must be the best guess for the composition of the present song. The song was first published in June 1805 in Vienna by the Kunst und Industrie Comptoir, as part of op. 52. The final two stanzas of the poem were not included.

The poem appeared in the Göttingen *Musenalmanach*, which Bürger was then editing, in 1788, and a year later in a collection of Bürger's poems. This was also published in Göttingen, the university town which had at the time an enviable reputation as a centre of youthful intellectual and poetic endeavour. The almanac version of the poem states that it was written in 1782. Bürger had married Dorette Leonhart in 1774, but fell almost at once for her sister Auguste, who is the 'Molly' of his poems, as well as the eponymous *Das Blümchen Wunderhold* (p. 85). Dorette died of consumption in 1784 and Bürger married Auguste, who had borne him a son the previous year. The poem is unusual in that Bürger's feelings are expressed through the mouthpiece of his girlfriend, who is made to give voice to her passion in physical terms which would certainly have seemed immodest at the time. The two final stanzas were omitted in the first publication, but are reinstated by Helga Lühning, editor of the Henle edition, who believes they were omitted simply through lack of space.

Beethoven's setting is simple and wistful. Beethoven, ever the innocent, fails to take notice of the passionate tone of the verse and would assuredly have been shocked to discover that Bürger's sister-in-law may have been carrying the poet's child when the poem was written. *Mollys Abschied* is a slight song, which could easily have been printed on two staves, as the vocal melody never departs from the top line of the accompaniment. In this respect it is wholly of the eighteenth century, rendering further support for an early date of composition. The reviewer of the Viennese *Allgemeiner Musikalischer Anzeiger*, writing in 1830, also reads the poem at a superficial level, praising Beethoven's setting as 'a simple, touching song in accord with the poetic sentiment'.

Users of the Henle edition should note a misprint at the beginning of bar 3 – B for A in the piano, left hand.

NÄHE DES GELIEBTEN The nearness of the beloved
Johann Wolfgang von Goethe

spring 1799 D major Bia 176 sketches

Ich denke dein, wenn mir der Sonne
  Schimmer
  Vom Meere strahlt,
Ich denke dein, wenn sich des Mondes
  Flimmer
  In Quellen malt.

Ich sehe dich, wenn auf dem fernen Wege
  Der Staub sich hebt;
In tiefer Nacht, wenn auf dem schmalen
  Stege
  Der Wandrer bebt.

Ich höre dich, wenn dort mit dumpfem
  Rauschen
  Die Welle steigt.
Im stillen Haine geh ich oft zu lauschen,
  Wenn alles schweigt.

Ich bin bei dir, du seist auch noch so ferne,
  Du bist mir nah!
Die Sonne sinkt, bald leuchten mir die
  Sterne.
  O wärst du da!

I think of you, when the sun's shimmering
  rays
  Are reflected on the sea,
I think of you when the moon's gleam

  Colours the springs.

I see you, when the dust rises
  On some distant track;
In the depth of night, when the wanderer
  shudders
  On some narrow bridge.

I hear you, in the dull roar

  Of the rising flood.
In the quiet grove I often go to listen
  When all is silent.

I am with you, however far away you may be,
  You are close to me!
The sun sinks, soon the stars will shine on
  me.
  If only you were here!

Goethe's poem first appeared in Schiller's *Musenalmanach* in 1796. It was inspired by Zelter's setting of a poem by Friederike Brun, itself derived from Matthisson's *Andenken* (p. 72), which opens with the same three-word formula. The process is well documented and gives an insight into Goethe's attitude to music. The poet wrote to Frau Unger on 13 June 1796 that he is no judge of music, lacking knowledge of compositional technique, but that music can affect him deeply at times. He goes on to explain how his first encounter with Zelter's song moved him instantly and led to the writing of this poem: 'Seine Melodie des Liedes: *Ich denke dein*, hatte einen unglaublichen Reiz für mich, und ich konnte nicht unterlassen selbst das Lied dazu zu dichten' (His melody to the song *Ich denke dein* [Brun's poem] had for me an incredible appeal, and I couldn't refrain from writing this poem myself to fit the music). Perhaps it is the poem's original musical inspiration which has made it so popular with composers. Max Friedländer (*Das deutsche Lied im 18. Jahrhundert* II, p. 200) refers to some 80 settings.

Beethoven made extended sketches for a setting of *Nähe des Geliebten* in the first half of 1799 (Berlin, DSB: Grasnick 2, pp. 37ff.). The neglect of these fascinating sketches can be explained only by the confusion generated by the fact that Beethoven used his third sketch for the first stanza as the theme for his piano duet variations, WoO74 (see *Ich denke dein*). This situation has been aggravated by both Schmidt (SV46) and Johnson (*The Beethoven Sketchbooks*, p. 87) in referring only to sketches for WoO74 in their listings of the contents of Grasnick 2, whereas Virneisel's facsimile edition and transcription (Bonn 1972–74) clearly shows a full five pages of sketches for a solo song. Nottebohm (*Zweite Beethoveniana*, p. 486) described the sketches accurately, but gave little impression of their full extent and importance.

It is clear from the sketches that Beethoven was aiming to produce a through-composed setting on a an ambitious scale, mirroring the words of each stanza through tonal analogue, and returning to a varied version of the opening music for the final stanza, prolonged by a climactic coda. The resulting song would have been 'Gesang' rather than 'Lied', and possibly akin to the celebrated 'cantata' *Adelaide*, composed a few years earlier.

Significantly, the first stanza is sketched only three times, and the third version of this stanza, which combines and refines ideas from the earlier two versions, is virtually identical with the theme of the piano duet variations (WoO74). Beethoven was clearly satisfied with this stanza. Each of the remaining three stanzas is sketched at least four times, with individual phrases set repeatedly. The third stanza is given particular attention, and adumbrated accompaniment figures show the composer seeking to illustrate the 'dull roar of the rising flood' with rapid semiquavers in a pattern of rise and fall. Starting and finishing in D major, the sketches are not shy to explore other tonal regions, from G major to C major (labelled as such in the autograph) and even C sharp major. Broken diminished seventh chords are used generously both for modulation and expression. That a coda was intended is clear from the fact that the phrase 'O wärst du da!' is set more than twenty times within four settings of the final stanza.

Beethoven clearly valued his sketches, as many sketchbooks were preserved through all the ups and downs (and house removals) of his life. Apart from the piano duet variations, he never returned to this song, but a sympathetic modern composer attuned to Beethoven's idiom and familiar with his working methods should have little difficulty in producing a convincing completion.

NAHE WARD DER TRENNUNG SCHLAG
The painful hour of separation drew close
unknown   1792–93

?E minor SV295 unfinished sketch

This fragmentary sketch is found on a single sheet in Vienna (GdM: A65), following the melody sketch for a high-pitched Minuet in F major. It is negligible at first sight, but the baroque effect of the opening bass line and the third-bar interlude is striking, as is the use of a fully palindromic musical phrase for the first vocal entries, to identical words ('usw' indicates 'etc.'). The short sketch is only erratically texted and above an adumbrated instrumental interlude Beethoven has written: 'zum Schluß fängt die Singstimme noch einmal an' (at the end the voice starts up again), typical of the 'memos to self' in which his autographs abound. Paper studies have dated the sketch leaf to the composer's earliest months in Vienna.

NEUE LIEBE, NEUES LEBEN
New love, new life (final version)
Johann Wolfgang von Goethe   1809
C major Op. 75/2 Peters 18 Henle 41 GA XXIII/219

Herz, mein Herz, was soll das geben?
Was bedränget dich so sehr?
Welch ein fremdes, neues Leben -
Ich erkenne dich nicht mehr.
Weg ist alles, was du liebtest,
Weg, warum du dich betrübtest,
Weg dein Fleiss und deine Ruh' -

Ach, wie kamst du nur dazu?

Fesselt dich die Jugendblüte,
Diese liebliche Gestalt,
Dieser Blick voll Treu' und Güte
Mit unendlicher Gewalt?
Will ich rasch mich ihr entziehen,
Mich ermannen, ihr entfliehen,
Führet mich im Augenblick
Ach! mein Weg zu ihr zurück.

Und an diesem Zauberfädchen,
Das sich nicht zerreissen lässt
Hält das liebe, lose Mädchen
Mich so wider Willen fest;
Muss in ihrem Zauberkreise

Heart, my heart, just what is happening?
What is oppressing you so greatly?
What a strange, new life!
I no longer recognise you.
Everything you loved is gone,
All that made you sad is gone,
Your diligence and your inner peace –
    all gone.
Oh, how did you reach this point?

Are you ensnared with ineffable force
By blossoming youth,
By this charming figure,
This gaze full of constancy and goodness?
If I seek to tear myself away from her swiftly,
To force myself to flee her charms,
In a moment, alas, my path
Leads me straight back to her.

And by this little magic thread
Which cannot be broken
The dear coquettish girl
Holds me thus against my will;
I must now live after her fashion

Leben nun auf ihre Weise.	In her enchanted circle.
Die Veränderung, ach, wie gross!	How enormous, alas, is the change!
Liebe! Liebe, lass mich los!	Love! Love, let go of me!

Goethe's poem first appeared, with *Mailied* (Beethoven's *Maigesang*), in Jacobi's *Iris* in 1775. It is tempting to imagine that Beethoven found them both while leafing through this attractive, pocket-sized volume rather than in a later edition of Goethe's writings. The two poems have little in common. *Mailied* was an outpouring of innocent joy; all Nature seemed to reflect the poet's undiluted happiness in his love for the guileless Friederike Brion who inspired him to new creative achievements. In *Neue Liebe, neues Leben* Goethe's 'diligence and inner peace' have been disrupted by his love for Elisabeth (Lili) Schönemann, the 17-year-old daughter of a Frankfurt merchant. The simple pastor's daughter has been usurped in his heart by a young society beauty. Her attraction is irresistible, like a magic spell; the poet is confused.

The poem has tremendous vitality. The poet addresses his oppressed heart with urgent questions and complaints. The thrice-repeated 'weg' (gone!) stresses what he has lost because of his changed feelings. The exclamation 'ach!' is similarly heard three times. Exactly half-way through the poem, Goethe begins to address himself directly – he can no longer deny his own heart. The final appeal is to Love itself.

The poem had an immediate appeal to composers. Zelter's setting is of particular interest, as he achieves vitality by using a syncopated accompaniment, identical in kind with that of Beethoven's *Ein Selbstgespräch*, also in E major, in which the poet Gleim is agitated as he too has fallen in love despite himself. Zelter's setting actually postdates Beethoven's. In a letter to Goethe of 25 April 1812, Zelter explains to Goethe that he has finally got round to composing settings of *Rastlose Liebe*, *Mailied* and *Neue Liebe, neues Leben*, adding a wry comment which may refer obliquely to Beethoven's settings of the two latter poems: 'Sadly I am very late, as always, in getting on with beautiful things, since other composers have already given them a proper mauling ('sich krumm und dumm daran komponiert haben'). If you don't like the songs, I don't feel any better about them myself. But where am I to find restless love, new love, new life, at my age?' (Zelter was then 54).

Beethoven's familiar setting of Goethe's poem was published in October 1810 by Breitkopf und Härtel in Leipzig as the second song of op. 75, dedicated to Princess Kinsky. This publication was synchronised with the English edition of the song, published by Clementi in London, registered in August 1810. The English translation, beginning 'Say fond heart, what pains torment thee' and ending 'Prithee, prithee, let me go', lacks Goethe's vitality and required some adjustment of the melodic line. The original autograph is in Bonn (BH: Bodmer Mh34) and has been dated '1809' by the composer.

Beethoven, aside from an expressive 'ja', hardly ever changed the actual words of a poem, but *Neue Liebe, neues Leben* is a prime example of the almost cavalier manner in which he often repeats words, phrases and entire stanzas to fit with his musical mould. The setting matches the mood of the text well – but is it still Goethe's poem, or has the song, whose structure is hugely more extended than the poem's, simply devoured the text? This is not a mere quibble, but points to a forward-looking aspect of Beethoven's song technique, for Romantic and post-Romantic composers were to impose their personal interpretation and style on texts to a degree unimaginable in the eighteenth century. It has certainly not affected the popularity of this fine song.

Beethoven succeeds triumphantly in combining an exciting musical pulse with slower reflective moments, written as recitative, without affecting the overall unity of the setting. It was a technique which Schubert acquired in his maturity; the racing pulse here reminds us of *Willkommen und Abschied* (D767), but the seamless integration of recitative within an unvarying pulse is reminiscent of a song such as *Am Feierabend* (D795/5).

There is subtlety in Beethoven's dynamic and expressive markings. The song opens quietly, with *sforzando* accents suggesting the poet's unease. The loud complaint as the poet laments his inability to work ('Weg dein Fleiss') is followed immediately by a subdued phrase for the loss of his inner peace ('und deine Ruh'). A short interlude slows the mood towards the recitative, and as the movement is taken up again, the marking is dolce as the poet recalls Lili's charms, before a delicate, sighing phrase on 'dieser Blick' leads into a long *crescendo* as he recalls the force by which he is enslaved. The alternation of quiet and loud moments continues throughout the song and is suggestive of the poet's wracked emotions.

The repetition of the entire first two stanzas gives plenty of scope for exploiting the possibilities of recurring melodic patterns. It would be overstating the case to talk of *leitmotiv*, but the reuse of the sighing phrase (bars 29–32, 85–8) on 'dieser Blick' to set 'zu ihr zurück' (bars 46–9, 104–7) cleverly suggests the link between the girl's physical attractiveness and the poet's enslavement. The third stanza opens to a constantly moving quaver accompaniment, and aural images of a spinning wheel or a merry-go-round are appropriate to the 'magic thread' and the 'enchanted circle'. Although the song ends with an outburst, the frequent repetition of 'lass' suggests despair rather than defiance. The song ends as it began, quietly.

Following the composer's markings in this song, rather than rattling it off, will always yield results. Above all, it must not be taken too fast; the marking is 'lively, but not too lively'.

NEUE LIEBE, NEUES LEBEN
New love, new life (first version)
Johann Wolfgang von Goethe   1798–99

C major WoO127 Supp V/8 Henle 18 Not in GA/Peters

See final version (previous entry) for text and translation.

This early setting of Goethe's poem was published by Simrock in Bonn in 1808, together with *Der freie Mann* and *Opferlied*. There is a full melody sketch for the present version on a double sheet which has now been divided, half owned by the Schott publishers' archive and half in private ownership. Sketches in Berlin (DSB: Grasnick 1), dated to the end of 1798, show the composer trying out various endings for the song.

Although this setting has the distinction of being the first published, it has very much the status of an ugly sister whose place was swiftly usurped by the much improved revision, published as op. 75/2. Indeed, during the nineteenth century this first version was virtually forgotten, or simply assumed (as in Nottebohm's catalogue of 1868) to be identical with the op. 75 setting. Crucially it was not included in the *Gesamtausgabe*, which became the basis for other 'complete' song editions. In 1930 Otto Erich Deutsch drew attention to it in an article entitled 'A Forgotten Goethe Song by Beethoven' ('Ein vergessenes Goethelied von Beethoven', in *Die Musik* XXIII, 1930), but it was not reprinted until Willy Hess included it in his *Supplemente*, vol. V, in 1962.

The setting has the same essential outline as the familiar version, but gives the impression of a first draft. It is virtually certain that Beethoven did not authorise its publication in 1808. The most striking evidence for this is the total lack of dynamic markings, such a significant feature of the later version; Beethoven would certainly have added these for publication, had he been given the chance. It was probably the unsanctioned publication of this early draft which encouraged him to return to the song for the numerous revisions which produced op. 75/2, and studying the two versions allows us to see the process of revision from draft to finished article with rare clarity. Melodic modifications always improve the shape of the phrase in the later version. The second recitative is absent here, as is the parenthetical repetition of the first line to introduce the recapitulation of the first two stanzas. Perhaps the only feature whose omission from the later version is regrettable is the running semiquaver phrase in the piano's right hand at 'mich ermannen, ihr entfliehen' which gives a delightful image of attempted flight.

O CARE SELVE O beloved woods
Pietro Metastasio   1794–95

G major WoO119 Not in Peters Henle 78 GA XXV/279

Coro:
O care selve, o cara
Felice libertà!

Una voce / Argene (solo):
Qui, se un piacer si gode,

Chorus:
O beloved woods, o beloved
And happy liberty!

Argene (Solo voice):
Here, if pleasure is enjoyed,

Parte non v'ha la frode,	Deceit has no part of it,
Ma lo conduce a gara	But love and constancy
Amore e fedeltà.	Lead it in friendly rivalry.
Qui poco ognun possiede,	Here everyone owns but little,
E ricco ognun si crede;	And yet all think thimselves rich;
Né, più bramando, impara	Nor, ever more covetous, do they learn
Che cosa è povertà!	The meaning of poverty.
Senza custodi o mura,	Without guardians or walls,
La pace è qui sicura,	Here peace reigns secure,
Che l'altrui voglia avara	Since avaricious desire of others
Onde allettar non ha.	Fails to entice it hence.

The poem is from the first act of Metastasio's *L'Olimpiade*, a 'dramma per musica', where it is performed by the Princess Argene and a chorus of shepherdesses. The drama was originally written in 1733, but this was one of many poems by the prolific librettist and dramatist which had become familiar outside its original context by the end of the eighteenth century.

The full autograph in the Kafka Album in London (BL: Add.Ms. 29801) is on the reverse of the autograph to *Der freie Mann* and is reproduced by Kerman (*An Autograph Miscellany*). The text and directions are added, strikingly, in red ink and in Roman script. An autograph fragment in Vienna (GdM: A75/9) appears to be based on the London manuscript and can be dated to 1794–95, the period when Beethoven was engaged in a thorough study of counterpoint with Albrechtsberger. The Viennese fragment is designated as 'No. 10' and was at one time intended as the final item in op. 52, with *Der freie Mann* as the other extra item; in the event, only eight songs were included in the opus. *O care selve* had to wait for publication until 1888, when it was printed in the Supplementary Volume XXV of the old complete edition.

The song is of modest scope. The original pastoral context of the poem is reflected in the 6/8 time signature, the dolce marking, and the naive simplicity of the vocal line, with a unison 'chorus', favouring small intervals and never straying outside the compass of an octave. A neatly rounded postlude completes this miniature essay in the Italian style. Although only one stanza is texted, Beethoven no doubt expected the other stanzas to be performed, and the whole piece ends with a clearly marked repeat of the refrain.

O HOFFNUNG O Hope
Christoph August Tiedge
spring 1818
G major WoO200 Not in Peters Henle GA

O Hoffnung, du stählst die Herzen,   O Hope, you strengthen our hearts,
Du milderst die Schmerzen.   You soften our pain.

This modest theme of four bars is included here for the sake of completeness. Beethoven wrote it as an exercise for his aristocratic composition pupil Archduke Rudolph, as the theme for variations. The young Archduke certainly did his homework on this occasion, and his set of forty variations was published by Steiner in December 1819. The title of the publication gave Beethoven generous credit for his modest contribution to the whole: 'Exercise, composed by Ludwig van Beethoven, with forty variations, dedicated to the composer by his pupil A.D.R.'.

For the words, Beethoven returned to Tiedge's *Urania* (see *An die Hoffnung*). As the composer's sketches, both musical and written, frequently indicate, he was fond of preserving pithy quotations such as this couplet, when he could relate them to his own situation or outlook. He certainly regarded Hope as an essential human ideal and indeed duty: consider the boldly delineated declamation of 'Hoffen soll der Mensch!' in the second version of *An die Hoffnung*, op. 94, a song which ends as this fragment begins, with a prayer to Hope: 'O Hoffnung!'

ODI L'AURA CHE DOLCE SOSPIRA
Hear the breeze which sweetly sighs (duet)
Pietro Metastasio   1809
E major Op. 82/5 Peters 27 Henle 50 GA XXIII/220

Soprano (Venere):   *Soprano (Venere):*
Odi l'aura che dolce sospira;   Hear the breeze which sweetly sighs,
Mentre fugge scuotendo le fronde,   Stirring the branches as it flees away.
Se l'intendi, ti parla d'amor.   If you understand it, it speaks of love.

Tenor (Pallade):   *Tenor (Pallade):*
Senti l'onda che rauca s'aggira;   Hear the wave which billows noisily,
Mentre geme radendo le sponde,   Brushing the river banks as it groans.
Se l'intendi, si lagna d'amor.   If you understand it, it complains of love.

Duet (a due):   *Duet:*
Quell'affetto chi sente nel petto,   Whoever feels this fond emotion in his
                                          breast

Sa par prova se nuoce, se giova,   Knows from experience if it be harmful or
                                          beneficial,

Se diletto produce o dolor.   Whether it engenders delight or sorrow.

The text is taken from an 'azione teatrale' by Metastasio, entitled 'La pace fra la virtù e la bellezza', although it is unlikely that Beethoven knew the context and the characters are not named in the song. He was not a fluent reader of Italian, although he realised the importance of learning the language, as a diary entry from around 1813 testifies: 'immer im Italienischen übersetzen und bloß wegen Zweifel hie und da die Woche ein zweymal den Universitätslehrer der italienischen Sprache fragen' (Keep translating from Italian and just consult the Italian professor at the university a couple of times a week if occasional doubts occur). This diary entry, T12 in Maynard Solomon's 'Beethoven's Tagebuch of 1812–1818', is preceded (T11) by an actual attempt at translation from Italian. Solomon also reminds us that some Italian grammars and a German–Italian dictionary were found among Beethoven's effects. Despite the fact that a knowledge of Italian was *de rigueur* for Viennese composers at the time, Beethoven's renewed interest in the language may have been fuelled by his love for Therese Malfatti, who was of Italian ancestry.

The song was published in London by Clementi in February 1810 with the Italian text only. The continental edition was published by Breitkopf und Härtel in Leipzig in July 1810 with the title 'Duett. Lebens-Genuss' (Enjoyment of life) as the fifth and final song of op. 82, with Italian and German words. Once again, the translator Christian Schreiber produced a German text which bears little relation to the original poem and requires metrical adjustment. It is to be avoided. The five songs of op. 82 are rarely heard in performance, but have such an authentic aura and polished fluency that they must surely merit an honorary place among the masterpieces of Italian song. Both the sheer quality of the word setting and the use of meaningful tonal analogues make singing in Italian essential.

Apart from the bland setting of *Merkenstein* (op. 100), this is Beethoven's only vocal duet with piano. The duet form is given by the text, of course, but fully exploited by the composer. Even before the soprano enters, we hear the gently sighing breeze in the first bar, evoked by shimmering demisemiquavers high in the keyboard. The message of the breeze is stated in recitative, before shimmering notes in the lower range of the keyboard introduce the tenor, as he sings of the billowing wave. The keyboard figure is then split into couplets which alternate between the pianist's hands, before a recitative in minor mode speaks of the waves' complaining (notice how the couplet figure joins in with the recitative at bars 30–1).

The two singers are clearly thinking along similar lines and it is wholly appropriate that their voices should join in duet (bar 34) to make the general point of the last stanza. Their oneness is suggested by the exchanging of vocal lines in the repeat of the stanza, where a lower accompaniment transfers prominence to the tenor (bars 41f.). In a brief coda, there is a charming evocation of 'diletto' (bars 52f.), as first the two voices and then the piano rise stepwise through almost four octaves of a broken E major chord; then a shared melismatic languishing on 'dolor', before a pedalled falling and fading arpeggio allows the music to close as delicately as it began. It would be hard to imagine a more intimate or sensitive love duet.

OPFERLIED   Sacrificial hymn (final version)

Friedrich von Matthisson   late 1798

E major WoO126 Peters 42 Henle 17 GA XXIII/233

Langsam und Feierlich

Die Flamme lodert, milder Schein	The flame leaps up, a gentle glow
Durchglänzt den düstern Eichenhain,	Shines through the dark oak grove,
Und Weihrauchdüfte wallen.	And aromas of incense waft through the air.
O neig ein gnädig Ohr zu mir	O bend your gracious ear to me
Und lass des Jünglings Opfer dir,	And let the young man's sacrifice
Du Höchster, wohlgefallen!	Be well-pleasing to you, o highest one!
Sei stets der Freiheit Wehr und Schild!	Be ever freedom's shield and defence!
Dein Lebensgeist durchatme mild	May your life-giving spirit breathe gently
Luft, Erde, Feu'r und Fluten!	Through air, earth, fire and water!
Gib mir, als Jüngling und als Greis,	Grant to me, in youth as in age,
Am väterlichen Herd, o Zeus,	At your paternal hearth, O Zeus,
Das Schöne zu dem Guten!	Beauty allied to goodness!

Matthisson's poem was first published, along with *Adelaide*, in the *Musenalmanach* for 1790, edited by Johann Heinrich Voss. It is not known, however, whether Beethoven found Matthisson's two poems in the *Musenalmanach* or in the third volume of the poet's works, published in 1794. The first fragmentary setting of the poem (see below, Hess 145) dates from 1794, although the present composition can be dated from the sketch in Berlin (DSB: Grasnick 1) to the very end of 1798. Beethoven returned to the poem in 1822, composing a setting for three soloists with choir and small orchestra, and again in 1825, when this setting was adapted for soprano solo, choir and orchestra (see next entry, op. 121b).

The poem describes, in the first person, a young man's initiation ceremony. The exact context of the ritual is left unclear. There are clear references to Bardic lore (the oak grove), to established religion (incense), to Greek myth (Zeus) and to the ideals of the Enlightenment (beauty, truth and goodness). Mention of the four elements and the Highest One give additional overtones of freemasonry. It is clear that the poem was of central importance to Beethoven. Nottebohm (*Beethoveniana*, 1872) emphasises the composer's constant interest in the text and describes it as a kind of guiding prayer throughout his life: 'ein Gebet für alle Zeiten' (a prayer for every occasion). This view is reinforced by the fact that Beethoven twice set the final line, with its plea for beauty and goodness, as a canon: in September 1823 for Marie Pachler (WoO202), and in May 1825 for Ludwig Rellstab (WoO203). It is not a huge leap of the imagination to believe that the composer saw himself as the hero of the poem, dedicating his life to beauty, truth and goodness, and took the final line as a personal motto.

This familiar setting of the poem was published in 1808 by Simrock in Bonn, together with *Der freie Mann* and the first version of *Neue Liebe, neues Leben* (WoO127). On 2 May 1810 Beethoven wrote to Franz Wegeler in Koblenz (EA256 / BB439) asking for a copy of a song of his which he did not possess and which was apparently being sung in Wegeler's freemasons' lodge. Wegeler explained in his *Biographische Notizen* that this was merely *Opferlied* with adapted words of his own; a similar process had occurred with *Der freie Mann*. Wegeler includes his own words to both songs in an appendix to the *Biographische Notizen*, and it is clear from the opening that they needed little adaptation to suit a freemason's initiation: 'Das Werk beginnet! Heil'ge Glut / Erhebe froh des Neulings Mut' (The work begins! Let holy fire cheerfully bolster the novice's courage).

Beethoven's setting, marked 'slowly and solemnly', reflects the ritualistic tone of the text. Indeed, the whole song has the effect of a chorale and is well suited to performance by a male-voice chorus in unison. The bare octaves at the opening, along with the fall through the notes of the arpeggio, recalls the opening of the Gellert song *Die Ehre Gottes aus der Natur*, also a hymn, although of a very different species. The strophic song is generally printed with repeat marks. The Henle edition authentically prints the whole song as a continuum, with the postlude to the first verse appearing as an interlude. This is necessary only because of Beethoven's altered prosody in the second stanza. In setting the first stanza only the third and sixth lines are repeated, but in the second stanza the unexpected, but deliberate repetition of 'O Zeus' disturbs the established word–note relationship. At such a slow speed this hardly matters, but it seems surprising that Beethoven chose to emphasise the name of a Greek god ('Zeus') at the expense of a favourite modern ideal ('das Schöne').

OPFERLIED Sacrificial hymn (first version)
Friedrich von Matthisson   1794–95

E major Hess 145 Supp V/6 Henle 101 Not in GA/Peters

See final version (previous entry) for text and translation.

The incomplete autograph of this earlier solo setting of Matthisson's *Opferlied* is in Berlin (DSB: Grasnick 8), and a related sketch in the Kafka Album in London (BL: Add.Ms. 29801). Both use the same manuscript paper, which has been dated to the end of 1794 or the beginning of 1795. Readers who wish to appreciate fully the importance of paper studies in determining chronology are referred to Johnson, Tyson and Winter, *The Beethoven Sketchbooks*, where details of watermarks and rastrology (the layout and dimensions of the musical staves) are given.

This earlier setting of *Opferlied* was not published until 1962 in volume V of the *Supplemente*, edited by Willy Hess. Hess, having assembled his own catalogue of the works, did Beethoven a great service in publishing material not included in the first complete edition, although his critical notes ('Revisionsbericht') are inadequate by modern standards of scholarship. Admittedly his erroneous statement that the Berlin autograph had been lost since 1945 was corrected in the 1980 reprint of volume V (although the error was compounded by the authors of Hess2 in 2003), but he still dates the song casually to 'around 1796'.

The first setting opens with a variant setting of the poet's first line (see above), but that is the only essential difference. The manuscript, which has only one stanza underlaid, is complete until the end of the vocal line, but then only four bars of postlude follow, in right hand alone. Helga Lühning, in the Henle edition, prints as usual only what Beethoven wrote, but Willy Hess reasonably completes the postlude in line with the final version and underlays both stanzas. The first setting will never be more than a curiosity in performance, but is further evidence of Beethoven's lifelong obsession with this text.

OPFERLIED Sacrificial hymn (choral version)
Friedrich von Matthisson   autumn 1824
E major Op. 121b Supp V/65 Henle 97 Not in GA/Peters

Mit innigem, andächtigem Gefühl, in ziemlich langsamer Bewegung

See final solo version (p. 228) for text and translation.

Beethoven returned to Matthisson's text in 1822, producing a version for three solo voices, choir, two clarinets, horn, violas and cellos. This version was first performed in Bratislava on 23 December 1822 in an 'Akademie' concert organised by the tenor Wilhelm Ehlers. The programme stated that it had been expressly composed for this occasion as an act of friendship. This is the version which was offered to several publishers, including Peters (EA1137 / BB1570), Lissner (EA1177 / BB1647) and Probst (EA1266 / BB1783), between February 1823 and February 1824.

The work was revised and extended in the autumn of 1824, for soprano solo, choir and full orchestra, and it was in this form that the work was offered to Schott in Mainz in November of that year (EA1321 / BB1901). A piano reduction as an alternative to the orchestral accompaniment was planned from the beginning, and this appeared simultaneously with the orchestral version when the work was published by Schott in July 1825. Scattered sketches in Berlin, Krakow and Bonn all confirm the dating. An autograph of the piano part alone is in Berlin (DSB: Aut.56).

It was no doubt the solemnity of the text and its personal significance for the composer which persuaded Beethoven to share it with a wider audience through the choral medium, although his enthusiastic advocacy of it in letters to Leipzig,

Paris, St Petersburg, Mainz and London suggest that he was also motivated by the marketability of a larger concert work.

In each of the two verses, the soloist sings the whole stanza, repeating the third and sixth lines, as in the solo version. Beethoven seeks to convey the sense of the words, notably in his generous use of melisma to describe the wafting aromas of incense, but the same figure cannot be well adapted to the corresponding line in the second stanza, and throughout there is less natural fluency than in the solo versions.

The chorus repeats the final three lines of each verse, and there is interest in Beethoven's manipulation of the text. In each verse the altered compression of the final line produces a very personal plea, strengthening the view that this poem had a deep-seated personal significance for the composer. 'Lass des Jünglings Opfer dir wohlgefallen' (Let the young man's sacrifice be well-pleasing to you) suggests his humble submission to his artistic calling, while 'O gib mir das Schöne zu dem Guten' (O give me beauty allied to goodness) is the heartfelt prayer of an idealist and creative artist. Small wonder, then, that the work is directed to be performed 'with feelings of inward devotion'.

ÖSTREICH ÜBER ALLES Austria above everything
Heinrich von Collin   1809
D major SV59/126 sketches

Maestoso

Wenn   es   nur   will____   ist   Ös-ter-reich

Wenn es nur will,
Ist immer Östreich über alles!
Wehrmänner, ruft nun frohen Schalles:
Es will! Es will!
Hoch Österreich!

If it only has the will,
Austria will always be on top!
Soldiers, shout out with joyful sound:
We have the will!
Long live Austria!

Weil es nun will,
Seyd stolz und sicher, Östreichs Bürger,
Ha! Was vermag noch der fremde Würger,
Wenn Östreich will.
Hoch Österreich!
(Folgen 5 Strophen)

Because it now has the will,
Be proud and secure, Austrian citizens,
Ha! What else can the foreign tyrant do,
If Austria has the will.
Long live Austria!
(5 further stanzas)

This is the final poem in a set of 16 *Wehrmannslieder* (Soldiers' songs) which Heinrich von Collin wrote in 1808–9. His younger brother Matthäus von Collin, in a fulsome biography appended to Heinrich's collected works (vol. VI, Vienna 1814), evokes the atmosphere which engendered these songs: 'Gradually everything in Austria took on the appearance of war. Preparations for a national army were made, all able-bodied men were drilled in warfare . . . Collin, through his friend the former Major Catinelli had received the commission from the highest level to compose suitable songs for the new army . . . He had never received a more sacred commission, nor one which so closely matched his dearest desires.' Matthäus goes on to describe the reception which the songs received when they were performed on 28 March 1809 in the Grosser Redoutensaal in Vienna before a packed audience, in musical settings by Joseph Weigl: 'A tumult of delight seized the assembled crowd; the utterly wild enthusiasm to which some succumbed was accompanied by the tears of others, who forgot themselves in the joyful emotion of the atmosphere among the people and their leaders, and considered this the happiest day of their lives.' The patriotic euphoria was short-lived, as the French entered the Vienna suburbs on 9 May. According to Ferdinand Ries, when the French bombarded the inner city two days later, Beethoven hid in the cellar at his brother Carl's house.

Collin's sixteen poems justify defence of one's country from every possible angle. 'Der Greis' is spoken by an old man who is happy for his son to die on the battlefield, as they will be reunited in Heaven; the bridegroom in 'Der Bräutigam' explains to his new wife that the defence of his fatherland must come first, as otherwise foreign troops might come into their house and do unmentionable things (literally unmentionable, as his wife's likely fate is represented by dashes!). In an appendix to his poems, Collin thought it necessary to include an apologia for the cycle, explaining that the songs had to be written in a style comprehensible to all classes and were designed to encourage soldiers to sing and thereby fill them with a lively sense of their noble calling. It is important for us to understand this specific historical context in order to understand their appeal for Beethoven.

The sketches in Berlin, listed by Schmidt as SV59 (DSB: Landsberg 5, p. 19), date from the spring of 1809, at a time when patriotic fervour reached its peak with the Austrian declaration of war on the French on 9 April 1809. The sketch quoted above (Bia 477) extends to 11 bars and is followed by a longer sketch, also marked 'maestoso', with adumbrated interludes which hint at significant contrapuntal development:

Maes[toso]

This page of the sketchbook, which gives every impression of being scribbled down in haste, carries a defiant footnote: 'Beethoven ist kein Bedienter – Sie wollen einen Bedienten – den haben sie nun' (Beethoven is nobody's servant – they want a servant – well, they've got one now). The sketch for 'Östreich über alles' is followed later in the sketchbook (p. 41) by a further sketch, occasionally referred to as misleadingly as an independent song sketch, headed 'Auf die Schlacht: Jubelgesang-Angriff-Sieg' (Into battle: song of triumph-attack-victory) (Bia 478):

auf die Schlacht Jubelgesang

Notwithstanding the marking 'als Gesang' (as song), this is probably an embryonic idea for an extended programmatic piece, possibly with chorus, rather than a solo song. The tripartite subheading supports this interpretation. Indeed, it seems likely that all the Berlin sketches were written down with a grand cantata-like composition in mind, but, with the swift submission of Austrian resistance, Beethoven missed the moment.

A sketch for the same words in Bonn (BH: Mh79v), listed by Schmidt as SV126, is further evidence of Beethoven's desire to set these patriotic words at this time:

Boettcher (table VIII) mistakenly lists the sketches as being in F major. Although they lack clef and key signature, the Berlin sketches are unequivocally in D major, and the Bonn sketch also begins to take shape if two sharps are assumed.

PETRARCH Sonnets
Francesco Petrarca

1804

SV29 sketches

Sonnet 12:   Wenn sie erscheinet unter anderen Schönen
                Quando fra l'altre donne ad ora ad ora
                When she appears among other beauties

Sonnet 125:   Wohin sich nur mein müdes Auge wendet
                Ove ch' i posi gli occhi lassi o giri
                Where'er I turn my weary eyes

Beethoven made two very short sketches (Berlin, SPK: Aut.19e, f. 35v) for the opening lines of two of Petrarch's sonnets, probably between April and June 1804. Streckfuss's *Gedichte* (poems) had appeared in Vienna in the spring and included a number of translations from Petrarch. It is one of the volumes found among Beethoven's effects after his death in 1827. Like the frequent underlinings in these volumes, fragmentary musical sketches, even if they possess minimal inherent interest, are solid evidence of the composer's discriminating literary interests. The conversation books show that he scoured the newspapers for details of latest publications and he actively sought out authors from the past and from other languages as they became available in translation. The number of different translations of Petrarch and Shakespeare which appeared at this period indicate that the composer was not alone in his enthusiasm, which is witnessed too by his fascination for Voss's translations of the Homeric epics (see 'Homer').

The two sonnets which Beethoven began to compose are Sonnet 12 and Sonnet 125. The first line of each is given above in Streckfuss's German translation as set, in the original form and in English.

PUNSCHLIED Punch song
unknown   c.1791–92

G major WoO111 Supp V/18 Henle 73 Not in GA/Peters

Wer nicht, wenn warm von Hand zu Hand	Who never felt a keener sense of pleasure,
Der Punsch im Kreise geht,	When the warm punch is passed
Der Freude voll're Lust empfand,	From hand to hand round the circle:
Der schleiche schnell hinweg.	Let him slink away swiftly.
Wir trinken alle hocherfreut,	We all drink in the happiest of spirits,
So lang uns Punsch die Kumme beut.	As long as the bowl still has punch to offer.
Chor:	*Chorus:*
Wir trinken alle hocherfreut,	We all drink in the happiest of spirits,
So lang uns Punsch die Kumme beut.	As long as the bowl still has punch to offer.

The author of this self-conscious and utterly predictable stanza is unknown, although the song is clearly related to the 'drinking song of farewell', *Erhebt das Glas mit froher Hand*. The use of the north-west German dialect word 'Kumme' (for 'bowl') is further proof, were it needed, that the song is a product of Beethoven's later Bonn years. The autograph fair copy in Berlin (DSB: Artaria 171) has been dated to 1791 or 1792. A note on this autograph indicates that Beethoven knew at least seven stanzas; he states that in the second, third, sixth and seventh stanzas the chorus should be omitted and the postlude ('das kleine ritornell') follow the solo verse directly. Only one stanza survives. The instruction is of interest, as it shows the composer seeking to incorporate variety into a strictly strophic composition.

The song was first published in 1925, in the first edition of Ludwig Schiedermair's detailed study of the composer's early years (*Der junge Beethoven*, Leipzig 1925), although it was omitted in later editions. It has since been reprinted by Willy Hess (Supp V/18), and by Helga Lühning (Henle).

Marked 'fiery', the song gallops along pleasantly in 6/8 time. With its frequent use of broken chords of G major, it sounds for all the world like a hunting song with horn effects. But in the world of German social singing, many basic themes can often be combined with little close differentiation: a list would certainly have to include hunting, drinking, friendship, loyalty and patriotism.

QUE LE TEMPS ME DURE How time drags for me

Jean-Jacques Rousseau   spring 1793

C minor–major WoO116 Supp V/3/4 Henle 100 Not in GA/Peters

Que le temps me dure I

Que le temps me dure II

Que le temps me dure,	How time drags for me,
Passé loin de toi!	When spent distant from you!
Toute la nature	The whole of nature
N'est plus rien pour moi!	Means nothing to me any more!
Le plus verd bocage,	The greenest of groves,
Si tu n'y viens pas,	If you do not appear there,
N'est qu'un lieu sauvage,	Is but a wild place
Pour moi sans appas.	With no appeal for me.
Hélas! si je passe	Alas, if I spend
Un jour sans te voir,	A day without seeing you,
Je cherche la trace	I seek your image
Dans mon désespoir.	In my despair.
Quand je l'ai perdue,	When I have lost it,
Je reste à pleurer;	I am left to weeping;
Mon âme éperdue	My distraught soul
Est prête d'expirer.	Is ready to expire.
Le cœur me palpite,	My heart beats furiously
Quand j'entends ta voix,	When I hear your voice,
Tout mon sang s'agite,	All my blood is in turmoil
Dès que je te vois!	The moment I behold you!
Ouvres-tu la bouche,	If you open your lips,
Les cieux vont d'ouvrir,	The very heavens have opened,
Si ta main me touche,	Should your hand touch me,
Je me sens frémir!	I feel myself quivering!

Rousseau's poem 'Que le jour me dure' was first published in *Les Consolations des Misères de ma Vie, ou Recueil d'Airs, Romances et Duos* (Paris 1781) with a setting by the poet based on only three notes (G, A, B). Both this melody, the so-called 'Air de trois notes', and the poem enjoyed an extraordinary vogue. The original melody was reharmonised; new poems were written to Rousseau's air; the original poem was set (as here) to different music; it was translated into German by Friedrich Wilhelm Gotter and others, and set to music in divergent styles by Corona Schröter, Carl Loewe and many others; still other composers experimented with three-note melodies of their own. Rousseau's air is printed and its impact outlined in Friedländer's *Das deutsche Lied im 18. Jahrhundert* (II, pp. 292f.).

Beethoven's two sketches for the song in Berlin (SPK: Aut.28, f. 3) have been dated to spring 1793. The first sketch was published in *Die Musik* in March 1902, along with *Romance*, by J. Chantavoine ('Zwei französische Lieder Beethovens'); the second sketch was reproduced in Max Unger's article 'Von ungedruckter Musik Beethovens' in *Zeitschrift für Musik*, November 1935, and Unger also published a realisation of both sketches in a separate music supplement (Nos 10b and 10c). Henle (1990) reproduces the two sketches as seen. Willy Hess (Supp V, 1962) realises the sketches for performance with minimal editorial intervention (although his 'correction' of Beethoven's clearly marked B natural to a B flat in the second bar is as presumptuous as it is dubious).

Perhaps it was respect for Rousseau, the man who had inspired the most recent generation of German writers and thinkers, which led Beethoven to approach this little poem with such circumspection. The first sketch is in the minor mode and in 6/8 time and opens with a languishing, self-contained four-bar prelude, which sets the mood with rising semiquaver figures merging into lingering appoggiaturas. Although the sketch is on two staves only and the accompaniment is not fully notated, there are sufficient indications to make realisation of the song a simple matter, including a note 'etc. this accompaniment goes on to the end' and a fragment of figured harmony. Beethoven was, after all, sketching for himself and not for posterity, and this musical shorthand is just a personal 'aide-mémoire'. The only problem with the song as sketched is the fitting of words to melody: 'loin' and 'rien' are both set as two syllables.

This is corrected in the second sketch, with the less enterprising, but more amenable 2/4 time signature. The use of the major mode in the second sketch, together with the accuracy of the prosody, make this the less problematic of the two attempts, but also the less ambitious. At the bottom of the autograph, Beethoven has added four bars in C minor and in 2/4 time, marked as 'No. 1'. These hybrid bars may have been intended as a bridge between the two settings, to be sung consecutively (C minor yielding to C major would not be at all unusual, although here there is no change of mood in the words set), or may have been Beethoven's first attempt at a setting which would merge the best features of both sketches.

Beethoven's choice of key can often be revealing (see Introduction). Here, the use of C minor for the first sketch provides a remarkable match and exemplar for Schubart's description of the key in his *Ideen zu einer Ästhetik der Tonkunst*, with which Beethoven was familiar: 'C-Moll, Liebeserklärung und zugleich Klage der unglücklichen Liebe. Jedes Schmachten, Sehnen, Seufzen der liebestrunkenen Seele liegt in diesem Tone' (C minor, declaration of love and at the same time lament of unhappy love. All the languishing, yearning, sighing of the soul intoxicated with love resides in this key). Despite the greater success of the second setting as word-setting, the composer would have been reluctant to abandon the ideal key of his first sketch, but failed to reach a satisfactory synthesis of the two settings.

RASTLOSE LIEBE Restless love
Johann Wolfgang von Goethe 1796

E flat major Hess 149 sketches

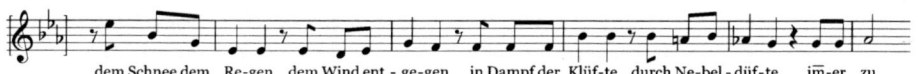

dem Schnee dem Re-gen dem Wind ent - ge-gen in Dampf der Klüf-te durch Ne-bel - düf-te im̄-er zu

Dem Schnee, dem Regen,	Against the snow,
Dem Wind entgegen,	The rain and the wind,
Im Dampf der Klüfte,	In vapour-filled ravines,
Durch Nebeldüfte,	Through wafting fog,
Immer zu! Immer zu!	Onwards! Onwards!
Ohne Rast und Ruh!	Without rest or peace!
Lieber durch Leiden	I should rather fight my way
Möcht' ich mich schlagen,	Through a world of sorrows
Als so viel Freuden	Than bear such a multitude
Des Lebens ertragen.	Of life's joys.
Alle das Neigen	All this attraction
Von Herzen zu Herzen,	Of heart to heart,
Ach, wie so eigen	Ah, what a very particular
Schaffet das Schmerzen!	Pain it creates!
Wie – soll ich fliehn?	What – am I to flee?
Wälderwärts ziehn?	Retreat to the woods?
Alles vergebens!	All, all in vain!
Krone des Lebens,	Crown of life,
Glück ohne Ruh,	Happiness without peace of mind,
Liebe, bist du!	This is you, O Love!

Goethe's celebrated poem was written at Ilmenau on 6 May 1776. Although Goethe's brief engagement to Lili Schönemann (see *Neue Liebe, neues Leben*) had been broken off only the previous autumn, the poet was already under the thrall of another lady, Charlotte von Stein, a lady-in-waiting at the Weimar court. Frau von Stein was ultimately to have a calming influence on the young poet, but here he expresses his lovelorn state in passionate terms, although the second stanza pretends to explore the nature of love more philosophically. Despite the romanticising of the landscape, the poem is based on direct personal experience. It was written, as one might say, 'on the hoof', as Goethe was travelling on horseback in the vicinity of the Thuringian Forest and it had indeed been snowing steadily. Riding back towards Weimar, he pondered briefly whether he should turn back into the forest, seeking Romantic escape in the life of a woodland hermit or some such, or continue to Weimar. A letter to Frau von Stein written the same day as the poem makes it clear that the woodland idyll was the merest fancy: 'I shall meet you again when I get back! It's all just too wonderful!'

Beethoven's letter to Goethe of 8 March 1823 (EA1136 / BB1562) promises a setting of this poem: 'Es dörften bald vieleicht mehrere ihrer immer einzig bleibenden Gedichte in Töne gebracht von mir erscheinen, worunter auch "Rastlose Liebe" sich befindet' (Perhaps soon several of your unrivalled and unique poems should be appearing in my musical settings, among them 'Rastlose Liebe'). There are extensive sketches in Vienna (GdM: A67) which Johnson (*Fischhof Miscellany*) has transcribed. Despite detailed melody sketches and adumbrated accompaniment figures, the sketches, which predate the letter to Goethe by several years, were never polished for publication.

The text was widely set to music in the late eighteenth century. Interestingly, if Beethoven had revised his sketch in 1823, his final version would still have postdated Schubert's setting of the text (D138), written in 1815 and published in 1821. Could it be that Beethoven's encounter with Schubert's song was the reason his own project was abandoned? While he never heard any of Schubert's songs performed, it is inconceivable that Beethoven did not at some time leaf through copies of songs by his younger colleague in the music shops of Vienna.

Beethoven's embryonic setting begins with a phrase which ignores the dynamic stresses of Goethe's verse. The poet, like Schubert, stresses 'snow', 'rain' and 'wind' with equal force, but Beethoven stresses only 'rain', the least dramatic of the elements, and momentum is not established. Beethoven later matches Goethe's forward-thrusting metre more closely than Schubert in setting 'immer zu' to two quavers and a minim, however, and both composers agree in their dactylic setting of the central stanza.

Jean Chantavoine first published the sketch and a tentative completion in *Revue d'histoire et de critique musciales* (Paris 1902), pp. 409–14. Recently the sketch has been realised by Willem Holsbergen, whose completion can be heard at www.unheardbeethoven.org.

RESIGNATION Resignation
Paul Graf von Haugwitz   1817

D major WoO149 Peters 56 Henle 67 GA XXIII/246

Lisch aus, mein Licht!   Go out, my light!
Was dir gebricht,   That which you need
Das ist nun fort,   Has now gone.

An diesem Ort	You will not find it again
Kannst du's nicht wieder finden!	In this place.
Du musst nun los dich binden.	You must now work yourself free.
Sonst hast du lustig aufgebrannt,	You used to flare up so brightly,
Nun hat man dir die Luft entwandt;	But now they have taken the air from you.
Wenn diese fortgewehet,	When this is finally dispersed,
Die Flamme irre gehet,	The flame goes astray,
Sucht – findet nicht –	Seeks – and does not find –
Lisch aus, mein Licht!	Go out, my light!

As the earliest known printing of the poem is in the *Frauentaschenbuch für das Jahr 1817*, published in Nuremberg, and Beethoven had been considering the text since 1814 or 1815, it seems that the composer used a manuscript copy of the poem. The text had probably been given to him by Johann Schickh, editor of the periodical in which the song first appeared, with a specific request to set it to music. According to Schindler, not always a reliable witness, Beethoven actually asked Schickh to thank Haugwitz for 'providing the impulse for such a happy piece of inspiration'.

The poem clearly had a personal appeal to Beethoven, prone to fits of self-examination and self-pity, but always resigning himself anew to his fate. Haugwitz begins and ends with an appeal for extinction and the whole poem is based on his metaphor of the candle's flame as the spirit of life, which must work itself free of the 'mortal coil' now that it is deprived of air (inspiration?). The image of the flame sputtering as it is slowly but surely deprived of the oxygen which it needs to survive is particularly vivid. The anthropomorphic image of the flame searching and going astray, along with the poet's consistently familiar address to the candle, as though talking to a trusted old friend, give the metaphor a remarkable personal poignancy.

Beethoven's earliest sketches for the song date from the very end of 1814 (Tours Conservatoire, SV383), but the fragment's only significance is to confirm that Beethoven was considering the poem at this early date. The main sketches for the song in its final version were in the Boldrini pocket sketchbook of 1817, described by Nottebohm (*Zweite Beethoveniana*, p. 352), but lost since the end of the nineteenth century. A further sketch in Berlin (SPK: Aut.11/1, Bia 669) from the end of 1816 is of interest, as Beethoven here begins to sketch a four-part setting in G major (clearly marked 'mit vier Stimmen'). It is astonishing that the composer should once have considered setting a text of such intimate personal significance as anything other than a *Lied* for solo voice and piano.

The song was first published in Vienna in the *Wiener Zeitschrift für Kunst, Literatur, Theater und Mode* for 31 March 1818. The second edition from Sauer und Leidesdorf, published in Vienna in February 1823, incorporated a number of corrections.

In this song, Beethoven pays extremely close attention to the declamation of the text. The expressive direction reads: 'to be performed with feeling, but still resolutely, firmly accentuated and as if speaking'. The instruction to imitate natural speech rhythms is of particular interest in this highly intimate utterance. It is not just the poet but the composer too who is identifying his own fate with that of the dying flame.

The outer sections of the song, which is in ternary form, are dominated by the interval of a falling minor third, a miniature but vivid piece of structural *leitmotiv* which provides an unmistakable tonal analogue for the dying flame, be it of the candle or of life itself. In the vocal melody, this interval is frequently bridged by a passing appoggiatura, adding the expressive suggestion of a world-weary sigh. Extreme and sudden dynamic contrasts suggest the alternation of protesting despair and weary resignation, and in the middle section the contrast between the full flame of life in former times and present exhaustion. The music moves conventionally from D major to G major, and thence by way of the mediant to B minor, but the suddenness of the return to G major and thence to C major (with G the only tonal pivot) at the end of the first section is surprising, suggestive of the poet's disturbed emotional state.

The second section is prefaced by two triumphant bars of repeated C major chords, as the poet recalls the former fullness of life. An accelerated intensification is achieved by filling out the chords (six notes becoming eight notes), by sharpening the metrical pulse, and by dynamic augmentation (*f* to *ff*, underlined by *sf* accents). Hearing these bars, we are not surprised to learn that the principal sketches for the song (see above, Boldrini) directly preceded sketches for the 'Hammerklavier' Sonata (op. 106), a work in which Beethoven exploits every resource of the latest piano to grand effect. For one glorious moment we are taken back to the exultation of *Die Ehre Gottes aus der Natur* from the Gellert songs. And yet the exultation is swiftly revealed as a memory only, and the image of the flame's wandering search for nourishing air concludes with significant harmonic dislocation, and an utterly unexpected falling fourth at 'findet nicht'. The note, when found, is a C sharp and is strongly interpreted in the following bars as the third of the dominant seventh chord of D major. Thus, the futile search for renewal ends with a resigned return to the home key, and the musical recapitulation suggests capitulation, a bowing to the inevitable.

The song ends as it began, quietly, and with the minor thirds in the vocal melody falling in four steps through an octave from high to low F sharp. There is no song which Beethoven invests with more intimate care and attention to detail. Despite the strict discipline of the song's formal outline (16 + 16 + 16 bars, plus final chord), it is a moving utterance because it speaks at every turn of the composer's personal commitment to the text.

ROMANCE Romance
unknown   1798–99

G major WoO128 Supp V/9 Henle 81 Not in GA/Peters

Adagio

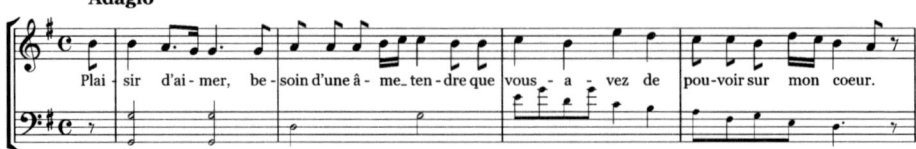

Plaisir d'aimer, besoin d'une âme tender	Pleasure of loving, need of a tender soul,
Que vous avez de pouvoir sur mon coeur.	What power you possess over my heart!
De vous, hélas, en voulant me défendre	Alas, in wishing to defend myself from you,

Je perds la paix sans trouver le bonheur.　　I lose my peace of mind without finding
　　　　　　　　　　　　　　　　　　　　happiness.

We can only speculate as to why the composer turned to a rather undistinguished French text in 1798 or thereabouts. The poem is known only from Beethoven's setting. A sketchbook in Berlin (DSB: Grasnick 1) contains, on different leaves, assorted melody sketches with variant versions, and a sketch for piano alone. The sketchbook is dated to 1798–9.

The song was first published in *Die Musik* in March 1902 (pp. 1078–82), in a completion by Jean Chantavoine, accompanying his article 'Zwei französische Lieder Beethovens'. He takes the piano sketch as the basis for his reconstruction, a reasonable process, as the upper (melody) line is written with stems upwards when it corresponds to text setting, and stems downwards when it forms part of the instrumental interlude and postlude. Willy Hess published a similar completion in more accessible format (Supp V/9) in 1962. By incorporating two bars from one of the melody sketches, repeating the words of the final line, Hess extends his completion to thirteen bars.

In the early 1970s, a slim volume of songs in contemporary copies was discovered in the Oettingen-Wallerstein Library collection, formerly at Schloss Harburg and now in the university library in Augsburg. This volume, dated on paper evidence to about 1800, includes the present song in a complete version, under the title 'Romance par Louis van Beethoven'. This version, comprising eleven bars and corresponding closely to the Berlin sketches, appears to be based on a lost autograph and is the version included by Helga Lühning in the Henle edition of 1990. The copy is reproduced and the song's history thoroughly discussed in an article by Gertraut Haberkamp in Dorfmüller's *Beiträge zur Beethoven-Bibliographie*, pp. 68–72.

A conventional poem is perhaps responsible for the essentially formal mould of the song, which retains its foothold in the eighteenth century. Expressive and contrasted dynamic indications are characteristic of Beethoven and further evidence that the copy was based on a once extant autograph. The postlude is akin to an ornate *ritornello* and suggests the harpsichord as accompanying medium, although, that said, similar passages abound in the slow movements of the piano sonatas. The postlude is one of the features which link this song to the more fluent *Mollys Abschied* of 1795.

RUF VOM BERGE　Call from the mountain
Friedrich Treitschke　　　　　　　　　　　　　　　　　　　Dec. 1816
　　　　　　　A major WoO147 Peters 51 Henle 65 GA XXIII/242

Etwas lebhaft

Wenn ich ein Vöglein wär',
Und auch zwei Flüglein hätt',
   Flög' ich zu dir.
Weil's aber nicht kann sein,
   Bleib' ich allhier.

Wenn ich ein Sternlein wär',
Und auch viel Strahlen hätt',
   Strahlt' ich dich an.
Und du sähst freundlich auf,
   Grüsstest hinan.

Wenn ich ein Bächlein wär',
Und auch viel Wellen hätt',
   Rauscht' ich durchs Grün,
Nahte dem kleinen Fuss,
   Küsste wohl ihn.

Würd' ich zur Abendluft,
Nähm' ich mir Blumenduft,
   Hauchte dir zu.
Weilend auf Brust und Mund,
   Fänd' ich dort Ruh'.

Geht doch kein Stund' der Nacht,
Ohn' dass mein Herz erwacht
   Und an dich denkt,
Wie du mir tausendmal
   Dein Herz geschenkt.

Wohl dringen Bach und Stern,
Lüftchen und Vöglein fern
   Kommen zu dir.
Ich nur bin festgebannt;
   Weine allhier.

If I were a little bird
And had two little wings,
   I would fly to you.
But since that cannot be,
   I'll remain here.

If I were a little star
And had lots of rays,
   I would shine on you.
And you would look up with a smile
   And return my greeting.

If I were a little brook
And had lots of ripples,
   I would babble through the countryside,
I would approach your dainty foot
   And probably kiss it.

If I turned into an evening breeze,
I would take up the scent of flowers
   And waft towards you.
Resting on your bosom and mouth,
   There I would find peace.

Not an hour of the night passes
But my heart awakes
   And thinks of you,
How you offered me your heart
   A thousand times over.

Brook and star do indeed find a way,
Breeze and bird from afar
   Come to you.
I alone am kept captive,
   And weep here.

This is Treitschke's much expanded adaptation of a German folksong which first appeared in Herder's collection of folksongs, later entitled *Stimmen der Völker* (Voices of the peoples), first published in 1778, and was given even greater currency by its inclusion in *Des Knaben Wunderhorn* (The boy's magic horn), the huge collection of over seven hundred folksongs collected by Achim von Arnim and Clemens Brentano, published between 1805 and 1808. The folksong consists of three stanzas. The first was used word-for-word as the first stanza of Treitschke's poem, while the third is adapted as the fifth stanza of the later poem. The second stanza, describing the lover's seeing and talking to his beloved in his dreams, was not used by Treitschke.

The folk melody, described by Herder as 'appropriate to the content, light and flowing', consists of a balanced twelve bars, achieved by the repetition of the fourth line of each stanza, but lacks any introduction or postlude, whereas Beethoven's melody consists of only ten bars (with no repetition of words), but makes the four-bar introduction, the four-bar postlude and final ritornello essential compositional features. The folksong is printed in collections such as Ludwig Erk's *Deutscher Liederschatz*, published by Peters, where it appears as No. 118. The familiarity of the folksong allowed its use as a universal point of reference in both literature and music. In Goethe's *Faust* (Part 1, 'Wald und Höhle'), Mephistopheles describes the lovesick Gretchen singing the song as she watches the clouds float beyond the city walls, while Schumann paid tribute to the folksong by adapting it, with a completely new middle section, as a vocal duet in ternary form (op. 43/1).

Treitschke's poem first appeared in June 1817 in a collection of his poems, published by Wallishauser in Vienna, with Beethoven's setting also published for the first time as a music supplement, part of a separate volume in landscape format. Beethoven clearly received the poem in manuscript from Treitschke, whom he knew well enough to address in letters in the same jocular tone he used habitually in letters to his publisher friends Anton Steiner and Tobias Haslinger. A letter to Treitschke of 9 June 1817 (EA782 / BB1130) indicates that the poet was in possession of an autograph copy of the song and also that Steiner had undertaken the engraving of the music supplement. Beethoven asks the poet to return the manuscript to Steiner so that significant errors in the engraving can be corrected (a series of puns render this and other letters of the period virtually untranslatable).

The autograph is no longer extant, but a faithful copy, made for Aloys Fuchs, survives in the music archive at the Benedictine Abbey in Göttweig. It is dated 13 December 1816 and bears the ironical title: 'Ruf vom Berge, von einem aus der Tiefe' (Call from the mountain, by someone from down below). Beethoven's roguish humour is also evident in the dedication 'Für Sn Wohlgeboren Hrn. v. Treitschke, ersten Trachter und Dichter / von den Ufern der Wien bis zum Amazonflusse' (For the noble von Treitschke, the foremost striver and scriber / from the banks of the Wien to the Amazon).

A single sheet in Bonn (BH: NE34), headed 'Auf'm Berge', shows a version of the melody which differs slightly in the first and third bars. Fanny del Rio describes in a diary entry for 20 December 1816 how Beethoven wrote this out for her sister Anna at the end of a pleasant evening.

Beethoven's song is full of vitality. The mood is set at the start with a chirpy four-bar introduction which lies high in the piano. It suggests the delicate song and movement of the tiny bird, and underlines the whimsical nature of the entire poetic conceit. After a repeated rising figure, the melody descends to its lowest note as the poet imagines the bird's coming in to land, on a pause, next to his beloved. After the pause, the voice feigns nonchalance, although this rising figure is too jaunty for the sentiments of the final stanza, and sensitive treatment will be required from the singer here.

A four-bar postlude echoes the final four bars of the vocal melody and leads directly back into each successive stanza, but this is extended after the final stanza into a seven-bar ritornello, a technique perfected in several of the folksong arrangements which Beethoven made for George Thomson.

SCHILDERUNG EINES MÄDCHENS
Description of a girl
unknown   c.1783

G major WoO107 Peters 37 Henle 1 GA XXIII/228

Tempo giusto

Schil- dern, willst du, | Freund! soll ich__ | dir E-li - sen? | Möchte U -zens | Geist in mich | sich er- gie - | ßen!

Schildern, willst du, Freund, soll ich	So you want me to describe
Dir Elisen?	Elise for you, my friend?
Möchte Uzens Geist in mich	May the spirit of Uz
Sich ergiessen!	Be poured out upon me!
Wie in einer Winternacht	Just as on a winter's night
Sterne strahlen,	The stars beam,
Würde ihrer Augen Pracht	Even so would Oeser
Oeser malen.	Paint the splendour of her eyes.
Finden wirst du voll und rund	You will find her cheeks
Ihre Wangen	Full and round,
Und den Purpur auf dem Mund	And on her mouth. the crimson
Herrlich prangen.	Gleaming resplendently
Und den stolzen Thron der Lust	And Cythera itself,
Sich zur Ehre,	To its credit,
Bildete nach ihrer Brust	Modelled the proud throne of delight
Selbst Kythere.	Upon her breast.
Wie sich, wenn ein Zephyr weht,	Just as small clouds rise
Wölkchen heben,	On a gentle breeze,
Scheint das Mädchen, wenn sie geht,	So she seems merely to glide
Nur zu schweben.	As she walks.
Sahst du je der Grazien	If you ever saw the youngest
Jüngste hüpfen:	Of the Graces at play,
Oh, so hast du sie gesehn	Then you have seen
Tanzend schlüpfen.	Elise dancing.

Welcher Reiz dem Körper noch,	What attraction could possibly
Sag es, fehle?	Be missing from her body?
Zehnmal findst du schöner noch	Yet you will find her soul
Ihre Seele.	Ten times lovelier still.
Wenn sie weit auf Gottes Flur	Whenever she surveys the expanse
Umher blicket,	Of God's creation,
Wie wird sie durch dich, Natur!	How wholly enraptured she is
Ganz entzücket!	By thee, O Nature!
Fern ist sie von niederm Schmähn,	She is far from all spite,
Fern von Neide,	Far from envy;
Glücklich alle Welt zu sehn,	Her greatest joy would be
Wär' ihr Freude.	To see everybody happy.
Für ihr Herz, das edel denkt,	How it honours her
Welche Ehre,	Noble-thinking heart
Wenn sie Menschenelend schenkt	When she sheds a tear
Eine Zähre.	For human misery.
Hält sie einst von Liebe warm	When she holds me
Wie die Sonne	In her tender arms,
Mich in ihrem weichen Arm:	As warm with love as the sun:
Welche Wonne!	What bliss!

This is Beethoven's first surviving song. It is not known where Beethoven found the text, and the poet's identity and that of the incomparable Elise are also, perhaps thankfully, unknown. No autograph survives. The setting appeared in 1783 in the weekly journal *Blumenlese für Klavierliebhaber*, published by Heinrich Philipp Bossler in Speyer, together with a little Rondo in C major WoO48 (this Rondo in 3/8 has a similar lilt to the song, but less vitality). The music to the song covers two of the short stanzas, and in the original edition only two stanzas appear below the music. The whole poem, as above, was printed in a separate collection of texts to accompany the songs for 1783, but most modern editions follow the original in printing only the first two stanzas. The whole text is reinstated in the Henle edition. The odd number of verses means that the whole poem cannot be sung without slight adaptation; repeating the final verse would be a sensible option.

The first edition claims that Beethoven wrote the song at 11 years of age: 'Von Hrn: Ludw: van Beethoven alt eilf Jahr'. Beethoven was 12 when the song was published, but may well have composed it before his 12th birthday in December the previous year. On the other hand, this could be attributed to the confusion which had existed since a concert announcement in 1778 docked a year from the composer's age; a notice published in 1783 by Beethoven's teacher Christian Gottlob Neefe described his star pupil inaccurately as 'a boy of 11 years'.

The song is wholly in the mould of the later eighteenth century, printed on two staves, with the voice doubling the keyboard melody. There is little attempt to fill out harmonies, with occasional sixths and thirds adding little of interest, and the throbbing bass line dully predictable. Neefe, whose songs were much published in song collections and almanacs, will have seen this song prior to publication, and an autograph would have helped us to identify improvements which the teacher may have recommended to his pupil. Did the teacher, for example, suggest the short interludes which balance out the three-bar vocal phrases?

It must be admitted that Beethoven set himself an uphill task with this particular poem; even the invocation of the Anacreontic poet Johann Peter Uz (1720–96) and the Hungarian-born painter Adam Friedrich Oeser (1717–99) fails to raise the tone of the verse, and the awkward syntax of the verse is immediately problematic. Despite everything, we have a song full of youthful exuberance and vitality, although the young composer shows self-discipline beyond his years in marking the song *tempo giusto*, requiring a strict and steady pulse. An ingenuous, but charmingly individual touch is the high note on 'Sterne' (stars), followed in the next bar by a brilliant outburst of piano figuration which certainly lights up the night sky.

SEHNSUCHT Longing
Christian Ludwig Reissig   1815–16

E major WoO146 Peters 48 Henle 62 GA XXIII/239

Mit Empfindung, aber nicht zu langsam

Die stille Nacht umdunkelt	The silent night hides valley and hill
Erquickend Tal und Höh',	In refreshing darkness,
Der Stern der Liebe funkelt	The star of love shines gently
Sanft wallend in dem See.	Amid the ripples of the lake.
Verstummt sind in den Zweigen	Nature's songsters are silent
Die Sänger der Natur;	Now in the branches;
Geheimnisvolles Schweigen	A mysterious silence reposes
Ruht auf der Blumenflur.	Upon the flowery meadows.
Ach, mir nur schliesst kein Schlummer	Alas, no slumber closes
Die müden Augen zu:	My tired eyes, mine alone:
Komm, lindre meinen Kummer,	Come, ease my sorrow,
Du stille Gott der Ruh'!	Thou silent God of peace!
Sanft trockne mir die Tränen,	Gently dry my tears,
Gib süsser Freude Raum,	Make room for sweet delight.
Komm, täusche hold mein Sehnen	Come, fondly deceive my longing
Mit einem Wonnetraum!	With a blissful dream!

O zaubre meinen Blicken	Oh, conjure up an image
Die Holde, die mich flieht,	Of the lovely girl who flees from me.
Lass mich ans Herz sie drücken,	Let me press her to my heart
Dass edle Lieb' entglüht!	That a noble love might be kindled!
Du Holde, die ich meine,	O lovely one, object of my thoughts,
Wie sehn' ich mich nach dir;	How I long for you.
Erscheine, ach erscheine	Appear, oh, appear before me
Und lächle Hoffnung mir!	And let your smile bring me hope!

Reissig is remembered today only as the provider of texts for eight songs by Beethoven (and one by Schubert), but this fine poem can stand alone and reminds us that Reissig was more than just another poetaster. We are used to Romantic scenes of twilight and moonrise, but here the utter stillness and solitude of midnight is evoked in the run-on couplets of the first stanza, with the darkness relieved only by the evening star reflected in the lake. Yet night brings gentle rest and renewal to the natural world, whereas the lovelorn poet is alone denied the boon of sleep which he craves. He longs for the 'sweet deceivings' of sleep, as only in his dreams can he hope to recapture the smiling image of the girl who has deserted him. His pathetic, self-conscious 'longing' is not for physical reunion, but for illusion and false hopes. Beethoven, himself unlucky in love, clearly responds to the poet's sentiment and devotes extraordinary care to the setting of this text.

The poem was not published separately until 1815, when it was included in the third edition of Reissig's *Blümchen der Einsamkeit* (Flowers of solitude), but had previously appeared in 1810 in a musical setting by Reichardt, in a collection of eighteen Reissig poems in settings by various composers. This volume had included three songs by Beethoven (see *Der Jüngling in der Fremde* for details). Despite some bad feeling which had been generated in 1810 by what Beethoven considered to be the unauthorised publication of his songs in this collection, the composer set the present text and *Des Kriegers Abschied* some years later and allowed their publication in similar collections. *Sehnsucht* was published by Artaria in Vienna in June 1816 in a collection of three Reissig settings, the other contributions coming from Gyrowetz and Seyfried.

An autograph in Berlin (DSB: Grasnick 18) shows the laying out of the work in several stages: voice part in ink; the adumbration of the piano part in ink; the filling out of the piano part in pencil; going over the finalised piano part in ink; and finally the insertion of the text. For a detailed scholarly description of song autographs German-speaking readers are referred to the Critical Report by Helga Lühning (1990) which accompanies the Henle complete edition of the songs.

The song has attracted an unusual degree of attention owing to the extensive rhythmic sketches in the Scheide sketchbook (Princeton, NJ), which show Beethoven experimenting with metrical patterns for the opening words. Nottebohm (*Zweite Beethoveniana*, pp. 332–3) quotes fifteen examples, and Lewis Lockwood (in *Beethoven Studies I*, pp. 97–122) transcribes twice that number. Lockwood seeks to revise the traditional image of Beethoven as an artist who chiselled away laboriously, revising, rejecting and adapting sketches until a work of art slowly appeared from the labour pangs. He suggests rather that these sketches seem to have been written 'rapidly and consecutively' and represent 'the rapid tumbling out of ideas, one after another'. From the resulting mass of sketches, Beethoven was then able to select the most appropriate one for the words, rather as a professional photographer would select the best print from a whole sheet of images. This would then be worked up (one might say: 'developed') into the final song.

Beethoven seemed fascinated by the question of prosody and rhythmic analogy precisely because he did not have an instinctive feeling for poetic metre. There are several examples of his writing out the metre painstakingly above a text; an example is the opening of the *Badelied* fragment, where the metre is superimposed despite the fact that it appears totally unambiguous.

In the present case, Beethoven was clearly concerned to find a musical figure which would not only match the poetic metre but be appropriate to the scene of utter stillness described in the first stanza and adaptable to the poet's thematic development in the remaining two stanzas. As this song retains an identical vocal verse throughout, leaving modification to the accompaniment, finding the right metre for the vocal melody was of paramount importance. The chosen metre works well. Beethoven's decision to run on to the third line without a pause is initially surprising, but allows him to create a sense of urgency where this is needed in subsequent stanzas. Hans Boettcher (*Beethoven als Liederkomponist*, p. 96) feels that the composer has captured the internal metre of the verse by managing to think independently of bar lines.

After the homophonic stillness of the first stanza, Beethoven varies the piano figuration meaningfully in the stanzas which follow. In the second stanza, alternating rests between the pianist's two hands suggests a disruption to the poet's sleep pattern, while the flowing triplets (or sextuplets) of the third stanza conjure up in imagination the image of the beloved. The strophic modification and intensification through variation of the piano figuration anticipates the use of the technique in the song cycle *An die ferne Geliebte*, which was sketched immediately after the present song, and may also be regarded as a preliminary study for *Abendlied unterm gestirnen Himmel* of 1820.

The key of E major, a similar movement and melodic shape, and the variation aspect have often led to a comparison between this song's opening bars and the final movement (*Gesangvoll mit innigster Empfindung*, originally marked just 'Gesang') of the Piano Sonata op. 109, but this analogy must not be taken too far.

SEHNSUCHT (Nur wer die Sehnsucht kennt)
Longing
Johann Wolfgang von Goethe   Late 1807–8
WoO134 Peters 60/1–4 Henle 32–5 GA XXIII/250

Nur wer die Sehnsucht kennt,	Only one who knows longing
Weiss, was ich leide!	Knows what I am suffering!
Allein und abgetrennt	Alone and cut off
Von aller Freude,	From all joy,
Seh' ich ans Firmament	I look thitherward

Nach jener Seite.	Up to the heavens.
Ach! der mich liebt und kennt	Alas, he who loves and knows me
Ist in der Weite.	Is far away!
Es schwindelt mir, es brennt	I grow dizzy, my bowels
Mein Eingeweide.	Are aflame.
Nur wer die Sehnsucht kennt,	Only one who knows longing
Weiss, was ich leide!	Knows what I am suffering!

Goethe's celebrated poem, written in 1785, is incorporated in his novel *Wilhelm Meisters Lehrjahre*, where it occurs at the very end of the 11th chapter of the fourth book. Wilhelm, injured while fighting off a band of marauding robbers, has been rescued by a beautiful lady and her companions. Having brought him to safety, she rides off at once, and in his fevered state, Wilhelm ponders who his attractive rescuer might be (little suspecting that they will be married by the end of the novel). The narration continues: 'Er verfiel in eine träumende Sehnsucht, und wie einstimmend mit seinen Empfindungen war das Lied, das eben in dieser Stunde Mignon und der Harfner als ein unregelmässiges Duett mit dem herzlichsten Ausdrucke sangen' (He lapsed into a dreamy state of longing, and the song which Mignon and the Harper sang at that very moment as an irregular duet, with the most heartfelt expression, seemed to chime with his emotions).

Beethoven owned a copy of *Wilhelm Meisters Lehrjahre*, which he recommended to Therese Malfatti in a letter of 1810, offering to send her the book (EA258 / BB442). Thus he would have been familiar with the context of the poem and the true identities of the characters involved, although this background knowledge hardly informs these relatively slight compositions. He would also have been familiar with Reichardt's settings of the poems, as these were inserted into the text in early editions. Those rather bland settings do not reflect the emotional complexity of the poems. Reichardt's splitting of Goethe's single stanza into two verses may have led later composers to regard the poem incorrectly as a two-stanza poem. Three of Beethoven's settings are weakened immeasurably by being set strophically, leading to such inconsistencies as 'Von aller Freude' being set to the selfsame music as 'Eingeweide'.

The text was set innumerable times during the nineteenth century. Tchaikovsky's impassioned 'None but the lonely heart' is perhaps the most popular setting, although (or more likely because) it imposes a heady emotional effusion on Goethe's more directly expressed, if impassioned text. The text fascinated Schubert, whose six settings are crowned by the duet setting (D877/1) of January 1826, which conveys all the desolation and pain of the text, while the duet form honours its original context. Schubert's setting for male voice quintet (D656) of April 1819 also follows every emotional contour of the text, enabled by the subtle colouring of the chosen vocal forces.

At least the first three of Beethoven's four settings of Goethe's text were probably written expressly for the periodical *Prometheus*, in which the first setting appeared (see below). The editors, Leo von Seckendorf and Joseph Ludwig Stoll, clearly commissioned a song from Beethoven, although we cannot know whether they also determined the text. Beethoven was pleased to have had his work published in this periodical and later offered *Andenken* for publication, but *Prometheus* ceased publication in September 1808.

Beethoven's autographs in Bonn (BH: Bodmer Mh33) include all four settings. In the right-hand margin Beethoven has written: 'Nb: Ich hatte nicht Zeit genug, um / *ein Gutes* hervorzubringen, / daher Mehrere Versuche / Ludwig van Beethowen' (I didn't have time to produce *one good one*, so here are several attempts, B.). This comment suggests that Beethoven was meeting a tight deadline and did not have the time required to refine a single masterpiece. The point is strengthened in sketches for the song (BH: Bodmer Mh75), where Beethoven writes: 'Es mangelte an Zeit, um dieses Lied *nur einmal* zu kürzen' (There was no time to shorten this song *even once*).

A long letter of 27 October 1819 (EA979 / BB1348) makes a rather similar point about its being easier to ramble than to be concise when time is limited: 'Denn schon Cicero entschuldigte sich, dass er *um kurz zu* seyn zu *wenig Zeit gehabt* hatte' (For Cicero once apologised for *having had too little time* to *be brief*). These remarks throw an interesting light on Beethoven's attitude to composition. He is stating clearly that something small and perfectly formed, be it a letter or a song, requires effort and cannot be rushed.

As the fourth and most extended setting of the song is on a separate bifolum, it may be that this version was finished later at leisure and may not have been offered to Seckendorf with the others. The editors of *Prometheus* chose the first version and this was duly published in the third volume of the periodical by Geistinger in Vienna in April 1808. All four settings were published in Vienna and Pest by the Kunst und Industrie Comptoir on 19 May 1810. Simrock published the songs in Bonn very shortly afterwards, in an edition which differed from the original only in the use of the treble clef for the voice (formerly soprano clef, as in the manuscript).

First setting (G minor)

Unusually for this period of Beethoven's song composition, none of the four settings has a piano introduction, making the songs seem even more compact. Through generous spacing, Peters manages to allocate them a page each; only the final non-strophic setting has its own page in Henle.

In the first setting, the *poco agitato* marking is underlined by a syncopated accompaniment, but this sits uneasily with the steady *andante* tempo. Emotional subtlety and tension are conspicuously absent. The voice rises above *p* only in the central three bars (to 'aller Freude'), but sinks again to end in a mood of passive resignation.

Second setting (G minor)

The second setting, in compound 6/8 time, comes close to capturing the 'dreamy state of longing' of the listener, Wilhelm Meister. The low-lying piano accompaniment, written almost throughout in bass clef and with a well supported flow of quavers, gives greater opportunity for emotional effect. Nevertheless, the choice of strophic form interrupts the emotional flow as the song restarts, and there is no attempt to convey the powerful image, with its Biblical overtones, of the burning in the bowels.

Third setting (E flat major)

The third setting, cast unexpectedly in a major key, is the least successful of Beethoven's 'attempts'. The song, with its neatly formed melody in ABA form, the doubling of voice and piano, and the jog-trot accompaniment of the central section, seems to hark back to a much earlier stage of Beethoven's career. It is certainly not equal to the emotional weight of the text.

Fourth setting (G minor)

The fourth setting is in ternary form and improves and expands the second setting. The two settings share key, time signature and aspects of the accompaniment figuration. This is the slowest of the settings, marked *assai adagio* and here alone Beethoven allows himself time to mirror the emotional tone of the text.

The expansion of the first phrase to a full four bars, as opposed to the fore-shortening of the second setting, allows the composer to emphasise 'weiss', 'was' and 'leide'. The stress on 'weiss' here draws the listener into the emotional complex as one who shares the experience of longing; this was clearly Goethe's intention.

The separation, through quaver rests, of the syllables of 'al-lein und ab-ge-trennt' produce an audible image of estrangement from life's pleasures (*Die laute Klage* exhibits a similar meaningful use of separated syllables, while the technique also recalls the quartet 'Mir ist so wunderbar' from *Fidelio*, I/iv). The melody then rises as the singer looks to the heavens for solace, before sinking again as she recalls the source of her pain, a heady mix of lovesickness and homesickness. The ensuing suddenness of the *crescendo*, accompanied with semiquaver chords, conveys the acute burning pain which comes with the memory of her plight. Beethoven is not content with a simple recapitulation of the opening phrase, but echoes this with a final varied repetition, immeasurably strengthened by the alteration of A to A flat at 'was (ich leide)'. The composer introduces the repetition by adding an extra syllable of his own on the upbeat (this insertion of an expressive 'ja' for intensification of feeling is a favourite technique).

One wonders on what criterion the first setting was selected for publication by the editors of *Prometheus*. This final version is clearly the most satisfying setting of Goethe's text, but may not have been available to the editors (see above). While most editions of the songs sheepishly reprint all four versions (despite the fact that the omission of other fine songs renders their 'complete' editions in any case incomplete), editors of song selections may be more discerning. This fourth setting is the only one included, for example, by Franz Abt in the venerable *Beethoven Album* from Litolff in Braunschweig, which provided my own earliest acquaintance with Beethoven's songs.

SEHNSUCHT Longing
Johann Wolfgang von Goethe 1810
B minor–B major Op. 83/2 Peters 29 Henle 52 GA XXIII/221

Was zieht mir das Herz so?	What is tugging so at my heart?
Was zieht mich hinaus?	What is drawing me outside?
Und windet und schraubt mich	Wrenching and propelling me
Aus Zimmer und Haus?	Out of my room, my house?
Wie dort sich die Wolken	Just as the clouds there
Um Felsen verziehn,	Disperse around the highest rocks,
Da möcht' ich hinüber,	I too long to pass over them,
Da möcht' ich wohl hin!	That's where I long to go!
Nun wiegt sich der Raben	And now the ravens swoop low
Geselliger Flug;	In sociable formation;
Ich mische mich drunter	I join in amongst them
Und folge dem Zug.	And follow their flight.

Und Berg und Gemäuer	And we swoop over
Umfittichen wir;	Mountain tops and lofty edifices;
Sie weilet da drunten;	She is down there somewhere;
Ich spähe nach ihr.	I look out for her.
Da kommt sie und wandelt;	There she comes strolling along;
Ich eile sobald,	I fly swiftly towards her,
Ein fliegender Vogel,	A flying bird,
Zum buschigten Wald.	Towards the bushy forest.
Sie weilet und horchet	She lingers and listens
Und lächelt mit sich:	And smiles to herself:
'Er singet so lieblich,	'He is singing so prettily
Und singt es an mich.'	And singing for me.'
Die scheidende Sonne	The sun's departing rays
Vergüldet die Höhn;	Gild the hilltops;
Die sinnende Schöne,	The beautiful girl ponders
Sie lässt es geschehn.	As she enjoys the scene.
Sie wandelt am Bache	She strolls through the meadows
Die Wiesen entlang,	That border the stream,
Und finster und finstrer	And the path, dark and ever darker,
Umschlingt sich der Gang.	Fades into its own embrace.
Auf einmal erschein' ich,	Then suddenly I appear,
Ein blinkender Stern.	A twinkling star.
'Was glänzet da droben,	'What is shining up above,
So nah und so fern?'	So near and yet so far away?'
Und hast du mit Staunen	And no sooner have you marvelled
Das Leuchten erblickt;	At the sight of the sparkling light,
Ich lieg' dir zu Füssen,	Than I am lying at your feet.
Da bin ich beglückt!	Then I am truly happy!

Goethe's poem first appeared in the *Taschenbuch auf das Jahr 1804* and was reprinted in 1806 in Cotta's edition of his works in Tübingen. The image of a poet's longing taking the form of a bird is not unique to this poem – consider, for example, Schubert's *Die Taubenpost*, or Beethoven's own *Ruf vom Berge* – but is here developed as a storyline over five stanzas. The bird, moreover, seems to represent the poet and not just his longing. Romantic poets tended to focus upon unrequited longing, which can come across as a form of emotional self-gratification; the longing is the thing, and for longing to be satisfied would break the spell. Goethe does indeed break the spell at the end of the poem when his journey's end is described not in the conditional, but in the present tense. One wonders whether Goethe's poem is intended as a rather ironical commentary on the Romantic cultivation of 'Sehnsucht'.

Sketches for Beethoven's setting in Krakow (BJ: Landsberg 11), dating from October 1810, indicate that the composer was consistent in his thinking on this song, which was planned from the start in B minor and in 6/8 metre. An autograph in Paris (BN: Ms. 21) contains heavily corrected versions of all the songs of op. 83. The three songs of op. 83 were published by Breitkopf und Härtel in Leipzig in October 1811. The first edition follows the manuscript in printing 'fliegender Vogel' (third stanza, l.3). The old complete edition and hence Peters chose 'singender Vogel' as in the original poem, but Henle has reverted to Beethoven's version.

The song opens with a 'gathering note', followed by semiquaver runs which suggest the unease which drives the poet to leave the confines of his room. (These semiquaver meanderings seem to prefigure Schubert's *Am Feierabend* from *Die schöne Müllerin*, and a further similarity to this song is found in the punching rhythm – two quavers plus rest – which occurs in the third stanza of Beethoven's song and throughout Schubert's). The song is of varied strophic form, the variation in the first four stanzas being created by the figuration of the piano accompaniment. This variation seems to be for variety's sake alone for the most part, but there is an amusing attempt to convey the swooping flight of the ravens in the second stanza. The trills which begin the interludes between stanzas are the merest adumbration of birdsong. In the final stanza the music brightens with a turn to B major and a high-lying accompaniment as the bird is transformed into the likeness of a twinkling star and the girl gazes in wonder.

This is one of Beethoven's jolliest songs and useful to refresh the audience's musical palate between some of the weightier offerings of a song recital.

SEUFZER EINES UNGELIEBTEN / GEGENLIEBE
Sigh of one who is unloved / Love returned
Gottfried August Bürger   1794–95
E flat major–C major WoO118 Peters 63 Henle 79 GA XXIII/253

Seufzer eines Ungeliebten

Hast du nicht Liebe zugemessen
Dem Leben jeder Kreatur?
Warum bin ich allein vergessen,
Auch meine Mutter, du! Natur?

Wo lebte wohl in Forst und Heide
Und wo in Luft und Meer ein Tier,
Das nimmermehr geliebet würde?
Geliebt wird alles ausser mir!

Wenngleich in Hain und Wiesenmatten
Sich Baum und Staude, Moos und Kraut

Sigh of one who is unloved

Have you not allotted love
To the life of every creature?
Why am I alone forgotten, O Nature?
Surely you are my mother too!

Where in forest or heath, in sky
Or sea did there ever live an animal
Which was never loved?
Everything is loved except me!

Although, in grove and meadows,
Trees and bushes, mosses and plants

Durch Liebe und Gegenliebe gatten,	Are joined together through mutual love,
Vermählt sich mir doch keine Braut.	No bride joins me in wedded bliss.
Mir wächst vom süssesten der Triebe	Honeyed fruits never ripen for me
Nie Honigfrucht zur Lust heran,	From the sweetest shoots of desire,
Denn, ach! mir mangelt Gegenliebe,	For, alas, I lack that returned love
Die eine nur gewähren kann.	Which only one can grant me.

Gegenliebe

Love returned

Wüsst' ich, wüsst' ich, dass du mich	If I could but know that you
Lieb und wert ein bisschen hieltest	Love and esteem me just a little
Und von dem, was ich für dich	And that you feel just the tiniest part
Nur ein Hunderteilchen fühltest;	Of what I feel for you;
Dass dein Dank hübsch meinem Gruss	That your thanks might graciously meet
Halben Wegs entgegenkäme	My protestations halfway,
Und dein Mund den Wechselkuss	And that your lips might gladly accept
Gerne gäb' und wieder nähme,	And return my kisses,
Dann, o Himmel, ausser sich	Then, oh bliss, my uncontrollable heart
Würde ganz mein Herz zerlodern!	Would simply burst into flames!
Leib und Leben könnt' ich dich	You could demand my body or my life,
Nicht vergebens lassen fodern!	They would not be denied you.
Gegengunst erhöhet Gunst,	Returned feelings intensify feelings,
Liebe nähret Gegenliebe	Love nourishes a loving response
Und entflammt zur Feuersbrunst,	And fans what might have remained
Was ein Aschenfünkchen bliebe.	A dying ember into a raging fire.

The two poems combined here as one *Doppellied* were originally written and published separately. Both appeared in the Göttingen *Musenalmanach*: *Gegenliebe* appeared in 1774, in the almanac for 1775, and *Seufzer eines Ungeliebten* the following year. In collected editions of Bürger's poetry, they were printed consecutively. It seems certain that Bürger conceived *Seufzer* as a prelude to *Gegenliebe*, as the word 'Gegenliebe' appears twice in the later poem. Haydn set only *Gegenliebe* in the second part of his *Lieder für das Clavier* (1784), although his coy strophic setting does not come close to matching Bürger's impassioned verse.

Bürger's poetry comes from not so much from the heart as from the loins, and his very direct and impassioned protestations of love must have caused the raising of many an eyebrow. In *Seufzer*, human love is compared to the animal instinct which leads to coupling among all Mother Nature's creatures, and the poet seems to be seeking physical satisfaction first and foremost. In *Gegenliebe*, the modest wish for a little reciprocation in the first stanza is rapidly intensified into a willing exchange of kisses, the offering of life and body, and a raging fire of passion. Bürger's view of sexual union as something natural and therefore right is by no means unique to these poems. Indeed, a sonnet entitled *Naturrecht* 'Natural right' aims specifically to justify his view that 'Menschensatzung' (human convention and law) should not prevent him from enjoying blissful physical union with his girl-friend.

We can only speculate whether Beethoven fully recognised and shared Bürger's sentiments. The sketches for the song in Vienna (GdM: A35), Berlin (SPK: Aut.28) and London (BL: Add.Ms. 29801) all date from 1794 or 1795, when Beethoven was a young man of 24, enjoying his early years in Vienna, away from home. The London sketch, from the Kafka album, is helpfully transcribed by Kerman (*An Autograph Miscellany*) and shows clearly that the intention was from the first to combine the two songs, with indications of the transition. On the other hand, there is no hint of the opening recitative which is a striking feature of the published version and a definite improvement on the composer's original idea of setting the whole of the first song in 3/4 time, which presented problems of prosodic declamation.

The song was listed, along with other early unpublished works, in a price list which Beethoven prepared in 1822 (See Tyson, 'A Price List of 1822'), where it is identified by first line of each poem and the key, which Beethoven gives debatably as 'C minor, C major'. It was finally published posthumously by Diabelli in Vienna in April 1837, together with *Die laute Klage*. No autograph survives, and so we cannot assess whether Diabelli, himself a composer, made any alterations to the composer's text. The suspicion remains, as Diabelli certainly added embellishments to *Die laute Klage*, as well as to several of the Schubert songs which were appearing in posthumous editions at a similar time.

The song is conceived on an ambitious scale. Lesley Orrey (*Beethoven Companion*, p. 419) feels that the song corresponds to the Italian operatic form of the 'cavatina-cabaletta' and compares the song to the more extended concert aria *Ah! perfido* (op. 65) of 1796. There are clear echoes of the *Andantino* from *Seufzer eines Ungeliebten* in the slow Aria section, also in E flat and in 3/4 time, of *Ah! perfido*, as well as general structural similarities. Unusually in the early songs, the piano accompaniment plays a full role, generally independent of voice-doubling, and occasionally suggests an orchestral conception in short score. There is also much more emphasis on purely musical considerations as regards the structure, balance and transitions of the song. Words are repeated in patterns which satisfy purely musical values, rather than to illuminate their intrinsic meaning.

The song begins with a recitative, apostrophising Mother Nature, which starts solidly in C minor, but modulates rapidly to B flat major. This in turn introduces the main *Andantino* section in E flat, which opens with an eight-bar piano introduction, prefiguring the opening bars of the vocal melody. The *Andantino* progresses fluently, with a particularly memorable musical phrase at bar 40 ('Wenngleich in Hain und Wiesenmatten'), initiating the stream of quavers which gives the section such forward thrust. The first poem is through-composed, and although the start of each stanza is delineated with a newly coined idea, the mangling of the poet's words within each stanza suggests strongly that Beethoven's watchword here is 'prima la musica (e poi le parole)'. The prosody is sound, but the repetition of words and phrases is dictated by musical considerations alone.

At the end of the recitative and *Andantino* section, which sets *Seufzer eines Ungeliebten*, there is a clear link to the final section, which sets *Gegenliebe*, with the opening words of the latter poem ('Wüsst' ich') heard twice above eight bars of postlude and a cadenza, which elaborate the dominant seventh of C major. The final *Allegretto* section, in C major, has such a memorable theme that it can have aurally the effect of a Rondo, although in fact there are simply two repeated sections, with some variation in the repeat of the second section.

Beethoven's later use of the music of *Gegenliebe* in his grand Choral Fantasia (op. 80) in 1808, setting very different words which speak of the civilising power of music in ideal terms, demonstrates that the music is not intimately bound to Bürger's words in the present song, and that the composer fully appreciated its potential for larger forces. The similarity of outline between this music and the melody which sets Schiller's *An die Freude* in the Ninth Symphony (1823) is less surprising when the idealising words of the Choral Fantasy are considered, but illustrates too the enduring impact of this important early song.

SO ODER SO The one or the other
Karl Gottlieb Lappe   1816 – early 1817

F major WoO148 Peters 54 Henle 66 GA XXIII/244

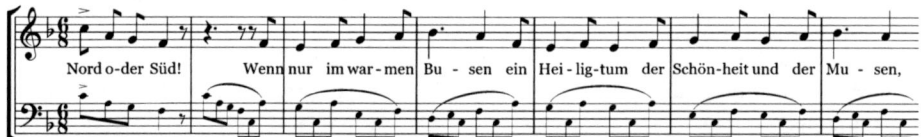

Nord oder Süd! Wenn nur im warmen Busen / Ein Heiligtum der Schönheit und der Musen, / Ein Götterreicher Himmel blüht!

Nord oder Süd! Wenn nur im warmen Busen	North or south! So long as, within a warm breast,
Ein Heiligtum der Schönheit und der Musen,	A sanctuary to beauty and the muses,
Ein Götterreicher Himmel blüht!	A god-filled heaven can blossom!
Nur Geistesarmut kann der Winter morden,	Winter can kill only intellectual poverty,
Kraft fügt zu Kraft und Glanz zu Glanz der Norden.	The north adds strength to strength and lustre to lustre.
Nord oder Süd!	North or south!
Wenn nur die Seele glüht!	So long as the soul is aglow!
Stadt oder Land! Nur nicht zu eng die Räume,	Town or country! If rooms are not too cramped,
Ein wenig Himmel, etwas Grün der Bäume	A bit of sky, a few green leaves on trees
Zum Schatten vor dem Sonnenbrand!	To shade us from the burning sun!
Nicht an das Wo ward Seligkeit gebunden.	Pure bliss was never bound to location.
Wer hat das Glück schon ausser sich gefunden?	Who ever found happiness outside of himself?
Stadt oder Land!	Town or country!
Die Aussenwelt ist Tand.	The outside world is cheap show.

(Knecht oder Herr! Auch Könige sind Knechte.
Wir dienen gern der Wahrheit und dem Rechte.
Gebeut uns nur, bist du verständiger.
Doch soll kein Hochmut unsern Sinn
    verhöhnen.
Nur Sklavensinn kann fremder Laune
    fröhnen.
    Knecht oder Herr!
    Nur keines Menchen Narr!)

Arm oder reich! Sei's Pfirsich oder Pflaume!
Wir pflücken ungleich von dem
    Lebensbaume.
Dir zollt der Ast, mir nur der Zweig.
Mein leichtes Mahl wiegt darum nicht
    geringe.
Lust am Genuss bestimmt den Wert der
    Dinge.
    Arm oder reich!
    Die Glücklichen sind gleich.

Blass oder rot! Nur auf den bleichen
    Wangen
Sehnsucht und Liebe, Zürnen und Erbangen,
Gefühl und Trost für fremde Not!
Es strahlt der Geist nicht aus des Blutes
    Welle.
Ein andrer Spiegel brennt in Sonnenhelle.

    Blass oder rot!
    Nur nicht das Auge tot!

Jung oder alt! Was kümmern uns die Jahre!
Der Geist ist frisch, doch Schelme sind die
    Haare.
Auch mir ergraut das Haupt zu bald.
Doch eilt nur, Locken, glänzend euch zu
    färben,
Es ist nicht Schade, Silber zu erwerben.
    Jung oder alt!
    Doch erst am Grabe kalt!

Schlaf oder Tod! Willkommen,
    Zwillingsbrüder!
Der Tag ist hin; ihr zieht die Wimper nieder.
Traum ist der Erde Glück und Not.

(Servant or master! Kings are servants too.
We willingly serve truth and justice.
Do command us, if you are more intelligent.
But no arrogance should belittle our
    minds.
Only a slavish mentality can humour
    foreign whims.
    Servant or master!
    Just nobody's fool!)

Poor or rich! Whether peach or plum!
We pick unequally from the tree of life.

The branch for you, just the twig for me.
My modest meal does not seem frugal for
    all that.
True enjoyment determines the value of
    things.
    Poor or rich!
    Happy people are all equal.

Pale or ruddy! Only on pallid cheeks do we
    behold
Yearning and love, anger and fear,
Feeling and comfort for the distress of others.
The spirit does not shine forth from
    coursing blood,
A different mirror burns in the sun's
    brightness.
    Pale or ruddy!
    Just so long as the eye is not dead.

Young or old! What do the years matter to us!
Our mind stays youthful, but our hair is a
    rascal.
My head too is greying all too soon.
But hasten, hair, to adopt a shining new
    tint,
There is no shame in acquiring silver.
    Young or old!
    But cold only in the grave!

Sleep or death! Welcome, twin brothers!

The day is over; you close our eyelids.
Earth's joy and misery are but a dream.

Zu kurzer Tag! Zu schnell verrauschtes Leben!	O day too short! O life that fades too quickly!
Warum so schön und doch so rasch verschweben?	Why so beautiful and yet so swift to vanish?
Schlaf oder Tod!	Sleep or death!
Hell strahlt das Morgenrot.	Brightly shines the rosy dawn.

The Pomeranian schoolmaster Karl Lappe is best remembered today through two celebrated settings of his verse by Schubert, *Im Abendrot* (D799) and *Der Einsame* (D800), both composed in January 1825. Throughout the nineteenth century, however, his fame rested on *So oder So*, a rather quizzical poem which encourages readers to come to terms with their lot by setting up a series of contrasting situations, and then demonstrating that it is how one copes with one's current situation which really matters. The third stanza, contrasting servants and masters, was omitted in all early editions of the song. This omission may have been due to the controversial subject matter, as with *Der freie Mann*, or to the fact that this is the only stanza which presents problems of scansion (line 3). It may have been already expurgated in Beethoven's copy of the poem, which had been printed shortly before in the *Zeitung für die elegante Welt* in Leipzig, in May 1816.

The song was first published in February 1817 as a 'special supplement' to the *Wiener-Moden-Zeitung und Zeitschrift für Kunst, schöne Literatur und Theater*, printed by Anton Strauss in Vienna, and republished later that year by Simrock in Bonn. Peter Simrock had visited Beethoven in June 1816 and obtained copies of *An die Geliebte* and *Das Geheimnis*, which had already been published as supplements to periodicals and which were quickly reprinted by Nikolaus Simrock. It is unclear whether at the same time Peter Simrock obtained a manuscript copy of *So oder so* or a promise that the projected song would be sent to him in Bonn.

A lost autograph, formerly in the Artaria collection, was dated '1817' in Thayer's chronological index of Beethoven's works (Berlin 1865). J. Fischhof stated, in an article in *Caecilia* XXVI published in 1847, that Beethoven had written a fascinating note on tempo and interpretation on the manuscript: '100 nach Mälzel, doch kann diess nur von den ersten Takten gelten, denn die Empfindung hat auch ihren Takt, dieses ist aber nicht ganz in diesem Grade (100 nämlich) auszudrücken' (100 MM, but this can apply only to the opening bars, since feeling also has its own beat, but this cannot be completely conveyed at this level (ie: 100)). This is reminiscent of the performance direction for *Der Mann vom Wort*, where Beethoven asks for dynamics to be matched to the poetic content, and also explains the careful directions for the performance of the final two stanzas, where Beethoven twice suggests a slight hesitation ('etwas verzögernd') before returning to the original tempo ('erstes Zeitmass').

Brief sketches for the song are found in the vicinity of sketches for the Piano Sonata op. 101, composed in 1816 (See Johnson, Tyson and Winter, *The Beethoven Sketchbooks*, pp. 251, 345), and there is an unmistakable similarity of melodic and rhythmic outline between the opening bars of the song and the sonata. This is apparent in the rising melodic figure (song: bar 3) and the wheeling 6/8 motion, and is reinforced by similar tempo indications: 'Etwas lebhaft' (sonata), 'Ziemlich lebhaft' (song).

The song finely captures the poem's mix of declamation, popular philosophising and gentle irony. The poem's unusual metre is turned to musical advantage. The initial declamation of the opening dichotomy, underlined by a short rest in the vocal line, is followed by a purely syllabic, but smoothly flowing setting of the remaining two-and-a-half lines. These eight bars (3–10) would function quite well as a solo piano piece, as the voice is doubled in the pianist's right-hand, the bass line incidentally duetting with the melody while constantly returning to low C as a passing pedal note. Thereafter the song builds to a dynamic climax at the peroration of the poet's argument (line 5), before the declamation of the first bar is heard again, along with the final tag line. A two-bar postlude leads directly back to the next verse in all but the final stanza, when a single extra bar is considered sufficient to rein the energetic pulse of the music.

SOLL ICH'S NUR DEM IRRTHUM DANKEN
Should I attribute it to a fallacy
unknown 1809

E minor SV59 sketch

This 8-bar fragment (not 6 bars, as Boettcher states in *Beethoven als Liederkomponist*, table VIII) is in the Landsberg 5 sketchbook (Berlin, SPK, p. 63), dating it to 1809. It is strange that an abortive sketch such as this should date from the same year as the polished settings of Reissig poems, which represent Beethoven at his most fluently inspired. The words, from an unidentified source, read: 'Soll ich's nur dem Irrthum danken, dass die Liebe (?nirgends) . . .' (Should I attribute it to a fallacy that love (?nowhere) . . .) and make little sense in the absence of the remaining lines. The fragment is included here for the sake of completeness.

As is usual, the sketch is difficult to decipher because of the casual placing of the heads of the notes, and the transcription above differs slightly from that of Clemens Brenneis. Boettcher lists the sketch as 'G major', but there is a stronger case for reading it as E minor, a key of nostalgic lament, otherwise used by Beethoven only for *Der Bardengeist* and the second section of Hölty's Klage.

SÜSSER RUHEGESANG – FRIEDENSGESANG
Sweet song of repose – song of peace

SV30 1826 instrumental

This sketch in the 'Kullak' desk sketchbook (SPK: Aut.24, f. 41v), which Beethoven used in late 1825 and throughout 1826, is listed by Schmidt under the heading of 'songs' on the basis of the supposed title (see above), but this is merely a descriptive heading for what was to have been an eighth movement for the String Quartet op. 131. The movement was, however, dropped from op. 131 and taken up as the theme for the slow movement of op. 135 (I am grateful to Barry Cooper for this information). The direction for the movement as published *Lento assai, cantante e tranquillo* accords closely with the German heading as above.

Although this sketch is not for a vocal composition, then, it does remind us how frequently Beethoven used vocal designations for later instrumental works: in piano sonatas, the 'Klagender Gesang' (Song of lament) of op. 110, the 'Arietta' of op. 111, and the 'Gesangvoll' (originally just 'Gesang') of op. 109; in string quartets, the 'Cavatina' of op. 130 or the 'Heiliger Dankgesang' (Holy song of thanksgiving) of op. 132. Just as Beethoven did not hesitate to incorporate instrumental techniques into songs (see *Adelaide*), so he expanded the expressive range of instrumental compositions with techniques and styles acquired from vocal composition.

T'INTENDO SÌ, MIO COR I hear you, my heart
Pietro Metastasio   1809
D major Op. 82/2 Peters 24 Henle 47 GA XXIII/220

Adagio ma non troppo

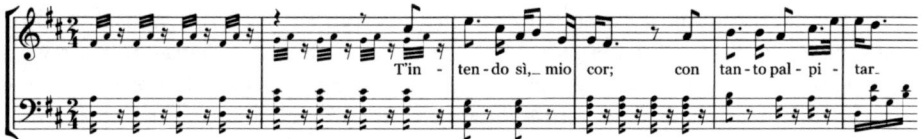

T'intendo sì, mio cor;	I understand you well, my heart;
Con tanto palpitar	From your vigorous throbbing
So che ti vuoi lagnar	I know you wish to complain
Che amante sei.	That you are in love.
Ah! Taci il tuo dolor;	Ah, do not reveal your sorrow;
Ah! Soffri il tuo martir:	Ah, bear your anguish:
Tacilo, e non tradir	Keep it silent, and do not betray
Gli affetti miei.	My fond feelings.

The text is found in Metastasio's cantata *Amor Timido*. Both the Italian and the Viennese public seem to have had an insatiable appetite for such stylised expressions of love in all its manifestations. Here the poet addresses his beating heart, setting up the sort of internal dialogue which recurs frequently, both in Italian verse and in German poetry. One thinks, for example, of Goethe's *Neue Liebe, Neues Leben* or Ernst Schulze's *An mein Herz* (To my heart), the latter addressed to a restlessly beating heart. The rate of the human heartbeat is a fundamental feature of tonal analogue, and it is fascinating to compare Beethoven's energetic settings of the Goethe text and Schubert's tempestuous setting of Schulze's poem (D860) with the slowly sighing, almost sobbing figure used in the present setting to suggest a heart which suffers but must ever keep silence.

No autograph survives, although there are extensive sketches for the setting in Berlin (DSB: Landsberg 5), suggesting late 1809 as a likely date of composition. The song was published by Breitkopf und Härtel in Leipzig in July 1811, with

Italian and German texts, as the second song of op. 82, which consists entirely of Italian songs. The German translation by Christian Schreiber was entitled 'Liebes-Klage' (Love's lament). Clementi had published the songs of op. 82 separately, and, since Härtel's edition was delayed by a dispute over Beethoven's fee, the English edition appeared in London in February 1811, five months before the German edition.

Clementi included the Italian text only. Although he had commissioned English translations for the German texts of op. 75, he no doubt thought that Italian was more familiar to his potential customers, rendering an English translation superfluous. As a notable musician himself, he probably also realised that these wholly authentic-sounding Italian settings need to be sung in their original language. The German translation, reprinted in the old complete edition and in Peters, but omitted by Henle, sounds out of place, even when one leaves aside such matters as metrical irregularities. This is a tribute to Beethoven's mastery of the Italian arietta form, inspired at this time in his life by his burgeoning love for Therese Malfatti and perhaps technically perfected by consultation lessons with Antonio Salieri.

Beethoven finds a rising demisemiquaver couplet figure, separated by short rests, as an analogue for his suffering heart. This touching figure, suggestive of sighing or sobbing, a persistent tug at the heartstrings, opens and closes the song, and recurs in regular short interludes, lending the song musical and semantic unity. The fact that the figure is not replicated in the vocal melody and hardly overlaps the voice creates a real sense of dialogue: the piano is the beating heart, to which the singer responds with his first phrase and with whom he maintains an emotional exchange throughout. The usual rhetorical devices of Italian song and the gestures of *opera seria*, appoggiaturas, turns and roulades, achieve a rare emotional impact in this slow-paced setting. The chosen key of D major prevents the song from descending into black despair, but there is an extraordinary poignancy in the turn to D minor and thence to B flat (key of the flattened submediant, beloved of both Beethoven and Schubert) at bars 26 and 27.

Hans Boettcher (*Beethoven als Liederkomponist*, p. 155) points to a remarkable echo of Mozart's *Marriage of Figaro* (from the Countess's aria from act III) in bars 19–22, attributing this to the fact that both composers were exposed to similar examples of Italian *opera seria*. Needless to say, Beethoven will also have had frequent opportunities to hear *Figaro* in Vienna.

TRAUTE HENRIETTE Dearest Henriette (fragment)

unknown   1790–92

D major Hess 151 Supp V/5 Henle 98 Not in GA/Peters

traute Henriette	Dearest Henriette,
holdeste brünette	Loveliest of brunettes,
hast du lieb für (mich?)	Do you love (me?)
heitre mein gemüthe	Cheer my spirits,
sänftge mein geblüte	Calm my raging blood:
Mädchen liebe mich	Maiden, love me!

The autograph of this fragmentary song is in the Stadtbibliothek in Vienna (WStB: MH 1844/c) and is reproduced in the Critical Report to the Henle edition (p. 109). Paper studies (which identify the manuscript paper used by watermark and rastrology) have dated the song to 1790 to 1792, making it one of Beethoven's last Bonn works or one of his earliest Viennese works. The song was first published in a completion by Adolf Erler (a.k.a. Alfred Orel) in the *Österreichische Musikzeitschrift* IV in 1949. Willy Hess includes a sympathetic realisation of the song in his Supplementary Volume V (1962), but the Henle edition includes only a direct transcription of the sketch.

The Hess realisation at least renders the song performable as a curiosity, but it would have required a great deal more work prior to publication. Despite clumsy phrasing and a stop-start effect in its movement, the song has points of interest even as a fragment. The entry of the voice, unaccompanied, in the first bar, appears deliberate, as rests are correctly notated in the piano part, and represents an innovative experiment in song. The rhythmic figure of the first bar is then transferred to the piano in bar 7 to introduce the second section of the song. Similarly, the phrase at 'liebe mich' (bar 14) is echoed by the pianist in bar 18.

The sketch thus provides an interesting insight into Beethoven's attempts to effect coherence in a song through related metrical and melodic phrases. This time, hampered also by the inadequacy of the text, it did not produce a 'finished' *Lied*, in either sense of the epithet.

URIANS REISE UM DIE WELT
Urian's world trip
Matthias Claudius   uncertain date
A minor–major Op. 52/1 Peters 9 Henle 4 GA XXIII/218

In einer mäßigen, geschwinden Bewegung mit einer komischen Art gesungen

Wenn | jemand eine | Reise tut,   so | kann er was ver | zählen;   drum | nahm ich meinen | Stock und Hut

Wenn jemand eine Reise tut,	When someone makes a journey,
So kann er was verzählen;	He has some tales to tell;
Drum nahm ich meinen Stock und Hut	So I took up my hat and stick,
Und tät das Reisen wählen.	And set off on my travels.

Tutti (vv. 1–13):
Da hat er gar nicht übel dran getan;
Verzähl Er doch weiter, Herr Urian!

Zuerst ging's an den Nordpol hin;
Da war es kalt, bei Ehre!
Da dacht' ich mir in meinem Sinn,
Dass es hier besser wäre.

In Grönland freuten sie sich sehr,
Mich ihres Orts zu sehen,
Und setzten mir den Trankkrug her;
Ich liess ihn aber stehen.

Die Eskimos sind wild und gross,
Zu allem Guten träge;
Da schalt ich einen einen Kloss
Und kriegte viele Schläge.

Nun war ich in Amerika;
Da sagt' ich zu mir: 'Lieber!
Nordwestpassage ist doch da;
Mach dich einmal darüber!'

Flugs ich an Bord und aus ins Meer,
Den Tubus festgebunden,
Und suchte sie die Kreuz und Quer,
Und hab' sie nicht gefunden.

Von hier ging ich nach Mexiko;
Ist weiter als nach Bremen;
Da, dacht' ich, liegt das Geld wie Stroh;
Du sollst'n Sack voll nehmen.

Allein, allein, allein, allein,
Wie kann ein Mensch sich trügen!
Ich fand da nichts als Sand und Stein
Und liess den Sack da liegen.

Drauf kauft' ich etwas kalte Kost
Und Kieler Sprott' und Kuchen
Und setzte mich auf Extrapost,
Land Asia zu besuchen.

Der Mogul ist ein grosser Mann
Und gnädig über Maßen

Chorus (vv. 1–13):
That was a jolly good thing to do.
Tell us more, Herr Urian!

First I visited the North Pole –
That was a bit cold, my goodness!
I thought to myself,
You're better off at home, lad.

In Greenland they were delighted
To see me in those parts.
They offered me the local drink,
But I did not partake.

The Eskimos are wild and large
And too lazy for anything worthwhile.
I called one a great lump
And got myself beaten up.

Then I reached America
And said to myself: 'Now, old lad,
The North-West Passage is around here.
Let's cross it!'

Quick as a flash I was on board
And out to sea with my trusty telescope.
Looked high and low,
But couldn't find it.

From there I went to Mexico;
It's a bit further than Bremen.
There's gold a-plenty there, I thought;
Grab yourself a bagful.

And yet, and yet, and yet, and yet . . .
How wrong can a fellow be?
I found nothing but sand and rock
And left the bag behind.

Next I bought a few cold snacks,
Cake and some sprats from Kiel,
And jumped on the express coach
To visit Asia.

The Mogul is a great man
And gracious beyond anything,

Und klug; er war itzt eben dran,	And clever; he was just having
'n Zahn ausziehn zu lassen.	One of his teeth extracted.
Hm! Dacht' ich, der hat Zähnepein	Hm, thought I, he has toothache
Bei aller Gröss' und Gaben! -	For all his magnificence.
Was hilft's denn auch noch: Mogul sein?	What's the good of being a Mogul?
Die kann man so wohl haben.	Anybody can have toothache.
Ich gab dem Wirt mein Ehrenwort,	I promised the landlord
Ihn nächstens zu bezahlen;	That I would settle up very soon
Und damit reist' ich weiter fort	And then continued on my way
Nach China und Bengalen.	To China and Bengal.
Nach Java und nach Otaheit	Thence on to Java and Tahiti,
Und Afrika nicht minder;	Not forgetting Africa,
Und sah bei der Gelegenheit	And I saw lots of towns
Viel Städt' und Menschenkinder.	And peoples on my travels.
Und fand es überall wie hier,	And found everywhere the same as here,
Fand überall 'n Sparren,	Everywhere some sticking point.
Die Menschen grade so wie wir	The people just the same as us,
Und eben solche Narren.	Just as big idiots.
Tutti: Da hat er übel, übel dran getan;	*Final chorus:* That was a bad thing to do.
Verzähl Er nicht weiter, Herr Urian!	Don't tell us any more, Herr Urian!

Claudius's whimsical poem first appeared in the Hamburg *Musenalmanach* for 1786, although Beethoven probably encountered it in Bossler's *Blumenlese für Klavierliebhaber* for 1787. This was, after all, the journal in which his earliest surviving songs had been printed: *Schilderung eines Mädchens* in 1783, and *An einen Säugling* in 1784. The dating of Beethoven's setting is uncertain; a related melody sketch in Moscow (CMMC: Wielhorsky sketchbook) dates from 1802–3, but Franz Wegeler, in the biographical notes which he wrote in collaboration with Ferdinand Ries, mentions it as one of the composer's very first songs. Johnson (*Beethoven's Early Sketches*) dates it as early as 1790–91 since a melody sketch appears alongside *Die Liebe* in an autograph in Koblenz (Sammlung Wegeler, SV329), but Lühning (*Kritischer Bericht*, p. 11, n. 4) questions the identification of this melody sketch. The song was finally published in June 1805 by the Kunst und Industrie Comptoir in Vienna, as the first of the eight songs of op. 52, in which Beethoven assembled some of his best essays in song from the last decade of the previous century.

'*Urians Reise um die Welt* ist ein guter Spaß, gemacht, eine lustige Gesellschaft zu unterhalten' (*Urian's world trip* is good fun, designed to entertain a jolly assembly), as a reviewer stated in the Viennese *Allgemeiner Musikalischer Anzeiger* in 1830. This brief mention in the first surviving review of op. 52 sums up the aim and the appeal of the song, pre-echoing De Curzon's description of it as an 'amusette' (*Les Lieder*, p. 15). *Urians Reise* is one of several early songs written for a soloist with a choral refrain. Some of these are solemn affairs, like *Der freie Mann* with its statement of the idealists' creed, or warlike, such as the *Kriegslied der Österreicher* and its companion piece *Abschiedsgesang an Wiens Bürger*, written for the Viennese volunteer force. Others are purely convivial, such as the song of personal farewell *Erhebt das Glas* or the later wedding cantata *Auf Freunde, singt dem Gott der Ehen*. The present song and the celebrated Flea Song (*Aus Goethe's Faust*) both set out to amuse as well as to entertain.

Both German and English listeners are entitled to wonder as to the identity of the eponymous Urian. A typically long, cross-referenced entry in *Grimms Dictionary* fails to solve the problem completely. The name was sometimes used simply to indicate a person whose name could not be called to mind ('old so-and-so'), but more often disparagingly. In this case it seems to indicate a grumpy old codger who criticises everything and everybody. 'Urian' was used occasionally as a 'Nick'-name for the Devil, most notably by Goethe in *Faust*, where Herr Urian presides over the Witches' Sabbath. This is unlikely in the present case – a pity, as it could have provided a neat link with Mephistopheles' *Flohlied*!

Beethoven nicely captures the comic tone of Claudius's poem, with a simple, balanced and highly singable melody, spiced with cheeky semiquaver half-bar mini-interludes in the pianist's left hand. The verse is in A minor, the chorus in A major with fuller harmony and bass octaves supporting the new vocal forces. Beethoven requests that the song should be sung 'in a comical manner'. In the hands of a singer with dramatic flair, the song should be a comical *tour de force*. It is important that the soloist should sing all fourteen verses, to give the world tour its full impact. As it is seldom practicable to have a chorus on stage in performance, why not encourage the audience to join in the *tutti*? This would certainly help to create the highly convivial mood intended by poet and composer.

WECHSELLIED ZUM TANZE
Alternating song for dancing
Johann Wolfgang von Goethe

1799

E flat major Bia 194 / SV46 sketch

Die Gleichgültigen:

Komm mit, o Schöne, komm mit mir zum
Tanze;

Tanzen gehöret zum festlichen Tag.

The indifferent ones:

Come with me, my beauty, let's away to the
dance;

Dancing is part and parcel of a festive
occasion.

Bist du mein Schatz nicht, so kannst du es werden,
Wirst du es nimmer, so tanzen wir doch.
Komm mit, o Schöne, komm mit mir zum Tanze;
Tanzen gehöret zum festlichen Tag.

Though you are not my sweetheart, you can become so,
If you never do, we can still dance anyway.
Come with me, my beauty, let's away to the dance;
Dancing is part and parcel of a festive occasion.

Die Zärtlichen:
Ohne dich, Liebste, was wären die Feste?

Ohne dich, Süsse, was wäre der Tanz?

Wärst du mein Schatz nicht, so möcht' ich nicht tanzen,
Bleibst du es immer, ist Leben ein Fest.

Ohne dich, Liebste, was wären die Feste?

Ohne dich, Süsse, was wäre der Tanz?

(Folgen 2 Strophen)

The truly affectionate ones:
What would festivities be without you, my dearest?

What would a dance be without you, sweetest one?

If you were not my sweetheart I would not choose to dance;
As long as you remain so, life is one long party.

What would festivities be without you, my dearest?

What would a dance be without you, sweetest one?

(2 further stanzas)

The poem was first published in 1789 in volume VIII of Goethe's collected works. The four stanzas are spoken alternately by the 'indifferent' and the 'truly affectionate' partners, the frivolous flirting of the former contrasted with the solid fidelity of the latter.

Beethoven sketched only the first stanza, appropriately employing the characteristic 3/8 tempo of the *Ländler* or waltz. The entire twelve-bar sketch is reproduced above. While fragmentary, it is in effect a complete melody sketch, since the first four bars are repeated, as the verbal underlay indicates, and would no doubt be used again with a closing cadence when the first two lines are repeated as the final couplet. We can only speculate as to how Beethoven would have changed the tone of the music for the different persona of the second stanza. Reichardt, in his 1794 setting, achieved this contrast by a change of tempo, from 3/8 to 2/8. Thus far, then, Beethoven has followed the example of the older composer. It would be left to Johannes Brahms in his 1864 setting for vocal quartet, op. 31/1, to find the perfect musical equivalent for Goethe's poem; Brahms splits his quartet into two couples, with the rather stiff and arch style of the 'indifferent ones' set against the smoothly lyrical warmth of the 'affectionate ones', all within the context of a continuous slow waltz on the piano.

Beethoven's sketch is in the Grasnick 2 sketchbook (Berlin, SPK, p. 31) and can be dated to the first half of 1799. The sketchbook has been published in facsimile (1972) and transcription (1974) by the Beethoven House in Bonn, edited by Wilhelm Virneisel.

WONNE DER WEHMUT The joy of melancholy
Johann Wolfgang von Goethe 1810
E major Op. 83/1 Peters 28 Henle 51 GA XXIII/221

Trocknet nicht, trocknet nicht,	Never dry, never dry,
Tränen der ewigen Liebe!	Tears of eternal love!
Ach! Nur dem halbgetrockneten Auge	Ah, how desolate, how dead the world appears
Wie öde, wie tot die Welt ihm erscheint!	To eyes that have even half-dried!
Trocknet nicht, trocknet nicht,	Never dry, never dry,
Tränen unglücklicher Liebe!	Tears of unhappy love!

Goethe's poem was written around 1775, during the age of sentimentality, but published in a revised form only in 1789, in the eighth volume of his collected works. Both in this poem, and in a contemporary poem *Im Herbst 1775* (revised as *Herbstgefühl*), tears are presented as life-giving and life-preserving. In *Im Herbst 1775* it is the poet's gushing tears of love ('Der ewig belebenden Liebe / Voll schwellende Tränen') which nourish the lush vines growing under his window; and in *Wonne der Wehmut* tears are again presented as life-giving, since their absence would lead (lines 3–4) to a barren and dead world landscape. In neither poem are the tears the result of simple human love. Although the revised version of *Wonne der Wehmut* (above) refers to 'unhappy love' in the final line, the original version referred to 'holy' and 'eternal' love alone. The poem acquires a sense of universality when this is realised, and it would be misleading to read it as a mere Romantic expression of human love-longing. The solemnity of Beethoven's setting suggests that he realised the true nature of Goethe's poetic statement.

The song exists in two settings, which differ only in the accompaniment, notably in the distribution of the notes within particular chords. The first version (Hess 142) was first printed by Willy Hess (Supp V/13) in 1962 and is reprinted in Henle (No. 85). The autograph of this version is in the Goethe–Schiller Archive in Weimar. It came into the possession of Goethe, who put it in front of the 12-year-old Mendelssohn when he visited the poet in October 1821, to test his sight-reading ability. This no doubt tested the young composer's ability to decipher a very messy autograph rather than his pianistic skills. That he succeeded is witnessed by a copy of the song he made from the autograph during a later visit.

An autograph containing the three Goethe songs of op. 83 is in Paris (BN: Ms. 21). Sketches in Krakow (BJ: Landsberg 11) can be dated with some confidence to late October 1810 as they follow directly on the autograph of the String Quartet op. 95, which is dated October 1810. Some of the sketches for *Wonne der Wehmut* indicate that Beethoven smoothed and simplified his original ideas to produce the noble simplicity of the final setting, which was published by Breitkopf und Härtel in Leipzig in October 1811 as the first song of op. 83, together with *Sehnsucht* (*Was zieht mir das Herz*) and *Mit einem gemalten Band*. This opus was dedicated to Princess Kinsky. Beethoven had wished her to receive the dedication of the previous opus from the same publishers (op. 82), but this had not happened.

Beethoven's choice of a steady tempo (*Andante espressivo*) gives his setting nobility and a sense of universality, but the song must not be taken at an excessively slow speed, to avoid stasis. Flowing tears have traditionally been expressed through the means of falling musical couplets, and Beethoven exploits and develops this *topos*. The second half of the first vocal phrase is such a couplet, and the falling scale which follows in the accompaniment is best heard as a succession of falling couplets. Indeed, this falling scale, which occurs four times, is a self-defined motto or tonal analogue. Starting out as a semi-independent accompanimental figure in the first two bars, it is fully integrated with the voice in bar 5, and in an extended form closes the song with what we may now interpret as a flow of undrying tears.

A further sequence of falling couplets is used to set '(Ach! Nur dem) halbgetrockneten Auge', but the following phrase significantly refuses to depart from a repeated G, the monotone suggesting the desolate and dead world which would result from dry eyes, while sharply accented chords evoke the pain which would arise from ceasing to lament and facing reality. The isolated, unaccompanied pleas 'Trocknet nicht!' which follow, on a *pp* monotone and coincidentally in the dotted rhythm of the quail (see *Der Wachtelschlag*), speak of a world of sorrow. Beethoven was clearly drawn to the pathetic tone of the text, and moments such as this suggest his personal identification with the sentiments, supporting Kinsky's claim (KH, p. 223) that the song may have been composed for Therese Malfatti. It was written in 1810, the year in which Beethoven probably considered proposing to Therese, only to suffer a rejection which plunged him 'from the heights of the most sublime ecstasy down into the depths' (EA254 / BB445). The composer's letter to Gleichenstein, in which he laments that friendship and emotions bring only pain, is closely contemporary with this song.

The voice rises despairingly at 'tears of unhappy love', but finally falls back into resignation (bar 18) with a carefully managed *decrescendo* on the highest note of the song. The singer closes with yet another (the eighth) utterance of the injunction 'Trocknet nicht', falling from A to the tonic E, before the pianist echoes the phrase, adding a further octave of tremulous lament. The whole song exudes confidence and demonstrates mastery of the new style of *Lied*, where voice and piano form an equal partnership and where a composer develops meaningful musical motifs to offer a heightened and often intensely personal recreation of the poetic text.

The poem has been set by many other composers. Schubert's setting in C minor (D260) was written in the August of 1815, when at least a song a day was the rule, during a Goethe spree (*Heidenröslein* was composed the previous day). The tempo ('Etwas geschwind') is surprisingly jaunty and the deeper nature of love's tears seems to have eluded the 18-year-old composer; but falling couplets are used to good effect, notably in the four-bar postlude. Zelter's setting in B minor (marked 'Langsam und versunken') deserves to be better known. Interestingly, only Beethoven chose a major key for his setting, demonstrating that the major can be rendered as poignant as the minor mode.

WUNSCH Wish
Friedrich von Matthisson

c.1804

C sharp minor Bia 433 sketch

Wunsch (i)

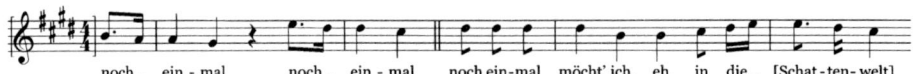

Noch einmal möcht' ich, eh in die Schattenwelt	Once more, before my blessed spirit descends
Elysiums mein seliger Geist sich senkt,	Into the shade world of Elysium, I would like
Die Flur begrüssen, wo der Kindheit	To greet those fields, where the heavenly dreams
Himmlische Träume mein Haupt umschwebten.	Of childhood hovered around my head.
Der Strauch der Heimat, welcher des Hänflings Nest	The native thicket, which gave cooling shelter
Mit Kühlung deckte, säuselt doch lieblicher,	To the linnet's nest, rustles more delightfully,
O Freund! Als alle Lorbeerwälder	O friend, than all the forests of laurel
Über der Asche der Weltbezwinger.	Upon the ashes of world-conquering heroes.
Der Bach der Blumenwiese, wo ich als Kind	The stream through the flowery meadow, where
Violen pflückte, murmelt melodischer	As a child I gathered violets, bubbles more musically
Durch Erlen, die mein Vater pflanzte,	Through the alders which my father planted
Als die blandusische Silberquelle.	Than the silver source of antiquity.
Der Hügel, wo die jauchzenden Knabenreihn	The hill, where whooping hordes of young lads
Sich um den Stamm der blühenden Linde schwang,	Chased round the trunk of the lime tree in blossom,
Entzückt mich höher als der Alpen	Fills me with greater rapture than the dazzling

Blendende Gipfel im Rosenschimmer.	Peaks of the Alps with their rose-tinged glow.
Drum möcht' ich einmal, eh in die Schattenwelt Elysiums mein seliger Geist sich senkt,	And so, once more, before my blessed spirit descends Into the shade world of Elysium, I would like
Die Flur noch segnen, wo der Kindheit	To bless those fields, where the heavenly dreams
Himmlische Träume mein Haupt umschwebten.	Of childhood hovered around my head.
Dann mag des Todes lächelnder Genius Die Fackel plötzlich löschen; ich eile froh Zu Xenophons und Platons Weisheit, Und zu Anakreons Myrthenlaube.	Then let the smiling spirit of death suddenly Lower his torch; I shall hasten joyfully Towards the wisdom of Xenophon and Plato, And to the myrtled arbour of Anacreon.

Although his sketches were never refined into a completed song, Beethoven was clearly attracted to Matthisson's charming, idyllic remembrance of childhood. The poet wishes to revisit the scenes of boyhood pleasures once more before death takes him to join the heroes of his maturity. These adult heroes are poets and philosophers of Classical Greece, and the Classical verse form and references to Elysium, the world of shades and laurel wreaths form a deliberate and effective contrast with the specifically local and homely images which populate the childhood memories (violets, birds' nests and alders) whose true value the ageing poet now recognises.

According to Gustav Nottebohm, who was a pioneer in the study of the composer's sketchbooks and seems to have seen most of them (including some now lost), Beethoven made several attempts to compose Matthisson's poem. The first example above is a tiny, isolated sketch among many (GdM: A36), but the composer then retained and expanded the melodic germ in the significant sketches (GdM: A39) which cover two pages and indicate an ambitious scheme for a through-composed setting of the poem.

Each stanza of the poem is clearly indicated ('Strophe I', 'Str: 2', etc.) and the opening lines of each stanza are set and texted. There are only occasional adumbrations of a keyboard accompaniment, including decorative interludes in semiquaver triplets in the treble and a final arpeggiated descent over three octaves in the bass to a firm close in C sharp minor. The vocal melodies for the opening of each stanza are closely related, but there is clear differentiation. At the end of the second stanza the composer has indicated an a close in C sharp minor ('Schluss in cis-moll') and at the end of the third stanza a close in F sharp minor. There is a clearly indicated recapitulation of the entire first stanza at the end; not only has Beethoven written 'D.C.' (da capo: from the top), but he has written out the words to the first stanza in full below the music, followed only by the argeggiated ending described above. Sadly, the gaps in the sketches are such that only the composer himself could realistically have produced a completed song from this musical shorthand.

Otto Biba, Director of the GdM Archive, who kindly provided copies of these sketch leaves, refers to the sketches generally as mere 'Idee-Notationen' (letter to the author). This neatly formulates an essential aspect of the creative process in Beethoven, but in this case a completed work is not too far away.

ZUR ERDE SANK DIE RUH' VOM HIMMEL NIEDER
Peace sank down to earth from heaven
unknown   1803
C major Bia 380 / SV60 sketch

Beethoven's sketch, quoted in its entirety above, is in the 'Eroica' sketchbook in Krakow (BJ: Landsberg 6, p. 1). The song occupies half a line at the opening of the 182-page sketchbook, which includes extensive sketches for the Third Symphony, *Leonore* and the 'Waldstein' Sonata, and illustrates in an exceptionally graphic way the dwarfing of Beethoven's songs by his works in larger forms. It is included here for the sake of completeness.

If one assumes soprano clef, which Beethoven frequently employed for sketching vocal melodies around this time (including *Das Rosenband* and *Lebensglück* in this very sketchbook), the melody assumes a satisfying shapeliness and is well suited to the meaning of the words, which evoke both the quiet of night-fall and the achievement of inward peace. As with other similar fragments, notably *An die Abendsonne* and *Gott allein ist unser Herr*, it seems likely that the words are the composer's own, taking shape during one of his beloved country walks.

II *The poets*

(* An asterisk following a name indicates that the person is the subject of a separate entry in this section.)

ANON. See 'Unknown' at end of this section.

BEETHOVEN, Ludwig van (1770–1827). In Beethoven's lifetime, it was not at all unusual for a composer to write poetry, particularly 'occasional' verse to mark a particular event. Similarly, artists from other disciplines, such as the painter Moritz von Schwind and the writer Franz Grillparzer, tried their hand at musical composition. The two poems here both mark occasions – the birthday of the young Prince Ferdinand Lobkowitz, and the departure of Archduke Rudolph from Vienna – and can be attributed to Beethoven with some confidence. Neither of the texts can be regarded as 'poetry' in any meaningful sense, lacking both rhyme and any metrical pattern. They are purely functional. It is likely that the composer also produced the words to some of his more fragmentary sketches (see 'unknown' below).

Es lebe unser teurer Fürst
Gedenke mein!

BONDI, Clemente (1742–1821). Italian-born poet and translator. After the suppression of the Jesuits in 1773, Bondi became first a librarian at Mantua and then moved to Milan, where he was befriended by the governor general of Lombardy, Archduke Ferdinand, and his wife. He followed them to Brünn (Brno) and thence to Wiener Neustadt, becoming the Archduchess's librarian, and finally settled in Vienna in 1810. His translations from

Virgil and Ovid were more celebrated than his original verse, which included several occasional pieces such as the cantata for the name-day of Dr Johannes Malfatti.

Cantata Campestre

BREUNING, Stephan von (1774–1827). Born in Bonn in August 1774, making him Beethoven's junior by four years. During his Bonn years, Beethoven was a frequent guest at the Breunings' house, and Frau von Breuning became almost a second mother to him. Breuning studied law and went in 1800 to Vienna, where he lived for the rest of his life. Here he was in the service of the Hofkriegsrat (court war council), becoming a Hofrat (court councillor) in 1818. He was Beethoven's most loyal friend, and both men were happy to heal a prolonged rift which had developed after a quarrel. Breuning's 1806 revision of the libretto of *Leonore* is a more important contribution to Beethoven's work than this single translation from a French *opéra comique* (see Hoffman). Stephan's son Gerhard (1813–92) preserved some important reminiscences of Beethoven's final years in his book *Aus dem Schwarzspanierhaus* (Vienna 1874).

Als die Geliebte sich trennen wollte

BÜRGER, Gottfried August (1748–94). Born in Molmerswende, Harz, the son of a pastor. Bürger studied theology in Halle, where he led a rather wild life, and then law at Göttingen. He was appointed magistrate at Altengleichen, near Göttingen, in 1772, and encountered the young student poets who founded the *Göttinger Hainbund* (see Hölty), although he was never an actual member. He edited the *Göttinger Musenalmanach* from 1778, after the students had gone their separate ways and Goeckingk* had joined forces with Voss* in Hamburg. Bürger's hugely popular ballad *Lenore* was published in 1774. In the same year he married Dorette Leonhart, but fell at once for her sister Auguste, who is the 'Molly' of his poems, as well as the eponymous 'Blümchen Wunderhold'. Dorette died of consumption in 1784 and Bürger married Auguste, who had borne him a son the previous year. After her death a third marriage ended in divorce in 1792, and Bürger, since 1789 a professor at Göttingen, was much affected by this public scandal, as also by a savage review of his collected poems by Schiller,* which may have hastened his death.

Beethoven may well have been introduced to Bürger's poetry by his Bonn teacher Neefe, who subscribed to a collected edition of Bürger's poems in 1778 and included seven settings of the poet in his collection *Vademecum für Liebhaber des Gesangs und Klaviers* of 1780.

An die Menschengesichter
Das Blümchen Wunderhold
Minnesold
Mollys Abschied
Seufzer eines Ungeliebten /
Gegenliebe

CARPANI, Giuseppe (1751–1825). Italian poet, critic and librettist, born near Como. After first studying law, he came to Vienna in 1796 when the French occupied northern Italy. He lived in Vienna from 1796 until 1801 and from 1805 until his death, receiving in his later years a pension from the Emperor. In addition to translations of French and German operatic texts into Italian and original poetry, he wrote one of the first biographies of Joseph Haydn (*Le Haydine*, Milan 1812). His poem 'In questa tomba oscura' was written in 1805; Tranquillo Mollo published a collection of 63 settings of the text by a

total of 46 composers a couple of years later. Carpani was personally acquainted with Beethoven, and was responsible for introducing Rossini to the composer.

In questa tomba oscura

CLAUDIUS, Matthias (1740–1815). Born in Reinfeld, Holstein, son of a pastor. Studied theology and law in Jena. From 1771 to 1776 he edited the newspaper *Der Wandsbecker Bote* (The Wandsbeck Courier). He was the main contributor to the newspaper, and his homely and gently humorous style, with content marked by religious orthodoxy combined with tolerance, achieved popularity without any hint of vulgarity. He became so completely identified with the publication that he himself acquired the nickname of 'Der Wandsbecker Bote'. Herder* procured an administrative post for Claudius in 1776, but Claudius chose to return in 1777 to Wandsbeck, where he enjoyed a happy marriage and prepared his works for publication. Much of his verse has the naturalness of folksong and is firmly embedded in the German cultural heritage. Thanks to Schubert, his best known poem is 'Death and the Maiden', and in Britain he enjoys an annual outing as the author of 'We plough the fields and scatter'.

Urians Reise um die Welt

COLLIN, Heinrich Joseph von (1771–1811). Viennese poet and dramatist, a civil servant by profession. Collin wrote a series of verse dramas on historical themes, which were given at the Burgtheater. His most popular play was *Regulus*, but his *Coriolan* was given a boost in 1807 by Beethoven's overture. The composer considered Collin as a potential collaborator in an opera, but nothing came of it. Collin's dramas glorify patriotism and the struggle for freedom, as does his collection of patriotic songs written to inspire the Austrian defence forces at the time of the Napoleonic threat, *Lieder österreichischer Wehrmänner* (Songs for Austrian soldiers) of 1809. Heinrich's brother Matthäus von Collin (1779–1824) wrote in a more lyrically Romantic vein and inspired Schubert to five fine songs.

Östreich über alles

DÖRING, Johann von (1741–1818). Born in Lüneburg, Döring worked as a senior civil servant in various North German towns. From 1781 he was a royal Danish chamberlain at Altona (Hamburg). According to Gerhard Hey in *Die Beiträger des Voss'schen Musenalmanachs* (The contributors to Voss's Musenalmanach) (Hildesheim 1975), Döring had a total of thirty-one poems published in almanacs under the editorship of Voss,* first in Göttingen and later in Hamburg, between 1776 and 1785. In the Göttingen *Musenalmanach* for 1779, where Beethoven found the poem *An einen Säugling*, Döring signs himself 'Ws.', an abbreviation for his usual but unexplained pseudonym 'Wirths'.

An einen Säugling

FRIEDELBERG, Josef (?1781–1800). The few sketchy details which are known of Friedelberg's life suggest that he was a heroic patriot in the mould of Theodor Körner. A number of his poems appeared in the *Wiener Musenalmanach* between 1794 and 1796. He quickly rose to become an Unterleutnant (sub-lieutenant) in the Korps der Wiener Freiwilligen (Viennese volunteer corps), subsequently joining the de Ligne infantry regiment. He is said to have died from the effect of earlier battle wounds in September 1800. The two poems set by Beethoven are full of patriotic fervour and warlike defiance.

Abschiedsgesang an Wiens Bürger
Kriegslied der Österreicher

GELLERT, Christian Fürchtegott (1715–1769). Although Gellert is remembered today principally for his collection of popular fables (*Fabeln und Erzählungen*, 1746 and 1748) and his volume of religious poems (*Geistliche Oden und Lieder*, 1757), his complete works occupy considerable shelf-space. They include a voluminous correspondence in addition to comedies, a novel, didactic writings and even a guide to letter-writing with model letters. The rare conjunction of reason and sentiment, as well as their natural fluency and sincerity of expression, attracted many composers to his *Geistliche Oden und Lieder*, and a few survive in German hymnbooks today. Despite Gellert's unwavering message that passions should be subjected to reason and that people should be content with their lot, his moral lectures at Leipzig University attracted huge audiences and people of all classes. He was ever prepared to give advice on moral issues to those who sought it, and no letter went unanswered. He never married.

Bitten
Busslied
Die Ehre Gottes aus der Natur
Die Liebe des Nächsten
Gottes Macht und Vorsehung
Vom Tode

GLEIM, Johann Wilhelm Ludwig (1719–1803). During his student years in Halle, Gleim met Uz und Götz, and the three young men developed an ostensibly neo-Anacreontic poetry, with stylised verse extolling the virtues of love, wine and song. Gleim's *Versuch in scherzhaften Liedern* (Essays in lighthearted verse) of 1744 was the first-fruit of this preoccupation. In 1747 Gleim, whose modest lifestyle did not mirror at all the hedonistic suggestions of his early verse, became a Canon of Halberstadt, where he spent the rest of his life. Gleim's patriotic 'Prussian songs of war and victory' (*Kriegs- und Siegeslieder der Preussen*) appeared in 1758, at the time of the Seven Years War, and temporarily enhanced his reputation as a poet. Towards the end of his long life, 'Vater Gleim' (the affectionate nickname recalls that of 'Papa Haydn') was known for his hospitality and kindness towards young, aspiring writers.

Flüchtigkeit der Zeit
Ein Selbstgespräch

GOEBLE, H. Nothing whatsoever is known about this poet, despite the fact that his text provided the inspiration for one of Beethoven's greatest songs. Nottebohm christened him 'Heinrich', seemingly with no more evidence than the popularity of the name. In his maturity Beethoven received numerous poems from aspiring writers or the publishers of periodicals for his consideration. Goeble's *Abendlied* evoked an immediate and powerful response.

Abendlied unterm gestirnten Himmel

GOECKINGK, Leopold Friedrich Günther von (1748–1828). Born in Groeningen near Halberstadt, Goeckingk studied in Halle before becoming a Prussian civil servant. During his posting in Halberstadt, he met and befriended Gleim.* After Voss* had left Göttingen, Goeckingk was drafted in to edit the *Göttinger Musenalmanach* from 1776 to 1778. Meanwhile Voss had begun to publish a new almanac in Hamburg and, having convinced Goeckingk that the market was too small for two rival almanacs, persuaded him to join him as co-editor. Bürger* then took over the editorship of the Göttingen version, and a rivalry did indeed develop. Goeckingk and his wife Sophie contributed a popular series of love poems to the almanac, using the pseudonyms 'Amarant' and 'Nantchen', although Goeckingk probably also wrote many of the female 'Nantchen' lyrics

himself. The collection *Lieder zweier Liebenden* (Songs of two lovers), published in 1777, established Goeckingk's reputation as a poet and is still in print.

An Amarant. Krank vor Liebe
Der gute Fürst

GOETHE, Johann Wolfgang von (1749–1832). Goethe was recognised in his own lifetime as the greatest living writer in German, or indeed any other language. His contribution to literature was enormous, comprising drama, poetry and prose, in addition to technical and scientific treatises on a wide variety of subjects. His long life enabled him to live through and participate in diverse literary movements, and it can be difficult to reconcile, for example, the highly impassioned 'Storm and Stress' of *Die Leiden des jungen Werthers* (The sorrows of young Werther) with the Classical poise of *Iphigenie auf Tauris*. Goethe wrote model works in most genres, from the epistolary novel to autobiography. The originality of his verse extends to bold word coinage; in this, he had an impact on the development of the German language comparable only to Luther's translation of the Bible into everyday German.

Beethoven met Goethe at Teplitz in July 1812. The two men had little in common apart from a recognition of the other's greatness in his field of endeavour. Beethoven considered that Goethe was too deferential towards the aristocracy, too much the courtier; Goethe deplored Beethoven's excessive gruffness, but realised immediately that the composer's deafness affected his social interaction rather than his composing. Like innumerable composers before and since, Beethoven sought to set Goethe's verse to music in a worthy manner. In addition to the songs, he composed *Meeresstille und glückliche Fahrt* (Calm sea and prosperous voyage) (op. 112), an aria from *Claudine von Villa Bella* for bass voice

'Mit Mädeln sich vertragen' (Getting along with girls) (WoO90) and music for the play *Egmont*. Beethoven's stated ambition to compose *Faust* remained a pipe dream.

An den Mond
Aus Goethes Faust
Bundeslied
Der edle Mensch
Die Trommel gerühret
Erlkönig
Freudvoll und leidvoll
Gesang der Geister
Gretchen am Spinnrade
Heidenröslein
Ich denke dein
Kennst du das Land
Maigesang
Marmotte
Mit einem gemalten Band
Nähe des Geliebten
Neue Liebe, neues Leben
Rastlose Liebe
Sehnsucht (Nur wer die Sehnsucht kennt)
Sehnsucht (Was zieht mir das Herz so?)
Wechsellied zum Tanze
Wonne der Wehmut

HALEM, Gerhard Anton von
(1752–1819). Poet, dramatist, historian and translator. Son of a lawyer, Halem studied law himself in Frankfurt an der Oder and Strasbourg. After working in his father's practice, he moved back to his native Oldenburg in 1775 and occupied high legal office. Regarded as a collaborator for his work in Hamburg during the French occupation, he was transferred to Eutin in 1813 as a Regierungsrat (county councillor) and died there in 1819. Halem is an important figure of the Enlightenment in northern Germany. The literary club which he founded in Oldenburg quickly became a centre of intellectual debate. He published a number of influential journals and corresponded with key writers of the day. Halem's interest in historical and

theological themes exhibited itself in plays and verse epics, as well as academic studies.

Gretels Warnung

HAUGWITZ, Paul Graf von
(1791–1856). Haugwitz was born at Reichenbach and died in Dresden. He appears to have been a Landrat (district councillor), but nothing more is known about him. Like so many middle-class civil servants, he no doubt found poetry a fashionable form of escape from a humdrum career. Could he be the son of the writer Otto Graf von Haugwitz (1767–1842), who was orphaned at an early age, studied at a Catholic grammar school in Breslau and at universities in Halle, Göttingen, Berlin and Vienna? If so, Paul will, like his father, have led the life of a dilettante on the family estate at Falkenau in Silesia.

Resignation

HERDER, Johann Gottfried
(1744–1803). Influential poet, thinker, critic and translator. Of humble origins, Herder managed to attend a grammar school and then Königsberg University. After teaching and preaching at Riga, Herder travelled in France and Germany, finding a wife and writing a series of brilliant essays. In 1776 Goethe* procured for him a position at the court of Weimar, where he stayed despite a souring of his relationship with Goethe in later years. Herder's influence on the poets of the *Sturm und Drang*, including the young Goethe, whom he had met in Strasbourg in 1770, as well as on subsequent writers, was crucial to the development of German literature. His own most durable literary achievement is his massive collection of so-called *Volkslieder*, which comprised not only German folksongs but translations from many languages, including Oriental verse. The collection, which appeared in 1778–79, set out to exemplify his many writings on the

true nature of poetry. German poets should aim to shake off the restrictions and artificial conventions of art and recapture the vigour of the earliest folk poetry. This was a sharp reaction to the primacy of reason in the writings of the Enlightenment.

Der Gesang der Nachtigall
Die laute Klage
Die Schwestern des Schicksals

HERRMANN, Franz Rudolph

(1787–1823). Herrmann (or Hermann) was born in Vienna, but studied for his doctorate in Breslau, where he was to die in an asylum. He worked as a private teacher and writer, and his works included a dramatic trilogy about the Nibelungs, together with stories, poems, essays and textbooks.

Der Bardengeist

HERROSEE, Karl Friedrich Wilhelm

(1754–1821). Born in Berlin, son of a cantor. Herrosee studied at the University of Frankfurt an der Oder and became a private tutor in Berlin, before being appointed 'Superintendent' (pastor) at Züllichau in 1788. He seems to have spent the rest of his life happily at Züllichau, where he died. He wrote a number of hymns and poems, and the libretto for an oratorio by Johann Heinrich Rolle, which has passed into oblivion. The one poem for which he is remembered, thanks to Beethoven's setting, is a fashionable expression of the joys of shared married bliss.

Ich liebe dich

HOFFMAN, François Benoît

(1760–1828). Born in Nancy, Hoffman was a prolific French librettist, critic and playwright. The award of the Nancy Academy's poetry prize in 1784 persuaded him to seek his fortune as a writer in Paris. The first of many dramatic successes was with *Phèdre* in 1786. His musical collaborators included Cherubini, Kreutzer

and Méhul. Jean Pierre Solié provided music for some of his lighter libretti, including *Le Secret*, which contains the French original of the poem set by Beethoven in the German translation by Breuning.* Although Hoffman managed not to upset the political establishment during the revolutionary upheavals, he did not shun confrontation with theatre management, championing the rights of the author and active in the Société des Auteurs Dramatiques (Association of dramatic writers). As a critic, he proved a man of independence and integrity.

Als die Geliebte sich trennen wollte
(French original)

HÖLTY, Ludwig Christoph Heinrich

(1748–76). Hölty was born in Mariensee, near Hanover, son of a pastor. He studied theology at Göttingen University and contributed poems to the *Göttinger Musenalmanach*, founded by Boie in 1770. He was a founder member and the most notable poet of the *Göttinger Hainbund* (Union of the grove), a group of young poets who swore eternal friendship as they processed round an oak grove by moonlight in September 1772. They met weekly 69 times between 1772 and 1773, reading and discussing Klopstock* and presenting their own work for critical comment and communal revision. Hölty's nickname in the Hainbund was 'Haining', named after a bard in a Klopstock ode. Hölty's own poetry, although often cast in Classical metres, is a sensitive and often nostalgic celebration of love and nature in blossom, but tinged with a sad awareness of death's inevitability. Hölty's health was never robust. He returned to Mariensee, working as a translator and private tutor, but died young of tuberculosis. His scattered poems were edited (and frequently amended) for publication by Voss* and Stolberg in 1783.

Klage

HOMER (seventh or eighth century BC). No biographical details can be obtained for such an ancient author, but the mystery is part and parcel of the Homeric cult. Homer has frequently been portrayed as a blind bardic singer, and the survival of *The Odyssey* and *The Iliad*, two gigantic works, each in 24 cantos, is truly remarkable. The sheer scale of these heroic epics will have appealed to the composer. Beethoven probably encountered the Homeric epics as a teenager in Bonn, when he was welcomed into the cultured household of the Breuning* family. His well attested admiration for the Greek poet was shared by other intellectuals of the time. Such figures as Homer and the supposed bard Ossian were much promoted by Herder,* who influenced the taste of a generation, for producing works which are closest to nature: the genuine 'voice of the people'. The celebrated German translations by Voss* afforded Homer a new lease of life at just the right time in literary history. Beethoven's determination to set Homer did not progress beyond isolated fragments.

JEITTELES, Alois (1794–1858). Physician in Brünn (Brno), where he was born and died. He was a medical student in Vienna when Beethoven set his six poems as a song cycle. He was probably introduced to Beethoven by Ignaz Castelli, who had published some of his work in his almanac *Selam* and with whom he was to collaborate on *Der Schicksalsstrumpf* (The stocking of fate), a parody of fate tragedy. His cousin was the writer Ignaz Jeitteles (1783–1843), with whom he co-edited a Jewish weekly journal *Siona, encyklopädisches Wochenblatt für Israelisten* in 1819. After Beethoven's death, Jeitteles wrote a poem, *Beethoven's Begräbniss!* (Beethoven's burial), which was adapted to music as a four-part chorus by Ignaz von Seyfried to music by Beethoven

(published by Haslinger the same year, 1827).

An die ferne Geliebte (song cycle)

KLEINSCHMID, Friedrich August (1749–1838). Writer and senior police official, born in Steinheim in Westphalia. He came to Vienna in 1776 to study law. Kleinschmid rose through the ranks to become Director of Police in 1791, and director of Vienna's prison by 1812. He was also a cultured poet and a distinguished art collector. Interestingly, the publisher Diabelli passed on some of Kleinschmid's poems to Schubert via the composer's brother (letter from Ferdinand to Franz Schubert of 4 August 1825), but Schubert did not set them.

Der Mann vom Wort

KLOPSTOCK, Friedrich Gottlob (1724–1803). Born in Quedlinburg, Klopstock acquired a classical education and a sympathy for Pietism at boarding school in Schulpforta. Milton's *Paradise Lost* inspired him with the declared ambition to write a religious epic, and this he achieved with *Der Messias* (The Messiah), although the publication of the twenty cantos in classical hexameters extended over 25 years. Of even greater importance were his odes, comprising love poems to 'Fanny' (a cousin he adored) and to 'Cidli' (actually his wife Meta, who died four years after their marriage), in addition to ecstatic utterances in free verse expressing awe at the majesty of God revealed in all creation. The odes had a powerful influence on the young Goethe* and the student poets of the *Göttinger Hain* (including Voss,* Hölty* and Miller*), who adopted Klopstock as their patron. Klopstock's uninhibited expression of sentiment and his image of the poet as bard or priest, defined the age of *Sturm und Drang* in poetry, and had an influence which extended into the Romantic movement of the next century. Beethoven read Klopstock and regarded him as one of the 'immortal poets', linking his name with Homer and Schiller* in a letter of 23 January 1824.

Neefe had published a collection of Klopstock settings in 1776 (*Oden von Klopstock mit Melodien*). This may be one reason why Beethoven produced only three fragmentary settings of this favourite poet. He wished to avoid comparison with his early teacher, whose name was so closely associated with the poet.

> *Das Rosenband*
> *Die frühen Gräber*
> *Edone*

LAPPE, Karl Gittlieb (1773–1843). Born in Wusterhausen. Described in Kosch's *Deutsches Literaturlexikon* as 'the most important poet of Pomerania'. It is indeed striking how many of Beethoven's chosen poets came originally from the north-eastern part of Germany. Lappe wrote a large number of lyric poems, published as *Gedichte* (Poems) in 1801, and *Blüten des Alters* (Blooms of old age) in 1841. The poem set by Beethoven enjoyed a prolonged vogue in the nineteenth century. Lappe became a secondary school teacher and later a farmer in Stralsund, where he lived until his death. The survival of his memory today rests upon the present song and two fine settings by Schubert: *Der Einsame* and *Im Abendrot*. Both these latter poems paint a picture of solitary contentment

> *So oder so*

LESSING, Gottfried Ephraim (1729–1781). Dramatist, poet and critic, born at Kamenz in Saxony. Lessing was educated at boarding school in Meissen. He went to Leipzig to study theology, soon transferring to medicine, although literature and the theatre became his main interests. He earned his living as a journalist, theatre critic and librarian. In addition to numerous essays on the theatre, aesthetics and moral issues, Lessing was an innovative dramatist. He established the form of the *Bürgerliches Trauerspiel* (domestic tragedy) with *Miss Sara Sampson* and *Emilia Galotti*, breaking with tradition by showing middle-class characters and employing prose. He also wrote the first modern German comedy, *Minna von Barnhelm*, and a celebrated drama of religious tolerance in *Nathan der Weise*. His support for freedom of speech, his belief that people are judged by their actions and his anticipation of an ideal state of humankind when morality will become instinctive make him a central figure of the German Enlightenment or *Aufklärung*, despite his often critical stance towards his own contemporaries.

> *Die Liebe*

MATTHISSON, Friedrich von (1761–1831). Matthisson was born at Hohendodeleben, near Madgeburg, studied at Halle University, and then taught for four years at the Philanthropinum, a school established by the educational reformer Basedow in Dessau. After travels in Germany as a private tutor, he was ennobled by Duke Friedrich of Württemberg in 1809, becoming his theatre director and librarian. His poised verse, sentimental without becoming emotionally taxing, often tinged with a fashionable melancholy and frequently employing classical metres, was standard reading among the lettered classes during his lifetime. It attracted the attention of many composers, inspiring what is probably Beethoven's most popular song, as well as a rich harvest of early masterpieces from Schubert.

> *Adelaide*
> *Andenken*
> *An Laura*
> *Badelied*
> *Opferlied*
> *Wunsch*

MEREAU, Sophie Friederike
(1770–1806). Poet, translator, novelist and
editor, born in Altenberg, née Schubert. She
married Friedrich Ernst Karl Mereau,
professor of philosophy at Jena, in 1793,
acquiring the name by which she is generally
known. They were divorced in 1801 and
Sophie married the poet Clemens Brentano
in 1803. Well regarded as a poet, novelist and
translator from Italian and English, she was a
regular contributor to Schiller's annual
Musenalmanach. Schiller* wrote
introductory verses to her collected poems,
published in Berlin in 1800 and 1802. Her
epistolary novel *Amanda und Eduard*
attracted Schiller's particular attention and
extracts appeared in his periodical *Die
Horen*. Sophie edited the *Göttinger
Musenalmanach* for 1803. She died in
childbirth in October 1806 at Heidelberg.
  Feuerfarb'

METASTASIO, Pietro (1698–1782).
Born in Rome, as Antonio Domenico
Bonaventura Trapassi, and renamed by his
adoptive father, he came to Vienna as court
poet in 1730 and stayed until his death. He
befriended the composer Salieri, who
arrived in Vienna from Venice in 1766, and
Salieri habitually used extracts from his
fellow Italian's works as word-setting
exercises for his students, including
Schubert and Beethoven. Unaccompanied
vocal works by both composers survive
from their time as students of Salieri.
Metastasio's fame and productivity as a
writer of Italian texts for operas, oratorios
and dramatic pieces for all occasions were
unrivalled. It has been estimated that some
eight hundred operas were composed to his
texts. Inevitably, settings of identical texts
by different composers abound. For
example, *La Partenza* was set by Mozart as
an accompanied 'Notturno' for two
sopranos and bass (K436) and by Beethoven
as a solo song (WoO124). In addition to the

songs listed, Beethoven composed *No, non
turbarti* (WoO92a) and *Ne' giorni tuoi felici*
(WoO93) as respectively a solo and a duet
with orchestral accompaniment.
  Ah! perfido
  Grazie agl'inganni tuoi
  L'amante impaziente (buffa)
  L'amante impaziente (assai seriosa)
  La partenza
  O care selve
  Odi l'aura che dolce sospira
  T'intendo sì, mio cor

MILLER, Johann Martin (1750–1814).
Born in Ulm, son of a pastor. From 1770
until 1774 Miller studied theology in
Göttingen, perhaps a surprising choice of
university for a South German lad, but
indicative of the university's high
reputation. There he met an enthusiastic
group of young poets, including Boie, Hölty*
and Voss,* and became a co-founder of the
Hainbund. He was the secretary of the
Bund, keeping minutes at their weekly
meetings. His predilection for love songs in
a simple folksong style and his interest in
medieval *Minnesang*, earned him the
nickname 'Minnehold'. He wrote a number
of highly sentimental novels, including the
bestseller *Siegwart, eine Klostergeschichte*
(Siegwart, a monastery tale) in 1776. The
resulting 'Siegwart fever' was similar in kind
to the 'Werther fever' which had gripped
literary Europe two years previously. Miller
returned to his South German roots,
teaching at the grammar school in Ulm,
before taking a country parish at Jungingen
in 1780, whence he finally returned to Ulm
to work as a deacon at the Minster.
  Die Zufriedenheit

PETRARCH (Francesco Petrarca)
(1304–74). Born in Arezzo, Tuscany. Italian
scholar, poet and humanist, whose thirst for
literature and love of Classical writers led
him to search for forgotten manuscripts in

the manner of a modern scholar, and whose intense poems to the idealised figure of Laura laid the foundations of modern lyric poetry. His family moved to Avignon when he was eight, following the exiled Papal court. Petrarch studied law successively at Montpellier and Bologna, at his father's insistence, but his father's death in 1326 allowed him to follow his own path. He was ceremonially crowned as a poet in Rome in 1341, but also became heavily involved in politics, diplomacy and polemics. Beethoven's library included an 1804 translation by Streckfuss of several sonnets, included in Streckfuss's poems as 'Blumenlese aus Petracas Sonette' (Poetic garland from Petrarch's Sonnets), and the composer began two settings, although these embryonic pieces hardly do justice to his enthusiasm for the poet.

PFEFFEL, Gottlieb Konrad
(1736–1809). Born and died in Colmar, Alsace. Studied law at Halle. Despite becoming blind at the age of 22, Pfeffel managed to pursue an active career, combining literature with educational administration, and founding a Protestant school in his native town. His voluminous original writings were supplemented by his activities as a translator into and from French. He was a regular contributor to the Hamburg *Musenalmanach* which Voss* edited from 1776 to 1800. His *Fables*, published in 1783, demonstrate his sympathy with French revolutionary ideals. He was clearly a man of firm convictions and significant moral fibre.
Der freie Mann

REISSIG, Christian Ludwig
(1783–1847). Born in Kassel. Reissig arrived in February 1809 in Vienna, where he joined the Austrian army as a volunteer. He was seriously wounded after three months' service and invalided out of the army, but

stayed in Vienna. Poems from his collection *Blümchen der Einsamkeit* (Flowers of solitude) were widely set to music, although this was generally at the specific request of the poet, who then had the songs published in collections, with extravagant dedications, and pocketed the lion's share of the profits. Almost forty composers were variously inveigled into providing settings, including Giuliani, Hummel, Reichardt, Salieri and Zelter. Beethoven was furious when Reissig had his setting of *Gesang aus der Ferne* (WoO137), composed for the poet as a favour, engraved without his permission. Reissig even claimed, falsely, to have paid Beethoven for the setting, which went totally against the composer's sense of personal honour. Nevertheless, Reissig's poems inspired the composer to some of his most fluent utterances in song, and, notwithstanding his fulminations against Reissig in 1810, he was to return to the poet to set further poems, including *Sehnsucht*, which he set with great care in 1816.
An den fernen Geliebten
Der Jüngling in der Fremde
Der Liebende
Der Zufriedene
Des Kriegers Abschied
Gesang aus der Ferne
Lied aus der Ferne
Sehnsucht (Die stille Nacht)

ROUSSEAU, Jean-Jacques (1712–78). Born in Geneva, son of a watchmaker. His mother died giving birth to him and his father left home when he was ten. He enjoyed little formal education and after failed apprenticeships and some aimless wanderings, he was taken under the wing of Mme de Warens and made up for lost time, reading books on history, philosophy, science and mathematics. Fascinated by music, he composed, devised a new method of musical notation and compiled a dictionary of music. In lean times, copying music became his principal source of income. His main writings include philosophical works, the influential novel in letters *Julie ou la Nouvelle Héloïse*, a treatise on 'natural education' *Emile*, and several autobiographical works, including the *Confessions*. He criticised the existing social order, constructively but ruthlessly, preaching a return to a more natural state, and made himself many enemies in the process. Ostensibly a product of the French Enlightenment, the sensibility and love of nature which permeates his writing makes him a forerunner of *Sturm und Drang* in Germany, and ultimately of the Romantic movement in European literature.

Que le temps me dure

RUPPRECHT, Johann Baptist
(1776–1846). Born in Wölfelsdorf in Silesia (now in Poland). He was a successful businessman in Vienna until 1809. When his firm collapsed under the impact of the Napoleonic invasion, he renounced business to take up writing and horticulture. The garden of his house at Gumpendorf was celebrated for its chrysanthemum shows. He wrote many patriotic poems which appeared in various Viennese journals, in addition to articles on economics and natural history. Rupprecht, who appears to have been on friendly terms with Beethoven, was asked to make German translations of the Scottish folksong settings, op. 108, although the composer became very impatient with the poet's dilatory approach to the task and finally looked elsewhere. Beethoven reacted enthusiastically to Rupprecht's request for him to compose 'Merkenstein', producing two settings of the poem.

Merkenstein

SAUTER, Samuel Friedrich
(1766–1846). Sauter was born and died in Flehingen, Baden. He worked as a village schoolmaster in Flehingen and in neighbouring Zaisenhausen. His verse was in a simple style, and the titles of his two poetry collections suggest that he deliberately cultivated a folksy image: *Volkslieder und andere Reime* (Folksongs and other rhymes) of 1811, and *Die sämtlichen Gedichte des alten Dorfschulmeisters S. Fr. Sauters* (The collected poems of the old village schoolmaster . . .) of 1845. If this was disingenuousness, it certainly backfired, as his more wooden and naive poetry, attributed to a 'Gottlieb Biedermaier', was held up to ridicule in the Munich weekly *Fliegende Blätter*. Sauter's involuntary pseudonym, as 'Biedermeier', was to become the generally derogatory label for an age of homely, middle-class, apolitical parochialism.

Der Wachtelschlag

SCHILLER, Friedrich (1759–1805). Swabian poet, dramatist and historian, born in Marbach near Stuttgart. In 1773 he entered Duke Karl Eugen's newly founded military academy near Ludwigsburg, studying law initially, but happier when allowed to transfer to medicine. After leaving the academy in 1780 Schiller became a field surgeon, but preferred writing plays. *Die Räuber* (The robbers) preached freedom from oppression in true *Sturm und Drang* style, and the resulting furore forced him to flee to Mannheim in 1782. After a difficult period, including an unhappy love affair with a married woman, he settled in Leipzig and completed *Don Carlos* (1787). His historical writings had impressed Goethe,* who helped Schiller become professor of history at Jena in 1789. Over the next four years he wrote a popular history of the Thirty Years War. Schiller now preached spiritual freedom rather than revolution. His 'sentimental' poetry is often overly philosophical in comparison with the pure lyric impulses of the 'naïve' Goethe and has proved a barrier to many composers,

Beethoven included, but his plays have been adapted into celebrated operas (*Wilhelm Tell, Maria Stuart, Don Carlos* and others), and, while Beethoven failed to complete a single solo song to a Schiller text, he was to respond magnificently to the poet's idealistic vision of human brotherhood in the Ninth Symphony.

An die Freude
Das Mädchen aus der Fremde

STEIN, Anton Joseph (1759–1844). Born in Bladen, Upper Silesia. After teaching at various schools in Vienna, he became professor of Classical philology and literature at the University of Vienna from 1806 until his retirement in 1825. His pupils there included the writers Grillparzer and Bauernfeld. In retirement, Stein wrote poems in German, Latin and Greek, which appeared in a collected edition in 1843. He was a friend of Cajetan Giannatasio del Rio and wrote for him the text for Beethoven's wedding cantata, performed at the wedding of Cajetan's daughter Anna to Leopold von Schmerling in February 1819.

Auf, Freunde, singt dem Gott der Ehen

STOLL, Joseph Ludwig (1778–1815). Viennese poet and dramatist. After the early death of his father, the celebrated doctor Maximilian Stoll, Joseph travelled with his guardian for some years, including stays in Berlin and London. Stoll settled briefly in 1801 in Weimar, where he wrote comedies for the court theatre. In 1807 he accepted the post of resident dramatist at the Burgtheater in Vienna. In 1808 he and Leopold von Seckendorf founded the journal *Prometheus*, which ran for only a year. Meanwhile Stoll had lost his position at the Burgtheater, probably because of his known sympathy with Napoleon. Financial hardship forced Stoll to lay all his hopes on a trip to Paris, and Beethoven, ever moved by the plight of suffering fellow artists,

wrote on his behalf to Joseph Hammer-Purgstall to ask for help in arranging the journey and also offered to stand guarantor for a loan. Grillparzer regarded Stoll as merely a good versifier and expressed contempt for his general fecklessness.

An die Geliebte

TIEDGE, Christoph August (1752–1841). Born in Gardelegen. A writer of philosophical and didactic verse. His most celebrated work is the 'lyrisch-didaktisches Gedicht' *Urania*, which appeared in 11 editions between 1810 and 1837 and was the source for the poem *An die Hoffnung*, set twice by Beethoven. Beethoven met Tiedge at Teplitz in August 1811. He was captivated by Tiedge and readily acceded to the poet's later proposal that they call each other 'du' in their correspondence to seal their friendship. From 1804 Tiedge had been living with the poetess Elisa von der Recke, whose earlier marriage had been dissolved, and they had settled in Dresden. Countess Elisa sent Beethoven copies of Tiedge's *Urania* and his *Elegien* in 1811, together with some of her own verse. The composer's promise to set some of her poems to his 'feeble strains' ('ohnmächtigen Tönen') came to nothing.

An die Hoffnung
O Hoffnung

TREITSCHKE, Georg Friedrich (1776–1842). Born in Leipzig. Poet, playwright and theatre director. Treitschke came to Vienna around 1800 and quickly became producer and librettist at the Kärntnertor Theatre. At the time of the French invasion in 1809, he was deputy director of the Theater an der Wien. As a 'mover and shaker' in the opera world, Treitschke probably met Beethoven for the first time in 1805, when revisions to the libretto of *Fidelio* were first discussed. He struck up a friendship with the composer around 1811 and they discussed

plans for new operas. Although these were to
come to nothing, Treitschke successfully
revised the libretto to *Fidelio* for its second
revival in May 1814. Beethoven was delighted
with the new libretto, and his setting of *Ruf
vom Berge*, published as a music supplement
to Treitschke's poems in 1817, was no doubt a
small gesture of thanks, along with settings of
'Germania', the final number from
Treitschke's *Singspiel Die gute Nachricht*
(The good news) (WoO94), and 'Es ist
vollbracht' (It is finished) from *Die
Ehrenpforten* (The portals of honour)
(WoO97).

    Ruf vom Berge

UELTZEN, Hermann Wilhelm Franz
(1759–1808). Born in Celle. Poet, tutor and
priest. After attracting attention at school
for his talent for poetry, Ueltzen studied
theology at Göttingen from 1777 to 1780,
before becoming a private tutor in Bremen
and Oldenburg. In 1789 he became the
priest of Langlingen near Celle, where he
lived until his death, acquiring a reputation
as a fine preacher. He contributed to
prestigious journals and almanacs. His most
popular poem *Ihr* ('Namen nennen dich
nicht') was widely admired, although
Goethe* detested it. His *Liedchen von der
Ruhe* was set to music by numerous
composers, including Daniel Gerstenberg,
Peter von Winter and Michael Haydn. In
addition to the solo song, Beethoven set the
first line of the poem as a canon (WoO159).
Many of Ueltzen's other poems are written
to fit familiar German hymn tunes.

    Das Liedchen von der Ruhe

VOSS, Johann Heinrich (1751–1826).
Born into rural poverty at Sommersdorf in
Mecklenburg. After his schooling in
Neubrandenburg, Voss could not afford to
attend university and became a private
tutor. Heinrich Christian Boie noticed some
of his poems and enabled Voss to attend

university at Göttingen, where he became a
founder member of the *Göttinger Hainbund*
in September 1772. He visited Klopstock*
as representative of the *Bund* in 1774. In
1775 Voss took over the editorship of the
Göttinger Musenalmanach and, after
leaving the university, published his own
Musenalmanach in Hamburg, later
supported by Goeckingk.* He became
headmaster of schools in Ottendorf and
Eutin, where he remained for 23 years. His
greatest achievement was his translation of
Homer's epics into German hexameters,
supplemented by translations from the
Latin poets. Voss has been criticised for his
over-enthusiastic editing of the poems of his
friend Hölty,* but he certainly saved many
fine poems from oblivion and was following
normal *Hainbund* practice in making
considered improvements to a colleague's
work, as reading and communal discussion
and amendment of new verse was a key
feature of the group's weekly meetings.

    Minnelied
    Homer translations

WEISSE, Christian Felix (1726–1804).
Born in Annaberg, Saxony. Government
official, dramatist, librettist, editor,
children's author. Son of a headmaster,
Weisse studied theology and philology at
Leipzig from 1745, later changing to law. In
Leipzig he met men of letters, including
Lessing,* Gottsched and Gellert.* After a
spell as a private tutor, Weisse became a tax
collector in Leipzig, where he spent the rest
of his life in comfortable propriety. His
gently humorous verse had been initiated
by a friendly competition with Lessing, and
his early verse was published in 1758 as
Scherzhafte Lieder (Comical songs). After a
volume of patriotic verse, he turned his
hand to historical drama and to the
Singspiel, in collaboration with the
composer J. A. Hiller. He also attempted to
improve on Shakespeare with a trimmed

adaptation of *Romeo and Juliet*. His final creative phase was devoted to literature for children, including the didactic collection *Kleine Lieder für Kinder* (Little songs for children) and a popular periodical *Der Kinderfreund* (The children's friend).

Der Kuss

WENNINGTON, William (active around 1800). Little is known of Wennington, who appears to have been a dilettante writer and music lover of independent means. He probably met Beethoven in Vienna late in 1798, perhaps at Lichnowsky's residence and may have commissioned this setting. A novel which Wennington translated, *The Man of Nature, or Nature and Love*, has a Preface dated 'Vienna 1798' and includes a 'Prince Linhouski' among its subscribers. Alan Tyson ('Beethoven's English Canzonetta', Musical Times CXII, 1971) has used entries made by Wennington at Stationers Hall, staking his copyright to minor literary works and libretti, to narrow the writer's Viennese visit to the period 'between the latter half of 1798 and the former half of 1799'. A *Translator's Defence*, of which the Preface is dated December 1799, is written 'upon my return to my native country after an absence in which persuits (*sic*) commercial and literary may be said to have participated'.

La tiranna

WESSENBERG, Ignaz Heinrich Carl von (1774–1860). Born in Dresden, of old noble stock, Wessenberg grew up on family estates in Feldkirch and Ampringen (hence his adopted pseudonym Heinrich von Ampringen). He studied theology, philosophy and literature in Dillingen, Würzburg and Vienna. Family connections ensured his early appointment to cathedral posts in Augsburg, Constance and Basle. In 1800 he became Vicar General of Basle and an outspoken figure of the Enlightenment.

He resigned in 1827 following major disagreements with Rome and devoted himself to his writing and charitable causes in Constance. He donated his own books to the town to form a public library. His work in the field of church politics overshadows his literary efforts, but he found time to write over a thousand poems, four plays, verse epics, as well as hymns, and works on history, theology and literary theory.

Das Geheimnis (Liebe und Wahrheit)

UNKNOWN. Beethoven certainly turned to 'Anon.' with some frequency. It is significant that many of the songs listed here are fragmentary sketches, and it may be that Beethoven simply used his own words for some of these. Two are dialect folksongs. The list also includes specific occasional pieces: two drinking songs, and an elegy on a dead poodle. The only text of real literary merit among them is *Man strebt, die Flamme zu verhehlen*; perhaps only here is the anonymity a source of regret.

Adorata, o Nice
An die Abendsonne
An Gott
An Minna
Das liebe Kätzchen
Der arme Componist
Der Knabe auf dem Berge
Dimmi, ben mio, che m'ami
Elegie auf den Tod eines Pudels
Erhebt das Glas mit froher Hand
Gott allein ist unser Herr
Ich sah sie heut, o Liebe
Languisco e moro
Lebensglück
Man strebt, die Flamme zu verhehlen
Punschlied
Romance
Schilderung eines Mädchens
Soll ich's nur dem danken
Traute Henriette
Zur Erde sah die Ruh vom Himmel nieder

Appendices

Appendix I *Publication of the songs*

Songs with opus numbers

Op. 32   Published by the Kunst und Industrie Comptoir (Bureau des Arts et d'Industrie) in Vienna in 1805.
   An die Hoffnung (first version)

Op. 46   Published by Artaria in Vienna in 1797.
   Adelaide

Op. 48   Six Gellert songs from his *Geistliche Oden und Lieder*, published by Mollo in Vienna in 1803.
   1 *Bitten*
   2 *Die Liebe des Nächsten*
   3 *Vom Tode*
   4 *Die Ehre Gottes aus der Natur*
   5 *Gottes Macht und Vorsehung*
   6 *Busslied*

Op. 52   Published by the Kunst und Industrie Comptoir in Vienna in 1805, but assembled from songs written in the last decade of the eighteenth century.
   1 *Urians Reise um die Welt*
   2 *Feuerfarb'*
   3 *Das Liedchen von der Ruhe*
   4 *Maigesang*
   5 *Mollys Abschied*
   6 *Die Liebe*
   7 *Marmotte*
   8 *Das Blümchen Wunderhold*

Op. 75   These six songs were published by Breitkopf und Härtel in Leipzig in 1810, with separate English editions published simultaneously in London by Clementi. The two Reissig settings (R) had previously appeared in an Artaria edition of settings of Reissig texts by various composers. See individual entries for details.
   1 *Kennst du das Land*
   2 *Neue Liebe, neues Leben*
   3 *Aus Goethes Faust*

4 *Gretels Warnung*
5 *An den fernen Geliebten* (R)
6 *Der Zufriedene* (R)

Op. 82   These five songs were published by Breitkopf und Härtel in Leipzig in 1811, with separate editions published a few months earlier by Clementi in London. The German edition carried texts in both German and Italian, with German titles for the songs, while the Clementi edition had texts in Italian only.
1 *Dimmi, ben mio, che m'ami*
2 *Tintendo sì mio cor*
3 *L'amante impaziente (Arietta buffa)*
4 *L'amante impaziente (Arietta assai seriosa)*
5 *Odi l'aura che dolce sospira*

Op. 83   Three Goethe settings, published by Breitkopf und Härtel in Leipzig in 1811.
1 *Wonne der Wehmut*
2 *Sehnsucht (Was zieht mir das Herz so)*
3 *Mit einem gemalten Band*

Op. 88   Published by Löschenkohl in Vienna in 1803, as *Das Glück der Freundschaft.*
Lebensglück

Op. 94   Published by Steiner in Vienna in 1816.
An die Hoffnung (second version)

Op. 98   Song cycle, published by Steiner in Vienna in 1816.
An die ferne Geliebte

Op. 99   Published by Steiner in Vienna in 1816.
Der Mann vom Wort

Op. 100   Published by Steiner in Vienna in 1816.
Merkenstein (duet version)

Op. 121b   Published by Schott in Mainz in 1825, simultaneously with the full orchestral version.
Opferlied

Op. 122   Published by Schott in Mainz in 1825, simultaneously with the full orchestral version.
Bundeslied

Op. 128   Published by Schott in Mainz in 1825.
Der Kuss

Other works published in Beethoven's lifetime

These are identified by WoO (Werk ohne Opuszahl), meaning a work without an opus number. In the thematic catalogue *Das Werk Beethovens* by Georg Kinsky and Hans Halm published in 1955, the solo songs are allocated numbers between WoO107 and WoO151, roughly in chronological order of their composition.

WoO107	*Schilderung eines Mädchens*	*Blumenlese für Klavierliebhaber*, Speyer, 1783
WoO108	*An einen Säugling*	*Blumenlese für Klavierliebhaber*, Speyer, 1784
WoO117	*Der freie Mann*	Simrock, Bonn, 1808
WoO121	*Abschiedsgesang an Wiens Bürger*	Artaria, Vienna, 1796
WoO122	*Krieglied der Österreicher*	Artaria, Vienna, 1797
WoO123	*Ich liebe dich*	Traeg, Vienna, 1803
WoO124	*La partenza*	Traeg, Vienna, 1803
WoO125	*La Tiranna*	Broderip and Wilkinson, London, 1799
WoO126	*Opferlied*	Simrock, Bonn, 1808
WoO127	*Neue Liebe, neues Leben I*	Simrock, Bonn, 1808
WoO129	*Der Wachtelschlag*	Kunst und Industrie Comptoir, Vienna, 1804
WoO132	*Als die Geliebte sich trennen wollte*	*Allgemeine musikalische Zeitung*, Leipzig, 1809
WoO133	*In questa tomba oscura*	Mollo, Vienna, 1807
WoO134/1	*Sehnsucht (Nur wer die Sehnsucht)*	*Prometheus*, Vienna, 1808
WoO134/1–4	*Sehnsucht (Nur wer die Sehnsucht)*	Kunst und Industrie Comptoir, Vienna, 1810
WoO136	*Andenken*	Breitkopf und Härtel, Leipzig, 1810
WoO137	*Gesang aus der Ferne*	Breitkopf und Härtel, Leipzig, 1810
WoO138	*Der Jüngling in der Fremde*	Artaria, Vienna, 1810
WoO139	*Der Liebende*	Artaria, Vienna, 1810
WoO140	*An die Geliebte*	*Friedensblätter*, Vienna, 1814
WoO140	*An die Geliebte* (version in C major)	*Lieder Kranz*, Gombart, Augsburg, 1826
WoO142	*Der Bardengeist*	*Musen Almanach*, Gerold, Vienna, 1814
WoO143	*Des Kriegers Abschied*	Mechetti, Vienna, 1815
WoO144	*Merkenstein* (solo version)	*Selam*, Vienna, 1816
WoO145	*Das Geheimnis*	*Wiener Moden-Zeitung*, Vienna, 1816

WoO146	*Sehnsucht (Die stille Nacht)*	Artaria, Vienna, 1816
WoO147	*Ruf vom Berge*	*Gedichte von Friedrich Treitschke*, Vienna, 1817
WoO148	*So oder so*	*Wiener Moden-Zeitung*, Vienna, 1817
WoO149	*Resignation*	*Wiener Moden-Zeitung*, Vienna, 1818
WoO150	*Abendlied unterm gestirnten Himmel*	*Wiener Moden-Zeitung*, Vienna, 1820

Songs published posthumously

Some songs not included in the Kinsky catalogue were catalogued by Willy *Hess* (Wiesbaden 1957).

1836–72

WoO140	*An die Geliebte* (second version)	*Reliquie . . .*, Scheible, Stuttgart, 1836
WoO118	*Seufzer eines Ungeliebten/ Gegenliebe*	Diabelli, Vienna, 1837
WoO135	*Die laute Klage*	Diabelli, Vienna, 1837
WoO130	*Gedenke mein*	Haslinger, Vienna, 1844
WoO105	*Auf Freunde* (as 'The Wedding Song')	Ewer & Co., London, 1858
WoO106	*Es lebe unser teurer Fürst*	*Neue Briefe Beethovens*, Stuttgart, 1867
Hess133	*Das liebe Kätzchen*	*Neue Briefe Beethovens*, Stuttgart, 1867
Hess134	*Der Knabe auf dem Berge*	*Neue Briefe Beethovens*, Stuttgart, 1867
WoO131	*Erlkönig*	*Beethoveniana*, Leipzig, 1872

1888 Songs first published in the supplementary volume (Vol. XXV) of the complete Beethoven edition (GA), Breitkopf und Härtel, Leipzig.

WoO109	*Erhebt das Glas mit froher Hand*
WoO110	*Elegie auf den Tod eines Pudels*
WoO113	*Klage*
WoO114	*Ein Selbstgespräch*
WoO115	*An Minna*
WoO119	*O care selve*
WoO120	*Man strebt, die Flamme zu verhehlen*
WoO141	*Der Gesang der Nachtigall*

1902–56 Miscellaneous publications, predominantly in musical journals and yearbooks.

WoO141	*Der edle Mensch sey hülfreich und gut*	*Musikgeschichtliches*, Berlin, 1900
WoO116	*Que le temps me dure* (C minor)	*Die Musik*, 1902
WoO112	*An Laura*	*Musikautographen*, Cologne, 1916
WoO111	*Punschlied*	*Der junge Beethoven*, Leipzig, 1925
WoO125	*Auf Freunde* (in A major)	*Der Bär*, 1927
WoO116	*Que le temps me dure* (C major)	*Zeitschrift für Musik*, 1935
WoO103	*Cantata Campestre* (German text)	*Jahrbuch . . . (Hess)*, Winterthur, 1945
Hess151	*Traute Henriette*	*Österreichische Musikzeitung*, 1949
Hess 144	*Feuerfarb'* (first version)	*Musik im Unterricht*, 1955
Hess 146	*Der freie Mann* (first version)	*Musika*, 1956

1962 Songs first published in volume V of the *Supplemente zur Gesamtausgabe*, ed. Hess, Breitkopf und Härtel, Wiesbaden.

WoO128	*Romance (Plaisir d'aimer)*
Hess 140	*Dimmi, ben mio, che m'ami* (first version)
Hess 142	*Wonne der Wehmut* (first version)
Hess 145	*Opferlied* (first version)
–	*Languisco e moro*
–	*Lied aus der Ferne* (see entry)

1990 Songs first published in volume XII/I of the new complete edition, ed. Lühning, Henle, Munich.

W113	*Klage* (first version)
–	*An die Geliebte* (fragment)
–	*Die laute Klage* (first version)
–	*Gretels Warnung* (first version)
–	*In questa tomba oscura* (first version)

This list does not include all sketches and fragments, the publication of which has been piecemeal. Gustav Nottebohm, who had unrivalled access to several major autograph collections, describes the contents of sketchbooks selectively in his *Beethoveniana* (Leipzig 1872) and notably in his *Zweite Beethoveniana* (Leipzig 1887), but generally quotes only the opening bars of song sketches. A number of valuable facsimile editions of autograph collections and complete sketchbooks with helpful transcriptions have been published, enabling study, reconstruction and completion of various sketches, and these are referred to *passim*. The administrators of the 'Unheard Beethoven' project seek to trace every fragment of Beethoven's music and make it available for listeners on their website: www.unheardbeethoven.org.

Appendix II *Der Gute Fürst*

Melody in E flat, from BL: Add.Ms. 29801, f. 133r

L. V. Beethoven,
Realisation by Paul Reid

Bibliography

Song editions

(GA) *L. van Beethovens Werke: Vollständig kritisch durchgesehene überall berechtigte Ausgabe* (Gesamtausgabe). Complete edition of Beethoven's works, published by Breitkopf und Härtel, Leipzig, in the 1860s in 24 volumes, with a later supplementary volume following in 1888. Previously published songs appear in volume 23 (1864) and previously unpublished songs in the supplementary volume 25 (1888), ed. Eusebius Mandyczewski. *Ludwig van Beethoven: Songs for solo voice and piano* (Dover Publications, New York 1986) is a photographic reprint of volume 23 only, but includes English prose translations and a helpful 'Glossary of German Terms' (performance directions, etc.).

(Henle) *Beethoven Werke XII/I: Lieder und Gesänge mit Klavierbegleitung*, ed. Helga Lühning (Munich 1990). Complete song edition in one large hardback volume, published with a Critical Report (*Kritischer Bericht*), in German, giving details of sources of texts and music. Also available in three separate softback volumes, without Critical Report and omitting fragmentary songs and alternative versions. Note that the numeration, identical from 1 to 69, varies slightly thereafter.

(Peters) *Beethoven. Sämtliche Lieder für eine Singstimme mit Klavierbegleitung*, rev. Max Unger (Frankfurt, London, New York, 1936). Not the complete songs with piano, as claimed, but the songs published in volume 23 of GA, plus three orchestral songs with non-authentic piano reductions.

(Supp) *Beethoven. Supplemente zur Gesamtausgabe*, ed. Willy Hess. Works not included in GA. The songs are in *Band V: Lieder und Gesänge mit Klavierbegleitung, Kanons und musikalische Scherze* (Wiesbaden 1962; revised edition 1980) (references to the revised edition).

Catalogues

Nottebohm, Gustav: Thematisches Verzeichniss der Werke Ludwig van Beethovens (Leipzig 1865).

(KH) Georg Kinsky and Hans Halm: *Das Werk Beethovens. Thematisch-bibliographisches Verzeichnis seiner sämtlichen vollendeten Kompositionen*

(Munich/Duisburg 1955). The standard thematic catalogue, highly detailed, but includes completed works only. In German. Works are listed by opus numbers (op.) and as works without opus number (WoO).

(Bia) Giovanni Biamonti: *Catalogo cronologico e tematico delle opera di Beethoven* (Turin 1968). Thematic catalogue which attempts to list all known works, including sketches for unfinished works, in chronological order. In Italian.

(Hess) Willy Hess: *Verzeichnis der nicht in der Gesamtausgabe veröffentlichten Werke Ludwig van Beethovens* (Wiesbaden 1957). Catalogue of Beethoven's works not published in GA, made in preparation for his supplementary volumes. In German.

(Hess2) *The New Hess Catalog of Beethoven's Works*, ed. James Green (West Newbury 2003). An expanded and updated edition of the Hess catalogue. In English.

(Klein) Hans-Günter Klein: *Ludwig van Beethoven. Autographen und Abschriften* (Berlin 1975). Catalogue of autographs and copies in SPK, Berlin.

(SV) Hans Schmidt: *Verzeichnis der Skizzen Beethovens* in *Beethoven-Jahrbuch VI* (Bonn 1969). Summary catalogue of the sketches, giving a comprehensive overview of collections.

Other sources

(EA) *The Letters of Beethoven*, translated and edited by Emily Anderson (3 vols) (London 1961).

(BB) *Ludwig van Beethoven. Briefwechsel. Gesamtausgabe*, ed. Sieghard Brandenburg (8 vols) (Munich 1996). German edition of complete letters, including letters written to Beethoven.

(Nohl) *Neue Briefe Beethovens nebst einigen ungedruckten Gelegenheitskompositionen*, ed. Ludwig Nohl (Stuttgart 1867). Important early collection of letters and some first music publications.

(T) Maynard Solomon, 'Beethoven's Tagebuch of 1812–1818' in *Beethoven Studies 3* (ed. Tyson) (Cambridge 1982) (T – indicates the number allocated by Solomon to entries).

Brenneis, Clemens (ed.), *Ein Skizzenbuch aus dem Jahre 1809 (Landsberg5)* (2 vols) (Bonn 1993).

Johnson, Douglas *Beethoven's Early Sketches in the 'Fischhof Miscellany'*, Berlin *aut.28* (2 vols) (Ann Arbor 1980).

Kerman, Joseph (ed.), *Autograph Miscellany from circa 1786 to 1799. British Museum Additional Manuscript 29801, ff. 39–162 ('The 'Kafka Sketchbook')*, vol. 1: facsimile, vol. 2: transcription (London 1970).

Virneisel, Wilhelm (ed.), *Beethoven, Ein Skizzenbuch zu Streichquartetten aus Op. 18* (2 vols), facsimile and transcription (Bonn 1972, 1974).

References

Boettcher, Hans, *Beethoven als Liederkomponist* (Augsburg 1928) (reprinted Sändig 1974)

Clive, Peter, *Beethoven and his World. A Biographical Dictionary* (Oxford 2001)

Cooper, Barry, *Beethoven and the Creative Process* (Oxford 1990)

Cooper, Barry, *Beethoven's Folksong Settings* (Oxford 1994)

Cooper, Barry, *Beethoven* (Oxford 2000)

Cooper, Barry, 'Beethoven's "Abendlied" and the "Wiener Zeitschrift"', *Music and Letters* 82/2 (2001)

Curzon, Henri de, *Les Lieder et Airs détachés de Beethoven* (Paris 1905)

Dorfmüller, Kurt, *Beiträge zur Beethoven-Bibliobiographie* (Munich 1978)

Friedländer, Max, *Das deutsche Lied im 18. Jahrhundert. Quellen und Studien* (3 vols) (Stuttgart/Berlin 1902) (reprinted Olms 1970)

Frimmel, Theodor, *Beethoven Handbuch* (2 vols) (Leipzig 1926)

Garland, Henry and Mary (eds), *The Oxford Companion to German Literature* (Oxford 1976)

Glauert, Amanda, 'Beethoven's Songs and Vocal Style', in *The Cambridge Companion to Beethoven* (Cambridge 2000)

Johnson, Douglas, Alan Tyson and Robert Winter, *The Beethoven Sketchbooks. History, Reconstruction, Inventory* (Oxford 1985)

Kerman, Joseph, 'An die ferne Geliebte', in *Beethoven Studies* (ed. Tyson) (London 1974)

Krones, Hartmut, 'Tonartensymbolik im Biedermeier unter dem Aspekt der musikalischen Temperatur', in *Musizierpraxis im Biedermeier* (ed. Boisits and Hubmann) (Vienna 2004)

Kunze, Stefan, *Ludwig van Beethoven. Die Werke im Spiegel seiner Zeit. Gesammelte Konzertberichte und Rezensionen bis 1830* (Contemporary reports and reviews) (Himberg 1987)

Lockwood, Lewis, 'Beethoven's Sketches for *Sehnsucht* (WoO146)', in *Beethoven Studies* (ed. Tyson) (London 1974)

Marston, Nicholas, 'Voicing Beethoven's Distant Beloved', in *Beethoven and his World* (ed. Burnham and Steinberg) (Princeton 2000)

Nottebohm, Gustav, *Beethoveniana* (Leipzig 1872)

Nottebohm, Gustav, *Zweite Beethoveniana* (Leipzig 1887)

Orrey, Leslie, 'The Songs', in *The Beethoven Companion* (ed. Arnold and Fortune) (London 1971)

Parsons, James (ed.), *The Cambridge Companion to the Lied* (Cambridge 2004)

Reed, John, *The Schubert Song Companion* (Manchester 1985)

Robbins Landon, H. C., *Beethoven* (London 1970)

Rosen, Charles, *The Classical Style* (London 1971)

Rosen, Charles, *The Romantic Generation* (London 1996)

Schürmann, Kurt (ed.), *Ludwig van Beethoven, Alle vertonten und musikalisch bearbeiteten Texte* (The complete texts to all of Beethoven's vocal works) (Münster 1980)

Schiedermair, Ludwig, *Der junge Beethoven* (Leipzig 1925) (2nd revised edition, Weimar 1939)

Smeed, J. W., *German Song and Its Poetry 1740–1900* (London 1987)

Solomon, Maynard, *Beethoven* (New York 1977)

Stoljar, Margaret Mahony, *Poetry and Song in late Eighteenth Century Germany* (London 1985)

Steblin, Rita, *A History of Key Characteristics in the Eighteenth and Early Nineteenth Centuries* (Rochester 1996)

Stuber, Robert, *Die Klavierbegleitung im Liede von Haydn, Mozart und Beethoven. Eine Stilstudie* (Biel 1958)

Tyson, Alan, 'A Beethoven Price List of 1822' in *Beethoven Essays* (ed. Lockwood and Benjamin) (Cambridge, Mass., 1984)

Wegeler, Franz, and Ferdinand Ries, *Biographische Notizen über Ludwig van Beethoven* (Koblenz 1838)

Index of songs by title

Note: Page numbers in bold refer to main entries. Familiar alternative titles are cross-referenced.

First line index

Note: this index cross-references first lines with titles (see Index of songs by title)

Lightning Source UK Ltd.
Milton Keynes UK
18 November 2010

163090UK00002B/6/P